GUERNS

GUERNSEY GREEN

The Life and Times of
Guernseyman
Bill Green

William M. Bell

First published 1992

Made and printed in Great Britain by
The Guernsey Press Co. Ltd, Guernsey, Channel Islands.

ISBN 0 952 0479 0 X

CONTENTS

ACKNOWLEDGEMENTS

The Author gratefully acknowledges the help, advice and information willingly given by the following persons. Without their assistance the scope and accuracy of the book would have been severely curtailed.

Harry Bisson.
Mrs Edna Butt.
Wake Clark.
John Ferbrache.
Alec Forty.
Charlie Froome.
Bill Green.
Mrs 'Mabs' Green.
The late Allan Grut.
Richard Hardwick.
The late Les Lane.
Frank Le Cocq.
Hubert Nicolle.
The late Harold Le Parmentier.
Mrs Elsie Patterson.
Charles Pratt.
Lloyd Robilliard.
Fred Short.
Mrs Maureen Sparkes.
Edgar Stacey.
'Dreamy' Stranger.
Frank Stroobant.
Mrs Jacqueline Stuckley.
Margaret Talbot-Cull.
Jackie Upham.
Miss R.Wilkes.
The late Lloyd Warry.
Herbert Winterflood.

ILLUSTRATIONS

FOREWORD

by Bill Green

I class it a great privilege to have perused my 'Obituary' whilst I am still alive.

I have thoroughly enjoyed reading the manuscripts of this book, and the many sessions I shared with the author and his tape recorder, which brought flooding back memories and phases of my life, which otherwise would have remained forgotten.

The book, Guernsey Green, is surprisingly frank - almost recklessly so in places! However, I am extremely grateful to the author for his selectivity in certain areas, particularly in relation to my love life, about which another book could be written, but can't !"

I believe the author knows more of me and my life than I know myself. He has by his research, which has been extremely thorough, reminded me of many incidents and activities which as far as I was concerned were long gone and totally forgotten. Whilst he has dug around my past, with great tenacity, I still have some secrets!

It is reputed that when Sir Winston Churchill was well into his seventies, someone once enquired of him, "How are you enjoying the evening of your life ?" "Evening", he bellowed, "late afternoon perhaps !" That is how I feel. I have enjoyed my life, I have enjoyed the book, but I have the feeling and the hope, that for me, the best is yet to come.

Chapter 1

LIFE IN SMITH STREET

At the turn of the century Guernsey was a tranquil haven, backward perhaps, with a community of placid, hard working Islanders, seemingly content with their leisurely way of life, which was slow, casual and almost crimeless.

The island in those days was largely dependent for its prosperity on the export of granite and the cultivation of grapes, tomatoes and flowers. St Peter Port, with its bustling harbour, was the hub of the island's commercial activities. Sailing boats and steam colliers berthed alongside the Quay in the old harbour, discharging their cargoes while, close by, clanged and clattered the double decker electric trams which ran between Town and St Sampson.

It was however the age of horse drawn carriages, from the pony and trap, to the wagonette and the 'four in hands' char a banc. While youths ran barefoot through the streets, men without hats were considered improperly dressed. Women in their long dresses and bonnets were a distinctive part of the Edwardian scene.

The sound of a barrel organ, the rhythmic beat of the horses hooves, the clatter of wheels on cobbled streets, the whistling of errand boys, the cries of the French onion sellers and the chatter of islanders conversing in patois, all contributed to the centuries old atmosphere of St Peter Port.

Guernsey in the decade before the Great War provided a surprising variety of entertainment, from a leisurely stroll around the harbour to a wealth of distractions at St George's Hall. The bandstand in Candie Gardens was the setting for many concerts, while Belvedere Field was the scene of the colourful King's Birthday Parades, in which both the Guernsey Militia and the Fort George Military garrison took part. Cycle clubs attracted numerous members on their outings into the country parishes and the swimming clubs at the Valette pools were popular, despite bathing being segregated.

The island was benignly governed by the Lt. Governor, the King's representative, together with the Bailiff, the Royal Court and the States of Deliberation. The ten parish Rectors and the twelve Jurats were the mainstay of the States. The recently introduced Peoples Deputies were at best tolerated, but certainly did not have any significant role to play in the government of the island. Democracy in Guernsey was still very much in its infancy.

It was into this Edwardian era that I was born at 44 Fountain Street, St Peter Port, on the 19th August 1909, in the flat above Mr F.J.Hubert's Seed Merchant business. My parents were employed as part time caretakers of the premises. Although christened William after my Father, I have been known as Bill throughout my life. In 1973, when I retired from business, I held a party for my staff in the same premises. The flat was by then a Restaurant, so I was able to say, in my short speech, that;

"I was born in this building some 63 years ago."

My sister, Daisy, was 17 years old when I was born, so really I was like an only child with three parents! I was obviously a mistake then and have been one ever since! Dad was 43 years old when I was born. I was, however, a very much loved and cherished late child, with parents who were wonderful people

Born in 1866, my Father was brought up in Sheffield. He joined the regular Army and became a Lance Corporal in the Kings's Own Yorkshire Light Infantry. He saw service in Ireland, being involved in the Irish riots which were provoked by Gladstone's Home Rule Bill. I can still 'hear' him telling me of his experience, when, with his bayonet fixed, he chased an Irishman down an alleyway and cornered him in a doorway. The Paddy tore his shirt apart and yelled;

"Stick it in! Stick it in!" which, of course, my Dad did not have the nerve to do.

Dad's great friend in the Army was Frank Wilson. They were posted to Guernsey, with the garrison in 1887. Here they met, courted and married, two Guernsey sisters, Ada and Emma Jane Renouf. My Aunt Ada and my Mother. These two soldiers were such buddies that they bought plots of land alongside each other in the Foulon Cemetery and that is where they are today, with their families. With one exception of course, and I am grateful for being that exception.

Mum came from a family of nine children, her father lived to a ripe old age, but her mother died at the early age of 39. My Mother's elder sister, Aunt Lil took on the job of looking after the family. Some of Mum's brothers and sisters were very young when my grandmother died.

My Mother was a typical Guernsey lady, plump and short, and I take after her! She had two children, my sister Daisy, and myself. Aunt Lil never married, but she had five brothers and for a time, they all lived together at The Campernells, Bailiffs Cross. We were a very close family, although my Mother and my Aunt Lil never got on too well. Later in life, when neither of them could walk very well, they both had walking sticks to help them. When they were in the same room I had to keep their chairs well apart, otherwise these two elderly ladies inevitably ended up doing battle with their walking sticks.

Mum was a real mother and a wonderful cook. She spent all her time looking after the family and nothing else. Woman's work was very hard in those days, there were no washing machines, nor any of the modern labour saving devices. There was a wash copper in the yard that was lit every Monday morning. The washing was boiled and then rubbed on a scrubbing board reminiscent of the lavoirs in France.

Mum was about the same age as my Dad and she lived on to 94, surviving him by 20 years.

When Dad left the Army, he and my Mother oscillated quite regularly between Sheffield and Guernsey before eventually settling in the island. I think that Mum persuaded him to put his roots down in Guernsey, a decision he never regretted. He came to love the island and was proud that it was his and his family's home. For some years he worked as an engraver for a firm in Smith Street, Lovell and Cox. Later he worked for Mr H.T. Lock, who was a Cycle Agent. He had premises next to the Old Government House Hotel where later, the Motor House garage was situated. Mr Lock held the Royal Enfield Cycle agency for the island.

Dad, who was never a fit man, became very ill sometime around 1904 or 1905. Old Dr R.E. Gibson, our family Doctor, was very interested in his, and indeed the whole families wellbeing. He recognised Dad's considerable ability, particularly with his hands. He knew that it was my Father's ambition to run his own business and he believed in him! Dr Gibson lent him five pounds, with which he set himself up in business. On the 6th November 1905 Dad opened his Cycle Shop.

In Smith Street, next to the Prince of Wales Hotel, which was run by Jimmy Travers and his family, was a passageway which led to a large room owned by Madame E.W. Dupre, of Doyle Road. That room was where Dad started his business, equipped with the tools which he bought with the money from Dr Gibson. He traded as W. Green, The Progressive Cycle and Motor Works.

On the front page of the Evening Press a Notice appeared stating:-

> 'W. Green, late with H.T. Lock, Cycle and Motor manufacturer, having commenced business on his own account at the Progressive Cycle Works at the top of Smith Street, hopes by personal attention to all repairs, to merit a share of his friends and the publics' patronage. Highest class plating and enamelling, repairs of every description to cycles, perambulators, typewriters, phonographs, electric bells etc. Charges moderate. Tel. 688.'

Sometime after Dad had set up in business Mr Lock, his former employer, went bankrupt and left Guernsey. Dad went down to the boat to see him off and offered Mr Lock some money, as he thought he was probably in severe financial difficulty. Mr Lock, however, pulled a wad of notes out of his pocket and said;

"It is not always a bad thing to be a Mason!"

Dad obtained the Royal Enfield agency, which became available as a result of Mr Lock's bankruptcy.

When I was almost a year old, Mum and Dad gave up their job as caretakers and the family moved from Fountain Street to Smith Street, into a flat above what is now the Midland Bank Trust Corporation. My Father's cycle business had prospered and it moved into the bigger shop, below our flat at 22A Smith Street. These were the premises that the Cycle business of 'Greens' were to occupy for well over half a century. Dad's new shop was three doors down from his old premises.

Green's Progressive Cycle Works pre 1914.

From then on, naturally, I was interested in bicycles. Dad built me a little bike which was unique in its day. Small cycles then were unheard of and mine was the only one in the island. Because everybody wanted to ride my bike, I became the 'Pin Up' of the school and in consequence gained many friends. After I eventually grew out of it, Dad hung it outside our shop. It was a novel and effective advertising sign, which was to remain there until the German occupation in 1940.

Our new home was the flat over the shop. I had my own bedroom, overlooking the Street and the harbour. There were two attic rooms, which I used as play rooms. When I was older I used climb out of one of the rear attic windows and walk along the gutters to the bedroom window of my friend, Mickey Travers, who lived over the Prince of Wales Hotel. That was until Dad caught me in the act one day and 'persuaded' me not to do it again, other than if there was an emergency, such as a fire. Mickey however, continued to visit me by our 'skyway.'

Our flat was not particularly large, there was a bedroom for my parents, one each for my sister and myself, a living room and kitchen. The furnishings were simple, a few chairs, a table and beds. People didn't have a lot of material possessions in those days. We had a big kitchen table, very ordinary by modern day standards, which Dad made when he worked for Lovell and Cox. He turned the legs on one of their lathes. It was a plain wooden topped table, which was constantly being scrubbed by Mum.

Our meals were served on place mats, tablecloths only appeared when we entertained visitors. In the kitchen there was a large range which was kept going permanently. In the corner on the wall hung our large tin bath, which on bath night would be placed in front of the range and filled with water. The water was heated in big saucepans on the range. We did not bath too often because it was a considerable task organising the heating of the water and filling the bath. Monday was generally bath night, because it was also wash day. Some of the hot water from the wash copper would be used in the bath.

Mum often told the story of how she insisted that my sister take me out in my pram. Daisy apparently objected, she did not want to be seen pushing a pram - everybody would think I was her child! So she would take me as far as the pump in Smith Street and abandon me while she went off with her boy friend. She would leave me in my pram kicking up hell and screaming my head off. Daisy had a boy friend for a long time, a lad called Mahy, who worked at Lovell and Cox, but nothing came of it. Perhaps having a baby brother 17 years younger than her did not help!

Daisy always took delight in reminding me of how Mum would tie me to the kitchen table leg. Apparently as a very small boy I was always running around and escaping from Mum and in danger of falling down the stairs.

Dad went to an auction sale and bought, very cheaply, a big old fashioned grandfather's clock. The reason that it was so cheap was that it was broken, but that didn't bother Dad. He took the clock to pieces and restored it to full working order. It was to remain in the family for many years. Dad loved the clock so much so that he christened it 'Old Joe'.

When I was a little boy it used to stand on the landing at the top of the stairs. 'Old Joe' would 'make' chocolate for me. Dad would take me on to the landing, open 'Old Joe's' door which concealed the two large weights, and I would say;

"Please 'Old Joe' make me a piece of chocolate".

I would then have to sit and wait patiently on the stairs for about ten minutes. Dad would come back and reach up inside 'Old Joe' and, if I had been good, sure enough 'Old Joe' would have made me a bar of chocolate, complete with wrapper! But if I had been naughty 'Old Joe' would let me down.

One day when there was nobody about, I fancied a bar of chocolate. I opened the door of the grandfather clock and requested 'Old Joe' to make me a piece of chocolate. As I couldn't reach up inside, I climbed onto the ledge of the door. Over came 'Old Joe' and we went down the stairs together. Of course when Dad came home he knew exactly what had happened. Dad repaired 'Old Joe' but it was a very long time before he made chocolate for me again.

Not only did 'Old Joe' supply me with bars of chocolate, the interior was used by Dad to pin up all the interesting newspaper cuttings which he saved. When my Father died 'Old Joe' went to my sister. Before the grandfather clock was taken to its new home I removed all the newspaper cuttings. I still have them and they make interesting reading. One cutting recalls that my sister Daisy was the first lady in Guernsey to fly, others tell of events during the First World War. It is fascinating after all this time to see which events attracted Dad's interest.

My Father was an expert with his hands, he could make almost anything. When I was still very young he made me a little trolley. I had great fun riding it down Smith Street, which has quite a slope from top to bottom. I started at the top outside Dr Bostocks' house, which was later to become Hirzel House. The Doctor's garden, in which there were a mass of shrubs and trees, was in those days surrounded by a high wall. When the wall was lowered and the garden dug out in the 1960s, the basement of Hirzel House became the ground floor and the original ground floor, the first floor. The old front door is now a first floor window.

The house next door to Dr Bostock's was Maison Allaire, which was destined to become the headquarters of the States Controlling Committee during the German occupation. I would roll down the street towards the Royal Yacht Hotel which in those days was at the bottom, where Boots the Chemist is today. On the way down I would pass, on my right, first the Prince of Wales Hotel and then Gaudin's stationery shop, run by the Davis family. Immediately before reaching our cycle shop was Rowcliffe the Tailor, which soon became C.H. Hollis, the Optician. Next door to our shop, still going down the street, was Mr G.J. Good's book business.

Smith Street water pump - today it is just a museum piece.

Then I would pass Boots The Chemist's original shop, which later became part of the Gas Company premises. Although I don't remember it, Stonelakes were the tenants of the property before Boots.

By now I would have travelled half way down the Street to the point where there is a recess, which leads by way of a flight of granite steps to Le Marchant Street. There today are the offices of Advocates Ozanne, Van Leuven and Perrot. In those days it was the Guernsey Press Company premises, where the Evening Press was printed. The paper continued to be printed there until the late 1970s.

At the bottom of the flight of steps stands a water pump. Up to and during the first world war it provided the main water supply for the residents of Smith Street - today it is just a museum piece. It was from this pump that we obtained our water. When I was a little boy, Dad fetched the water for all our needs, cooking and washing, from this pump. We had a number of water carriers and Dad had to hump them up all the fifty two stairs to our flat. It really was a heavy task, as I found out when I was older. Then I quickly learnt to be very careful with the amount of water I used.

There was another pump just beyond the Royal Court and Dad preferred the taste of the water from there. Being further away we only occasionally obtained our water from that pump. It was surprising how the water varied from pump to pump.

Further down the street, I would pass Mr C. Stutchbury's Grocery Shop. I can remember my sister, Daisy, being sent by Dad for some pigeon's milk. I can see Mr Stutchbury searching all over his shelves only to realise that he was having his leg pulled. He was furious. Dad roared his head off. My Father loved his bit of fun and I think I have taken after him. We were both mischievous in our own way and we both had a touch of devilment in us.

Then I passed Tozer's the newsagent and printer, who later moved to the Pollet. Towards the bottom of the Street was first the Press Company Shop, then the Banana Market and finally W.T. Pealing's fish shop, which later became Le Riches.

I had now reached the Royal Yacht Hotel and the bottom of Smith Street, where it joined with both the High Street and the Pollet.

The Royal Yacht Hotel was originally the home of Sir Isaac Brock, the Guernseyman and British General who saved Canada for the Empire. Today a plaque on the wall commemorates that association.

The Royal Yacht was an impressive Hotel, with a recessed foyer and an all white facade on the lower part of the building, with granite above. It had an impressive entrance porch. I used to ride my little trolley down Smith Street and sometimes go right into the Hotel foyer. I remember getting 'shooed' out of there many times by the Commissionaire. I never intended going into the Hotel, but the brakes of my trolley were not very efficient, so I used to try and stop by putting my feet against the door. Sometimes the door would open inwards and I would end up right inside the foyer.

The brake on my trolley consisted of a lever which, when pulled, pressed a piece of wood against one of the back wheels. I would try to help the brake by putting my feet against the front wheels, but this never worked satisfactorily. Starting at the top of the Street, outside Dr Bostock's, my speed was such that the only way I could stop was by running into something or someone. When Dad realised the problem, he insisted that I start from outside our shop so that I would not get up too much speed by the time I reached the Royal Yacht Hotel. Fortunately there were not many people in Smith Street to get in the way in those days - you certainly couldn't do it today!

Having ridden my trolley down the street, I then had to haul it back to the top in order to enjoy my next ride. Being a very little boy, that presented me with a real difficulty, so in consequence I became very adept in obtaining assistance from passers-by.

On the way back up the street, I would pass on my right the imposing Capital and Counties Bank, which in July 1918 was to become Lloyds Bank. Today the green copper dome dominates the area. I can remember when it gleamed and sparkled in the sunlight, the copper looking newly polished. Then I would pass Alf Thompson's shop which became Wolf's the clothing store, and later Stonelake's, the chemist. Their Landlords were Mr De Carteret and Mr Le Patourel. It was the Mr Le Patourel whose son, Wallace, was to win the Victoria Cross in the second world war.

Further up the street I would pass Lovell and Cox. They had an arcade or alleyway, which led to their work rooms at the rear of the shop.

Dad greatly admired the facade of the then Lovell and Cox building with its vast amount of delicate lace type cast iron decoration. He explained to me that the original arches, columns, rails and pinnacles were cast at the tram sheds at Les Banques in the 1880s. Because of my Dad's interest, I became fascinated and today I still admire it for its intricate workmanship. Over the years it has been regularly painted and maintained, and adds to the great character and charm of the Street.

In between Lovell and Cox and the Main Post Office is one of the boundary stones, Les Barrieres de la Ville, of the old walled town. There are five or six of these granite stones around the town and each marks the site of a gate in the old town wall. The next shop was Gallery Nowela, which sold ladies gowns and later became the extension of the Main Post Office.

Then I came to the Singer Sewing Machine premises. Mr Hancock ran it during the first war. He was a very good artist and painted for a hobby. One of his pictures, a beautiful sea scene hung in my home for many years before it mysteriously disappeared!

Then opposite our shop was the Misses Frecker Berlin Wool Depot shop. Although it was to become the German Book shop during the occupation, with a big portrait of Hitler in the window and today is Button's Book shop, the magnificent original shop front still exists.

Next to the Misses Frecker shop at the top of the Street, there was a walled garden belonging to the Travers family from the Prince of Wales Hotel. As boys we were allowed to play there. It seemed much larger in my youth than it does today, but it is still an oasis in a desert of buildings. In front of the garden there is a paved area which was lit by a gas lamp. It was here before the first world war that a German Band gave concerts on fine summer evenings. With their fiddles and cellos, they would play the favourite melodies of the day. Mum always enjoyed their rendering of the Skater's Waltz. I can clearly recall my Father, although he would have been in his late forties, and old Mr Stevens from the Banana Market, warming pennies on a shovel in the fire and throwing them down from the window. The German bandsmen were picking up the red hot pennies only instantly to drop them again. Both these grown men were laughing their heads off. They did not like the Germans then, even before the first world war.

In those far off days, a considerable number of people lived in Smith Street since almost every shop had living accommodation on the upper floors. There was a tremendous community spirit, everyone knew everyone else and knew most of their business. We were all great friends. The children played together and used the street as a playground. Adults were also very close and were always in and out of each others homes.

Dad rented all the property in our block, which included the flat below ours. This he sub-let to two dear old ladies, Maud and Gertie Mackie. They were very friendly and took a great interest in me as a young boy. When old enough, I ran errands and fetched water for them and would often be given a bar of chocolate as a reward.

After the two Miss Mackies left, the flat was taken over by Mr and Mrs Kramer. He was involved in the bulb business in the island. Mrs Kramer, a delightful person, was unfortunately an alcoholic. She would come downstairs into Dad's shop soon after it had opened in the morning, shaking like a leaf and give me some money to get her a bottle of gin. My friend Mickey Travers from the Prince of Wales Hotel would get a bottle from his father and I would take it up to Mrs Kramer, hidden in a shopping basket. She would come down later as steady as a rock after her daily dose of gin. It was a sad story because she was a lovely lady.

My parents used to run what could only be called old-fashioned parties. I remember Dad would string different coloured ribbons around various parts of the building. We had to get hold of a ribbon and follow it to it's destination, where a note told you to go somewhere else. There were a lot of stairs in our home and we used to have great fun with these old fashioned party games. I can remember very many of these parties being held in our Smith Street flat, with what seemed like half the residents of the street joining in.

There were quite a little gang of children living in and around Smith Street. Mickey, who was to become a lifelong friend, and his sister Nig Travers lived just up the road from me. We used to call her Nig, which was not her real name, because she had a dark complexion. With the Dredge boys and the Gould boys, who lived in Le Marchant Street, we used to play some wonderful games.

We played games around the Plantation at the top of Smith Street. It did not become the War Memorial until well after the end of the first war, sometime around 1926. It was a genuine plantation with a mass of bushes and trees - a wonderful place for us to play 'Hide and Seek' and 'Kick the Tin.' That was a very popular game in my youth, and play would extend right into the centre of the Town.

Another favourite pastime we enjoyed was playing with hoops. There were both wooden and metal hoops. With the wooden ones, we used a stick and rolled them down the street, beating the hoop as we went, to make it go faster. Some of us were able to perform tricks with the wooden hoops, picking them up and swinging them around on the stick. Also there were metal hoops, which we used for hoop races, both in the street and at school. We had a piece of wood with a metal hook on the end and ran alongside the hoop controlling it with the hook. Almost every youngster in those days had a hoop.

Old Pop Travers, Mickey Travers grandfather owned a fleet of seven or eight horse drawn carriages. He kept the horses and some of the carriages in the livery stables at the top of Smith Street. It was in these premises that Huxster & Le Page and later Idon Critchlow held their Auctions. I remember going to an auction in the late 1970s and being able to recognize parts of the old horse stalls. Regrettably all traces of the stables have now disappeared.

As small boys, Mickey Travers and I would go and see the horses in the stables. It was great fun for us, seeing them being groomed and fed. When Pop Travers was short of business he would park his carriages near the plantation, with a board on them, indicating that they were available for hire.

My Father supplied Pop Travers with bells for his carriages. I can still recall the old chap driving down Smith Street in one of his carriages, with the bells going ding, dong, ding. The bells were, at Pop Travers insistence, all of different tones. This requirement caused Dad some considerable difficulty. He had to write to firms all over the place, before he managed to obtain them. The bells were large, with a big clapper and a striker which was activated by the driver pulling a lever. Old Pop Travers sounded the bells when he went around a corner. He used to drive right the way down Smith Street and High Street advertising his carriages for hire. Dad wasn't half proud to think that he supplied the bells.

In between what is now Burton's and Grut's in the High Street, there is a little alleyway. For some years it was the entrance to the Grove Cafe and, because of its popularity, customers often had to queue in the passageway and up the stairs in order to obtain a table. Up that alleyway at one time many years ago, was a stable. Old man Gould used to get one of his sons to take a horse up the alleyway, once a year in order to maintain its use as a right of way. I can remember accompanying one of the Gould boys, who was leading a horse up this alleyway. He tethered the horse in the old stable for a couple of hours and then led it out again. That apparently was sufficient to preserve the right of way.

The archway, by what was W.T.Pealing's fish shop and later became Le Riches, which leads up to Lefebvre Street, holds vivid memories for me. It was here, under the arch, where the lamplighters gathered before setting off on their rounds. In winter they would be well wrapped up against the weather, looking drab and stern. Just before dusk they would set off in their different directions with their long poles to light up St Peter Port. At the end of each of their poles there was a small cradle in which they placed the 'match' and a little bracket which was used to turn on the gas tap. The lamplighters became very adept at turning on the tap and lightning the gas in one movement. Later of course they had to go round again to turn off the lamps.

These lamplighters continued their 'profession' well into the nineteen twenties, before they were eventually replaced by the advent of the electric lamp. I can recall a time, in my early teens, sitting on the roof of a French Bleriot Car, being driven slowly up the Grange by my lifelong friend 'Dreamy' Stranger, turning off the taps of the gas lamps, undoing the work of the lamplighters. I can only put it down to youthful exuberance!

Like all parents of that era, mine wanted me to play a musical instrument. Dad was very keen that I learnt to play the piano, so I took lessons for a time until it was realised that I was neither musically inclined, nor enthusiastic. I well remember being required to practice for set periods each day. I also recall speeding up the clock so that I could get out to play with my friends. My sister used to tell a story of me, as a very young boy, learning to play the violin. Apparently I was sent down with my music and a music stand, into Smith Street to practice. As I practised the wind would catch the music and blow it all over the Street. I am reputed to have got into a terrible temper as a result. Daisy always concluded the story by adding that my playing sounded better in Smith Street than it did in our flat and would have sounded even better in the High Street.

My Mother's family name was Renouf. My Grandfather, John Renouf had a ginger beer and mineral water factory, called the Niagara Works, in the Truchot. Mum often recalled the times when she and Aunt Lil were kept home from school so that they could wash the mineral water bottles. The Works were located in the Truchot because of the supply of high quality spring water from a well on the site. Some years ago when the area was being re-developed the builders came across the well and had to bridge over it. The Lloyds International building today towers over the well and I believe that they still have trouble with water seeping into their basement. There is a wonderful story, which is often told but I cannot vouch for its accuracy, that the water from the spring in Candie Gardens comes from the Pyrenees. My old school master, J.P. Warren, wrote a book on the streams of Guernsey, in which he says, 'The water supplying Candie Gardens also drains into the same declivity as Vauxlaurens Brewery'. That water clearly also supplied the well for my Grandfather's ginger beer factory.

Grandpa Renouf was reputed to have invented the Niagara bottle, which had a patented self sealing stopper. The bottle contained a marble type glass ball sealed into the neck. As the bottle was filled with its fizzy contents, the glass 'ball' would rise against the rubber washer in the neck and seal itself. The seal could be broken by pressing down on the glass 'ball' and the drink poured out. These bottles were used for many years very successfully, until it was realised they were not all that hygienic. Dirt and dust accumulated on the top of the glass 'ball' and when the seal was broken it would all drop down into the drink. I drank gallons of the stuff, ginger beer and every sort of fizzy concoction, without it doing me any harm. As boys we would break the bottles to get the glass ball out and use them as marbles. I have, amongst my souvenirs, one of those ginger beer bottles with the name Renouf imprinted in the glass.

Whether my Grandfather rented or owned the Niagara Works I do not know, but I do know that it was later acquired by the family of my friend, Dreamy Stranger. It was then a jam and mineral water factory and officially called the Guernsey Aerated Water and Preserving Company, but always known as Stranger's Jam Factory.

The town was the main shopping centre for the whole of the island. Transport into town was not easy, people had to come on their bicycles, in their own horse and buggy, or rely on the horse bus.

For country people, Saturday was the great shopping afternoon and evening in town. They came into town in the afternoon and many left their bicycles in our Smith Street shop. They would stay until eight or nine o'clock in the evening and then return to Dad's shop, loaded with shopping, to collect their bicycles.

There were always crowds in town on a Saturday evening because the shops, all of which did a good trade, kept open until nine thirty. Shoppers flocked around the town, looking for bargains. There were no deep freezes or refrigerators, so perishable items of food, such as meat, had to be sold off, sometimes for as little as half price. As closing time drew near so the prices fell. Some shoppers became very adept in obtaining a bargain.

Saturday, for me was the great night of the week for reasons other than just shopping. Saturday was the night when there were a lot of drunks around. They fascinated me as a boy. The Police had a pair of hand trucks with which they used to remove the drunks from the town. It seemed to me they were constantly wheeling drunks up Smith Street. They would be making a lot of fuss and noise and sometimes the police had to strap them down for their own and indeed our safety. They would be taken down to the Town Hospital where there were cells for these chaps and there they remained until they were sober. It was all great fun for us boys to watch.

On Saturday nights Dad took the 'Bean Jar' down to Senner's Bakery in the Pollet to be cooked in the furze oven. I went down with Dad when I was very young, but later, when I grew up a bit, I would take it down to the Bakery. It was traditional that Sunday morning's breakfast was Guernsey Bean Jar. What was left over would last for two or three more days. Mum would make Bean Jar in an earthenware crock, which had a brown paper cover on the top, tied with cord. Mum's basic ingredients included pig's trotters, or any good meaty bone, haricot beans, onions, carrots, turnips, sage, parsley and thyme.

My Mother used to tell of the time when my Father had been unwell, and on doctors orders was kept without food for a period. He did not appreciate this treatment and one day got up and found a whole chicken that Mum had cooked. Dad ate the lot and pronounced himself fully recovered afterwards!

Mum and Dad were very keen on motion pictures. We all went, every Friday evening to St Julians Hall as it was then known. Later it was renamed the Gaumont. Our great favourites were Charlie Chaplin and Buster Keaton. My Saturday afternoons would be spent at Billy Bartletts, a cinema, at the top of St Julians Avenue, opposite Ann's Place. Later it was to be known as the Palace of Varieties. The trouble was when it rained you couldn't hear anything but the noise of the rain beating down on the corrugated iron roof. The seats, as I recall, were just bench forms.

I went there to see Pearl White and Eddy Polo epics. These famous film stars of their day featured in adventures which were shown by instalments. This week's instalment would end with Pearl White, who was always the heroine, hanging onto a cliff edge and the villain stamping on her fingers. The hero, Eddy Polo, would be coming along a tight rope to rescue her. It would then be announced that a further instalment would be shown next week. Of course, we couldn't wait until the next week to see what happened to Pearl White. The hero, of course, always succeeded in rescuing her.

Dominic Santangelo, who composed the music of what I consider to be Guernsey's National Anthem, Sarnia Cherie, was a friend of Dad's and became a great friend of mine. I have a signed original copy of his famous piece of music. He was a very fine musician and used to play the accompanying music for the films.

Sometimes the picture theatres were taken over for stage shows. I vividly recall a performance at St Julians Hall, depicting the sinking of the Titanic. The tragic sinking of the great ship on her maiden voyage took place in 1912. I must have only been three or four at the time of this re- enactment, but I can still visualize the scene on the stage even now. There was a very large model of the Titanic which was slowly up ended, As the great ship gradually slipped beneath the waves, I could hear the rumbling of the furniture and fittings falling about inside the hull of the ship. It was so realistic to a small boy, that I almost believed it was happening as I watched.

On Sundays I went to Sunday school at St. Paul's Church. When I came home, Mum and Dad would inevitably be sound asleep, one on the sofa and the other on the chaise longue. Sunday dinner, which we had in the evening and was always a roast, would be quietly cooking on the range. While my parents slept, I would creep out and go down to the harbour.

It was great fun playing amongst the boats, there was always something going on in the harbour. My friends and I would get up to all sorts of mischief, including throwing stones. Once or twice a policeman came and told Dad that he had caught us throwing stones into boats. There were big boat cradles on the Careening Hard and we used to play down amongst these for hours. I remember once when a boat was being tarred I went home with tar all over my clothes, which didn't make me very popular with Mum.

On Sunday evenings, people went to church, after which they paraded up and down on the Harbour walks and the Castle Emplacement, meeting friends and relations. The ladies would take note of what other ladies were wearing, and discuss the details at great length. It was the done thing to see and be seen. Girls would meet boys in a very restrained and almost formal way. My parents used to walk down there quite often and I would accompany them on my little bicycle. It was quite an occasion, all in our Sunday best.

My parents only went to church on special occasions. Arthur Couch, who worked for Dad as a mechanic and was more religiously inclined, often took me to St John's Church. We became firm friends and it was under his influence and guidance that I developed a life long interest in the Church.

When I was seven years of age, my grandmother Green died in Sheffield and I went with my parents to the funeral. She had been to visit us in Guernsey, but I didn't remember her. Some years later I found a photograph of her, which was unnamed. I recognised my grandma Green from having seen her in her coffin. In 1986 I went to Sheffield to see grandma's grave. I found it with the help of the Curator. I was there when I was seven and I was there again when I was seventy seven. It was really just a nostalgic visit.

On our way back to Guernsey, my parents took me to a picture theatre in London. The dense, dirty and yellowish smog, was so thick, not only outside but also inside the theatre, that they couldn't show the picture. The lamp they used in the projector was not powerful enough to project the picture through the smog onto the screen, so we were given our money back. When we went outside there were people walking in front of buses with flares. That was a London pea souper. In 1916 the factories in Britain were turning out armaments as fast as they could. It was the smoke from the factory furnaces that contributed to the smog. We, thankfully, have never had that kind of fog in Guernsey.

When my sister Daisy, left school she worked for Dad in the shop, doing many jobs, but particularly keeping the books. Daisy married Percy Trotter, at the Town Church in 1915. I can still remember the great fuss Mum and my sister made of the wedding arrangements. As always the ladies in the family, and there were plenty in my family, took a great interest in all the details. I looked upon it as a family event that this little boy had to suffer. Daisy, I learnt in later life, wore a dress made of Voile, which was a very light semi-transparent woven fabric. After their marriage

Pre First War Military Parade down Smith Street. Daisy Green looking out of Green's shop doorway (centre).

they lived in a flat above Smales, the sweet shop opposite Elizabeth College. Later they moved to Mount Row, where their eldest son Ian, was born.

A French Franc was given to me by Mum to put in baby Ian's hand. French money was legal tender in the island in those days. As we walked up the Grange we met my sister with baby Ian in his pram. I put the Franc into Ian's hand just as Mum had instructed. I was scarcely eight years old and was the baby's Uncle! Ian and I have remained very close over the years, I visit him at his home at Westbury in Wiltshire and he regularly comes to Guernsey. In 1922 Daisy's husband took a job as a school master in Siam, where his father was the Chief of Police. Daisy and her family lived out there for a number of years before returning to the island.

A newspaper cutting from the Guernsey Evening Press, dated 18th August 1917, which I found in 'Old Joe', reads:-

> 'Mr W. Green senior, the well known cycle agent from Smith Street, has just completed making some very fine Toy Models, including a war department motor trolley, a motor garage and a crane. All of these Models are on view in the window of his premises, in Smith Street. The trolley has rubber tyred wheels, a brass radiator and a metal bonnet, it can be steered and is fitted with electric lamps, the body is of wood and the tail board drops. The crane is perfect in every detail, there are four movements all connected by levers to a power handle, the load is let down on the brake as is the case of real cranes. The models which have been designed and made by Mr Green in his spare moments, show considerable merit in workmanship and detail.'

I still have those toys together with the load the crane carried, sacks of sawdust, which were hand sewn by my Mother. Dad made these toy models in 1917, a date confirmed, by the registration number on the Motor Trolley, which is 1917. The garage bears the name of 'Somme Garage', which commemorated one of the battles of the first world war. I am glad to say they are all still in first class condition. Sometimes I am tempted, even after all these years, to get them out and play with them !

My Father was a very clever man, with a great ability to work with both his head and his hands. He was continually inventing, adapting or rebuilding all things mechanical. He built and rebuilt a threewheeler car, he made working scale model toys for me, he built my little bike, and even just before he died in 1940, he was making a working model of Neville Chamberlain hitting Hitler on the head with an umbrella. The action was activated by putting a penny in a slot. He intended that the money raised would have gone to a war charity, regretfully he never finished that model.

Mum had to put up with the consequences of Dad's creative flair. She would find the brass knobs missing from her bed - they had been used to make lamps for a model truck Dad was making for me. There were times when Mother would return home to find the flat was being redesigned - a wall would have been demolished by Dad. Mum got used to this and learned to live with Dad's 'creativity'.

Dad spent many hours in his store in Hirzel Street, building a threewheeler car to his own design. The threewheeler was a 'concoction' of parts cannibalised from cars and motorcycle sidecars. It had two wheels in front, one behind and was powered by a Swedish Minerva motorcycle engine mounted at the rear. The apron, part of the body work and C-springs came from a great big motorcycle sidecar. The windscreen also started life on a motorbike. I think it was very probably that he used some old car parts for the steering, which was controlled by cables. The steering column had on the bottom end of it, a drum, around which were wrapped cables, which in turn were connected to each of the front wheels. As the steering wheel was turned, it would roll the cables and turn the wheels. Once, when we were out for a run, Dad caught the edge of the pavement and snapped one of the cables.

The steering wheel then, only turned one of the front wheels and it was impossible to drive the car. He could not repair it on the spot, so we all had to walk home.

Dad kept that car for years, rebuilding it many times. The oil lamps, which were made of brass, were beautiful and Father's pride and joy. Whilst nearly all of the rest of the car was eventually scrapped, the lamps were treasured. They were in the back store of my Smith Street shop, for many years, almost up to the second world war. When I came to look for them, they had disappeared, somebody no doubt had 'acquired' them.

The car was regularly used for family outings. One of our favourite haunts was Le Gouffre and on one visit Dad took a photograph of the car with Daisy at the wheel and Mum, with me as a two year old, on her lap. This photograph which was

The original photograph of the tricar, driven by Daisy Green, with young Bill Green on his Mother's knee.

taken in the spring of 1912, has appeared all around the world. It was also reproduced in the book 'Guernsey through the Lens'.

My nephew, Ian Trotter, came across a first day cover when he was in Los Angeles a few years ago, with the photograph of the car reproduced on the envelope. The car is described, as a 1913 Minerva and the original background, depicting Le Gouffre, had been replaced with the Town Church as the new setting. The first day cover bears a green Guernsey Europa stamp, which has been franked. I went to the Guernsey Postal Headquarters, to find out how the 'Cover' originated. They had no knowledge of them at all. I wrote to the shop where my nephew had obtained the first day cover and eventually obtained a further fifty covers. I had a shock when the account arrived for £300. That sum was many times more than the car had originally cost my Father to build. The mystery of the envelope remains, particularly as they were printed in Cheyenne U.S.A. !

The French came to the island in 1916 to examine the possibility of establishing a seaplane base in the harbour. I remember Dad relating tales of people who had been on the foreshore at Belle Greve Bay when the first seaplane arrived from Cherbourg. They thought that it resembled a giant bird as it landed on the water.

I remember seeing one of the French seaplanes flying over the Town Church and diving almost into the harbour and out again. I discovered many years later that the plane was flown by one of the French Aviators, L.V. Lambert. Long after the war Vic Lambert came to live in Guernsey. He was one of life's gentlemen and

First day cover featuring the 1913 Minerva Tricar.

was a very skilled Electrical Engineer. Later he became French Consul Agent in the island.

The Aviation Maritime Francaise, after their inspection, established a base on the site of the model yacht pond. The seaplanes, there were ten or twelve of them, soon became an everyday spectacle, both in the sky and on the water, in and around St Peter Port. They were forever being taxied in and out of the harbour. These small bi-planes, powered by a single engine, flew countless missions in search of German U-boats.

The blue French beret with the red pompon, worn by the aviators, quickly became a familiar sight in the town. Three hangars and a workshop were built on the site of the temporarily demolished model yacht pond. The seaplanes were

French seaplane base 1918. Note camouflaged merchant ship, top centre, and submarine moored in centre of harbour.

hoisted from the harbour by a crane and placed on trolleys and wheeled into their hangers. Kenny Bell was employed by the French to stand by in his boat when the seaplanes were taking off or landing, in case they needed assistance. Sometimes the pilots would fall into the harbour and it was Kenny's job to rescue them. Alongside the hangers six huts were erected as living quarters for the Frenchmen.

St Peter Port was a very busy harbour during the first World War. Not only was it used as a French seaplane base, there were also French submarines and many other warships. The mailboats still ran and there was the usual commercial shipping. Because there was considerable German submarine activity around our waters, the mailboats were armed and merchant ships, camouflaged.

I often rode my bike down to the harbour to see what was going on at the seaplane base. The Frenchmen were intrigued with me and my little bike. One of the pilots took a liking to me and encouraged my interest in the aircraft. On one occasion I was allowed to sit in the cockpit of a seaplane and work the rudder back and forth.

I used to watch the seaplanes bombing the Sardrette rock, which is just outside the harbour, with plaster of paris practice bombs. I believe that these practice bombs were the same size and weight, about a hundredweight, as the ones they used in action. They practised quite often, flying at low level around this rock trying to hit the centre of it. I can remember seeing the bombs missing and splashing into the sea. I don't know how they released these 'bombs' from the plane, I think they were just dropped over the side. There was no such thing as bomb bays in those days. The seaplanes used to roll, but I could not see the bombs leaving the plane, although I did see them hitting the rock or splashing into the sea.

My parents liked to go out to Mont Au Nord, a private house at Jerbourg, which was later to become the Idlerocks Hotel. It was empty during the first world war, so my parents and I went up there for picnics. It had a large well laid out garden, with a plateau where we would all sit, enjoying the magnificent view. We could see Herm, Sark, Jersey and on a clear day Alderney and the coast of France. My parents loved Jerbourg.

From our vantage point we watched seaplanes flying around the area. I vividly remember seeing two French aircraft bomb a German submarine just off St Martin's point. The submarine was just awash when the two seaplanes dropped their bombs. They missed the submarine, which quickly submerged below the surface and out of danger. Dad took a photograph with his Brownie Box Camera of one of the French aircraft dropping the bombs. For many years I treasured that photograph, but regrettably it became mislaid and lost.

Many years later Vic Lambert talked to me about his memories of the time when he was stationed in the island with the French seaplanes. He was the first pilot to land a plane in the harbour. Apparently he had been on a training flight and when he returned Vic found it impossible, due to the strong wind, to land in the roadstead outside the harbour. Flying in from Belle Greve Bay, he cleared the harbour wall and landed where the new jetty was later built.

Vic fascinated me with his tales of the French flying boats. When they first started operating from our harbour they had no wireless communications with their base. Instead they used carrier pigeons which, when released with their message, would return to Castle Cornet.

In June 1918, when on a reconnaissance mission with another seaplane Vic spotted a German submarine, as it surfaced. They were ten miles north west of the Les Hanois Lighthouse and immediately went into action dropping their bombs. The submarine was hit and seen to sink. That was, according to Vic, the only submarine officially sunk by the French airforce based at St Peter Port Harbour.

Another incident which Vic Lambert recalled was when one of the French pilots was flying over St Martin and accidentally jettisoned a bomb, completely destroying a vinery. All Pilots had been instructed not to fly over land when loaded with bombs, so the offending French officer was cashiered from the service.

Dad rented Number 7, The Quay, from Mr Benjamin Bailey Creasey and Mr Victor Creasey, for £24 a year. Interestingly the lease stipulated the rent be paid only in Guernsey money. English and French currency were also legal tender. He leased the store and office from Christmas 1915 until May 1919. He needed the storage space in order to have somewhere to keep his reserve stock of new bicycles. This store, which is now part of Creasey's shop basement, had, as I recall, a weather board across the front entrance as a defence against the sea coming over the Quay at high tides. If the wind was blowing from the east and there was a very high tide, the seafront and the store would be flooded. Dad also used the store as a workshop for many of his engineering projects.

When the tank was invented during the first war, its details were very secret. My Father, who had an inquiring mind, read as much as he could about this new weapon that the army were using in France. Although he had never seen a drawing or picture of it, he envisaged the shape of the tank very accurately. On the floor of the store on the Quay, he chalked a drawing of the tank, as he thought it would look. I remember his delight when eventually he saw a picture of a tank, his interpretation had been extremely accurate.

Father was so impressed with this new weapon that he built a scale working model of the tank. He spent many hours down at his store on the Quay, building a replica in wood, fabric, cardboard and three ply. It was beautifully finished with tracks made of wood slats and canvas. Dad fitted it with hand pedals and three dummy guns, which the driver could manipulate. Dad used carpet nails, which looked just like rivets, particularly when the completed model was painted. It was about six feet long, which was large enough for me to get inside and drive around

Model Tank built by William Green Snr. Young Bill Green on right of tank without cap.

the town. This model tank, painted grey, attracted great interest.

On Saturday, 23rd February 1918, in the Guernsey Evening Press, a photograph appeared of the tank, the description read:-

'A splendid model of a tank has been made by Mr W. Green Senior of 24 Smith Street to be used in street collections. It was in action for the first time last Saturday when nearly £15 was collected for the Children's Dinner Fund.'

The Children's Dinner Fund was created to provide meals for poor children during the first war. Surprisingly, in Guernsey there were people who were hungry, particularly children. A soup kitchen was set up and the tank was used to help raise some of the money required to meet the running costs.

Whilst I drove the tank under the guidance of my Father, my cousin Milly carried a tray of flags. People would take a flag and put money in her collection box. We raised quite a sum of money.

I drove the tank around the Arcade, which was on the level and sometimes ventured down the High Street and into Church Square. I was only eight at the time and fairly small for my age, so couldn't drive it very far without having to stop for a rest. Father had made it possible to stop one track and drive the other, so it could turn corners and manoeuvre as necessary. Dad constructed the tank so that as I hand peddled and steered I could look out to see where I was going. My vision was, however, very limited, so Dad always walked alongside instructing me to turn a little more to the left or to the right.

The cardboard and three ply eventually disintegrated, but not before the model tank had given good service and a great deal of pleasure to very many people, both in Guernsey and Jersey. Dad received a letter from the Chairman of the Jersey St John Ambulance Association Emergency War Committee, requesting that we take the tank over to Jersey to help with their fund raising. Their invitation was accepted and Dad and I took the tank over on the Great Western Railway steamer. We were met off the boat and a lorry transported the tank to Royal Square, where I drove it around to the great interest of everyone. A lot of money was raised. It was a most successful, enjoyable and, for me, exciting trip.

I have many vivid memories of the First World War, being five years old when it started and nine years old when it finished. There was no radio or television in those days and the Press was the great communicator. The Guernsey Evening Press was printed just down the road in Le Marchant Street. Every evening, I remember, there would be a crowd outside the Press office, overflowing into Smith Street, waiting for the paper to come out with the latest news of the war. As a very young boy, I would look out from my bedroom window and see these crowds of people.

When the first war started in 1914, great concern was felt that the Germans would intensify their naval activities in and around the Channel Islands. It was considered possible that a German military raid could take place on the island, so the Royal Guernsey Militia was mobilized. Many of the bays around the island, which were potential landing places, were protected with barbed wire and regularly patrolled. All along the west coast, from L'Eree to L'Ancresse, trenches were dug, all possible landing places were manned, machine gun posts were established and huts were built for the guards.

The strategically important telegraph cables which provided our link with both the Mainland and France came ashore at Telegraph Bay, Jerbourg. A hut was erected right down on the shore of Telegraph Bay and a guard was posted there in case there was a landing. A telephone line kept the guard in contact with the barracks at the top of the cliff. The threat of a German raid was taken seriously.

During the First World War there was an enlistment office next door to the Police Station. At the age of six, having seen many men of military age going to the office to enlist, I decided to join the Army. I can actually recall going to the enlistment office and being interviewed by Captain Cowley, who was the Recruiting Officer. He sat me at his desk and took down all my details. Later he came to see my parents and explained that I had enlisted in the Army, but had requested two weeks at home with Mum and Dad before being drafted. I remember my parents constantly relating the story to all our friends and relations, as of course proud parents are wont to do.

In 1916, the Royal Guernsey Militia was re-mustered as the Royal Guernsey Light Infantry. The new R.G.L.I. left Fort George and the island in June 1917 and quickly saw service as part of the famous 29th Division in France and Flanders. On the western front the R.G.L.I. fought gallantly at the battles of Cambrai in November 1917 and Lys, in April 1918, sustaining very heavy casualties. After that it was decided never again to send Guernseymen away as a unit. Many hundreds of men from the island were killed during the First World War. Their names are recorded on the memorial at the plantation at the top of Smith Street.

Father, who came to Guernsey as a Lance Corporal in the King's Own Yorkshire Light Infantry, was not well enough to re-enlist during the first war. A very patriotic man, he was bitterly disappointed at not being able to serve his King and Country.

My brother-in-law, Percy Trotter, served with the Royal Flying Corps, but was invalided out as a result of being injured when his aircraft crashed.

When the war ended I remember the crowds in Smith Street singing God Save The King. There was tremendous rejoicing, but nothing to the celebrations that took place at the end of the German occupation, in 1945.

The French Airforce was stationed at the harbour until the end of the war in 1918. There had been ten pilots, a dozen observers and over one hundred maintenance and back-up men in the French contingent. After they had all returned to France the equipment left behind was sold by auction. The aircraft floats, which were made of three ply, were bought by people who used them for having fun in the sea. The bodies of the seaplanes were broken up for fire wood.

Dad loved Jerbourg. When the opportunity occurred, he bought a plot of land at Jerbourg point from Mr Le Maitre, who lived in the farm opposite the Jerbourg Barracks. He paid sixty pounds for it - a bargain even in those days. After the war the six huts on the Castle Emplacement, that the French used as living quarters, were auctioned. I went down to the auction with Dad. He bid for almost all of

Seaplane Bungalow in 1919.

them, but they went for far more than he could afford. When it came to the last hut, Dad always said the auctioneer knocked it down to him 'a bit quick' because he knew him. He paid ninety pounds for the hut. They were built in sections, which were comparatively easy to dismantle.

William Green Snr., with French plaster of paris practice bombs at entrance to Seaplane Bungalow

Dad, with the help of a mechanic from his cycle business and an uncle of mine, took the newly acquired hut to pieces. The sections were then carted up to the plot he had bought at Jerbourg. Six drays, each drawn by four horses belonging to Harry Dredge, were used to transport the hut. Dad with the help of some members of the family and friends, re-erected the hut and it is still there to this day. For obvious reasons he called it Seaplane Bungalow. It is now well over seventy years old, so it has certainly stood the test of time.

After the war there were some of the French plaster of Paris bombs left down at the harbour. Dad managed to obtain a couple of them and cemented them into the top of the two pillars of the terrace at the front door of Seaplane Bungalow. They remained there until the Germans removed them during the occupation. As a family we moved from our flat at 22A Smith Street, to Seaplane Bungalow, Jerbourg Point, in 1919.

Chapter 2

A SUITABLE PUNISHMENT WAS ADMINISTERED

Schooling started for me at Amherst Junior School in the infant's class, under Miss Cohu. Later I went into the upper school where the Headmaster was Mr W. Stringer. He was succeeded by a remarkable man, Mr F.L. Dyson. Old man Dyson, as we all used to affectionately call him, was a tremendous teacher who did a great deal to shape my life.

Headmaster Dyson was without doubt a great patriot. On Empire Day, which was on May 23rd, he would parade all the boys to mark the occasion. In fact we paraded on all the occasions which were associated with the greatness of Britain, for in those days, Great Britain was the world's premier country. Sadly I have lived to see the greatness of Britain, wane.

As a result of old man Dyson's example and encouragement I have been a strong patriot throughout my life. The pride that he instilled in me and many other Old Amherstian's, is still with me to this day. Even as a little boy, when we went to the cinema and the National Anthem was played, encouraged by my Father, I would stand to attention.

After my seventh birthday I was allowed to ride my bike to school unaccompanied. One day I was riding home from school, along La Butte, to the junction with Elm Grove, when around the corner came a Frenchman in a Model-T Ford and knocked me off my bike. I was riding correctly, on the left hand side of the road, but he came around the corner on the wrong side. He was from the French seaplane base at the harbour and no doubt thought he was still driving in France.

He drove straight at me, I went to go to the other side of the road to avoid him, but he attempted the same manoeuvre and knocked me off my bike. Fortunately, Model-T Fords had a high ground clearance and I fell under the car and escaped injury. He had almost stopped by the time he hit me, but I was still scared. My little bike fortunately was un-damaged.

Miss Jackson, who was one of our school teachers, had seen the accident as she had been cycling along the road behind me. Up to then she was not one of my favourite teachers, in my eyes she was a bit of a tyrant. Miss Jackson came to my rescue and made sure that I was all right. Then she gave the 'unfortunate' Frenchman a real wigging, first in English and then in French, just in case he did not fully understand the English version. My estimation of Miss Jackson improved instantly. Her vigorous efforts on my behalf made me feel much better. For many years after that incident, I took Miss Jackson a bunch of flowers on Christmas day, it was my way of saying thank you.

Each morning I was seen off to school by Mum, who would wave and watch me riding up to the top of Smith Street. I returned at lunch time and then pedalled off again for afternoon school. After a time I became bored with school, I thought I would be much happier riding my little bike around Cambridge Park. So I decided that was just what I would do. I set off each morning, enjoyed playing in the Park and returned home for lunch. In the afternoon I again enjoyed the pleasures of the park. This apparently went on for some days before my form mistress called at the shop to enquire how I was and how long I would be off school. The game was up, but I must say that I was in some ways glad, as I found playing by myself for such long periods very boring. For once in my life I was glad to have been found out and returned to school quite willingly!

My first Headmaster, Mr Stringer, and I did not get on too well, in fact, to be truthful, I didn't get on very well with any of the masters, apart from Mr Dyson. My relationship with all masters was very much a love hate one. Whilst I appreciated their virtues, my complaint was that they did not appreciate mine and in retrospect I can well understand why. In consequence there was always some sort of confrontation between master and Bill! Looking back today, I can only admire those splendid gentlemen who had such a tremendous influence on me and my life.

Mr Stringer transferred from Amherst to the Intermediate School in Brock Road. He jumped ahead of me and was Headmaster when, as a new boy, I entered the Intermediate school. He remembered me only too well from Amherst and it wasn't to my advantage. I was not all that pleased to see him either. It was about my second day at the school when he spotted me and said;

"I hope you behave yourself a lot better than you did at your last school !" It proved a forlorn hope.

However Mr Stringer did not last too long at the Intermediate School and in January 1922, left to join the Inspectorate of the Board of Education. Our new Headmaster was F.E. Fulford. 'Fluffy' Fulford as we affectionately called him, would say;

"Now you boys, you do as I say, not as I would do if I was your age."

He was a splendid Headmaster and an all round sportsman. 'Fluffy' was an ex-amateur footballer, who had played for Clapton. He was a left hander and left footer and an extremely good swimmer. In fact he was a great sporting character, a very dynamic and decisive man, beloved by all and capable of giving as good as he got.

My great friend Frank Stroobant, often tangled with 'Fluffy'. On one occasion he was writing on the blackboard, when he heard 'Stroo' talking. He swung around and threw the chalk at 'Stroo', who caught it and threw it back. 'Stroo', who was very adept at all ball games and must have been about thirteen at the time, hit 'Fluffy' right between the eyes.

"Come out here!" roared 'Fluffy'.

'Stroo' came forward, as he did so 'Fluffy' swung around and kicked him right up the backside. 'Stroo' shot straight out the classroom door!

Good manners played a important part in our upbringing. At school we were taught that 'Manners maketh Man,' and this I think, had a tremendous influence on our behaviour. At home my parents were insistent on good manners. Regrettably, the schools and parents of today do not put the same emphasis on good manners and behaviour. Good manners, however, does not mean that you cannot have a sense of fun and enjoy life.

In life it is important to have a sense of humour since it enables you to get a laugh out of things and situations which are often far from laughable. Being blessed with both a sense of humour and a sense of fun, both of which I think I have fully exploited, I have thoroughly enjoyed life!

I am sure that we did all sorts of outrageous things in our childhood days. Youngsters of today are basically just the same as we were, but the fundamental difference is that we never damaged anybody else's property or person. We were just wicked little devils.

Frank Stroobant had a sense of humour and most certainly still does to this day. He had a gang, with Frank Gebhardt, Cyril Conway, Walter Plunket, George Ganower and many others as members. I was just a bit too young to be a member, but followed their 'questionable' activities with considerable interest and often admiration.

A whole crowd of them would go out together at night. Bill Head was a farmer who tethered his cattle at Beau Sejour. When it was dark, 'Stroo' and company moved the cattle down over the hill to the Cotils. They did this once or twice, then Farmer Head laid a trap and caught them.

Bill Head said;

"You know lads, you are not going to do any good doing this sort of thing. Why don't you do something useful? Why don't you come and help me tether the cattle?"

'Stroo' and his friends thought that was a good idea, so they went out with him one evening.

Bill Head was giving instructions on how to do this and that. He told them that it was necessary to stake the cattle and explained;

"It is important to drive the stake in accurately with one blow - I will show you how it is done and then each of you can have a try, if you like."

So they all gathered around in a semi circle to watch. Bill Head took up the large wooden mallet, swung it above his head and drove it straight into a great big juicy cow pat. They were smothered and the more they tried to wipe it off, the worse it became. Frank Gebhardt's mother made him sleep in the bath that night. 'Stroo' was covered from head to foot and as he has so often related since, had his mouth wide open at the wrong moment! There was a lot of talk in those days of making the punishment fit the crime - Bill Head successfully practised that philosophy !

Adjusting the school clock, in an effort to try and get the final bell rung a little early, was always a challenge as far as us boys were concerned. On one occasion, we were successful and the final bell was rung a full ten minutes early. The clock was positioned high up on the wall, so I had to get up on a cupboard to reach it. I needed assistance, which was always readily provided by other boys - that is until a master was approaching. On one occasion having climbed up, I was just about to adjust the clock when 'Fluffy' Fulford appeared. That required a long explanation.

We played all the known schoolboy tricks and a few more beside, which we invented. Inevitability we were always found out and a suitable punishment administered.

The School bell provided another challenge. At the school there were two staircases. You could go up one flight of stairs, along the passage, through the games room and down the other staircase. The Bell was rung by a cord which hung down over the staircase. The break period was ten minutes and after about five minutes one of us would nip up the stairs, give a tug on the bell cord and quickly run down the other stairs. We would then join the other boys who would be assembling and moaning about the shortness of the break.

Another schoolboy prank we engaged in concerned the lights. In the winter time, as it became dusk the lights had to be put on in the playground. Another boy and I discovered that if we slightly withdrew the fuses the lights would not operate. At a glance the fuses appeared to be properly in place. We had been reasonably successful with this dodge on a couple of occasions and could not resist a further attempt at disruption. My friend was bending over and I was standing on his back adjusting the fuses, when 'Fluffy' Fulford came round the door and took a running kick at my friends invitingly positioned rear quarters. He shot forward and I landed in a heap at the irate 'Fluffy's' feet. A further suitable punishment was administered.

Mr J.P. Warren, Jasper Warren, was one of our masters, who took our class for History before the morning break and for Geography on resumption. I wasn't very good at History, but not too bad at Geography. He would always collect our homework papers before break and leave them on his desk, so he could mark them during our Geography lesson. He often discovered that some of the class hadn't produced any homework. Jasper would call out the names of the boys whose homework was missing - all would declare that they had handed in their papers and of course they had. I also swore that I had handed in my paper. Jasper puzzled this out and discovered that during the break a number of papers would mysteriously disappear.

It quickly dawned on him what was happening when he discovered that young Green's was always one of the papers that was missing. Again a suitable punishment was administered. It usually consisted of vigorous use of a cane, it hurt at the time but you put on a brave face. I would take my punishment and then strut off. In a sense, because you could take your punishment like a man, you became something of a hero amongst the rest of the class. Actually I think that this punishment did us a lot of good, certainly it did me no harm.

Jasper Warren, who later became President of La Société Guernesiaise, was a very interesting man, who sought to teach me Geography. His approach was to turn theory into practice. I recall very well on one occasion he set us as homework, the task of drawing a map of our way home from school. I drew my map with cross roads here and cross roads there, in my usual slapdash way. When I presented my homework for inspection, Jasper Warren looked at it, studied it carefully.

"Green, I see you have drawn this map of 'your way home', where do you live?" he asked.

"Jerbourg Sir."

"Oh yes, have you got your bicycle?"

"Yes Sir."

"Well you and I, with the aid of your map, will cycle to your home this evening after school."

We started off from school, down Brock Road, through the Grange and along Queen's Road, that was fine. Then we branched off into Belmont Road, that is what my map showed, although I hadn't bothered to name the roads. I had just drawn a diagram. I said;

"We turn left here Sir."

"Oh no we don't, your map says turn right and that is the way we are going."

We went down the Vauquiedor, through the Brigade Road and eventually landed up out on the cliffs at the Gouffre.

"Well young Green we don't seem to have anywhere else to go?" Jasper said.

"Well Sir we are a long way away from where I really live."

"I know that - you will go home and tonight you will draw me a proper map. Next week we will follow your new map and see if we fare any better."

Of course I did another map, a proper map, which I traced out and put in all the details I had left out previously. He accepted my new map, but we never used it - he had made his point and I had learnt my lesson. He was a cunning old devil and a gifted teacher. Jasper Warren was also a gentleman of great charm, with a tremendous knowledge of Guernsey. He walked nearly every inch of the island and studied almost every aspect of the terrain!

At school, we boys were always up to some mischief or another. We discovered in the washroom area, a light switch, which, when touched, gave an electrical shock. There was a gang of us and any boy whom we disliked, we forced into the washroom, where we would push the victim's hand on to the light switch. We took a childish delight in seeing our victims jump in the air on receiving an electric shock.

Being a little knowledgeable, we stood on a rubber mat so that we didn't get a shock. We were doing this to a boy one day, when along came one of our masters, 'Titchy' Nordon, who enquired;

"What are you boys doing here ?"

The victim, whose hand we were trying to put on the switch quickly responded:

"Interfering with the light switch sir."

'Titchy' Nordon, of course, investigated to see if we had been interfering with the light switch. Without standing on the rubber mat, he took hold of the switch and shot straight up in the air! Another 'dose' of suitable punishment was administered.

C.J. Le Pelley was our Divinity master and on my very first day at the Intermediate School I fell foul of him. I was playing the fool and pushed another boy off the end of the bench. C.J. knew who was responsible, and came across and swiped me across the ear with a Bible. I took a poor view of that, as I always thought the 'Good Book' should not be used for such a purpose !

Mr Le Pelley owned a motorbike, a 3hp B.S.A., of which he was very proud. In order to get my own back I let down his tyres. His bike was fitted with Schrader valves - I knew how they worked from helping Dad in the shop. My success was short lived as it was obvious that only young Bill Green would know how to do such a spiteful deed. Once again a suitable punishment was administered.

C.J. and I never really got on. However, to his great credit, when many years later I first stood for election as a Peoples Deputy, an elderly gentleman got out of a car and, with the aid of a walking frame, struggled into the Douzaine room at the Castel. On his way past me he whispered:

"I have come to vote for one of my old boys!"

As I was the only old boy in the election, there was no doubt for whom C.J. was going to vote. So, of course, he became a very different character in my retrospective estimation.

In July 1921, King George V came to the island and inspected the massed parade of boys assembled in Cambridge Park. I can clearly recall the King in his Naval uniform, with white trousers. He looked very impressive, just as I thought a King should look. As the King was going to inspect the parade, the boys had been ordered to remove their caps. However because it was such a hot day the King suggested that the all boys be allowed to put their caps back on. I never wore a cap. A boy two down from me didn't have one either. The King stopped and inquired why he was not wearing a cap. I nearly died because I thought the King was going to stop and question me, but to my relief he passed on without a word. That moment of fear is my lasting memory of King George V and Queen Mary's visit to the island.

Later in the day when the Royal couple drove along the sea front, I noticed that Queen Mary was looking over the top of the crowd and wasn't taking too much notice of all the proceedings. She had been affected by the heat of the day, in fact it was later reported that she had nearly fainted. Every schoolboy and girl was given a mug with the portraits of the King and Queen to commemorate their visit.

The Intermediate School was for a time transferred from Brock Road to Vauvert, but as the woodworking equipment was still at Brock Road, we returned there on Thursday afternoons for our woodwork class. After assembling in the playground at Vauvert, we walked in single file to Brock Road where we reported to the Woodwork Master.

I discovered there was no check on our presence at either end and having by that time no great enthusiasm for woodwork, I said to my friend, Arthur Gillam;

"We needn't go to woodwork on Thursday. My Dad's business is closed on that afternoon, so we can go and get Dad's Indian motorcycle and sidecar and go for a ride."

Dad kept his Singer car and the motorcycle in the store in Hirzel Street, which he rented from Mr Guilbert who ran the nearby Box Factory. Dad had taught me to ride the motorbike and sidecar, very unofficially.

So that is what we did. We absconded from school and went for a drive on Dad's Indian motorcycle, Arthur in the sidecar while I rode the bike. There were very few policemen in those days and the odds of running into one was very low. The only trouble we encountered was when we put the motorcycle away, we found it had dripped oil all the way into the store. Arthur and I were there collecting together little piles of dust and putting them on each spot of oil when my Father came down to get out his car. As soon as he saw us he had a good idea what we had been doing. He went over and felt the cylinder of the motorcycle, it was still warm ! We got a 'mother and father' of a wigging for that escapade - we only did it once.

Despite my antics, Dad provided me with my first motorcycle. It was a two stroke Royal Enfield, Model-A, 225cc, with a two speed graduated gear. For a youngster of my age to own a motorbike in those days, was unique. I had my bike before my thirteenth birthday, which meant that I wasn't officially allowed to ride it on the road. However as things were easier in those days, I would take a chance and ride it. Dad was aware of what I was doing and did little to discourage me. When I became fourteen I was able to obtain a driving licence. In the early twenties no insurance or road test was required, in fact I have never taken a Driving Test in my life!

At the time I was the youngest motorcyclist in the island and Inspector Green, the Police Chief, thought he would personally acquaint me with the responsibilities of having a driving licence. I didn't tell him I had been riding a motorcycle around for quite a long time ! He was a very kindly policeman and I think he really liked the fact that my name was Green and so was his, although we were not related.

I was fourteen, possessed my own motorbike and a licence to ride it - and ride it I did, all the time and everywhere. The trouble was that I had to give up time from riding my prized possession, to attend school.

Motorcycle races were held on Vazon Sands on Thursday afternoons, at a time when I was at school, or supposed to be at school! One Thursday I played truant and rode down to Vazon to compete in the sand racing. My bike was only a small machine, but I had taken off the silencer, so it made a lovely sound. The full throated roar of a well tuned motorcycle was and still is to this day, music to my ear!

At fourteen, I raced my first of many races on Vazon sands. During all my years of sand racing, I rarely came off my machine and of course my first race was one of these times. The event was written up in the Press and it proclaimed that 'Young Bill Green came off his motorbike in the Vazon race!'

Being unhurt, I was back at school the next morning. My headmaster, my form teacher and my Father, all read the newspaper report and learnt for the first time where young Green had been on Thursday afternoon. I was in trouble, more for playing truant than for sand racing. Dad was proud that his son had ridden in a motorcycle race, although he did not let on to me at the time.

Frank Stroobant, who, like me, was motorcycling mad, has always said that my popularity at school was not on account of my personality but because of all the motorcycling equipment I possessed. He was probably right - Dad made sure that his son was always a good advertisement for his business. 'Stroo' was also the proud owner of a motorcycle but, as I remember, he had a great deal more difficulty in staying on them than I did!

Our school masters treated us both in the same sort of vein. 'Stroo' and I had the same brand of devilment in us and I am reasonably sure that the masters had a secret admiration for both of us. They did not, however, fully appreciate our antics because it disrupted the whole curriculum. You were either an academic or you were not. There was no argument about it, I was not. There were some boys who could fool around all term and then produce an excellent examination result. I fooled around all term and then turned in the most disastrous examination papers. I was not very good at absorbing information unless I was interested in the subject. If it was about engines or anything mechanical I was all right, but if it was in any way academic I was not interested. In consequence my popularity with the teachers was always at a pretty low ebb.

Frank Stroobant is two years older than I am and when you are at school that is quite significant. 'Stroo' was a school Prefect and as such, organised a swim from the Castle Emplacement to Fermain. He persuaded me and other boys, to enter for the swim. It would be quite safe, he assured everyone, there would be plenty of boats in case anybody got into difficulty. He said he had arranged with Fred Noyon the fisherman to provide six boats. There we were, all lined up, about forty boys, on the Castle walk ready for the swim and only two boats turned up. No matter, off we swam to Fermain.

'Stroo', managed to obtain two half flasks of brandy, so each boat had a supply in case of emergency. Colin Campbell, one of the swimmers, dived in, swam about forty yards and screamed for help. He was dragged into one of the boats and to help his recovery, was given a shot of brandy. He swigged the lot and was put back in the sea again. Another two hundred yards he yelled out again, this time he was pulled aboard the other boat. The second flask of brandy was consumed, by which time Colin was almost paralytic. Although he took no further part in the swim, he had more than his fair share of the 'enjoyment'.

The boy who won the swim, Bert Cleal, was sharp. He swam over to the Valette bathing pools and from there by easy stages made his way over the rocks. He reached Fermain long before anyone else. To get to Fermain, the rest of us had to swim well out to sea in order to keep clear of the rocks of Fermain Headland.

The arrangement 'Stroo' made was that when we completed the swim, we had to walk up to the Fort Road to the transport he had arranged for us to get back to the Castle Emplacement and our clothes

Being the youngest, I was a slower swimmer than the rest and was soon left behind by the other swimmers and the boats. I 'had' to swim to Fermain or drown, there was no alternative. So swim to Fermain I did. When I got there and walked up to Fort Road, the transport had departed. I either had to swim or walk back. In those days, there was no Val Des Terres to shorten the trek. I chose to walk back to my clothes, a long way in a wet bathing costume after a long swim for a little lad.

I must be fair however and say that 'Stroo's' organising ability was to improve in later life!

I went with the school to the British Empire Exhibition at the Wembley Stadium, London, in September 1924. The trip had been organised by our Headmaster 'Fluffy' Fulford. We travelled on the G.W.R. steamer Reindeer to Weymouth, where we were met by a party of our teachers and their wives: Captain and Mrs Steel, Mr and Mrs J.P.Warren, Mr C.W.Toke and Mr Nordon. We were all disappointed to see so many teachers, as we felt that it would restrict our ability to enjoy ourselves.

It was a tremendously successful exhibition, with exhibits from all over the world. There were displays from all the member countries of the British Empire. The Dominions each had their own exhibition pavilion: the Canada Pavilion, the Australian Pavilion and the New Zealand Pavilion. These exhibits depicted each Dominion's culture, with their industrial and commercial activities displayed and highlighted. The British Pavilion featured a reconstruction of the attack on Zeebrugge during the Great War.

At the exhibition, there was row upon row of slot machines and of course us boys could not resist that attraction. We had to use them despite the fact that we did not have any English money. Guernsey pennies were a little bit larger than their English counterparts but, being kids, we had to get the chocolate out so we forced our pennies into the machines. Inevitably there were complaints that the slot machines were not working. The machines were opened up and found to be jammed with Guernsey pennies. Somebody found out where the Guernsey contingent was staying and an official complaint was received. We were made to exchange all our Guernsey money for English coins.

Whilst in London we stayed at the Major Rufane Saunders Hostel, in a disused railway siding at Park Royal. It could accommodate almost five thousand children and it had a huge dining room which seated over three thousand. On the Sunday morning we were taken for a walk in St James Park. It had been raining heavily and as a result the trees were laden down with moisture. As we walked along in our 'crocodile', I took hold of branches, pulling them down, then releasing them. The result was that the boys further behind in the 'crocodile' were getting soaked. Unfortunately for me one of the masters also got a soaking. The consequence was that instead of going to Windsor Castle on the Sunday afternoon, I was left behind at the Hostel as a punishment.

Having nothing better to do, I wandered down to the tuck shop where there was a young girl serving with whom I became quite friendly and we went for a walk along the railway sidings. Ruby and I got on famously and I saw a great deal of her during our stay in London. She took a liking to me and that was to my advantage, because she provided me with free tuck. I came back to Guernsey but could not forget her. I had a yearning for Ruby and built up this wonderful image of her in my mind. They say that absence makes the heart grow fonder and it certainly applied to me.

Sometime later, being the proud owner of a motorbike, I could wait no longer, I had to go and find Ruby again. So, with my motorbike, I set off to look for her. I travelled to Weymouth on the G.W.R. Mailboat, R.M.S. Ibex, it took about three and threequarter hours to make the crossing. The cost was twenty eight shillings and an extra two shillings and six pence for my motorbike. In those day's you were required to drain the petrol tank before you were allowed aboard. They inspected the tank to make sure it was empty and an Automobile Association man met us at Weymouth to give us enough petrol to get to the nearest petrol pump.

Once I had filled up with petrol I rode my motorbike as fast as it would go all the way to London and eventually found Park Royal and the hostel. The hostel had, however, been converted into a factory and the gate was manned by a Commissionaire who refused to let me past, try as I might. I pleaded, I explained that I had travelled all the way from Guernsey, I told him the story of how I met Ruby, but he remained adamant and I remained outside the factory gate.

Being pretty desperate and distraught, having come all that way I just could not accept that I would have to go home without seeing Ruby. I prayed ardently for something to happen to help me out of my seemingly impossible situation, and it did. As I walked back to my motorbike two men came out of a side gate of the factory and I told them my tale of how I wanted to meet this girl again and how far I had travelled. They listened to me and then one of them said;

"Oh you need to see the lady who runs the canteen - she was here when it was a Hostel."

They took me past the Commissionaire, through the gate and into the factory. In the canteen, I met the lady, who said;

"What a strange thing, I had a letter from her today."

I did not know this girl's name, except it was Ruby. This lady took the letter out of her handbag, tore off the address and gave it to me. So the girl of my dreams name was Ruby Noakes, who lived at 30 Anstey Road, Reading. My prayers had been answered.

Back astride my motorbike once more, I travelled down to Reading and found Anstey Road. The lady who answered the door was obviously Ruby's mother and she told me that Ruby was working at Scrpell's Biscuit Factory. Finding the factory, which later became the world famous Huntley and Palmers, I approached the Commissionaire, who was as helpful as the one at Park Royal had been unhelpful.

He was a very kindly old man who listened to my story with great patience, then telephoned all over the factory to find Ruby Noakes. Eventually he said;

"Now my son, if you go to the bottom of those stairs over there, she will come down in a few moments."

Waiting at the bottom of the stairs I was in absolute ecstasy. At any moment the girl of my dreams would appear and walk down to me. The setting was perfect, then this girl appeared and she was as gorgeous as I had imagined. Absolutely stunning ! There was only one problem, however - she couldn't remember me from Adam, so that was the end of my first love affair !

By the time the First World War started, Dad's cycle business was well established. His gross turnover in 1914 was about £600 and net profit just in excess of £100. In today's terms it seems incredible that such a small turnover was sufficient to say that a business was successful. However by the standards of the day, my Father and his business were a success. Cycling was the 'in' thing in those days. Dad worked hard and established a very good reputation for the business and himself. The Royal Enfield agency was proving to be very satisfactory and profitable. I know that before Royal Enfield went out of business after the Second World War, we were the oldest Enfield dealer in the business and they were very proud of us.

Dad realised that in order to maintain the success of the business, he would have to expand into the new motorcycle market and during the war he obtained the agencies for Calthorpe, Douglas, Royal Enfield and Indian motorcycles. It was surprising that they were still being manufactured. His sales ledger, which I still have, records the sale of about 25 motorcycles during the war. I can still recall

Indian Motorcycle and sidecar 1920's.

Dad's delight in obtaining so many machines. He must have made a fairly good profit when he sold them.

After the war he specialised in Indian motorcycles, which were built at Springfield Massachusetts, U.S.A.. Indians at that time were reputed to be the elite motorcycle, made by the worlds largest manufacturer. They were equipped with dynamo lighting, electric horn, speedometer, three speed gears and three inch tyres. Indian's were the most silent and easily controlled motorcycle on the road. The machines, Dad received, were shipped to Guernsey in beautiful wooden packing cases and much of the wood, which Dad saved, was later used to improve and extend Seaplane Bungalow.

Sadly the first person to be killed on a motorcycle in Guernsey was a man called Capitain, riding a 5hp Indian motorcycle and sidecar. He was driving along Doyle Road towards the Grange and was killed when, after first colliding with a lorry coming up the Grange, he hit the wall on the far side of the road. Dad was extremely concerned because he sold Mr Capitain the Indian motorcycle that he was riding. In my Father's sales ledger there is the entry for the sale of a 5hp Indian motorcycle and sidecar, on the 28th. July 1915, to Mr Capitain of the High Street for £76.10.0d. The motorcycle was priced at £63.0.0d. and the sidecar £13.10s.0d.

Indian motorcycles were the first machines which used the twist grip control. Previously, motorcycles had lever controls, including all British manufactured machines. It was suggested at the inquest that Mr Capitain had opened the throttle instead of shutting it.

Royal Enfield Motorcycle and sidecar 1920's.

Soon after the First World War Dad was very keen to acquire a car agency. Mr Thompson in the Grange had obtained the Citroen agency and Father felt that he too should be entering the car market. At that time the French were further advanced than the British in the manufacture of cars, particularly small cars, so Dad went to France and agreed to take on the agency for a car called the Benjamin. Regrettably the Benjamin was the wrong choice, he only imported two cars and they proved to be pretty troublesome. Dad managed to sell one and the other car he kept for himself. The Benjamin was a very small car and I have very nostalgic memories of it as I was allowed to steer the car sitting on Dad's knee.

Dad also had a Singer car for some time and it had a 'dicky' seat at the rear which I would occupy on family outings. It was marvellous in fine weather, but when it rained I got a real soaking ! Dad would put up the hood which was all right for those in the car, but Bill sitting in the 'dicky' seat got 'blooming' wet !

Bob Kimber, the policeman, lived not far from me at Chefoo, along the Jerbourg Road and I passed his house every time I went into town. The Jerbourg Road was not very busy in those days. Coming home, once I had left the main Sausmarez Road and turned into Jerbourg Road, I had a long straight clear drive up to Seaplane Bungalow. It was always a great temptation, for any young motorcyclist like me, to race down the straight at a fair old lick.

One day 'Dreamy' Stranger and I had a bit of a 'beat up' between us as we streaked down the Jerbourg Road to Seaplane Bungalow. After 'Dreamy' had sped home on his motorbike, along came P.C. Kimber astride his pedal cycle. He parked it against the hedge, took off his cycle clips and proceeded up the path to our front door. I stood on the doorstep, trying to look the picture of innocence.

P.C. Kimber took his notebook out of his pocket, his pencil from behind his ear, licked the pencil and said:-

"You know young Green, I have been waiting a long time to catch you tearing up and down the Jerbourg Road. Today I have and I have also caught your friend. I have the numbers of both your machines and I am going to report you for speeding."

So that was that, P.C. Kimber put his pencil back behind his ear, his notebook back into his pocket, his cycle clips back on his trousers, mounted his bike and slowly pedalled back down the road.

After a while I got my motorcycle out and a little slower than usual, at least until I had passed P.C. Kimber's house and went to report to 'Dreamy' Stranger. I told him that we had been caught.

"What speed did he say we did ?" he asked.

"Forty miles an hour!" I replied.

"Bloody liar, I was doing sixty!"

We were very lucky, P.C. Kimber didn't report us but he'd made his point, he had meant it as a warning. He was a kindly old fashioned copper, who was very tolerant with the younger generation.

'Dreamy', Terry Bougourd and I were all motorcycle mad, not only did we race them on the roads, we also on occasions raced them in the the Commercial Arcade. We knew we should not race there because we had been told off times by friendly policemen. Nevertheless we still raced around the Arcade when there was nobody about. One night when we raced through the Arcade, there was P.C. Dave Browning sitting on the window sill of Le Cheminant's, the toy shop.

All of a sudden Dreamy Stranger flashed past him, Dave could not believe his eyes, then Terry Bougourd flashed by, I'm next and he couldn't believe what he was seeing. We all thought that he would be sure to report us. Next time I saw him in the street I thought I was in for it, but he never said a word, probably he never believed what he saw.

The general consensus amongst us boys was that Dave Browning was stupid. I must admit that we used to plague him, mainly I think because he had no sense of humour. I vividly remember one day when Dave was bringing a man he had arrested up Smith Street to the Police Station. His prisoner was struggling a bit, but Dave was walking him arm in arm up the street. The prisoner's hat fell off and he starts shouting;

"Let me go back and fetch my hat."

Dave Browning says;

"No, I know what you will do, you will run away. You stop here while I fetch it."

By the time I reached my fifteenth birthday, my enthusiasm for school had waned considerably. My interests were elsewhere, motorcycling, my Father's business and even one or two young ladies. School had become a very low priority in my life.

One day 'Fluffy' Fulford came to see Dad. I can remember him saying;

"Look Mr Green, we have taught him all that we can teach him, he won't learn any more, he has this urge to be out of school. I don't think there is any benefit in him staying, I suggest you take him away and let him do whatever he is going to do."

Dad wanted me to go on to college but Mr Fulford said;

"I think you would be wasting your money, Mr Green".

So that was that, I left school.

Chapter 3

RACING WAS MY RELIGION

When I left school at the end of the autumn term 1924, I went to earn my living, working for my Father. I was paid the princely sum of seven shillings and six pence a week.

I never really had any ambitions as far as work was concerned, my only real goal in life at that time was to race motorbikes. I previously worked part time for Dad while at school and during the holidays. As a schoolboy I had found the shop and anything mechanical fascinating. Dad was always only too willing to explain how engines and indeed anything else worked. He had great knowledge and infinite patience and I was interested and keen to learn. While still at school he had taught me the basic principles of the internal combustion engine.

Before leaving the Intermediate school, I went with my form to weekly Science classes at Elizabeth College. The master was very impressed with my knowledge of the internal combustion engine and told the class I knew more about it than he did. I drew diagrams on the blackboard to help him explain the working to the class. I explained the timing and how the spark took place at the top dead centre. The master claimed that he actually learned something from me. That episode

Young Bill Green astride a 350cc Royal Enfield watched over by Arthur Couch at Castle Cornet.

impressed on me just how knowledgeable my Father was and it gave me great encouragement to learn all I could from him.

Dad employed the three Couch brothers, Arthur, John and George. They taught me a great deal, particularly when I left school and was working full time. I started my working life doing general cycle repairs, repairing punctures, fitting valves, replacing mudguards, mending ladies dress guards, fitting replacement brake blocks, in fact anything and everything to do with a bicycle. I learnt how to re-bore motorcycle engines, something which is rarely done these days. Sometimes I was even allowed to serve customers in the shop, but often had to call Dad or one of the Couch brothers if I could not handle it.

Ladies' bicycles of that era had their rear mudguards drilled and eyeleted, so that dress cords could be fitted to prevent ladies dresses, which were voluminous, catching in the wheel. I often fitted the cords, which was a very tricky and tedious operation, requiring a great deal of patience. Hand grips on the handle bar ends were always needing replacing. After a time the grip would become brittle and merely by leaning the bicycle against a wall they would get broken. I remember fitting hundreds of these replacement grips at the cost of 1s.3d a pair. There was an art in replacing them, first you had to thoroughly clean the handlebar metal with emery paper, then fill the handle grip with water for three minutes, empty it out and quickly slide the sleeve home in one operation. If you failed to get the grip on in one push, it would stick and, once it did, there was no way of moving it. You had to cut it off and start again with another pair.

Cycle accessories were very lucrative business. Cycle pumps, pump connectors, cycle bells, cyclometers, lamp brackets, chain case covers, tyres, tubes, puncture repair outfits, tyre levers, saddles, oil cans, chains, brake blocks and shoes, cycle locks and much, much more were sold in considerable quantities.

Cycles in those days, were licensed and each had a registration number. We made the number plates, not only for our own sales, but also for most of the trade. We used a metal bending machine that Dad had constructed. A Cycle Licence cost 2s. 6d. for a year or 1s. 3d. for six months.

Most cycle agents of the day re-enamelled secondhand cycles with stove enamel. We had a huge stove enamelling oven in the attic above the Smith Street shop where this was done. The cycles were stripped down and the frames were vigorously rubbed down with emery paper. Everything had to be meticulous clean, Dad insisted on total cleanliness. Three coats of stove enamel were then applied, all baked in the oven. With the cycle frames re-enamelled and the spokes polished to a high standard, the cycles would look like new machines. The price of this operation in the late twenties was about £2 10s. 0d. In 1932, Hercules produced a bicycle for £3 19s. 9d. By 1934 Hercules were producing one thousand bikes a day and the refurbishing trade collapsed.

It was not long before I got bored stiff mending punctures. However I remained totally fascinated by the difference to the performance of a motorbike that a slight change in the shape of a cam would make. Dad explained how an altered contour would give a higher lift or a bit more overlap on the valve timing. I learned how small changes could dramatically improve the performance of an engine. He took a great interest in my racing bike and spent hours with me adjusting the contours of the cams and making other minor modifications. Dad was brought up in Sheffield and, because many members of his family had been involved in the production of cutlery he understood the tempering of steel very well. He taught me how to soften the cams and, after we had re-shaped them, harden them again.

Father took on the A.J.S. agency in 1922. He sold his first motorcycle, a 2.3/4hp 3 speed, A.J.S. on April 8th 1922, to Captain H. Penfold, who was at that time stationed in the island. The price recorded in my Father's sales ledger, was £85. In September 1953 Captain Penfold returned to the island as a visitor and I

Raring to go, Bill Green on a 350cc Royal Enfield.

showed him the original entry in the sales ledger. He was delighted and he hired a cycle from us for the duration of his stay in the island.

Dad built up a great deal of goodwill, particularly as he was prone to put service to his customers before profit. Nevertheless he was a good business man and ensured that he made a reasonable profit. Dad was very proud of the good reputation that he had worked so hard to earn.

I learnt a lot from Dad, he not only taught me about all things mechanical, he also tried to make sure that I had a sound knowledge of basic business principles. I am afraid the administrative side of the business did not interest me in the way my Father would have liked. He did, however, instil in me the basic financial disciplines which stood me in good stead throughout my business life.

Looking back over my business career, I can only say that it was very enjoyable and I believe successful. That enjoyment and success was a direct result of what Dad taught me in my early years. Not only did I have a good grounding, I also had what many people described as a great deal of luck. Luck is really only opportunities which you have the ability to recognise. People who have the ability to recognise opportunities are classified by others as lucky. That ability is an important factor in whether you are successful or not in any sphere of life. Dad's training, enabled me to recognise those opportunities and take full advantage of them.

A few years after we had moved to Seaplane Bungalow, Mrs Annie Bassett-Lowke and her husband, an electrical engineer from Northampton, acquired one of the adjacent large fields. They purchased four small circular tin huts, which had been used by the British army in the first world war. These were brought to Guernsey and erected in the field, in the pattern of a square, and were then connected to each other by the construction of small interconnecting passages. Later the central 'courtyard' area was covered over and the resulting 'structure' was used as a summer bungalow. The family, which included three daughters, came to the island and stayed for a couple of months each summer. They called their summer home, Le Planton.

Bassett-Lowke's brother ran the famous model engineering company, that built specialist scale working models. In mainline railway stations in England, there were working models of Railway steam engines displayed in large glass show cases. At Waterloo Station in London there was a model of one of the Mailboats which served the island. I still have a scale model of an artillery cannon which was made by the company and it is accurate in every detail

Bassett-Lowke and my Father became very friendly and as they were both engineers, one electrical and the other mechanical, they got on well together. Both were interested in the new phenomenon, the wireless. At that time the British Broadcasting Company had just been formed and started broadcasting in November 1922. Because he knew of my Father's great interest, Bassett-Lowke made a special trip over to Guernsey, bringing with him a wireless set he had built. Dad was very keen to see if the transmissions could be received in the island. We had a flag pole at Seaplane Bungalow so they hoisted the aerial to the top. The wireless which was huge, about the size of a desk, was positioned in our lounge at Seaplane Bungalow.

I remember the two of them huddled around the set with their earphones, adjusting the dial for hours before they finally heard the faint call sign, '2LO calling, 2LO calling.'

It was not too long before the Bournemouth Station, 6BM, started broadcasting. I can remember as if it were only yesterday, Bertram Friar, who was the first announcer, in his best B.B.C. voice saying;

"6.BM calling, Bournemouth station calling, 6.BM calling, Bertram Friar calling."

The station being so much closer to the island, the reception was pretty good. That started the wireless boom in Guernsey.

The company who manufactured A.J.S. motorcycles, began to produce A.J.S. wirelesses. Dad who held the A.J.S. motorcycle agency, also took on the A.J.S. wireless agency. Dad sold his first wireless on 9th November 1923 to a Mr Robilliard, who paid £22.7s.6d. for a three valve A.J.S. Symphony set. By the time a Mr Roberts of St John Street decided to buy a similar set, a week later, the price, according to Dad's old sales ledger had increased to £28.7s.6d.

Dad was keen to promote his new agency so, when the Trades Fair was held at St George's Hall, he hired a room and installed a wireless set. Crowds flocked to hear the broadcasts, some people staying there throughout the day, captivated by the novelty. It was a tremendous success and did a lot to popularise the new medium.

In the early days of broadcasting, motorcycle agents seemed to be the natural and obvious trade to undertake the sale and maintenance of wireless sets. It was probably because batteries were required and needed recharging, that the motorcycle trade seemed the suitable outlet. As wireless became more popular the trade drifted away from the motorcycle agents to the more specialist and permanent radio businesses.

Very soon after leaving school and joining Dad in the business, we obtained the contract for equipping the Cottage Hospital at Amherst with wireless. The Matron of the Hospital was very friendly with Advocate H.C. Ninnim and he generously offered to provide the equipment for the benefit of the patients. We had the job of wiring up the Hospital and providing headsets for the patients in every bed. We created a continuous circuit, with newly patented plugs and jacks. When the jack was withdrawn the two pins would close together maintaining the circuit without disconnecting every other patient. The Crawford jack, which was named after the inventor, seemed in those days to me to be a wonderful invention.

Part of the contract involved erecting an aerial on the roof of the building, which later became the Police Administrative Headquarters. I was working on the roof positioning the aerial, when I slipped and slid down the tiles, crashing through a sky light on to the floor below. Apart from the odd bruise I was unhurt. If there had been no skylight I would have most certainly slid off the roof and fallen to the ground three floors below. There was no way that I could have survived such a fall, I was extremely fortunate, as I have so often been in life.

The time came when Dad wanted me to learn a trade. The big question was, what training should I undertake. Bassett-Lowke told Dad that he was confident that he could train me to become a good electrical engineer. The idea attracted me. Having played about with batteries and electrical equipment in the shop, I found the prospect interesting. My father and I both had great respect for Bassett-Lowke's ability. I was sixteen in the August of 1925 and Dad gave me a new 275cc Royal Enfield Motorbike. In early October I left the island to go and train with Bassett-Lowke's Company in Northampton.

Mum made sure that I was suitably attired for my new venture and I was fully fitted out with new clothes, which included a suit and a trilby hat. However, I strongly objected to the trilby - I did not think it was 'Me', but Mother insisted and I had to wear it. My parents came down to see me off, and as the the mailboat was pulling away from the Quay, I was waving goodbye with my trilby and for sheer devilment I dropped it over the side. I was delighted to see it being carried away in the wash of the boat, I could see that Mum was furious, she was shaking her fist at me.

I lived with the Bassett-Lowke family, at Albion Place, Northampton. The three daughters, Vivien, June and Janet, all very good swimmers, swam at the baths nearby their home. The Bassett-Lowkes employed a swimming coach, Mrs Hughes who had great ability as a teacher and trained some of the British teams at the world famous Ilford Pool. The family often went to swim there and took me with them. The reason why I became a good swimmer stems, I believe, from the interest that Mrs Hughes took in me during my stay in Northampton. I owe her a great debt of gratitude for all she did in encouraging my interest in swimming. I have had a lifetime's enjoyment from the sport.

In the summer of 1926, the 'Ye Olde English Fayre' was held in Guernsey. Mrs Barrow, who was the grandmother of Deputy Valerie Renouf, was responsible for staging the Fayre in the grounds of the home of Miss Cox, at the original Beau Sejour House. The Bassett-Lowkes Company won the contract for the wiring installation for the Fayre. I was working in the factory at Northampton when I learned about this contract. By that time I had become very homesick, I missed Guernsey, I missed the sea, I missed my friends and to be honest I missed my parents. So I applied to return to Guernsey and work on the contract

My request was granted and with a man called Mr Darker I came back to the island. Between us we pretty well wired up the Fayre. Mr Darker was a great character who knew his job and knew quite a few shortcuts. When it came to safety he was only too ready to cut corners. Switching off the current to work on the installation took up time, so he regularly worked with live wires. I knew only too well the danger of standing on wet grass and handling live wires. Touch a live wire and you received a 'belter' of a shock.

One time Mr Darker was standing twisting a number of wires together to make a connection and I said to him;

"Aren't you getting a shock when you do that ?"

"Get a hold of my arm."

I took hold of his arm and I nearly looped the loop. How he could stand all that electricity going through him, I still do not understand.

The Ye Olde English Fayre, which included amusements and entertainment brought across from the mainland, lasted a week and was a tremendous success.

When the electrical contract was completed and I was due to return to Northampton, I decided that I was happier at home in Guernsey. So instead I went back into the business with Dad. I had been over in Northampton with the Bassett-Lowke's for just under a year. Whilst I never qualified as an electrical engineer, I learnt a great deal which stood me in good stead throughout my life.

I joined the Royal Guernsey Militia when I was seventeen. Training was compulsorily for all young men unless you had a disability. I look back on my period in the Militia with both pride and nostalgia. I learnt a great deal and thoroughly enjoyed the comradeship. We were required to attend evening training parades at the Town Arsenal and the three weeks annual camp, at what is now Les Beaucamps School.

The annual camp was, for many, the first time they had been away from their homes and their families. It affected people in different ways. Some of the lads hated it, others like me took it in their stride. Looking back on those camps, I can only conclude that they did a great deal to help to forge one's character. A young man of seventeen would enter the camp as a youth and after three weeks, return home as a man.

In camp we were all thrown together. We started off as a motley collection of individuals but after three weeks we became a unit with loyalties to our fellows, our Company and our hut. Nothing mattered but the honour of the Company. We learnt to salute the flag and we were trained to respect so much that is now disregarded. We learnt to say 'Sir' and had pride in our unit, our dress and our bearing. We became a body of men loyal to the King, our island, and each other. It was a great lesson in life and democracy.

Personally I greatly enjoyed my three weeks at camp, although I don't believe the 'authorities' enjoyed me all that much. I approached the Royal Guernsey Militia with the right attitude, I was going to have a jolly good time and enjoy myself. Perhaps my philosophy of life - that whatever else you do, set out to enjoy yourself, stood me in good stead. Like many of my contemporaries at that time, I resented being forced to do things, but if that's what you had to do, well you did it and made the best of it. Actually, when my period of service was completed, I didn't want to leave the Militia

When we attended the three week camp at Beaucamps, we marched there from the Town Arsenal in full uniform. I always found it difficult to wind my 'puttees' so that they did not gradually un-wrap themselves when we were marching. Puttees were a strip of cloth worn, wound around our legs from the ankle to the knee. On one occasion when we marched to camp, one of my puttees came undone and started to trail behind me and the other lads took delight in treading on it, to try and make me trip. Eventually Company Sergeant Major Butcher halted the Company so that I could rewind my puttee. I was not allowed to forget that incident for a very long time!

We had a character in our troop, Bunno Le Maitre, who later became a sergeant in the regular army. At the camp we slept in one of the many huts which had been erected on the site, and there were about thirty boys in each hut. One night a number of us were chucking boots about in the hut and Bunno said;

"Anybody else throws a boot at me, then it goes into the water tank outside my window."

That was a challenge. I crawled up and took his boots from the end of his bed and threw them at him - he promptly put them in the water tank. Next morning Bunno was looking everywhere for his boots. He was a wonderful character and between us we had a great deal of fun.

When the time came for a kit inspection we were always missing some item or other. Bunno would borrow the sergeant's sash and just before lights out, would go into one of the next door huts and yell:

"Put those lights out."

Then he would pick up a broom or a bucket or anything we were missing and return to our hut.

Dreamy Stranger and I both managed to take our motorcycles with us to the annual three-weeks camp. When we were off duty we would jump on our machines and go for a 'burn up'. We were the only two recruits who managed to wear out a pair of army boots during our three weeks training. I can remember the two of us going along the L'Aumone at night, on our motorbikes, trailing our boots on the metalled road surface. The studs in our boots sent up a cloud of sparks. We both enjoyed doing this, but wore out our army boots within a few days. The army was mystified how we managed to wear down our boots so quickly, they thought we had marched for miles and miles.

In the Militia we were taught how to handle a Lewis machine gun. I could dismantle and re-assemble the machine gun faster than the instructor. However when it came to firing the gun that was an entirely a different matter. I never really mastered the art of firing the machine gun, as an unfortunate fisherman found out to his cost. Once we had mastered the theory we were allowed to fire the weapon. In those days we used the Vazon Range for target practice. When my turn came I pressed the trigger without having a proper grip on the gun and sprayed bullets all over the bay. The target, was the only thing I missed. My aim was so bad that an unsuspecting fisherman quietly fishing in Cobo Bay, had to fling himself into the bottom of his boat. When he finally reached shore, his boat resembled a colander, it was riddled with bullet holes. He understandably, was extremely cross and came to see our Major to lodge a complaint. He said that he had been lying in the bottom of his boat with bullets flying all around. I believe he was compensated by the Army, who accepted that such accidents happen when men are being trained.

On the rifle range at Vazon we shot at targets and each company competed against the other companies for the 'Top Shooters' prize. We fired at the target and then by means of a pulley system the 'card' was delivered for our inspection. There was a gauge to measure the 'grouping' of the shots and when the target card had been assessed, we pasted coloured paper over the bullet holes so that it could be used again. A brush was supplied to apply the paste. We quickly discovered that the handle of the brush made holes exactly the same size and shape as the bullets.

'A' Company were soon returning some very good scores. It was not long before everyone was scoring bulls. I was, of course, in 'A' Company and we won the prize for the 'Top Shooters'. Somewhere at home I still have the medal I was 'awarded'.

The Royal Guernsey Militia was disbanded just before the German Occupation in 1940. Former Militia boys still meet every year for a dinner. I had the honour to be the Chairman of one of the annual reunion dinners when the then Lieutenant Governor, His Excellency Lieutenant General Sir Alexander Boswell and the Bailiff Sir Charles Frossard attended.

I used to take quite a lot of time off work to go to England or France with the Motorcycle and Light Car Club. Also I regularly went by myself, particularly to England. Dad encouraged me and turned a blind eye if I got into mischief, which I often did. As a youngster, Dad used to disappear and his family never knew where he was or when he would come back. He told me stories of how, when he lived in Sheffield, he would go wandering off across the Yorkshire Moors, leaving everyone to worry about him. He would get work at some engineering works and only return home when he felt like it. Whenever I disappeared for short periods of time on the mainland, he dare not remonstrate with me because he knew I could always point the finger at him.

I thoroughly enjoyed going to England and exploring on my motorcycle. Guernsey was rather restrictive, while the mainland provided plenty of straight roads and opportunities to put my bike to the test.

Whenever travelling to the mainland by boat there was a choice of two railway companies who were in competition with each other, the Great Western Railway and the London and South Western Railway. The G.W.R to Weymouth was the cheaper.

The cargo boats which plied between Guernsey and Weymouth at that time were the Pembroke, the Lynx and the Gazelle. Each boat accommodated twelve passengers and mainly sailed overnight. I tried to travel on one of those boats if I could, not only because they were cheaper, but the accommodation was excellent.

The Pembroke was a wonderful old ship, which saw service as a passenger boat prior to being converted to carry cargo. I travelled on her if it was at all possible, as I became friendly with the Chief Engineer who would take me down to see the engine room. Dinner on board the cargo boats was quite an event. Passengers dined at the Captain's table with the Captain, the Mate and Chief Engineer. The waiters were resplendent in evening dress with a white waistcoat, there were no half measures, they were all immaculately dressed. The service was on a par with the Ritz.

Besides the cargo boats there were the mailboats which regularly sailed between the island and Weymouth. The G.W.R. mailboats were the Reindeer and the Ibex, which travelled to Weymouth in three and three quarter hours. They crossed the Channel at eighteen knots and were very good sea boats.

I travelled regularly to Weymouth with my motorcycle and, having filled my empty tank with petrol, would just ride and ride. I enjoyed the freedom that my motorcycle gave me and travelled hundreds of miles, often only stopping to sleep. I slept under hedges, in railway waiting rooms, indeed anywhere I could put my head down for a few hours. When in London I stayed at Channel Islands House. A Guernsey family, called Golding owned a house in Russell Square and Channel Islanders could stay there, bed and breakfast costing 4s.6d.

In life everyone has their idols and I am no exception. As far as music is concerned, my idols, have without doubt, been Layton and Johnstone. Turner Layton and Clarence Johnstone the great American singing duo. They both sang and Turner Layton also played the piano. Their music, the sophisticated popular songs of the twenties and thirties, was instantly appealing. They were the tops, they were fabulous and in my opinion, they were one of the legendary musical acts of this century. I followed them all over England and was probably the greatest and most faithful fan they ever had.

I used to write to Columbia Records to find out where Layton and Johnstone were going to perform. Then I would save up my money so that I could go and see them. They were my passion and on my motorbike, I followed them from venue to venue. From the Birmingham Empire down to London and the West Ham Empire. Then back up to the Palace of Varieties in Leeds. Where they went I sought to follow, I would get there somehow.

The nearest I ever got to Layton and Johnstone was when they were appearing in the Mile End Road. I plucked up enough courage to go around to the stage door and saw their manager. I asked him to request them to sing one of their numbers for me.

"They only sing songs that they have rehearsed beforehand - which was the one you wanted?" he said.

I told him my favourite song was Alabami Bound.

"I will see what I can do.".

Well they sang it for me and I came out of the theatre in absolute ecstasy, ten foot tall!

I have what is probably the most complete collection of Layton and Johnstone records and cassette tapes in private hands. They used to make four records a month at the height of their fame and I believe they were the first singers to sell a million records, long before Sinatra, Crosby or the Beatles. They were probably at the height of their popularity during the late twenties and early thirties. Now, of course, quite a number of their songs have been produced on long playing records and cassettes, I have them all.

At one time I was the proud owner of a portable Columbia gramophone, the type which you wound up. In an attempt to charm my girlfriends, I would borrow Dad's car, take a stack of Layton and Johnstone records, my gramophone and a supply of needles. I played all their wonderful love songs and that, if my memory serves me correctly, had the desired effect on many of my girlfriends, provided that is, they shared my passion for Layton and Johnstone.

Layton and Johnstone broke up in the late thirties but their popularity continued until well after the Second World War and even today their records are played and enjoyed.

On my travels around England I went to the De Luxe Cinema in Gloucester, and saw and heard my first talking picture. It was the Jazz Singer and starred Al Jolson. He sang Sonny Boy and many of the songs he made famous. I remember writing to my Father from Gloucester, in the mid twenties and saying;

"Dad there is no doubt about it, the talkies have come to stay."

Motorcycle racing was a religion with me. From the day I played truant from school to take part in my first race on Vazon beach, I was hooked. Dad encouraged me and made sure that I was equipped with a suitable bike. He made sure that I did not have a too big and powerful motorcycle too soon. He believed that I should not ride beyond my ability or experience. He recognised my potential and sought to develop it, without putting me in any danger. Dad was a very shrewd old chap.

Having started my racing career on Vazon sands on a Royal Enfield 225cc., I rode that bike in every race possible. After a while Dad moved me up the ladder a little with a 275cc. Royal Enfield. A year later he provided me with my first A.J.S. machine, a 275cc side valve Model-G5. It was not a racing bike, but we tuned it up and it performed reasonably well. In fact it was quite quick for its day and I was a tolerably successful competitor and won a number of races.

My Father took Terry Bougourd, Tim Thoumine and myself to the Isle of Man, to watch the 1925 T.T. races. In the Junior T.T. Jimmy Simpson came in second on a 1925 350cc A.J.S. Dad took us all into the A.J.S. pits, which was a great thrill for a 15 year old motorcycling racing fanatic. He had been commissioned by Terry Bougourd's father to buy a racing motorcycle for Terry. Dad negotiated and bought the actual bike Jimmy Simpson had just ridden into second place. Terry raced it for some years, very successfully, how I envied him.

It was a wonderful piece of machinery. The rocker gear was made of duralumin, a light strong aluminium alloy containing copper. Duralumin was later successfully used in aircraft manufacture. The push rods were also made of duralumin, everything for lightness. The 350cc machine only weighed 190 pounds. It had twin fuel tanks fitted as it was built especially for the T.T. All in all it was a beautiful racing machine.

When I was 18, I graduated to a 350cc machine. It was an overhead camshaft A.J.S. model-K7, and the first overhead camshaft model that ever came out of the A.J.S. factory. As far as I was concerned it was not a very successful machine and I didn't race that bike for very long. It lacked power and acceleration at the lower speeds and it did not achieve full power until you were doing well over 50 miles per hour. Both on the sand and on the road, that was a drawback. In the islands we raced on short circuits, where full power was needed at much lower speeds. If I had known then what I later learnt, I might have been able to modify it satisfactorily. Looking back, it was probably the exhaust pipe length and the extractor action that was the key to greater power.

I developed the broadside method of cornering long before anybody else locally thought of it. When attending a dirt track race on the mainland I saw Claude Rye, who was later to become one of the largest mainland motorcycle dealers and a very good friend of mine, broadsiding around corners. I thought that it ought to be possible to carry out the same manoeuvre on sand. When I tried it, I soon discovered that it wasn't very easy to do, because sand was much heavier than the surface material of a dirt track.

I eventually geared my machine so that I could drop down low enough in the gears to get the revs going and have enough power on the back wheel to slide it. Then I would open up at the right moment and the bike would broadside around the corner. If I successfully controlled the slide, then I was faster than anybody else. With this great advantage, I beat off all opposition to establish my position as Number 1 racing motorcyclist in the Channel Islands. Of course it wasn't too long before others riders cottoned on to the idea. However I had perfected the broadside method of cornering, so while other riders sometimes kept up with me through a corner, no one ever got the better of me and my machine.

I never seriously injured myself racing, although I rode competitively for well

Ready for the 'Off' Vazon 1930's. Bill Green No.2, Bert Coutanche No.11. 6 & 7 from right.

over thirty years. I was fortunate to have a natural ability and developed a considerable degree of skill in the sport. Also, I possessed a certain amount of common sense and consequently always raced within my own capacity. If that wasn't good enough to win, I would accept the result and wouldn't take the 'extreme' chance which some other competitors often took and as a result sometimes beat me. They relied on luck and nine times out of ten it deserted them. I preferred to rely on skill and ability and always rode with my head. I felt that I was a better rider than most of my compatriots and could win races by ability. I convinced myself that I did not need to take chances to win. I freely admit to being a conceited youngster, but my record and the fact that I managed to avoid injury for so long must prove something.

I raced all around Guernsey and Jersey, not only on my own machine but also on any machine I could lay my hands on and in every race and competition that was held. Motorcycle racing was my life. From time to time I ventured to the mainland to race at such places as Southport. I was quite successful there, except for the presence of another rider, Fred Rist. He was dedicated to win regardless of the consequences. He beat me every time we raced, but I did have the satisfaction of taking second place on a number of occasions against a large and strong field.

I raced on the Brooklands circuit on two occasions before the war. They held meetings for amateurs and I was keen to compete on the world famous track. Tim Thoumine had attended meetings at Brooklands and he came back and encouraged me to enter the 'Clubman's Race' which was for riders with a certain amount of road racing experience. Although I only really had sand racing experience they accepted my entry, albeit under sufferance. I remember that there was quite a bit of correspondence flying back and forth before my entry was finally confirmed.

There were about twenty riders in each of the two races. Semi professionals like Freddy Dixon and Eric Fernhough took part. My bike and I were no match for them, with their superior racing machines. Fernhough, who was a well known amateur racing rider, could lap Brooklands at about 100 miles per hour. Freddy Dixon was also well known for his ability to race his Douglas machine at high speed. These two boys knew Brooklands like the back of their hands and fully used their knowledge to their advantage. They would get right up on the banking whilst I was still down below. Then they would swoop down the bank at great speed, creating the lead which won them the race. I tried going up the banking, but it was like going up hill for me. I learnt a great deal from my two races, but it would have taken many more 'outings' to have become as adept as they were in the use of the track. Racing at Brooklands was a great experience which I look back upon with considerable pride. There are not many former racing motorcyclists around today who can boast that they raced at Brooklands. I was there, I raced, I enjoyed it and I now treasure the memory.

Brooklands was a mecca for those of my generation who relished the thrill of speed. I went there a number of times to watch the motor racing. I saw many of the greats of that era, as well as the famous. I recall Billy Cotton the band leader racing in a Riley and whenever I heard him on the radio or watched him on the television after that, I always thought of Brooklands.

I was standing alongside Jane Baxter, the actress, when her husband Clive Dunfee, went over the top of the banking and was killed. There were the two brothers, Jack and Clive. They entered the 1932 500 mile race and were taking turns driving a big Bentley, speed six. The car won the previous year's race at the record speed of almost 120 miles per hour.

Clive had just taken over from Jack and had only completed a few laps of the two and a half mile circuit when the accident happened. Driving at over 130 m.p.h., he swerved to avoid another competitor, put a wheel over the edge of the Members' Banking and lost control of the car. It careered through the air taking the tops out of many of the trees at the top of the embankment. Dunfee was flung out of the car and hurled down the banking of the race track, narrowly missing another car in the race. He was killed outright. Despite wreckage being strewn across the track, the race was allowed to continue.

After the crash, while the race continued, I saw one man hanging on to the hand of another man at the top of the embankment, whilst using his free hand to stretch down to grasp hold of a branch of a tree which was lying on the race track. The crowd watched with bated breath while he pulled the large branch out of the path of other cars which were flashing past. When he regained the safety of the top of the bank a great cheer went up.

There were always large crowds on the Members' Banking and, in order to provide greater protection for them, a wood paling fence was built along the edge of the track to prevent any more cars going over the top.

The lap record holder at that time was Tim Birkin. I went up to see him race sometime after the Dunfee crash and watched him use the fence to his advantage by driving around the top of the banking with two wheels on the wood paling. In my book that was quite something - highly dangerous - but that was why he was the track record holder.

One of my regrets is that I never competed in the Senior T.T. race in the Isle of Man. I entered the amateur race on one occasion. My entry and fee had to be in many weeks before the event. Arthur Couch who was one of our mechanics and I travelled to Weymouth on the mailboat and rode the bike up to Fleetwood, where we caught the ferry to the Isle of Man. We took it in turn to drive, while the other rode pillion. On arrival, we stripped the bike of all the superfluous 'bits' in order to reduce it's weight for the race. The motorcycle was a pushrod 350cc A.J.S., which in my opinion was a pretty fast bike, that was until I saw the competition ! It was an amateur race but many of the competitors had a completely professional approach. By comparison my bike and I were totally unprepared.

The race was over six laps of the Isle of Man circuit, and there was a very large field of competitors. I had a good start and clocked a time of 42 minutes 38 seconds for my second lap, which was not up with the leaders but still a very respectable time. I had completed 3 laps and over half the race when valve bounce caused a push rod to jump out. It was a great disappointment at the time but I had the satisfaction of having competed in a T.T. race in the Isle of Man. Arthur and I set to, repaired the machine and rode it back to Guernsey.

After the Second World War, in 1949, I went back to watch the T.T. races. On the Sunday they closed the circuit to traffic and allowed motorcyclists to practice to their hearts content. The locals called it 'Mad Sunday'. I took the opportunity of having a burn up around the circuit and recorded laps of 33 and 34 minutes, approaching an average speed of 70 miles per hour which, I felt, was very creditable and a vast improvement on my pre war effort. Of course by then I had a more powerful machine and technology had made considerable advances.

While I raced motorcycles because I enjoyed it, Dad, encouraged me not only for that reason, but because it was good for our business. We were in business to sell motorcycles and my successes meant that customers would buy an A.J.S. from Green's of Smith Street, rather than a B.S.A. from Millards. There was considerable competition between my Father and Tommy Millard. While there were other dealers in the island, Millards were our main competitor as they had the B.S.A. agency and sold a considerable number of motorbikes. It is fair to say that they were at one time outselling us with their B.S.A. agency. In many of the races in which I competed, there were more B.S.A. than A.J.S. machines. However as Dad put it;

"Young Green and his bike usually wiped the board with them", and that was good for business.

The competition between dealers was not limited to the Racing Circuit, it spilt over into the advertising columns of the Guernsey Evening Press.

Millard's would advertise.

'Go down to Vazon on Thursday and watch the B.S.A.'s go by.'

Dad would respond with.

'Yes, go down to Vazon and watch the B.S.A.'s go by, you won't SEE the A.J.S.'s they'll be going too fast!'

Nothing very subtle about the advertisements, but just as competitive as the race track.

My racing activities, and the publicity obtained, kept the name of Green's and A.J.S. in the public eye. Greens and A.J.S. were synonymous and very successful. We were eventually selling more A.J.S's. than Mr Millard sold B.S.A's. which of course, was the object of the exercise.

I was not sponsored by A.J.S., I was racing purely as an amateur. However I did have a Guernsey pullover embroidered with the initials A.J.S. on it. It was a form of advertising, which helped our business. In comparison with today, advertising was in its infancy, but the general public of the island were fully aware that Green's were the agents for A.J.S. motorcycles.

Without doubt I could ride and race a motorcycle as well as any man in the Channel Islands. It was natural that I should want to progress further, even to the extent of turning professional.

Dad sent all my race results to the Managing Director of A.J.S. Motorcycles. My record was impressive and as we were one of their Dealers, they naturally took a keen interest. They sent their Racing Manager, Fred Neale, to watch me race in some of our local meetings. I must have impressed Fred, because not long after I was approached and offered training with A.J.S. at the Brooklands track, with a view to riding with the A.J.S. team. Obviously they felt that here was a young man with the potential to become a professional rider. Naturally I was flattered by the offer, it was the fulfilment of all my dreams.

I was 18 and my Father was well into his 60s. Although I did not appreciate it at the time, Dad was looking forward to retirement and to handing the business over to me. He was shrewd enough to realise that I would not come to too much harm racing in the islands, as an amateur. If, however, I was to become a professional with much more powerful machines, I would be encouraged to take greater risks and who knows what the consequences would be. Also if I was to join A.J.S. I would have to leave the island, and would not be around to take over the business he had so successfully built up. He believed that the business would stand me in good stead for the rest of my life, while professional motorcycle racing would only, at the most, be for a few years.

Dad therefore was very much against my accepting the offer from A.J.S., but dared not say so. I knew instinctively that he did not want me to go, but I desperately wanted to accept the offer. It was torment for me because I was tremendously fond of Dad and wouldn't have done anything to hurt him. I am proud to say I was that sort of person. Dad was a wonderful father and we were very close. He knew me pretty well, probably at that time better than I knew myself.

Dad solved the 'problem' in his own way. He organised a row between us. We used to argue like the devil about the future of the business. Dad, for his part, was happy to let the business continue the way he had run it for many years, very successfully. I on the other hand, wanted us to get bigger. I wanted to stock some special motorcycles but he didn't think that we should. I was the typical impatient youngster who wanted everything to happen there and then. We disagreed, we argued, but we respected each other's point of view. We never fell out to the extent that we lost our respect or love for each other.

How he 'set up' the row I do not know even to this day, but I can see him now, getting up from his desk and saying;

"Now look here my boy, You think you know everything about everything. You think you know how to run this business better than me. All right then, I am going to walk out of this business now, and it will be your responsibility. If you ever need me, then you can call me back."

He put his pen down on his desk, picked up his hat and coat and walked out, just like that! Being a conceited little so and so, which I obviously was and not being prepared to ask for or seek advice, guidance or help from my Father, I was left to run the business !

Chapter 4

DETERMINED TO MAKE A SUCCESS

Dad totally withdrew from the business. He busied himself at Seaplane Bungalow, where he built eleven additional bedrooms in the form of an annex. My parents ran it as a guest house, Mum did all the cooking and Dad did anything and everything that needed doing. Despite both being in their sixties, they developed it into a very successful little business. Together with other guest house proprietors on the Jerbourg peninsula, he formed an Association, of which he was President. Dad produced a map of the area on which were marked all the guest houses belonging to members. This was used to promote their businesses, with considerable success. My Father was a great Association man, for many years he was President of the Cycle Traders Association and a delegate to the Guernsey Chamber of Commerce.

I for my part, set about running the Smith Street business. Being eighteen, and determined to make a success of it, I quickly became totally absorbed in the business, working virtually day and night. Very reluctantly I turned down the offer from A.J.S. to race professionally. Oh how I would have liked to have competed on the British and Continental circuits. I realised, however, that the business was my future and that it had to come first.

When I took the business over from Dad in 1928 the turnover was just in excess of £5,000 a year, while the net profit was in the region of £400. That in those days was the measure of a very successful business. Father had set me up in a business that was reasonably profitable, left me with a well stocked shop and £300 in the bank. At the time I did not appreciate just how fortunate I was to have such a generous Father.

I reacted just as Dad hoped - knuckling down to the job in hand and at least for the time being, gave up the thoughts of becoming a professional racing motorcyclist. Years later when Dad let on to me about his ploy, he said that his great fear was that as a professional I would have been either 'very successful or very dead !' Dad told me that he had organised the row between us, knowing the character I was, so that I would set about showing him I could successfully run the business. Cunning old devil, Dad was no fool!

We always had a chat at the weekend about how the week's business had gone. He was interested in how many pushbikes we had sold and whether we had sold a motorbike or two. Dad kept a close watch on the bank account, he knew that was a good barometer of how I was running the show. Otherwise Father left me very much to my own devices as far as the day to day running the business was concerned. He knew that he had left me with a good staff who would see that I came to no real harm - I suspect that they would have told my Father if I had been doing anything way out of order. I am sure that they used to let him know from time to time how I was coping. Despite keeping away from the shop, I was aware that he was still keeping an eye on things. I paid him a 'return' on his financial involvement in the business.

When I took over from Dad, I inherited five staff, all very knowledgeable and loyal. Business in those days was very different from today, we were like a family, we stuck together and supported each other. Arthur and John Couch repaired cycles brought in by customers. The third Couch brother, George had left us. Lily Knight, who eventually married Arthur, was an excellent sales lady and worked in the front shop. Bert Coutanche, a young lad of fourteen had just been taken on by Dad, and was to stay with me for almost forty years. My other member of staff was John Langlois, whose brother was the hairdresser in the Arcade. John had been with Dad for a number of years and as a small boy I had been fascinated by his pocket watch. He was very proud of his watch, it was the big English lever type which struck the hour. He always wore it, whether he was working or not, with a waist coat and chain.

Arthur Couch who was much older than I was, had taught me to ride my little bike. He was a great character and in many ways was the mainstay of the business. Arthur taught me the art of splicing cycle tubes. If you had a 28" cycle tube and you required a 26" one, you would cut a piece out and splice it. It was quite a technical job to do it properly and that skill came in very useful during the occupation when there was an acute shortage of tubes. When I showed my wartime staff how to splice a tube they were amazed that I knew how to do it.

Occasionally I worked at the workbench alongside Arthur, but if there was office work requiring attention I would concentrate on that. I don't think the fact that I had taken over the responsibility for the running of the business had any adverse affect on the staff. I did not attempt to change things too much. There was no need to, as Father had built up a good business that ran well and was profitable.

Although I was now responsible for the business, I still competed locally in any and every motorcycle race in the Channel Islands. I tuned my bikes in the workshop upstairs, above the shop. Dreamy Stranger and I spent many evenings and weekends up there, getting our bikes ready for the next race. That was my interest, motorcycles were my life - I was dedicated to racing motorbikes. The priorities in my life at that time, were work, racing bikes and the ladies, in that order. The ladies had to take second place to my motorbikes at that time and that was to turn out to be one of my problems.

The cycle business remained profitable, as the late twenties were boom years. Motorbikes and cycles were selling well. We sold around a hundred cycles and a dozen or so motorbikes a year. The price of motorbikes varied from about £45 to well over £100. My old friend 'Stroo' bought an A.J.S. for £54.10s.0d. and Louis Guillemette, who later became the States Supervisor, a smaller machine for £45. Cycles by that time had been considerably reduced in price, in fact they had come down to less than half the immediate post First World War price. I vividly remember selling La Dame de Sark, a ladies Enfield Cycle with a three speed gear for £4.15s.9d.

When I took over the responsibility for running the business the A.J.S.Agency was well established and remained an important ingredient in our success until they finally went out of business after the Second World War. The original A.J.S. company was formed in 1912 by four brothers from Wolverhampton. The eldest brother was A.J.Stevens and his initials were used for the name of the legendary motorcycles. Originally their motorcycles were very much transport vehicles, but during the twenties A.J.S. built a reputation for racing machines. Their machines won many Tourist Trophy (T.T.) races, and their motorcycles were raced all over the world. In the 1920s they were, along with Norton, probably the leading British manufacturers of the era.

A.J.S., like many companies, was hit hard by the slump in business around the time of the depression. They sold out to the Collier brothers who ran the big

Matchless factory at Plumstead in London and the manufacture of A.J.S. motorcycles was transferred south.

In the early thirties I opened the shop at eight in the morning and closed at six in the evening. Thursday was half day closing, but we opened on Saturdays from eight in the morning until half past nine at night. It was a long and very tiring day, but it was the day that much of our business was done.

At that time electric lightning for bikes was taking over from the old fashioned carbide lamps. Saturday night for us had been the time of the week when we replenished the carbide in the lamps for cyclists. I can remember when I was a young boy working with my sister, Daisy filling carbide lamps for tuppence a time. I had the job of sieving the old carbide in order to save any of the larger lumps which were reusable. I learnt the art of selling the same item twice and as a result it was a very profitable trade. In the late twenties and thirties dynamo lighting sets become very popular and changed the whole pattern of Saturday nights. Instead of filling lamps we stored peoples bicycles for them while they promenaded around the Town.

Every morning the shopfront was washed down and the pavement swept, using a bucket of water and a broom. I did that myself because I wanted our premises and the street outside to look clean and attractive. I personally worked until about

A bedecked Smith Street. Note little bike, and signs for Hollis, P.R.Rabey, A.J.S. and Greens

half past ten, then I would nip down to Stainers, a restaurant at the bottom of the lower Pollet, for a cup of coffee and a chat. Looking back, I had a very carefree life in those far off pre war days. I was never afraid of hard work, in fact I used to thrive on it, but took plenty of time off to enjoy myself. Whether I was off to the mainland on any of my many exploits, racing or just nipping down to Stainers, the staff would carry on and keep the business going. They were always very loyal. I doubt if I fully appreciated their support and loyalty at the time. In retrospect they were a super team.

Stainers, which post-war became Da Nello's Restaurant, was as far as we youngsters were concerned, the 'in' place. We met there at all times of the day and night. It was run by old pop Stainer and Mrs Stainer and, when they retired, by Reg and Eileen Stainer. The restaurant opened very early in the morning, when passengers from the mailboat came in for breakfast. As soon as the mailboat left harbour all the dockers would be there, because in those days they had no other facilities.

I went down to Stainers regularly each morning. It was the the young business men's morning meeting place, I liked to regard myself as a business man. On the way down I would call in for Ralph Palmer who worked with his Father at the chocolate shop, which later became Machon the jeweller. There was always a crowd of us there including Eddie Bougourd from Motor House and Colin Munro, from the electrical shop. We would sit there enjoying the latest gossip and putting the world to rights.

They served a very good three course lunch for a shilling, consisting of soup, meat, two veg and potatoes, and some sort of sweet, which would often be rice pudding, or a choice of that sort. A cup of tea was tuppence. It was very good value even in those days. One thing about Stainers which still sticks in my mind was that there was always a vase of flowers on your table. A small point, but it is surprising how it has made a lasting impression on me.

There was an afternoon tea session, which attracted many shoppers. In the evening many of us would meet up there before going off to play table tennis at the Artisans club. Afterwards, when we were so tired that we could hardly stand up, we would return and recuperate with milk shakes. Other times we would meet there before setting out on a 'burn up' of the island on our motorbikes. In the evening there was a two course meal available for anyone who wanted it. They had residential rooms above the restaurant which were mostly used by commercial travellers visiting the island. All in all Stainers was quite an enterprise.

Reg Stainer was a pretty shrewd business man in my estimation, that is until one day he made what I can only describe as an error of judgement. He charged tuppence a cup for his tea, which was reasonable - no one complained, not even the dockers. Reg found a good source of quality tea at a very competitive price and decided that he would sell some of this tea, by the pound, to his restaurant customers at a very attractive price. He stacked packets of this tea on the counter and put up a sign saying;

> "This super tea I have found,
> makes 200 cups with one lb."

Clearly he anticipated selling his customers a lot of this tea. Ken Gould who was a docker and carter, a rough diamond if ever there was one, came in with his mates and read this notice. He rubbed his chin and thought for a moment, then boomed out at the top of his voice:

"Stainer you bloody rogue!"

Reg apprehensively inquired "What's the matter Ken?"

"Two hundred cups from one pound of tea and you are charging us chaps tuppence a cup."

The packets of tea rapidly disappeared from the counter!

There was a character, old man Bichard, who was a regular at Stainer's. One evening when some of us were in there drinking our milk shakes, two commercial travellers who were staying there got into a very heated discussion. They were arguing about Freud and I remember one of them saying; "If you take the moving atoms out of that fire place, it would cease to exist!"

None of us could comprehend this, we looked at the fireplace with absolute awe. These chaps were in a dimension way above us.

"Yes, but of course if you read your Freud it would be so and so......" The other commercial traveller replied.

Progressively these two became very heated and we expected blows to be struck at any moment.

Old man Bichard was sitting in his usual place beside the fire. He had heard all this and, when there was a pause in the argument, he spat in the fire and said, pointing to the ever present flowers in the vase on one of the tables;

"There's creation for you!"

The tension was broken and everyone laughed.

Pop Stainer was the Island Fire Chief and if the fire bell rang, he dropped everything and went and took command. The fire station and fire engine were in Upland Road. The procedure was that Joe Way, who drove the fire engine and ran a small garage next door to the restaurant, would get his car out and take old pop Stainer to the Station. Of course when the fire bell sounded, we would all dash out, grab our motorbikes and follow the fire engine to the fire.

Pop Stainer, having to rush off, would leave Reg Stainer in charge of the cafe. Reg would shout;

"Pay on the way out, pay on the way out."

We weren't bothered to pay as we were in too much of a hurry to follow the fire engine to the fire. We attended some wonderful fires.

One of the best of them was in the Market Square where Richings the grocers shop caught fire. Having arrived on my motorbike, I was standing with my back to the market, looking up the stairs. I could see butter stacked at the top of the stairs and, as the fire took hold, pounds of flaming butter started to slide down the stairs and right across the pavement. Very soon people were tiptoeing around in a sea of melting butter. We thoroughly enjoyed that fire.

Another spectacular fire occurred when the Piette Saw Mills went up in flames. From our point of view, that was a good fire as well. We followed the fire engine all around the island and witnessed many of the best fires.

At midnight on Friday nights, a group of us including 'Stroo', 'Dreamy', Andre Audaber and E.Lewis Troalic would set off from Stainers to race around the island, T.T style, on our motorcycles. We would start off by racing around the Banques towards the north of the island, and then follow the coast road around until we reached L'Eree. Then we would turn inland and come back over the hill to town. At that time of night there was no traffic about and never any policemen to dampen our enjoyment. The only accident that ever occurred was when 'Stroo' hit the back of a hay cart. What it was doing on the road at that time of night I do not know, but it didn't have a light of any description. 'Stroo' finished up in the hay cart, his pride more hurt than anything. We always returned to Stainers for a final cup of coffee before setting off for our homes when the restaurant finally closed at around two in the morning.

On one occasion when we left Stainers on one of our notorious 'burn ups', we almost finished up with egg on our faces. Dreamy and I set off to race down to Pleinmont and on the way Dreamy, who at the time was just in front of me, braked slightly to avoid a chicken. The chicken momentarily became caught up in his bike before running across the road. We both looked round and laughed and drove on to

Pleinmont. When we arrived there and dismounted, Dreamy spotted a perfectly shaped fried egg on the top of his exhaust pipe! We had to show all our pals this wonderful phenomenon, so Dreamy rode his bike back into town, as slowly and as gingerly as he ever rode a motorbike in his life.

After my disappointment over Ruby Noakes the ladies had taken a lower priority in my life. It was not that I wasn't interested, I most certainly was, but largely because I was very preoccupied with motorbikes and motorcycle racing. Girls, at that time in my life, had to take second place, but I think I can say with absolute certainly that in later years I have more than corrected that deficiency!

One of the pastimes which I enjoyed very much, was dancing. I regularly attended many of the dances held at the Channel Islands Hotel, which later became the Savoy. Bert Gallienne organised these and other social activities and we became very friendly. He had a girlfriend, Daisy Hayman. Her father was a deeply religious man, who went to church, two or three times every Sunday. He was very strict with Daisy, who was not allowed out after 10 o'clock at night, even though she was almost twenty-one.

At the dances Bert was always busy acting as Master of Ceremonies, so he would say to me;

"Bill will you run Daisy up to her house and bring her back?"

So I would run Daisy back to her home in Rue Poudreuse, on the pillion of my motorbike. She would go in and say;

"Good night Mum, good night Dad," and go up to her bedroom, but instead of going to bed she climbed out her bedroom window, slithered down the drainpipe and tiptoed along the garden path to where I was waiting. Then I would take her back to the dance and Bert.

Bert for some reason or other always had some clearing up to do after the dance, so I would be delegated to take Daisy home, often well past midnight. Whilst Daisy found it easy enough to escape out of her bedroom window, it was impossible for her to return the same way, so she had to go in the back door and up the stairs and do this without her father hearing. I always had a strong suspicion that her mother knew what was going on, but did not let on to her dad. As I remember, he took a very poor view of Bert and me, no doubt with good reason.

I would run Daisy almost up to her house, she would get off the bike and would walk up to the gate. Then I would drive my motorbike flat out past the house, making as much noise as possible which, as I recall, I did with great efficiency! After each run I would turn the bike around and go back down again whilst Daisy made progress towards her bedroom. First, she would open the gate and run up the garden path to the back door and wait, then on my next run she would get as far as the bottom of the stairs. As I raced passed again she went up three or four stairs. This went on until I saw a match struck in Daisy's bedroom window and I knew it was time for me to go home. Whilst Daisy was safely back in her bedroom the rest of the neighbourhood was by now wide awake and fuming at that noisy motorcyclist, who should know better at that time of night. Many times I did Bert the favour of taking Daisy home !

One favour I did for Daisy, however, led to my appearance in the Magistrates Court. One afternoon, as I drove up St James Street and into the Grange, I spotted Daisy on her bicycle and said;

"Jump in I will give you a lift home, I can wheel your bike while I drive." Daisy got into the front seat alongside me and, with one hand on the steering wheel and the other guiding the bicycle along side the car, I set off up the Grange.

I had not gone more than a hundred yards when Police Inspector Sculpher stepped out in front of the car and put up his hand for me to stop. I was summoned 'for driving a motorcar with want of care' and duly appeared in Court. I admitted the infraction and was fined twenty shillings and costs.

Late one wintcr's night I was on my way home and passed Bert's Douglas motorbike and sidecar parked outside Daisy' house. It had been snowing heavily and there was a covering of about a half inch. As I went past I could see a figure on Daisy's lawn, so I stopped and there was Bert on his hands and knees writing 'I love Daisy' in the snow.

Bert ran a garage at the bottom of the Colborne Road, opposite Prince Alberts Road. Passing late one night, I noticed the lights were on, and assuming that Bert must still be working, I stopped and went in. There was Bert pinned up against the wall at the back of the garage by a Model-T Ford which was ticking over. The old Model-T's had band gears which tended to slip if they weren't properly adjusted. Bert had apparently started it on the handle and it had crept forward pinning him against the wall. Fortunately the starting handle, which was between his legs, was taking much of the weight and prevented him from being crushed.

As I went in Bert yelled;

"Switch the 'f'ing' engine off,"

"All right," I said, but didn't hurry as I hadn't appreciated the seriousness of the situation.

"Switch the bloody thing off it's pressing against my chest!" he shouted.

I switched it off. "How long have you been there?"

"About thirty minutes."

"What were you going to do if I hadn't come along ?"

"I would have had to wait until the so and so petrol ran out, I suppose."

A gang of us used to rent a little hut, called the Nest, on the cliffs, at the top of Saints Bay for a fortnight in the summer. The boys would camp down in a tent and the girls slept in the hut. Daisy Hayman was one of our group and she had a cousin, Nesta Batt, who lived in the village of Drybrook in Gloucestershire. Nesta came to Guernsey on holiday for two or three summers running. She stayed with Daisy and joined our little group of campers. Nesta and I fell for each other.

I made many trips to see her in Gloucestershire and we got engaged on my twenty first birthday, the 19th August 1930. Drybrook, however was a long way away and having the responsibility of running the business and being dedicated to motorcycle racing, I could not get away as often as Nesta, or indeed I, would have liked. Besides, there were a lot of attractive girls here in Guernsey so in the circumstances, it was not surprising that our romance did not blossom.

On one of my trips to Gloucestershire to see Nesta, I encountered what is probably the coldest weather and worst driving conditions of my whole life. Before leaving Drybrook to return home Nesta's Mother gave me a large 'lump' of Christmas cake for the journey. I was driving along eating this cake as I went. Snow was banked up on the sides of the roads and there were deep drifts often reducing the road to less than pavement width. Suddenly I realised that a lorry was bearing down on me from the opposite direction, and I had to veer off road to avoid an accident. I drove into a very deep snow drift and as the bike went in, the snow pushed me off the back of my saddle.

As I picked myself up the lorry driver shouted;

"Are you all right mate?"

"Yes I am O.K. thanks"

I was unhurt, but I didn't know what a job it is was going to be to get my bike out of the snow drift, - I never did find the rest of my Christmas cake.

What finally broke up our engagement was when I met Ruth Lempriere and took her for an 'unforgettable' ride in my Father's car. Looking back now, I do not think I was in any way ready to settle down to the 'restrictions and responsibilities' of married life. In fact I was really only just beginning to enjoy the benefits of 'playing the field'.

I was walking up St Julians Avenue one evening, when I met Ruth Lempriere coming down the Avenue.

"Hullo where are you going?" I said.

Ruth replied, "I have been trying to get into St Julian's cinema but I can't get in, it's full."

"I was going there."

"You won't get in, I have just tried."

"Lets go for a walk up the road." I suggested.

We walked a little way up the road and I noticed Dad's car, an Austin Seven parked at the side of the kerb. As I knew he was at the pictures and would not be out for some time I suggested to Ruth that we went for a ride. I always had a good line with the ladies!

Ruth liked the idea, so we borrowed Dad's car and went for a drive out in the country. I was, of course trying to impress Ruth with my driving ability. I was convinced that I knew how to manoeuvre the car at speed through corners, that was until I had a little bit of bad luck and turned it over in the Talbot Valley. It wasn't too difficult to turn an Austin Seven over, they were not designed for cornering at speed. Of course I was going too fast around the bend, but that was all part of the process of impressing the young lady.

As the car turned over, I fell out and found myself standing up on my two feet on the roadside. I remember seeing the car going down the road rolling over and over, with its lights first coming into view and then disappearing again. The Austin Seven finally came to rest with Ruth still inside. I ran up to the car and pulled her clear, miraculously she was un-injured except for cuts on her leg. There we were stranded in the valley, with the car on its side and both of us shaken by the experience. My concern was that my Father was unaware that I had 'borrowed' his car, so that when he came out of the pictures he would find the car missing and report its disappearance to the Police.

Fortunately Mr Robilliard, the watch maker from the Pollet, came along and on seeing the road blocked, stopped to enquire if we were all right. He helped me push Dad's car on to the verge. Then he took Ruth home to St Sampson's and dropped me off at Stainers. In the restaurant there was a big mirror, so naturally I looked to see what kind of mess I was in after the accident. I was wearing a blue jacket, grey flannel trousers and a white shirt with a collar and tie. In those days I used to grease my hair - there was not a hair out of place. I turned around, I didn't have any mud on me anywhere, as far as I could see I was untouched by the accident.

When it was time for the performance to end I went up to St Julians Cinema to meet Dad.

He came out and greeted me.

"Hello my boy, what are you doing here?"

"I have come to see how I am going to get you home, Dad?"

"You can come home with me, I've got the car up the road."

"You haven't it is on it's side in the Talbot Valley!"

The first words my Father said were, "Are you all right, my lad?"

"Yes, I am O.K."

We took a taxi out to see the car, which was a write-off. My Dad, bless his heart, never said a word about my taking the car.

When I arrived home I took my jacket off in front of the big mirror in my bedroom and turned around. My shirt, at the back, had a whole circle of mud on it. I think that I must have fallen out of the car when the driver's door opened and bounced on my back before landing upright on my feet. My coat had obviously come up over my head as I went out the door and dropped down when I was deposited on my feet. When my jacket was down there was no sign of the mud to be seen. Otherwise I was completely un-marked and un- injured. I was extremely lucky, as was Ruth. My Dad was absolutely wonderful about the accident, we were great pals!

I first met Ruth when her guardian, Jack West, took her to the National Cycle and Motorcycle Association Dinner and Dance at the Richmond Hotel. Ruth must have been fifteen at that time. When I danced with her, I remember admiring her long hair, which was set in ringlets. My Father was very involved with the association and as a result I got the job of welcoming the guests. I was a young man and that was the first public speech I ever made.

After the accident I went down to see Ruth, and inquire whether she was alright. I really got to know her after being 'thrown' together by the crash and as a result Ruth became my regular girl friend. However motorbikes remained my first love. I spent a great deal of time in the evenings and at weekends down at the Smith Street shop, tuning or just playing about with my racing machines. Ruth would loyally hang around waiting for me to finish so I could take her out. Reg Randell, who was a friend of mine, used to come down and watch me working. When Ruth got bored Reg took her out for a spin on his motorbike, so that I could concentrate on my work. This proved fatal, because Ruth ended up marrying Reg Randell.

When I left the shop after work in the evening, I really enjoyed the ride back to Seaplane Bungalow. In those days the Jerbourg Road was not nearly as built up as it is today. So after a hard day, I would let my motorbike show me what it could do - that was my way of revitalising myself. Saturday night was different, I worked late and usually drove home in the dark.

Susie Osborne ran the pub by the Doyle monument, which in later years became the L'Auberge Divette. It was then called The Monument Tavern, although it was better known locally as 'Susie's Place'. Her brother Tom Jefferies, a road sweeper, was one of her regulars and he was renowned for getting absolutely plastered on his pay day, Saturday.

By the time I had closed the shop and cashed up, it was usually well past 10 p.m. Old Tom by this time would be fighting drunk and his sister would turn him out of the pub to sober up. Old Tom would stagger away from the Tavern and into the road, fall down and drop off to sleep. As often as not, I would pass him lying in the road, where he had fallen. Sometimes he would fall into the hedge, with his legs sticking out into the road. A number of times I nearly ran over him as I drove along the road. In those days the acetylene lightning on my motorcycle was not all that effective, particularly for forward vision. On Saturday nights I drove along the Jerbourg Road with a great deal more care than on other nights. Many a time I got off my bike and shifted old Tom to the side of the road.

One Saturday night, in 1935, I had my motorbike in bits, so Dad came to pick me up with the car. We arrived home just after ten o'clock, Mum had our regular Saturday evening meal of a conger steak and mashed potatoes with thick gravy ready for us on the table. That was one of my favourites in those days. We were tucking in to our meal when the telephone rang, it was the Police who told us that the shop was on fire. Dad and I immediately set off back to the shop. As we drove out of the High Street, into Smith Street, we were just in time to see the Fire Brigade go into action.

We could see the fire in the front part of the shop and it was well alight. As the Firemen played their hose on the shop window, the glass shattered with the force of the water and a row of cycle lamps, just inside the window, shot off the shelves as the firemen played the hose on the fire. Some of our tenants living in the flats above the shop were rescued by the Fire Brigade, while still in their night clothes. There was considerable damage caused to stock, not only by the fire, but also by the water and smoke. The fire also spread to Mr Rabey's bookshop, next door. We were never certain what caused the fire, but I had my suspicions.

Dad had a habit of lighting his pipe with a match and then holding on to it until it burnt his fingers. He would then drop the match, or throw it away. Dad often sat in bed with a match box between his knees, a pipe and a newspaper, and strike a match without taking his eyes off his newspaper. He would then, when the match was burning his fingers, without looking flick the match into a ashtray by his bed. I never saw him miss the ashtray. I think that it was probably one of his matches which caused the fire.

The Fire Brigade instructed us that we could not go back into the building until the assessor came. He had to come from the mainland and it was two or three days before we could start to clear up the damage. It was some time after that before we could re-open for business. The insurance compensation was around £600, a lot of money then, but we had lost a great deal of stock. Dad always insisted that we have adequate insurance cover - I was glad that I had listened to his advice.

Another occasion when the insurance company became involved in a claim was when the garage at Seaplane Bungalow caught fire. Dad had converted a section of the original French hut into a separate garage. One day the garage caught fire and was well alight when Dad and I returned home from one of our trips. Neighbours were throwing water on the fire in an attempt to put it out. Dad rushed up and said

"Let it burn, the garage is insured, it has almost had its day and I have always wanted to move it."

Dad built himself a new garage in a different position with the help of the insurance money!

Around 1932 the Guernsey Motorcycle club, which organised the racing in the island, waned badly. For a period there was very little motorcycle racing in the island, so I used to take my bike over to Jersey and compete there. It was not until 1934 or 1935 that racing re-commenced in Guernsey.

One of the consequences of the temporary demise of motorcycle racing was that Terry Bougourd gave up racing. I acquired his 350cc A.J.S., of 1925 T.T. fame and raced it for many years, very successfully. I kept re-conditioning the engine, both to keep it going and to modify it. The bike packed up frequently, but it was very fast when it went. It was a lovely piece of machinery to ride. I don't think I ever rode a better bike from the point of view of cornering. I could really slide it round a corner, it was a dream, so light you could almost lay it right down on its side, and then pick it up as easily as a bicycle. It was beautiful racing machine.

Despite my responsibilities of running the business, my dedication and enthusiasm for motorcycle racing was still un-diminished. By this time I had established quite a reputation for myself in the islands and I continued to win races and set many records. In 1935 Gallaher Ltd, the Cigarette Company, produced a set of cigarette cards of Sporting Personalities. I was included as number 18 in a series of 48.

"Island Sporting Celebrities"

W. GREEN.

"Guernsey's leading racing motorcyclist and a well known figure at Channel Island meetings on 350cc A.J.S. machines. Holds the fastest time for Dos D'Ane and Naux Hills Trophies, also fastest Vazon lap. A skilful and fearless rider, Green's cornering is brilliant but unorthodox, favouring the spectacular 'Controlled broadside'. Has raced at Brooklands and Southport and holds Guernsey Grass Track Cup."

Gallaher Ltd. Cigarette Card.

The photograph on the front of the card shows me on an A.J.S 350c. The Dos D'Ane Trophy was awarded for the Hill Climb at La Rue du Dos D'Ane, Castel. My time of 13.4 seconds, set in the late twenties on my first push rod A.J.S., is unlikely to be broken because the Hill Climb was abandoned a few years later. It was transferred first to Petit Bot and then later to Le Val des Terres.

I was very nearly prevented from setting that record. Before any racing could take place we had to set up the timing equipment and run various cables up the hill. As we were laying out these cables, an old Lady came out of a cottage on the hill and said in a pronounced Guernsey accent,

"Mister, is it that you are going to run the motors up yer today?"

"Yes" we said.

"Oh my husband, he is very sick, he won't like it if you runs the motors up yer today - he is very sick, him!"

So we had a chat about it amongst ourselves and decided that we would pack up all the equipment and call it a day.

As we were reeling up the last of the cables, she came out again and said

"Mister, it all right now for the motors, - he is dead!"

That is the day I broke the record and that is why I remember it so well.

That Gallaher Cigarette Card was to prove invaluable to me during the early part of the war.

Chapter 5

THE WEE MITE

On the 15th of September 1933, Cecil W. Noel made the first sustained flight in a Guernsey built plane. This was the culmination of a great deal of planning and hard work by a team of dedicated enthusiasts, led by Cecil Noel and Harold Le Parmentier. I was proud to be a member of the team, albeit on a fairly casual basis. I vividly remember standing on the beach at Vazon cheering when Cecil returned from his forty five minute flight. I, and two thousand Guernsey men and women who had come to see our local 'Hero' make the historic flight.

In 1929 Cecil Noel, who served as an Pilot in the Royal Flying Corps during the first war, became interested in gliding. He did some work on designing wings for gliders and from this conceived the idea of building a plane. He spent months drawing up plans for the aircraft. It was only then that he mentioned the idea to his friend Harold Le Parmentier. Known to all as 'Parmy' he was an engineer employed by Eddie Bougourd at his Motor House Garage. 'Parmy' later married Eddie's daughter, Doris and took over the management of the business.

'Parmy' had also been exploring the possibility of building a plane, so enthusiastically welcomed the idea of them co-operating on the project and together they planned every detail. Cecil purchased a 30-35 h.p. A.B.C. Scorpian car engine, second hand from the wreck of a fatal smash that had taken place at White Rock when a car crashed into a crane.

On the 11th April 1932, construction of the plane commenced in a shed in Doyle Road owned by the Motor House garage. All the parts of the plane were manufactured or constructed in the island, with the exception of the engine.

It was inevitable that rumours should start to circulate about what Cecil and 'Parmy' were doing in the shed in Doyle Road. No one in Guernsey had ever built a plane before, so speculation was rife. The most popular local belief was that it was a 'Hair Brain' idea. For test purposes the engine was mounted on a Ford Model-T chassis and of course it was said that they were trying to make a Ford fly !

By October, sufficient progress had been made on the construction of the plane for the fuselage, complete with engine, to be towed down to Vazon sands for trials. There were no wings, but the fuselage was driven up and down the sands for thrust and tail lift tests. These successfully completed, it was back to the Doyle Road shed for more work.

By this time there was a team of volunteer mechanics working in the evenings and at weekends. Harry Kaines and Eddie Edmonds were the principle assistants and I also went down and helped whenever I could spare the time. I wasn't directly involved with its construction, but made myself useful and found the whole concept fascinating.

Many trips were made to Vazon with the fuselage and on every occasion, permission first had to be obtained from the Police. That was a tedious requirement, but they were always most co-operative. When the fuselage was driven at speed along the beach, the tail lifted up off the ground. We would constantly make corrections and re-corrections. Eventually the wings were constructed, with the struts being made of tongued and groved plywood.

Cecil Noel made a propeller out of planks of teak laminated together, shaving and shaping the wood to form the propeller. I was working with him one night when he announced that he had finished the propeller, except for the final balancing. He and I took it up to Le Lacheur's Garage at Les Merriennes at three in the morning and broke into their paint shop, no doubt with permission. The propeller was put on a pin point in a vice and Cecil sprayed it with paint, a little here, an extra thickness there, a bit more paint on one side than the other, in order to obtain a perfect balance. When he finally finished, the propeller balanced like a pair of scales. The completed propeller was fitted to the plane but the result wasn't to Cecil's satisfaction. The pitch angle was not just as he wanted it, he was not satisfied, so another propeller was cast in aluminium. This propeller was much heavier and more difficult to balance, so in order to reduce the weight and obtain a perfect balance he drilled a series of holes in it, which he filled with cork. That propeller was finally completed to Cecil's satisfaction.

Many attempts, watched on virtually every occasion by hundreds of islanders, were made to get the aircraft into the air. On several occasions the machine was coaxed off the ground by Cecil's skilful handling. A few test hops, but no sustained flight was achieved. In April 1933, exactly one year after construction had been commenced, the plane made its first short flight at Vazon sands. It rose 12 feet into the air, but had only travelled about 45 yards before it was back on the beach. Cecil taxied along the beach and when he came to a halt, we all rushed over to hear how he had fared.

His first words were, "Well it flies!"

He had encountered great difficulty with engine vibration, in fact he said that he had never been shaken like that before. As always further adjustments were made which proved comparatively successful and another attempt to get the plane into the air was made.

Cecil and Roland Le Lacheur, from Le Lacheur's Garage, had previously fitted a reduction gear to the engine in order to try to increase the power, but the bolts had not been properly tightened.

Cecil Noel taxied along the sands, revved up, and was going along at about 40 m.p.h., when there was almighty bang. The plane had been just about to lift off, when the vibration caused one of the loose bolts to come free and jam the works. The propeller split into two, one section cartwheeled along the beach before finally embedding itself in the sand, whilst the other part remained attached to the engine and continued to rotate. The result was that the violent vibration caused considerable damage to the front end of the plane and the Scorpian engine was damaged beyond repair.

Cecil Noel became very downhearted as a result of this mishap. 'Parmy', who was a very skilful and knowledgeable engineer, gave a lot of thought to the problem. He was convinced that the original engine had been under powered. There was not sufficient forward thrust to maintain flight and the type of engine inevitably caused undue vibration. So without telling Cecil, he set about searching for a new and more suitable engine. When he was in London he was offered a choice of two French 9 cylinder 40hp. Radial Salmson engines, each with two wooden propellers, one four bladed and the other two bladed. He purchased an engine and two propellers for £46, complete with a certificate of origin, in French. 'Parmy' was delighted with the new engine, he said it ran as smoothly as a sewing machine. The engine's installation required considerable modifications to the plane. The front structure was completely re-built, the balance had to be re-distributed, the wings were back staggered to compensate for the 12 inch reduction in the length of the nose. By the autumn Cecil and 'Parmy' were confident that the plane would fly.

Everything was ready, and at 3 a.m. on September 15th we took the plane out of the store at Doyle Road and towed it down to Vazon. Whilst the team who helped to build the plane were confident, the public were still sceptical. They had seen so many attempts which had been unsuccessful, they still needed convincing. The plane had been named the Wee Mite by Cecil Noel, but the Guernsey public scornfully referred to it as the 'We Might'.

Whatever they thought, the public still wanted to come and see the attempted first full and unrestricted flight. If the Wee Mite was going to fly, then they were going to be there to witness the historic event. By nine in the morning over 2,000 people were watching everything that took place. The Wee Mite was a very resplendent monoplane, with detachable wings and a two bladed propeller. It measured 18 feet in length, had a wing span of 31 feet and weighed 650 lb. empty, with an all up weight of 970 lb. 'Parmy' had registered the aircraft and its registration letters, G-ACRL were emblazoned on the top of the wings and on the side of the fuselage.

At 9.15 a.m. a short flight was made successfully, Cecil just took the Wee Mite up and immediately put it back down on the sands. Certain adjustments were carried out and then a ten minute flight was made, following which Cecil pronounced himself totally satisfied. He then took the Wee Mite up for its first sustained flight. From a 150 yard run he took off at 50 m.p.h. At first it looked as if he was going to land on the neighbouring beach, but within a minute had risen to 240 feet. The Wee Mite climbed quickly and was soon just a small speck in the sky over Pleinmont. Cecil Noel took off at 10.35 a.m. and landed again at 11.20 a.m..

In his 45 minute flight he had climbed to 2,500 feet at the rate of 450 feet per minute, flown at 93 m.p.h., and circled over St Peter Port and L'Ancresse. The aircraft that had almost become the laughing stock was now, as it taxied back along the beach to the slipway, the toast of Guernsey. The crowd cheered and cheered, Cecil Noel was declared a genius and compared to the great pioneers of the air. It was one of the great days in Guernsey's long history. Such was the interest that the noon edition of the Guernsey Evening Press reported the details of the flight which had only been completed less than an hour previously. Newspaper sellers carried placards announcing the historic flight by Guernsey's first ever locally built plane.

The Wee Mite at Vazon Sands.

The real 'genius', in my opinion, was 'Parmy'. He was an outstanding engineer, who later became Rolls Royce's technical representative in Scotland. He himself said that by building the Wee Mite, which had cost him a great deal of money, he taught himself another trade, which he put to good use with Rolls Royce.

Cecil Noel, who had done so much to bring about the success of the Wee Mite, quickly lost interest after successfully completing the historic flight. He found other challenges to interest him, which was typical of the man. Cecil craved a challenge, and when that was surmounted, looked for the next.

'Parmy' was the owner of the Wee Mite and continued to fly it in and around the islands. I remember the delight in Alderney when it was seen flying around their skies. Each flight required considerable preparation. The plane was stored in the shed at Doyle Road and had to be towed down to Vazon and assembled. The wings were bolted on to the fuselage and this in itself, was quite a protracted exercise. Vazon beach could only be used when the tide was out, so careful planning and timing was required as the plane had also to be dismantled before the sands were covered by the incoming tide. The Police had to be contacted before each flight and their permission obtained. The fuselage and wings had to be transported by road and this was not an easy operation. With all the preparation and planning that was necessary, not as many flights were undertaken as there would have been if it had just been a matter of wheeling the plane out of a hanger.

Sadly The Wee Mite met its end in the autumn of 1936. The petrol tank on the aircraft was fairly small, in keeping with the need to restrict any unnecessary weight. The fuel gauge proved somewhat unreliable and this deficiency had only been overcome by filling the petrol tank before every flight. 'Parmy' decided that he would take the Wee Mite up for a short flight around Vazon bay. Previously it had been flown by another pilot and 'Parmy' broke the golden rule and took off again without refuelling. Almost as soon as he was airborne, the Wee Mite ran out of petrol and the engine stalled. The plane was only 50 feet in the air, it stopped climbing and nose dived into the pebbles on the beach. The nose of the Wee Mite was embedded in the pebbles, with the rest of the plane wrapped around it and 'Parmy' in the middle. The Wee Mite was a total writeoff, but 'Parmy' was uninjured, other than a gash on the bridge of his nose. He conceded "I ran out of petrol - it was as simple as that."

The Wee Mite, which had only flown a total of fifteen and a half hours, was never rebuilt.

My love for motorcycle racing and the thrill of speed naturally led to a desire to learn to fly. I had been allowed to sit in the cockpit of a seaplane down at the harbour during the first war by one of the French airmen and that had really caught my imagination. As a boy I had often visualised myself as a pilot, flying to the mainland or the continent. I saw myself as a real Biggles type character.

Dreamy Stranger had trained as a pilot and was regularly flying here, there and everywhere. He was always involved in some adventure, or mishap. I noticed, also, that the girls were always very impressed. There was no doubt in my mind, I definitely wanted to learn to fly.

Dad was not at all keen on the idea of his only son risking life and limb, defying gravity, in order to take to the 'Highway of the Sky', as he called it. Although I was still living at home, I was twenty-four and Dad realised that he had little control of the situation. In the past he had been concerned about my motorcycle racing and now I was set on learning to fly. Dad had something else to worry about.

Early in 1934, I went over to Whitchurch Airfield, near Bristol and took a considerable number of flying lessons. At seven and sixpence for a quarter of an hour, flying was a rich man's hobby. A flying lesson consisted of taking off in an old Tiger Moth, doing a circuit of the airfield and then attempting a landing. I did not take to flying in the same way I had taken to motorcycling. No way could it be said that I was a natural flyer, as my long suffering instructor reluctantly, but emphatically pointed out after my third attempt to land. Each time I approached and tried to put the plane down on the runway, I did it in such a way that we bounced about twenty feet back up in the air. He took a poor view of me and my attempts at flying.

Dad, who knew that I was away taking flying lessons, was desperately worried. Bristol was far from home and he did not know what was happening and knowing me he was right to be worried. He sent me a telegram to the effect that he wished I would give up my ambition of learning to fly.

He had no need to worry, as very soon my money ran out. I sent him a telegram saying.

> "Green, Seaplane Bungalow, Jerbourg, Guernsey.
> Flying finished, having good time. Bill. April 1934."

Mum said afterwards that Dad was very relieved when he received that telegram.

Dreamy Stranger has been a lifelong friend of mine. He is probably the most imperturbable and unflappable character I have known during my long life. He has always had a very lackadaisical attitude to life and speaks with a attractive drawl, which, no doubt accounts for his nickname. Over the years, whenever he has written to me, he has always signed himself - 'Dreamy' - his Christian name is Lloyd, but I have rarely heard it used.

Dreamy rode a motorcycle with real dash and style and he flew airplanes in much the same manner. He learnt to fly at Brooklands and Bristol's Whitchurch Airfield, where he was fortunate enough to afford a considerable number of lessons.

Part of his flying training was to make a solo trip from Bristol to Southampton, land at the airfield and return to Bristol. He completed this exercise, apparently successfully and a few days later he set off again, for Southampton, this time with his flying instructor.

As they were about to land, Dreamy said;

"Where is the other airfield that I landed at last week?"

"If you landed somewhere else, then you did not land at Southampton Airport." said the bewildered instructor.

Dreamy was always getting lost, so he would follow the railway lines and when he came to a station, flew as low and as slow as possible trying to read the name on the platform. He would often rely on this method to find his way home. The only problem was when the railway line entered a tunnel and Dreamy had to make a sudden ascent to avoid crashing. A wonderful flyer, but a hopeless navigator.

The first time Dreamy flew to Guernsey was on a Bank holiday. He hired an aircraft from the Brooklands aero-club, one of the conditions being that it was not to be flown over the sea. That condition did not worry Dreamy, he immediately set course for Guernsey. He was accompanied by a passenger who apparently, at the start of the flight at least, had total confidence in Dreamy's flying and navigational abilities.

They took off and crossed the English coast, heading for Guernsey. After flying over the sea for some time and not having seen any sign of land, even Dreamy was getting slightly concerned. He thought they should have been able to see Guernsey on the horizon. His passenger was by now showing definite signs of anxiety. Dreamy spotted a boat and declared;

"There's the Guernsey Mailboat."

So he followed that course for a little while and his passenger was, for a time, reassured. Dreamy however soon realised that it was a boat going God knows where, but it certainly was not the mailboat so he turned the plane around and headed in the opposite direction. By this time his passenger was no longer anxious, he was panicking. Fortunately it was not long before they saw land and Dreamy recognised Pleinmont. It then dawned on him that before he turned back, he had been trying to fly the Atlantic in a Tiger Moth !

I knew that he had intended to fly to Guernsey and when I saw a plane circling low over Jerbourg and Seaplane Bungalow, I realised that it must be Dreamy Stranger. He was so excited that he had flown the Channel and I was the first to know. I got on my motorbike and followed him as he flew. He 'buzzed' another friend, Geoff Cohen who lived in Mont Arrive. Geoff also set out on his motorbike to welcome Dreamy when he landed. By this time Dreamy's petrol was running low, so he decided it was time to land. He flew to Vazon, where he thought he could land on the beach but the tide was in, right up to the sea wall. He had to land somewhere and quickly. Dreamy spotted a field alongside the Chateau des Marais which, from the air, appeared suitable.

What Dreamy had not realised was that it was a hay field, with the grass almost ready for cutting. From the air it looked an ideal meadow in which to land. He put the Tiger Moth down on the top of the two foot high grass. As the Tiger Moth slid into the growing hay the grass grabbed around the axle and turned the plane over on its back. When I arrived there after driving back and forth across the island, Dreamy was sitting on the gate, while his passenger was standing beside him, dabbing his forehead with a handkerchief. He had bumped his head when the plane had turned over, but had not hurt himself too badly. The first thing Dreamy said to me was;

"Well Willie, I have flown the Channel!"

Dreamy and his passenger were fortunately in good shape, but the plane was in no condition to fly. It was upside down in a field which was totally unsuitable for either landing or taking off. There was a big row, not only because he had crashed the plane but because he had flown over the sea and was uninsured. Dreamy's uncle and a number of his friends, including myself, helped to dismantle the plane and it was shipped back to the Brooklands Aero Club. It cost Dreamy's father £250 to settle the matter. Fortunately his Dad was pretty well off - he had to be to have a son like Dreamy.

On another occasion when Dreamy Stranger flew to the island from Brooklands, he landed on the grass runway at L'Eree. In 1931 the Guernsey Aero Club had been formed and they acquired fields at L'Eree which were eventually used as the island airfield before the present one at La Villiaze was brought into use.

I was there to meet him and he greeted me by shouting out;

"Do you want a flight Willie?"

"Yes sure."

I was always interested in anything that involved speed and excitement. So he took me up and we did a circuit of the island, which included flying around the Hanois Lighthouse at Pleinmont. I was expecting Dreamy to gently bank the plane around the Hanois, but no, we went around with the wings almost vertically parallel with the lighthouse. I was sure that I was going to fall out, and hung on to the base of my seat like grim death. We finally landed and as he turned the petrol tap off, Jean Fulford, a lady friend of his, one of many, came up to him and said;

"Oh Dreamy give me a flight."

He, of course, was only too willing and I remember her getting into the plane. He started to taxi along the grass. I was petrified because I knew he had turned the petrol tap off. The petrol tank was in the wing and I could clearly see the tap, still in the off position. I thought 'Oh my God! Disaster!' He taxied along the grass runway and thank heavens, ran out of petrol before he was ready for take off. He got out, turned the petrol tap on, swung the propeller to re-start the engine, which you had to do in those days, and took off. Jean had her flight and they landed safely.

One of the events which I liked to attend from a business point of view, was the International Motorcycle show at Earls Court. It gave me the opportunity to meet our suppliers and see what was new in the motorcycling world. On one visit I met up with Dreamy, Bill Mauger and Tony Cohen. Tony was studying to be an Advocate at Caen University in Normandy. We had been at the show all morning and were just about to go off for lunch when Tony announced that he would have to go, as he had to get back to Caen. He said that he had just nipped over for a quick visit and if his father knew where he was there would be big trouble.

Dreamy said not to worry, he would hire a plane and fly him back. So after lunch we all went down to the Heston Aero Club. We thought we would all go and see Tony safely back to Caen University. Unfortunately Wrightson Hire only had available a brand new De Havilland Leopard Moth aircraft which would accommodate three, the Pilot and two passengers. Bill Mauger and I tossed up to see who would go, I lost, so off they went. I waited at Heston for their return.

With Dreamy's usual navigation skill, the airfield in France which they had intended to land, could not be found. Names of French railway stations did not, on this occasion, help. They were well and truly lost. Dreamy not to be beaten put the plane down in a field and Tony Cohen set off to find his own way back to Caen University. We heard later that it took him two days!

Dreamy and Bill Mauger took off and headed for the English Channel. By this time a roaring northerly gale had blown up which slowed them down. In fact it was so bad that all aircraft of Imperial Airways were grounded. In the middle of the channel the exhaust blew just where it connected with the engine. The result was that they were confronted with a constantly flickering flame from the exhaust port of the engine. Gradually the windscreen was covered with oil and by this time it was beginning to get dark. Dreamy was having increasing difficulty in seeing out of the windscreen.

They crossed the English coast near Folkestone and passed over Canterbury Aerodrome, which had its lights on. Dreamy, later recalling the flight, said that where he made his cardinal mistake was when they passed over Canterbury, he should have closed his throttle and glided down and landed. He chose instead to fly on towards Heston. Ten miles further on, it was getting dark as they were approaching the south east suburbs of London. Dreamy concluded that it was not going to be possible to reach Heston, so decided to land. He spotted a flat area of open ground which appeared suitable for a landing. He decided that he would land in the middle of the open area, which he successfully did. Dreamy recalls 'sitting' on the brakes as the plane rapidly approached a belt of trees at the far end of the open space.

Having survived from what even Dreamy called a 'Hairy' experience, they set off to find a telephone. Nearby they found a country pub. The barman asked Bill what he wanted.

"A brandy".

The barman poured out a small measure, but Bill demanded the bottle and poured himself half a tumbler full, which he immediately downed. Bill Mauger always said that Dreamy did a magnificent job flying that plane while hardly being able to see out of the windscreen and landing it successfully in a gale. He was very grateful to be back on the ground in one piece and said it was solely due to Dreamy's ability as a pilot.

All this time I had been waiting at the airfield for them to return. Then Wrightson Hire at Heston received a telephone message from Dreamy, saying that they were 'down' in a field. The Hire Company organised a car to go and find out what had happened to their aircraft. I went down with them and meet up with Dreamy and Bill in the pub. Dreamy then showed us where the plane had finished up and only then did he realise just how lucky he had been. Right across the middle of the open space was a ditch, which he could have only missed by a few feet. The Wrightson Hire pilot took one look at the plane and said;

"I don't know how you got this thing in here, but I can't fly it out!" Dreamy had once again caused a plane to be dismantled.

Chapter 6

SENSATION AFTER SENSATION

Early in 1935 the tranquillity of the islands daily life was shattered by sensational headlines in both our local newspapers. Alfred Brouard was found dead, with his throat cut from ear to ear!

Farmer and former school teacher, Alfred Brouard lived at his farm at Le Camp Jaonnet, Four Cabot, St Andrews. Although seventy six, he was in good health, reasonably active and still ran the farm. He was looked after by his housekeeper, Mrs Gertrude De La Mare. Gertie, who was twenty seven, had been employed by Mr Brouard for about two and a half years and was separated from her husband. She was paid eight shillings a week, out of which she had to buy food for herself and her daughter who lived with her. Not only was she required to do the housework, she also worked on the farm looking after the cows, cutting hay by hand, with a hay knife and doing various other labouring jobs.

Gertie had become aware that while her employer could only afford to pay her eight shillings a week, it was his intention, if she remained in his employ, to leave her the farm and all his property when he died.

On Wednesday the 6th February 1935, Mrs De La Mare found her employer dead in bed with throat wounds. The police at first believed it to be a case of suicide, but the more they investigated, the more suspicious the circumstances appeared.

There was a note, apparently left by the dead farmer, which contained a number of spelling mistakes. As Mr Brouard had at one time been a teacher of English, it was unlikely that he would have made such basic spelling mistakes. It was suggested that the note had been forged by Mrs De La Mare.

The Guernsey Police had little or no experience of investigating this type of case, so they called in the assistance of New Scotland Yard. Two Officers, Chief Inspector A. Duncan and Detective Sergeant W.R. Smart, arrived and started their investigation. Almost immediately Mrs De La Mare was charged with the forgery of the Will of Mr Brouard. She appeared in Court and was remanded in custody.

Shortly afterwards we learnt that Sir Bernard Spilsbury, the eminent Pathologist had been called in to assist in the case. The body of Mr Brouard was examined in the mortuary by Sir Bernard. On the Monday following the death of Mr Brouard an Inquest was held, when Sir Bernard and two local Doctors, Dr Bostock and Dr Montague, stated that in their considered opinion, the wound on the dead man's throat was not self inflicted.

Clearly then it was murder, but who was going to be charged ? What were the results of the two Scotland Yard Officers investigations ? The whole island was buzzing with speculation and I scanned every issue of the Evening Press and the Star for more sensational revelations. The case, as I remember, was almost the sole topic of conversation. The scene of the tragedy attracted the attention of many hundreds of people. Scores of cars passed the farm, with passengers satisfying their morbid curiosity, by gazing at the house, or catching an occasional glimpse of police officers at work.

Mrs De La Mare again appeared in court and was further remanded on the forgery charge. The two Scotland Yard Officers left the island. We were all expecting further developments, but for almost a week nothing more happened. Then the Yard men returned, apparently with important new information. A conference was held with the local Police and one of the law officers, it lasted until 9 pm. Next day, the 22nd February, Mrs Gertie De La Mare was charged with the murder of her employer, Mr Alfred Brouard. The local press had a field day with headlines such as.

"Charge of Murder. Sensational turn in St Andrews mystery, young housekeeper pleads not guilty!"

The Trial started on 1st April 1935. It was the first murder case to be heard in Guernsey since the trial of Private Joseph Humphries in 1916. We learned that there were going to be thirty six witnesses. The queue for seats in the public gallery started at 6 am. I arrived just before 8 am and managed to get one of the seats. I was lucky, as many who arrived later failed to gain admission.

Never before had a trial in our Royal Court been attended by so many reporters from the British Press. The case received full coverage in the national press, they wanted to report every development and every word. Throughout the trial there was a succession of well known people who had come to watch and listen. The author of 'The Barretts of Wimpole Street', Rudolf Besier, sat in the public gallery during one of the sittings and the Rt Hon J.R. Clynes, the former Labour Cabinet Minister sat, in the front row on another day.

During the thirteen day trial the Evening Press arranged to publish special editions. As well as the normal morning racing edition, they published editions at 1 pm, 1.30 pm, 2.30 pm, 4 pm and a late special published at the then usual time of 5.45 pm. Each edition contained a virtual verbatim report of the days proceedings up to the time of publication.

At the end of the first day's hearing the court adjourned and visited the site of the murder, Le Camp Jaonnet. Mrs De La Mare, the accused, the Advocates and the Royal Court spent almost two hours inspecting the scene. My friend Joe Way drove Mrs De La Mare and her wardress to the farm in St Andrews in one of his large hire cars with the blinds pulled down.

Whilst I tried to attend court every day there were a number of days when I could not get a seat, despite having joined the queue some hours before the start of the Court sitting. I was very friendly with Reg Randell, whose father Advocate H.H. Randell, was defending Gertie. He knew of my interest in the proceedings and my difficulty in getting a seat. One evening he said;

"Would you two lads like to come into court tomorrow? I think it might be a quite interesting day."

Of course we jumped at the offer and he got us into court. I don't know how he did it, but Reg and I both had good seats. The Court as always was packed.

Sir Bernard Spilsbury was called as a witness. Advocate Randell immediately raised an objection to him being heard as a Medical Practitioner. 'H.H.' as we all knew him, said that Sir Bernard had not been registered in the island as a Medical Practitioner, therefore he was not legally able to give medical evidence. He reminded the court that the case was the most serious that had been before the Royal Court for some time. 'H.H.' said that the first thing that Sir Bernard should have done on arrival in the island was to present his credentials to the Royal Court and apply for permission to practise in Guernsey.

Advocate H.H. Randell went on.

"It is my duty, and I hope that the Court will not think that I am frivolous, to protest against the calling in of a man to give evidence, when according to the laws of the island he has no more qualifications than a Witch Doctor or a Medicine

Man. Sir Bernard could give evidence as to what he did but in my view, could not express an opinion."

Mr Ambrose Sherwill who, it was officially announced in the London Gazette, on the third day of the trial, had been appointed His Majesty's Procureur, Guernsey's Attorney-General, said that he had foreseen the possibility of such an objection. He pointed out that any medical man practising without permission was liable to a fine of £20. He did not, however intend to prosecute Sir Bernard, as he had come to the island by invitation. He pointed out that Sir Bernard had been invited, as a matter of urgency and if he had waited for a sitting of the Royal Court it would have been several days before Sir Bernard could have commenced his investigation. The Procureur said that Sir Bernard was on a medical register and fully qualified.

Advocate Randell responded by saying;

"He is the most eminent man of his kind, if he were a nincompoop I would not have raised an objection."

His Majesty's Procureur suggested that there might be an injustice done to the defendant if Sir Bernard was not called. He maintained that, even if Sir Bernard had been fined for practising in the island, he was not de-barred from giving evidence as there was no such intention expressed in the Ordinance.

The Bailiff said there was an Ordinance prohibiting medical men from practising without permission of the Royal Court, nevertheless he thought the matter was a very grave one for the Court and it was essential that the Court should have the best evidence available.

The Jurats of the Royal Court agreed unanimously that the defending Counsel's objection should not be sustained. Sir Bernard was therefore called to give evidence. Asked by the Procureur for his qualifications, he said he was a Bachelor of Medical Science, a Bachelor of Medicine and Surgery and a Fellow of the Royal College of Physicians.

Sir Bernard said that, in his opinion, death would have been quick with such a throat wound, probably within twenty five seconds. Whilst Advocate H.H. Randell conducted his cross examination of Sir Bernard skilfully, with searching questions, there was no doubt that it was not suicide.

"One determined sweep of the knife did that cut." stated Sir Bernard. He agreed that the cut was one such as would have been made by a very determined man. He could not conceive that Alfred Brouard had inflicted the wound on himself.

With the possibility of suicide being excluded, the Court heard other damaging evidence against Gertie. The Manager of Midland Bank, Mr A.E. Le Masurier, related how he had told Mrs De La Mare of Mr Brouard's intention to leave everything to her when he died if she remained with him. He had explained to Mrs De La Mare that her employer was unable to pay her more than eight shillings a week.

"That is all very well, but has he made a will to that effect ?" she asked, adding that she could get better wages elsewhere, but he would not let her go.

Advocate Randell in cross examination, asked Mr Le Masurier whether he thought Mr Brouard had some hold over Mrs De La Mare in financial matters, which made her stay?

"Yes." was the short but intriguing answer.

"Can you say whether she had any faith in her employer's promise to leave her everything?"

"I should not say she had." was the reply.

The bank manager also gave evidence of Mrs De La Mare taking a letter to him, purporting it to be from the dead man, asking him to sign the enclosed Will. Mr Le Masurier said that he told Mrs De La Mare that he could not sign it as Mr Brouard was dead.

The Will was dated 1st November 1934, and it read.

'My Will, And my which, In case anything happens to me during such time Mrs Gertrude E. De La Mare is in my employed I leave everything to her, furniture, money, cattle and everything else, now the house building and the five fields I leave also to her but if by law she is not entitle to it the property must be sold and her to have half of the money rents due to me as to go to Mrs Gertrude E. De La Mare.

I the undersigned.

A. Brouard.'

Day by day the case continued to produce sensation after sensation. When the defendant's mother, Mrs Le Page was called to give evidence for the prosecution, everyone knew that we were in for yet another sensation. Gertie's mother began by saying that Mr Brouard told her on several occasions that her daughter would have everything when he died. Then she told of meeting her daughter and granddaughter when out walking on February 3rd, the Sunday before Mr Brouard death.

Mrs Le Page said that her daughter had told her;

"I have come with sad news, Mr Brouard is dead!" and added, "I went to call him this morning and he did not reply, so I went up and opened the door and he was down near his bed with his throat cut with a knife."

That evidence was supported by a French lady, Madame Jegou, who had been out walking with Mrs Le Page when she met her daughter. Madame Jegou confirmed the date of the meeting and the conversation. By the time Gertie De La Mare gave evidence on her own behalf, the case, in my view, was lost.

Gertie throughout the trial wore a long blue coat with a matching hat and always appeared armed with a pencil and a note pad. During the proceedings she listened intently to all the witnesses and I noticed that she took notes occasionally. When Gertie came to give evidence she was remarkably composed and said;

"Really I don't understand why my mother should speak against me. I could not even kill a mouse, let alone a man !"

It was during her evidence that the bed in which Mr Brouard died was set up at the Bar of the Royal Court. I found that to be a touch macabre.

Before one of the sittings of the Court which I attended, the Usher addressed the public gallery, expressing the hope that unlike the previous day, would we please refrain from strewing banana skins and orange peel on the floor. He told us that this made the cleaners work more difficult and that the banana skins and orange peel should be put into our pockets and taken home. The Usher's unusual request made just as much of a lasting impression on me, as did the murder trial.

The only card that Advocate Randell had left to play was the possibility that Mrs De La Mare was of unsound mind when the murder was committed. H.H. made a great play of the fact that Gertie's father had apparently suffered from a mental condition.

Advocate Randell spoke for three and a half hours in his closing address for the defence, but it was of no avail. The eleven Jurats first decided by six votes to five, that Mrs Gertrude De La Mare was sane at the time of the murder. Then, after retiring for forty five minutes, they unanimously found her guilty of the murder of Alfred Brouard. It was the thirteenth day of the trial when she was sentenced by the Bailiff to death by hanging.

On May 29th, Mrs Gertrude De La Mare, who had been reprieved by the Home Secretary, left the island to serve penal servitude for life in a mainland prison.

Chapter 7

A CAREFREE LIFE

At the top of Le Val des Terres there is a large granite boulder, with the inscription:

> 'Le Val des Terres. Cette route a ete inauguree
> par Son Altesse Royale, Le Prince De Galles.
> Le 24 Juillet 1935.'

It was a beautiful July day in 1935, when the Prince of Wales came to the island to open the Le Val des Terres, the new road built to connect the South Esplanade with Fort George. The road was built at the time of the depression and many of the island's unemployed were put to work on its construction.

My girl friend at that time was Gwen Robilliard and we spent the day following the Prince around the island. His programme had been published in the press and I had it weighed up, so that with my motorbike and local knowledge of the lanes, we could usually arrive at the Prince's next stopping place before the Royal party. I treated it as a challenge. We wore red, white and blue rosettes and carried a Union Jack which we waved vigorously. I think the Prince got to know us, to the extent that after a time he appeared to look for us and give us a special wave. Well Gwen liked to think it was a special wave just for us!

When the Prince drove through the Talbot Valley, we were there. When he got out of his official car and walked down to look out over Petit Port Bay, we were there, we followed, or rather preceded him wherever he went. We picked strategic positions so that we could get the best view of him. He went to St George's Hall, called in at the St Martin's Boys Club, visited Elizabeth College and paid his respects at the War Memorial. When the Prince, a slight figure in a light grey flannel suit and a straw hat, arrived at the top of the Le Val des Terres, we were only a few feet from the huge granite boulder upon which the inscription was engraved.

A big arch of welcome, decorated with flowers, had been erected for the ceremony. First the Prince of Wales unveiled the stone and its inscription, by pulling away the Union Jack, then he opened the new road by snipping the ribbon with a pair of golden scissors.

I heard him say as he cut the ribbon.

"Le Val des Terres" and then he added, as he turned to look at the inscription on the stone: "A very nice old block".

One of the official party explained that it weighed about 4 tons and had been brought from L'Eree on the other side of the island. I well remember his conversation stopping reply:

"Really" he said.

He drove down the newly opened Le Val des Terres and found over 5,000 cheering children waiting to greet him on the South Esplanade. The Prince cut short his visit, and left around 4 o'clock, which made him a little unpopular with the island authorities as he was due to visit a number of other places before concluding his visit. I heard afterwards that he rushed away in order to keep a dinner engagement with Mrs Simpson.

The Prince arrived in the island on board the Destroyer H.M.S. Faulknor, but left by a Royal Air Force Singapore seaplane. When Gwen and I realised that he was leaving we dashed down on the motorbike to the harbour and launched my small boat.

With my Seagull outboard motor, we were cruising up and down trying to get as near as possible to the Prince's seaplane. We both felt that we had almost got to know the Prince on his visit and wanted to give him a final wave. Suddenly a pinnace from the destroyer, with a small naval crew, was bearing down on us at high speed. They pulled alongside and a charming Naval Officer said:

"Excuse me Sir, you happen to be right in the fairway of the Prince's aircraft, would you be kind enough to move to a more northerly position."

If he had requested us to pull the bung out and scuttle our boat, I think we would have done it willingly, such was his charm. Gwen fell for him, hook, line and sinker, she was always very keen on the Navy after that incident.

As soon as we had moved our boat as requested, the Prince's seaplane and an accompanying aircraft were quickly airborne. The two planes flew in the direction of St Martin's point before lifting away into the sky and heading, at great speed, towards the mainland and Mrs Simpson.

My brother-in-law Percy Trotter owned a boat, which he kept in the harbour. Percy went away and he left me in charge of his boat, so I said to Bert Coutanche, who was working for me at the time.

"Lets go out boating tonight."

"Great!" said Bert.

The boat was kept at a mooring down where the lifeboat anchorage used to be and had fore and aft mooring ropes. When we took the boat to sea the practice was to tie the two mooring ropes together on a float. Late that night when we returned we couldn't find the stern mooring rope, so obviously I had not secured it properly and it had sunk. So there we were with the boat, only secured by the forward mooring. Unless we did something to secure the stern it would drift all over the place. So I rowed out in the punt and dropped the anchor at the stern to make it fast until we could get the other mooring rope from the harbour bed.

Bert and I rowed ashore to the New Jetty in the punt, tied it up to a railing and went to Stainers for a coffee, waiting there for the tide to go out so that we could retrieve the stern mooring rope. When, at 3 o'clock in the morning, we returned, we found that the punt had floated over into one of the 'squares' under the New Jetty and as the tide had gone out it was left in a little pond of its own. We tried every means to pull it out, but the punt was too heavy. So we had to sit there and wait until the tide came in again, before we were able to release the punt.

All our troubles with the punt had prevented us from going out on the low tide to look for the rear mooring. The tide the next day was not low enough for us to find the mooring rope from the punt, so I had to dive in and swim around the bottom of the harbour to locate it. After searching the bottom for some time, I retrieved it all right. Then we tried to lift the anchor, but it would not budge, try as we might. So I swam down the anchor rope to find out why. The former Lifeboat anchorage had two dead man weights, with a chain between the two and our anchor was underneath the chain. I dived down and standing on the bottom, tried to lift the chain and pull the anchor out, but without success.

I realised that the only way we were going to recover the anchor, was by attaching a rope to the chain, with Bert in the boat lifting while I pulled the anchor free. We finally retrieved the anchor, but just because I had failed to secure a mooring rope to a buoy, it had taken us days to tie up my brother-in-law's boat. It taught me to take a great deal more care with mooring ropes in the future. I put it all down to experience !

Percy Trotter's boat was equipped with an air cooled Petter Engine, which was started with claw type starting handle. The engine had a shaft with a keyway in it, on to which the claw starting handle located. Once the engine started, the claw handle would un-hook and release itself. Well that was the theory but in practice, occasionally the handle would stay on and only be released when the engine was finally shut off. The last movement of the engine was when it momentarily reversed itself and this was when the handle was released and catapulted away with great force. I have only ever seen two engines with this claw type handle arrangement, one on my brother-in- law's boat and the other was on the engine which generated our electricity at Seaplane Bungalow. My experience with the engine at home was that the only way to deal with the situation was to switch off the engine and run for cover. The handle would fly off, very often being hurled through the side of the shed, which was clad with asbestos sheeting.

One evening when Bert and I planned to take Percy's boat out, we started the engine and the blessed claw handle stuck on the shaft. We sat and looked at the handle going around and around. It was all right whilst it was going around, but the question was where was it going to go when we stopped the engine.

"Bert" I said,"I don't know what is going to happen, it will either go out through the bottom of the boat, or it will go into the sea and we will lose the handle. God knows what my brother-in-law will say."

We sat there for ages just looking at this handle going around and around, trying to fathom a way out. Eventually we realised that there is no way we could solve it, so we switched off the engine and took cover. The engine spluttered to a halt and suddenly went 'chup' and the handle flew off skywards. We followed its flight through the air and were very relieved to see it fall into a boat about a hundred yards away.

"You've got to have a bit of luck sometime." said Bert and we paddled over in the punt and retrieved the claw handle.

Boating was never really my scene, I was much happier with motorcycles or in the company of the opposite sex.

My parents were always fascinated by my string of girl friends. Whilst they never sought to interfere, in their own way they kept a close eye on my activities. Anybody I brought home was made most welcome by Mum, she would ply them with tea and cakes. I can say without hesitation that all my girl friends were nice respectable young ladies, but what their parents thought of me was perhaps another matter.

Gwen Robilliard's father was a very strict old boy, who was very protective of his daughter. She had to be in by half past nine every evening, that was his rule and Gwen complied with it, but that did not suit me. After I had seen her home, I usually went down to Stainers to meet the lads. In my view that was the place to be, far better than going home to bed. Gwen objected to me going there on my own, in fact she disliked Stainers and the friends I met there. I think it was mainly for this reason that we eventually parted.

In 1935 I became friendly with Elsie Stewart, she was quite a lot younger than me, but we got on well together. I had known her four brothers, who were all older than Elsie. Her father, who was a milkman, had been a long time customer of 'Greens'. Dad had sold him a big Royal Enfield motorbike and sidecar with which he delivered milk to his customers.

Elsie and I went to a number of dances together, but we did not always come home together. One particular dance which we attended was held at the Captain's Hotel in St Martin and I remember that having paid 2/6 for her ticket, she danced all night with Nev Brouard. I felt that was not a good return for my investment, so I said to Elsie :

"If you can dance all night with Nev, then you can go home with him !"

I knew that Nev did not have a car and that he lived at Saints, which was the opposite direction from Elsie's home in Brock Road. That night she walked all the way home by herself, it was a long way and Elsie was scared stiff.

Elsie and I went to a Sunday School party at St Andrew's Church in the Grange. She was a member of the church and her parson was the Reverend Rose. At the party he came over to me and asked:

"How old is Elsie ?"

"I think she is about sixteen!"

"How old are you?"

"Twenty six." I replied.

"You know you are a bit old for her, don't you think?"

I knew how to take a hint - he put me right off Elsie.

However, Elsie and I were to get together again, but much later in life.

One evening in May 1936, I was in Stainers with some friends enjoying a coffee, when Sammy Best accompanied by Snowy Henry came in and said: "Bill we have been looking for you everywhere, what are you doing tomorrow?"

"I really don't know, why?"

"Well we've got a boat and we want to go and see the Queen Mary arriving in Cherbourg on her maiden voyage, but we can't get the engine started. Will you help us. ?"

"O.K." I said "I will come and have a look at the engine for you."

Sammy's boat, the Isle of Lihou, was quite a nice looking forty footer. She had been up on the Careening Hard for a number of years and Sammy Best had just purchased her. There were gaping gaps in the deck planking about half an inch wide, but she had a beautiful old Kelvin engine. I worked all night on the engine and finally managed to get it going. It was decided, on my advice that the engine should be reliable enough to get us to Cherbourg. I telephoned Dad to let him and Mum know where I was going. He was quite used to me nipping off at a moments notice and said:

"Take care of yourself."

At eight the next morning, the 27th May 1936, we set off for Cherbourg. The sea was rough, but the old Kelvin was ticking over beautifully, it was a lovely old engine. Sammy Best was at the helm, and acted as our navigator. He was pretty knowledgeable about sailing and the sea. I had been taken along as the 'Engineer', because the boat was really in a very doubtful condition, particularly as it had been on the Careening Hard for so long. Snowy Henry and Edgar Guille were the other two members of our crew.

The going proved to be pretty rough, but we were making good progress, until we were just off Alderney, when the engine packed up. I went below and found a serious situation, the boat was leaking and the water had risen to the level of the flywheel. The flywheel had sprayed water everywhere and cutout the engine. I took a look at the bilge pump, it was not working, and apparently hadn't done so for years. So I set about bailing out with a bucket. I passed a full bucket to Sammy, he tapped on the under side of the aft hatch, Snowy took the hatch off and picked up the bucket and threw the contents over the side. Before Snowy could replace the hatch, another wave would hit the deck and put more sea water back in than we had bailed out. I said to Sammy

"This is no place for me, I am going back up on deck."

Up on deck I found Snowy Henry emptying the petrol out of a two gallon petrol can over the side.

"What the hell are you doing, Snowy ?"

"Well" he replied "If we are going to sink, I will at least have this can to hold on to, it will float."

I looked at Alderney and said;

"I don't need an old tin can, it would only impede me, I'm going to swim ashore."

I would have never reached land because the tidal race would have taken me miles passed the island. I didn't have a lot of experience in those days of tides and currents, but if I had tried to swim, I am sure that it would have been the end for me.

Sammy Best quickly assessed the situation and called out;

"Come on boys, get the sails up and lets get into Alderney where we can get things sorted out."

He was a very strong character and his leadership pulled us together. We hoisted the sail, which proved a difficult task because we were pitching and rolling about. Finally we got under way and sailed the boat into the safety of Braye Bay. We set to, bailed the boat out and I managed to get the bilge pump working. It was about two o'clock in the afternoon when we finally managed to get the old Kelvin engine ticking over. We set off again and made very good time.

As we were about to enter Cherbourg harbour there was a loud report and a column of water rose just in front of our bow.

"That was a shot across our bows." said Sammy.

We all thought it was, but it probably wasn't.

Edgar exclaimed, "Why are they firing at us, we have got the Union Jack flying?"

We never did understand what had happened.

Shortly afterwards a big French submarine passed us, on the surface, coming out of Cherbourg Harbour. We gestured our intention to enter the harbour and the French sailors in the conning tower, waved us on in the direction of the harbour. We sailed into Cherbourg and tied up at the wharf.

The Queen Mary was due in at about seven o'clock that evening. Just after six we decided that we would sail out to meet the great ship. It was a beautiful summers evening and after a little while I could see this huge ship, the Queen Mary, the pride of Britain, coming out of the mist. She was exactly like every photograph and every painting that I had ever seen. As the great ship came closer to us we could hear the sound of the passengers and crew singing 'Britannia rules the waves', drifting over the water.

We were flying our little flag at the stern, and Snowy said:

"We had better dip our flag."

"Do you think so?"

"Oh yes."

So we dipped our flag in salute. I can still see, in my mind's eye a sailor sprinting down the Queen Mary's deck as fast as he could go to the aft mast and in response to our salute he pulled the Queen Mary's Ensign down about thirty feet.

We were mentioned on the radio, when the commentator on the B.B.C. said that a small white British boat welcomed the Queen Mary as she entered Cherbourg Harbour on her maiden voyage. That was the Isle of Lihou, with us four Guernsey boys aboard.

We were not the only boat from Guernsey that travelled to Cherbourg to see the Queen Mary on her maiden voyage, the ferry St.Julien, and the New Fawn, were also there loaded with spectators. Mr J.E.B.Tetley, a Director and Manager of the Guernsey Brewery hired the Brittany, a motor vessel which plied between St Peter Port and France, and invited every publican in Guernsey, Alderney and Sark on board to see the Queen Mary. Of course the Brittany was loaded with beer. A friend of mine, Harold Hughes, the proprietor of the Farmer's Hotel, was aboard and he spotted me on the Isle of Lihou, and yelled:

"Hi there Bill, what the hell are you doing there ? Want some beer ?"

Well that's the only vice I haven't got, but before I could open my mouth to explain, Sammy yells out: "Yes!"

Harold and a sailor on the Brittany were soon letting out a rope and tying a bottle of beer about every six inches or so. Sammy and the others were hauling it aboard. Before long we had so much beer aboard that we were nearly as well stocked as the Brittany.

The Brittany, after they left us, sailed into Cherbourg harbour and around the Queen Mary and out again without paying any harbour dues. They were later fined by the French Authorities, the equivalent of £100 for that offence.

We eventually went back into Cherbourg Harbour and tied up. We met Judge French from Alderney, who asked if he could have a lift back to Alderney, because he had missed his boat.

"We're not" said Sammy, "going near Alderney because we have to go to the west of the Casquets due to the tide, but we will take you to Guernsey."

"That will have to do." said Judge French, "What time are you sailing?"

"Two o'clock in the morning on the tide." replied Sammy.

With that arranged, we all set off into the town of Cherbourg with different intentions in mind.

When I returned to the boat later that evening I found that the rest of the party had been at the beer and were very merry, to put it mildly. About 1 am, Snowy, Edgar and Sammy went below, curled up and fell fast asleep.

Not long after, Judge French returned and inquired whether we were still sailing on the tide at 2 am.

"Not tonight by the look of it" I said "look at this lot!" pointing out our sleeping drunks.

"Oh dear" said Judge French, "I need to get back - you can't start the engine, I suppose ?"

"Oh yes, that's what I do aboard."

"Fine" said the Judge, "I can navigate."

I started the engine and the Judge cast off. So we set sail with Judge French at the wheel. About six in the morning I was feeling tired and decided to have a lie down for a while. I was the first to wake up, it was about 2.30 in the afternoon, we were tied up in Alderney and Judge French had gone home.

What I did not know at the time of our trip to Cherbourg, was that Edgar Guille and Sammy Best were to be charged with the theft, the previous March, of a safe and its £125 contents from Mr Ernest T.Henry of the Hermitage, L'Ancresse. They were arrested in June and the trial took place in the following July. It was a major trial in which Advocates W.H.Arnold and H.H.Randall appeared for the defence, while His Majesty's Procureur, Ambrose Sherwill prosecuted.

The public gallery was packed, I had difficulty in getting a seat, but succeeded in being present for the whole of the trial. Twelve witnesses for the prosecution were sworn and heard, and three witnesses each for the defence.

It appeared that the safe had been taken from an outbuilding serving as an office and store at the Hermitage and transported to the common on Mr Henry's trolley. Sammy Best was known to Mr Henry and had his permission to use the trolley. Attempts had been made to open the safe on the common and evidence was found of green and grey enamel chippings in the area. Chisels and a hammer from Sammy Best's gravel pit were shown to bear the marks of green and grey enamel paint. A small chip of wood found at L'Ancresse fitted the shaft of Sammy's hammer precisely. It appeared there was little doubt that the tools used in opening the safe belonged to Sammy Best.

The clothes of both Sammy and Edgar were examined by the the police and samples taken from the turn ups. Mr Arthur Littlewood, the States Analyst, said in evidence that in one of the samples he had found small pieces of enamel. He had compared the pieces of enamel microscopically and found they agreed with those of the safe in all particulars, there was no difference whatsoever.

The sample which contained the damning evidence came from Edgar's trousers. Sammy's trouser sample gave a negative reaction and did not incriminate him.

Considerable evidence was submitted in respect of Sammy's bank account and other financial transactions. On the day before the robbery, he had a balance of 3s.6d. Soon afterwards amounts of £67.17s.6d., £35 and another £35 were paid into the account. Sammy did not give any satisfactory explanation of where these sums of money had come from.

The Bailiff, who presided, said in his summing up:

"The prosecution has admitted that the evidence against Best is not so strong as that against the other accused."

The Bailiff stressed that if the court had any doubt in their mind:

"It was far better that a guilty man should escape, rather than an innocent man be convicted."

The case against both defendants was basically the same, but the evidence was stronger in the case against Edgar. He had offered no explanation to account for the traces of enamel in the turnups of his trousers. Again the Bailiff stressed:

"The accused must have the benefit if there was any doubt in the minds of the Jurats."

On returning after 10 minutes absence, the Jurats unanimously found Sammy Best not guilty. However they returned a unanimous verdict of guilty against Edgar Guille who was sentenced to twelve months imprisonment.

I was in court when the verdict was announced. As I listened to his footsteps, as he descended the stone stairs from the dock, I remember thinking to myself:

"My God Sammy, your lucky!".

One evening, soon after the trial, Sammy was down at Stainers, discussing the outcome of the case and boasted;

"They couldn't have caught me, I sent my suit to Burtol's the cleaners. If the police had found any chippings of paint on me, I would have sued Burtol's for not cleaning the suit properly !"

There was no doubt in my mind that Sammy had got away with it, he was there with Edgar. In fairness to Edgar, who worked for Sammy, he was very loyal and did not let his friend and employer down.

I am sure that the Isle of Lihou, Sammy Best's newly acquired boat and our trip to Cherbourg to see the Queen Mary on her maiden voyage were financed by the proceeds of the robbery.

Part of the island's pre war social scene, were the regular dances held at St Martin's Parish Hall. I enjoyed them, largely because there were always a bevy of pretty girls over whom I could cast my eye.

One of the young ladies whom I met at these dances and who interested me, was Dora Johns. She and I became friendly and went out together on a number of occasions. Dora had a friend who also attended one of the dances at St Martin's Parish Hall, a very pretty young lady, Mabel Telford. I enjoyed dancing with these young ladies. I remember Harold Holmes, who was the leader of the band at the St Martin dances, saying to me;

"Bill you can't half pick 'em !"

Mabel, or Mabs, as she was known, was born in the very pretty little village of Armathwaite, near Carlisle and came to Guernsey as a Nursery Nurse to the Winkfield family. Colonel Winkfield's wife Margery was the elder daughter of the Bailiff A.W. Bell. They lived at Le Penage in Les Caches, St Martin.

Mabs' charge, was William Winkfield. Dora Johns, was also a nursemaid and together they would go for walks with their charges. Mabs and I went out together on a couple occasions. She was great fun, I liked her a lot, but regrettably she left the island when she went with the Winkfield family to Northern Ireland. I had her address and we wrote to each other a few times, then we lost contact. In those days I had a habit of using drawing pins to pin up all my collection of addresses on the woodwork in my office at the shop. Somehow I lost Mabs address, so I went to Dora to ask her if she had it. She didn't, so that was the end of that particular romance for the time being.

Chapter 8

WAR AND MARRIAGE

My life during the thirties was totally carefree and enjoyable. The business to a very considerable extent ran itself as my staff were very supportive, which allowed me to take off all the time that I wanted. Financially, the shop provided for my many and varied needs, although without too much to spare. I had not yet been struck by the saving habit.

I travelled to the continent and mainland on numerous occasions, following my many interests and enjoyments. I made a name for myself as a racing motorcyclist and developed very successful relationships with a number of young ladies.

Bill Green in action at Vazon, September 15th 1938.

I was still living at home, but allowed all the freedom I wanted. I enjoyed life, I enjoyed the company of my friends, male and female, I was totally happy and contented. I realised that it would not last for ever and it didn't, but there were days of complete and absolute ecstasy. The thirties were wonderful days and I remember them well.

I was in my office in Smith Street one evening in early 1938, when there was a knock on the door and in came Dora Johns.

"Do you still want Mabs Telford's address ?" she asked.

"Yes indeed, I do."

Mabs who had been working for Colonel Winkfield's family in Northern Ireland, left them when the Colonel was posted to India. She wanted to go with them, but her parents felt that she was too young to travel that far from home. Mabs had taken a job, again as a Nursery Nurse, working for the Mackie family at Gretna Green. I wrote to Mabs and I can still remember what I said, 'I suppose your present boy friend is tall dark and handsome.' I was checking to see if she had a boyfriend.

A letter came back saying that she did not have a permanent boyfriend, but there were one or two on the sidelines. That was sufficient encouragement for me and before long I was on my way up to Gretna. I crossed to the mainland on the Saturday and after a very long and hard ride on my motorbike, arrived in Gretna Green early the next morning. It was Sunday, and in Scotland, nothing was open and I was starving.

I found the Mackie's house, rang the bell, and asked for Miss Telford. Mrs Mackie, who was a lady of some substance, said:

"Well, I am sorry, Nannie is busy with the children at the present time, but it is her half day, come back at one o'clock."

Unknown to me, Mrs Mackie, who apparently knew all about me from my constant stream of telephone calls and letters to Mabs, rushed up the stairs to the nursery and told Mabs that Bill Green from Guernsey was inquiring after her and that he would be back at one o'clock.

Having nothing else to do and not being able to get any food, I went to church. A very friendly lady sitting next to me shared her hymn book, it appeared that they were in short supply. Even today, I can still recall the embarrassment of my tummy rumbling and making the most terrible noises. I was thankful when we sang a hymn because by singing with great gusto it temporarily relieved the hunger pangs! During the rest of the service, when we were not singing, my empty tummy was sending out increasingly audible complaints about lack of sustenance! Never since that day have I experienced anything quite like it, neither have I felt quite so embarrassed.

Well, at one o'clock I was back waiting outside the gate of the Mackie house. Once again I had travelled to the mainland to meet the girl of my dreams, once again I was waiting for her to appear. Ruby Noakes had not even remembered me - what would be my reception on this occasion ? Mabs came out and was delighted to see me standing at the gate and I got a wonderful reception!

Mabs had planned to go and see her parents on her afternoon off, so we went together. I hit it off with her parents, we got on well.

Later that summer I went over and stayed with Mabs and her parents and while there, I plucked up courage, proposed and was accepted. In August 1939 Mabs came over to Guernsey on holiday and we planned the details of our wedding.

I was now thirty and had been giving considerable thought to settling down. I was certain that Mabs, although ten years younger, was the right girl for me. She had a wonderful personality, was very loyal and was just the influence I needed to settle down. She was a lovely person, I loved her and still do!

My parents fully approved of our decision to get married. Mabs and I went house-hunting and found a house that was being built, opposite the entrance to Saumarez Park, in La Route de Saumarez. The cost of the house, when completed was £750. We put down a £75 deposit. We had planned to get married in the summer of 1940, but with the uncertainty the war caused, we felt, like many other couples at the time, that it was better to get married as soon as possible. So we decided to bring the date forward to February 1940.

Whilst my own personal outlook was one of sunshine and clear blue skies, the war clouds were gathering over Europe. Hitler's territorial and military ambitions would affect others, but they were unlikely to affect our little island of Guernsey. So we thought - how wrong we were.

War was declared on September 3rd 1939. Mum, Dad and I sat in the dining room at Seaplane Bungalow that Sunday morning and listened to Neville Chamberlain's announcement that we were at war with Germany. I was jubilant about it, being young, my thoughts were along the lines of getting rid of these Germans, who had been a nuisance long enough. Dad was more realistic, he thought that the war would last some time, much longer than my prediction of six months,

"Ah my boy, you will be involved in this war, more than you think."

We followed the news on our wireless set and read about it in the newspapers. We of course were interested, but it had little effect on our daily lives, certainly not during the autumn and winter of 1939/40. It was called the 'Phoney War', all talk but little action.

The first real effect the war had on islanders, was when petrol was rationed. This brought an immediate benefit to the business, it boomed. Everyone wanted new bicycles, or their's repaired. Supplies were still plentiful and we were ordering huge quantities of cycles and spares from our mainland suppliers. Other dealers were doing likewise and this was to prove very beneficial later on when replacement supplies became almost un-obtainable. Christmas 1939 was from a trade point of view, a bumper success, and we sold record numbers of push bikes. Dynamo Lightning sets and all types of cycle accessories were also in great demand.

Dad, who had always suffered a great deal of pain, was now seventy-three and decided to give up running the guest house. He and Mum had run it successfully for twelve years. Dad suffered from rheumatism and arthritis and when he was in a bad state I drove him down to Dr R.E.Gibson, who gave him a relieving injection of morphia. The morphia knocked him out, but afterwards he would be all right for some time.

I realised that we might need some petrol in an emergency and said to Dad; "We had better put in a stock of petrol, so we are able to get you to the Doctor if we need to."

So we stored some petrol in the old fashioned two gallon cans, about a dozen of them, in the garage at Seaplane Bungalow. Later an order was issued that no one should keep more than three gallons of petrol in store. "We had better" I said to Dad, " hide some of that petrol because we still might need it."

"Yes, all right my lad I will see about that."

One day I said to him, "Here, where's all that petrol gone ?"

"I've hidden it."

"Well, where is it? I'd better know as you mightn't be well enough to tell me."

"Well my boy, never light a fire in the lounge."

I knew immediately where he had hidden the petrol. Dad, many years before had built a fireplace into one of the lounge walls and extended Seaplane Bungalow by building a conservatory. Between the fireplace and the conservatory there were some weatherboards. By removing these boards access could be obtained to a recess around the rear of the fireplace. Dad stacked the cans of petrol in the recess and replaced the weatherboards.

While the rest of bungalow had been blacked out, the lounge wasn't. It was the biggest room in the house with a considerable number of windows, which Dad hadn't bothered to black out. Mum and Dad decided we wouldn't use the lounge during the winter of 1939/40, so in consequence the fire was never lit.

I kept in constant touch with Mabs, both by letter and telephone, I sent her presents and went across to see her as often as I could get away. Mabs and I set the date for our wedding. We planned to be married in the Church, at Johnstone Bridge, near Lockerbie, Dumfriesshire, on Wednesday 28th February 1940.

I went to see the Vicar of St Martin's Church to arrange for my banns to be called. The Rev R. Coulthard suggested most strongly that I should be confirmed before the wedding. I agreed and attended a series of confirmation classes in the Rectory. I felt very much out of place as I was, by far, the oldest candidate. However I was confirmed.

Ralph Palmer, a great character and a wonderful friend, agreed to be my best man at my wedding. I had known him since our schooldays, we played a lot of table tennis together at the Artisans club and we were both stalwarts at Stainers. Over the years we regularly swam together in all weathers. Ralph learnt to dive long before he could swim a stroke. We encouraged him to dive into the deep end of the pool on the promise that one of us would fish him out. I think that the only reason Ralph eventually learnt to swim, was because we left him in longer and longer before fishing him out. For a long time Ralph could swim better under water than on the surface. As a result he could hold his breath under water longer than any of us.

Ralph has always had a great sense of fun and a mischievous streak of devilment in him. He would go to great lengths to pull my leg. Some years previously, when the largest R.A.F flying boat ever to visit Guernsey taxied into St Peter Port harbour and tied up at a buoy almost opposite the model yacht pond, there was a general air of excitement.

At the time it entered the harbour, I had been riding my motorcycle along the Quay on my way to the bathing pools at Valette for my daily swim. On seeing the flying boat, I went to the Castle Emplacement to find out what was going on. As I could not get anyone with a boat to take me out for a closer look at the flying boat, and having my bathing costume and towel with me, I changed and swam out to it. I swam right around the flying boat, and chatted to the R.A.F. officers aboard.

On returning to shore I was met by a policeman who enquired :-

"Did you know that swimming in the harbour is forbidden ?"

"Oh is it ?"

"Yes, I am afraid that I will have to take your name and address."

Later in the day a policeman came and interviewed me and delivered a verbal message from Police Inspector Sculpher, saying, "Please don't swim in the harbour again, it is not allowed".

The next day when I went swimming at the Valette, there was a model of a seaplane floating in the pool. Ralph and a few of my friends persisted in asking me each time I came out of the water for my name and address. They pulled my leg unmercifully. Later a letter, signed 'Pro Bono Publico', appeared in the Press, expressing great apprehension about the delinquency of modern youth disobeying the laws of the island by swimming in the harbour. The letter did not name me but there was no doubt who they were getting at - Bill Green. I took great umbrage at the time, I was meant to of course.

I remember being furious about this criticism of me - what I wasn't going to do to the author of that letter when I identified him ! I decided to reply by writing to the Press. The letter, however, was never written because in the meantime, I discovered that my critic was none other than Ralph Palmer. I should have guessed.

Regretfully, none of my family were able to come to our wedding. My Father wasn't at all well and was unable to travel and Mum did not feel that she could leave him. There were travel restrictions and it was difficult to get the necessary travel documents unless you could prove an essential need to travel. Regretfully that meant that none of my relatives travelled across for our great day.

On the Friday prior to my wedding, Ralph and I set off on the overnight mailboat Normannia. We had been playing table tennis that evening and before we sailed, I went up to Seaplane Bungalow to say cheerio to Mum and Dad. They both wished me good luck and happiness. During war time, travelling across the English

Channel was a considerable undertaking. There was a danger from German submarines, so we crossed at full speed, about 19.5 knots, all blacked out, without any lights aboard. On the Saturday Ralph and I went to the Motor Show at Olympia. It was a marvellous exhibition and showed just how little life in Britain had been affected by the war up to that time.

After the Motor Show, Ralph and I travelled on the overnight train to Nuneaton, to see an old friend of ours, Jack Hessel. I remember there was terrible confusion at the station because it was the night that the clocks went forward and nobody knew what time the train was actually going to leave.

Jack Hessel was a former member of the swimming club who had moved to the mainland to take a job as a dental mechanic. As a boy he suffered with a bad stammer and had sought the help of a speech therapist who taught him to fill in with any words that he could always be sure of saying. Jack would often get stuck and could not get any further with what he was trying to say. The only two words that Jack could always be certain of saying were 'gosh' and 'blooming'. In consequence his conversation would consist of phrases such as 'I am going to the gosh blooming town.', 'I will catch the gosh blooming bus.' and 'Where have you put that gosh blooming bathing towel.' Of course the saying 'gosh blooming' went through the swimming club. Jack, took it all in good part and in consequence became the a very popular member of the club. He really was a super bloke.

After a very pleasant day with Jack Hessel, we caught the overnight train to Carlisle. In those days if I was travelling by train, I chose to go overnight as it saved the cost of an hotel room. When Ralph and I arrived at Carlisle on the Monday morning, we went straight to Mr and Mrs Telford's home, where Mabs handed me a telegram, one of those 'Priority' telegrams in a red envelope. It read.

> 'Dad very seriously ill, failing fast. Phone me.
> Signed. Percy (Trotter)'

I rang home, only to learn that Dad had died suddenly at 3 am. that morning. The funeral was to be on the following Thursday, the 29th February. Clearly I would have to return for the funeral, but there was no way that we could be married on the Wednesday and be in Guernsey for the funeral on the Thursday. Our first thoughts were that we would have to put off the wedding, but the more I thought about it the more I was convinced that Dad's wish would be that we should get married.

We consulted the Minister who was due to conduct the marriage service and together we explored every possible alternative. The Mackie family owned the Gretna Green Blacksmiths shop and getting married there was one of the options we considered. A qualification for being married at Gretna Green, was that one of the couple had to have been in residence for three weeks prior to the marriage. If we had chosen that option, there would have been no difficulty as Mabs fully qualified, having worked for the Mackie family. However neither Mabs nor I, or indeed her parents wanted us to get married over the famous anvil.

The Guernsey Ecclesiastical Law required that the banns had to be called on three consecutive Sundays. My banns had been called in St Martin's Parish Church for the third and final time on the previous Sunday and the Rev Coulthard had posted the necessary documents, but they had not yet arrived in Johnstone Bridge.

In the circumstances the Minister in Johnstone Bridge took Ralph Palmer's word that I was a single man and agreed to marry us on the Tuesday morning. So on the 27th February 1940, Mabs and I were married. We had one bridesmaid instead of two, the other arrived for the planned wedding the following day!

Mabs' banns were called three times on the Sunday before our wedding and according to Scottish law, they had to lay for forty eight hours. However that requirement was not entirely complied with, as we were married one hour early, at 11 am., in order that we could travel down to London on the Tuesday afternoon. So the old Minister broke all the rules - we were probably never properly married at all, if the truth were known.

We left the church and were on our way by taxi to catch the London train at Carlisle, when we were flagged down by an A.A. man outside the A.A. box in Gretna. Instead of leaving our Marriage Certificate at the Church so that it could be registered at the County Records Office, we had taken it with us. Without it being registered there was no way that Mabs could obtain her passport in her married name, so we handed the certificate to the A.A. Man who kindly arranged to get it back to the church.

All our invited guests came the next day to the reception, but the bride and bridegroom were missing. We never cut our wedding cake, we only saw a photograph of it.

We travelled down to London on the Flying Scotsman, all three of us, Mabs, me and my best man, Ralph Palmer. Our original plan had been for us to honeymoon in London and while there, to apply for a passport for Mabs. In those wartime days a passport was required for travel between Guernsey and the Mainland. Mabs couldn't come back home with me immediately because she had not yet obtained a passport. So, after staying the night in a London hotel, I very reluctantly had to leave my bride of one day, with Ralph.

I telephoned Syd Le Page, a friend of mine who worked for R.G. Davis the Guernsey Travel Agents and explained to him how desperate it was for me to get back to the island for my Father's funeral. He told me to go to down to Chichester and he would try to arrange a flight back to Guernsey from there. Mabs and Ralph came to the station to see me off. I was leaning out of the carriage window, waving to them as the train left the station. I had bought a 'Guide of London' for them, and as they were disappearing into the distance, I suddenly realised that I still had the guide in my hand. So I dropped it on the platform and poor old Ralph had to run miles along the station to pick it up. Ralph Palmer always said that, in some ways, he enjoyed his first 'honeymoon' better than his second!

I travelled down to Chichester, where I found that Syd Le Page had booked a seat for me on a flight to Guernsey. I landed in the island early on Thursday morning and was met by another friend of mine, Len Rouget, who took me straight to Seaplane Bungalow.

When I arrived I discovered that, at Mum's request, the funeral service was being held at home in Seaplane Bungalow. This apparently was Dad's wish and his coffin was resting on trestles in the lounge. My sister and her husband Capt. Percy Trotter were there, so were Dad's brother-in-laws, Harry and Harold Renouf, his nephew Peter Gallienne and his sisters-in-law, my Aunts Lil and Ada. Mother wasn't very well, naturally, and Aunt Ada, who was a very capable lady, had taken charge of the arrangements. As the service was going to be held in the lounge and it was a cold winter's day, Auntie built the biggest fire you could wish to see. It was obvious that she had decided that no one was going to be cold.

I took one look at the fire and thought 'crikey the petrol !' I didn't want to scare anyone, so I damped it down without explaining what I was doing. Later Auntie noticing how black the fire looked, stoked it up again. During the service the fire was roaring up the chimney. I thought 'My God we are going to cremate Dad if we're not careful'. The heat was so intense that the varnish on the end of Dad's coffin blistered.

After the service was over and everyone had left, I stripped away the weatherboards and removed all the cans of petrol that were hidden around the chimney stack. One of them was almost round as a result of the heat. Miraculously it hadn't burst, but if it had we would have all gone up.

Dad and I had enjoyed a great relationship, although he was forty three years old when I was born and was old enough to have been my grandfather. He and I were great pals, we always enjoyed each others company. He taught me so much and gave me great encouragement and support in whatever I did. I never knowingly did anything which I knew he would disapprove. He was a wonderful Father and, in my own way, I had tried to be a good son. I sorely missed him.

On my 28th birthday he presented me with a pair of gold cuff-links. Inside the display box he put a small handwritten note which read

> 'With love and best wishes for many happy returns to the
> staunchest pal I have ever known.
> Dad.
> 19th August 1937'

I still have the cuff-links, the box and his note. I was very fond of my old man and his gift is still my most prized possession.

I have only worn the cuff-links on very special occasions. I wore them when I was married, once when, as President of the Chamber of Commerce, I presided at their Annual Dinner, again on My President's night at Rotary. The Past Rotarians honoured me, by making me their President and I wore Dad's cuff links at their Dinner. Of course I wore them when I had the honour to meet Her Majesty the Queen when she came to the island. The last time I wore them was when Mabs and I went to Court to transfer our interest in Seaplane Bungalow to our daughter Margaret. All these were very special occasions in my life.

A few days after Dad's funeral, Ralph and Mabs, with her new passport, returned to the island. They had to wait until confirmation arrived in London from the Scottish County Records Office that Mabs had changed her name. I was of course overjoyed to see her and we quickly settled into the annex of Seaplane Bungalow. I was now a married man with responsibilities. Not only did I have a beautiful and charming wife, I was also responsible for looking after my Mother. Whilst I had run the business for over twelve years, Dad had always been there to give advice, to discuss difficult decisions and to take over the reins when I was absent, now I was on my own. Without doubt I now had thrust upon me a great deal more responsibilities than I ever had before. But more was to follow. It was not long before Mabs announced that she was expecting a baby. We were both delighted, but life was never going to be quite the same again. My halcyon days of youth had departed for ever.

Dad did not leave a will, so his property and possessions had to be divided in accordance with Guernsey Law. I, as the only son, received two thirds of the property, Mum received her dowry and chose to stay in Seaplane Bungalow. Dad had expected me to take care of Mum, which I happily did for the next twenty years. The business, which was still in Dad's name although I had run it for many years, was split up with my sister. The shop was well stocked, but as a consequence of buying Daisy's share, I was left with a substantial overdraft.

The war, which had not really affected Guernsey to any great extent, now started to make its presence felt in many ways. Petrol had been rationed for some time, but now other items, meat, bacon, butter and sugar, went on ration. The blackout, which had at first been willingly tolerated, now became something of a tedious chore. More and more islanders were leaving to join the forces or work in munition factories. The Germans invaded and overran Denmark and Norway. Their 'U' boats were having more and more success, sinking British shipping.

Mum decided that she would move into the Annex with us and let Seaplane Bungalow. I thought that this was a good idea, as it would allow Mum to increase her income from the letting. In fact it did not work out, as Mum and Mabs did not get on as well as I had hoped. Mum in some ways resented Mabs and on one occasion told her that she wished 'her Bill' had married a Guernsey girl. As a consequence of the growing animosity between her and Mabs, she moved out and went to live with Auntie Lil at 'The Campernells' in St Andrews.

We let Seaplane Bungalow to an R.A.F. officer and his wife, Gerry and Billie Smith. They were a very likeable couple and we got to know them well. Gerry was a great character and an excellent flyer. He was an Anson pilot, based at our airport. Mabs and I occasionally saw an R.A.F.Anson being flown at cliff top height just out to sea from the Jerbourg Peninsular. We discovered that it was Gerry Smith, signalling to his wife. Apparently if he gave the thumbs up signal as he flashed passed, Billie knew he would be home for lunch.

One day Gerry told me, very confidentially, that there was going to be a heavy raid that night on Italy, mounted from our airport. The information was so confidential that hundreds of people went up to the airport to give a Guernsey welcome to the R.A.F. flying crews as they relaxed on the grass waiting for the 'off'. Thirty bombers landed during the afternoon and were due to set off that night to raid the Fiat works in Turin. They broke their journey in Guernsey in order to refuel so they could reach their target and return to base in England. Gerry later told me that the raid was not an unqualified success as only four of the planes reached their target in Italy, the others having turned back as their wings iced up over the Alps.

When the island was demilitarized, Gerry Smith and his wife left Guernsey. Billie went by mailboat and he later flew out in his Anson. They had a dog, to which Gerry had become very attached and did not want to leave behind. Officially he was not allowed to take it with him in the plane, so he arranged with Mabs for her to take the dog up to a certain point on the perimeter of the airfield and wait. Gerry taxied his Anson alongside the perimeter hedge, got out and Mabs handed him the dog. Gerry got back into the cockpit with his dog and they both flew off.

I felt that I should be doing my bit to help the war effort. I served in the Royal Guernsey Militia when I was seventeen and, although I had enjoyed the comradeship, I did not really want to join the Army. Ralph Palmer and I decided to join the Royal Navy. Together, we visited the office at Government House and enquired if we could sign on for the Navy. Surprisingly, they could not help us and suggested that we try at the Town Arsenal. There they advised us to obtain forms from the Post Office. This we did and both filled up the forms and sent them off to the Admiralty. I volunteered for the Engineering Branch, in view of my mechanical knowledge and experience, while Ralph just wanted the opportunity of joining the Royal Navy and going to sea.

Ralph and I received official replies from the Admiralty saying that there were no problems, provided we were prepared to sign on for twelve years ! I was still of the opinion that the war was going to be over quickly, by the end of 1940, or at the very latest by the summer of 1941. There was no way that I was going to sign on for twelve years, - the duration of the war, yes, but certainly no longer. Ralph took the same view. The Royal Navy lost two keen recruits.

Ralph Palmer was still keen to go to sea and after trying to join the crew of almost every Merchant Navy ship which called at our harbours, was finally taken on as an Ordinary Seaman on the Onesimus Dorey's SS Sarnia, despite having no maritime experience or qualifications whatsoever. He had a very interesting war and wrote a short book about his experiences, which I found fascinating.

If I could not join the Navy, then perhaps I could put my skills to use by working for one of the great British engineering companies. I wrote to several different firms offering my services, but received replies to the effect that they would contact me when they had a vacancy. Len Rouget, who ran a small garage in Saumarez Street, had applied to work with Armstrong Siddeley in Coventry. He was accepted and said:

"Come with me Bill, you want to be an engineer, they are desperate for people."

I had a very good team working for me at the beginning of the second World War. Arthur Selous, Artie to us all, a highly skilled mechanic, was the mainstay of the business. He was too old to think of joining the forces. Bert Coutanche, was another excellent mechanic, but he left to join the Royal Air Force. Freddie Mudge and Mac Allen completed the team.

I decided to go and work for Armstrong Siddeley and Artie agreed to take charge of the business for the duration. I remember I increased his wages to £2.10s.0d. a week !

Len Rouget and I set off for Coventry. He left his wife Bunty behind and I left Mabs. The arrangement was that we would find somewhere to live and then send for our wives. Mabs was suffering from morning sickness due to her pregnancy and we both felt that she would be better with me in Coventry. She would be nearer her mother if anything was to go wrong.

Len and I travelled over by boat and when we arrived in Southampton, I realised that I had forgotten my passport. Len remembered his and had no difficulty. I, on the other hand, was trying to talk my way through Customs and Immigration, but the officer was not being at all co-operative. It began to look as if I would be refused entry and would have to return to Guernsey. Len Rouget stood there, casually opened a new packet of Gallaher cigarettes and pulled out the Cigarette Card. By a lucky chance, a 48-1 chance, it was number '18, W. Green', with my photograph.

Len turned to the Immigration Officer and said;

"Mr Green has not got his passport, but I have one for him - will this do?"

With that he handed the officer the cigarette card - he looked at it, read the back, looked at me, looked at the card again and said;

"Yes, I will accept that."

Saved by a packed of Gallaher cigarettes, despite never having smoked a Gallaher cigarette in my life!

We travelled up to Coventry, found some digs and went to work for Armstrong Siddeley. Day by day we listened to the news from France, day by day it got worse. At lunch times we went across the road to a pub for something to eat and to listen to the B.B.C.'s Home Service one o'clock news. We had only been in Coventry for a matter of two weeks when it was reported on the news that French resistance had disintegrated and the Germans were rapidly advancing towards the English Channel.

"That's it Len, I'm going back to Guernsey to get Mabs and Mum."

"I'm coming too, to get Bunty."

So we went straight back to the factory and told the Foreman;

"We'll be back, but we have got to go to Guernsey to fetch our wives."

"That's all right boys, we will see you soon."

We left immediately, straight after lunch on the Monday, not even waiting to collect our wages. We travelled down to London and of course all the traffic was going in the opposite direction since the evacuation was under way. We had a terrible job to get back to the island.

Len Rouget and I travelled home to Guernsey on the mailboat, from Southampton. As we sailed down Southampton Water near Netley Hospital, we heard the air raid sirens and before long we saw a German plane caught in the searchlights. The bomber jettisoned a stick of bombs in the estuary between us and the shore. The explosions caused the ship to vibrate violently and then pitch and roll for some time. There was a group of soldiers, aboard, one of them shouted:

"Who the hell is that - Jerry?"

"Yes" I said.

"Them Germans could never hit anything, we'll be all right, they will never hit us."

I immediately recognised the voice, it was Sid Logan, an old motorcycling adversary from Jersey. He was going home to Jersey, on leave, having just returned from Dunkirk.

We arrived back on Thursday 20th June and nobody understood, other than our families, why Len and I had returned.

Looking around, the island seemed empty. It was and I realised for the first time just how many people were being evacuated to England. Virtually all the children were being sent away, together with many of their mothers. The majority of men of military age had departed, or would do so in the next few days. Out of a population of forty five thousand, almost half left the island. There were many men who sent their wives and children away and who stayed behind to look after their businesses or property. Many intended to follow their loved ones as soon as they had settled their affairs.

The Press headlines that greeted me on my return declared that 'Guernsey Calms Down'. Many businesses were proclaiming that they were carrying on as usual. My own business, under the management of Artie Selous, had opened as normal and had done good business. Artie was proud of his management, he boasted that he sold five cycles in one day, which at the time was something of a record. He was doing a good job and I was happy at the prospect of leaving the business in his hands when I returned to Armstrong Siddeley.

On the evening before my return to the island, Mabs went down to St Martin's Parish Hall and registered herself and Mum for evacuation. She apparently misunderstood a newspaper announcement and thought that evacuation was compulsory. Mabs had not been able to register me as she did not know for sure that I was on my way back to the island. In fact she did not know of my intention of coming back to fetch her and Mum until I actually arrived on the doorstep. Communications between the mainland and the island were almost impossible. I had tried to telephone her on a number of occasions, but without success.

I read a notice in the Evening Press that an 'announcement' would be made at Victoria Pier that evening at 7 pm. regarding further evacuation details. I wanted to hear what the arrangements were as my first priority was to get Mabs, Mum and myself away before the Germans arrived.

When I tried to obtain sailing tickets, I soon discovered that only if I was prepared to volunteer for the forces would I get a passage, but even then I would not be able to take Mabs and Mum. I did not want to join up, I wanted to go back to Armstrong Siddeley and that meant that I had no priority.

Mabs and I went down to the Victoria Pier to hear the announcement about the arrangements for evacuation. There must have been well over three thousand people milling around on the Esplanade and the Pier waiting for the announcement. We arrived there at 7 pm. and by 7.30 nothing had happened. By a quarter to eight there was still no sign of any speaker or announcement. We gave up and decided to walk up to the shop in Smith Street. When we arrived outside the Press Office there was a crowd, and Ambrose Sherwill was just starting to speak.

He said that he knew nothing about a meeting at Victoria Pier, but that he had been telephoned by the Press and told that there were crowds there and outside the Press office. He understood that they were expecting him to speak. Apparently Mr Sherwill had been working late, but immediately agreed to come and address the crowd outside the Press office, where the necessary equipment had been set up. That response was typical of the man, he spoke for twenty minutes without notes and then offered to answer questions.

I can clearly remember standing, leaning against Lovell's shop front with Mabs, listening to his speech:

"Evacuation," he said, "is entirely voluntary, I do not know whether we shall get many away apart from the children and those of military age."

Mr Sherwill then stressed the need for everyone to keep calm.

"There have been signs that people had almost got into a panic, but we must all carry on as usual. The Bailiff, the Jurats and I are not going away at all, we are continuing our work and we will look after your interests. That there would be times of trouble ahead was possible. There will possibly be economic difficulties, there might be some difficulty over the food supplies, but hold your heads high like men and women." said Mr Sherwill.

He explained that men of military age should volunteer for the forces and get away as quickly as possible. They, he said, would be given priority.

"Do you mean" I called out, "you want me to go and leave my family here ?"

"Yes, that is what you are expected to do!" he replied through the megaphone.

"I am sorry," I said, "But I am not going to do what I am expected to do, I will go when I can take my family with me."

Mabs and I went home and held a family conference with Mum. We decided that we would all be evacuated together as a family or not at all.

Within the matter of a few days the evacuation of children and men of military age had been completed and there were empty spaces on the boats. Life was getting back to 'normal' to the extent that the mailboats were again running on Tuesdays and Fridays. The export of tomatoes, which had been suspended, was re-commenced. Like many people I was now not sure whether to go or to stay. I weighed up all the reasons for staying, then all the reasons for going. Each time I did that I came to a different conclusion. I could not grasp the idea that the Germans were coming, there was nothing for them in Guernsey.

The air of normality that had descended on Guernsey was largely a result of Ambrose Sherwill and his colleagues being very successful in re-establishing public confidence. Slogans like, 'Compulsory evacuation a lie!' 'There is no place like home!' 'Cheer up!' 'Keep your heads!' 'Don't be yellow!' 'Business as usual!' were appearing and had their effect.

At one moment I was convinced that the Germans would be unlikely to be interested in our little island. Their target was Britain, not 'off the beaten track' Guernsey. If they were to come, I told myself, it would not be for some time and we would be able to get away. Then when I had convinced myself that I would stay, I thought to myself that the Germans were only just across the water in Cherbourg and they could be here in a matter of hours. I changed my mind time and time again and everyone I spoke to had a different effect on my thinking.

I met one of my friends in Smith Street and asked his opinion about leaving. He was very firm with his advice :-

"Don't talk so silly, the Germans won't come here, there is nothing for them to come for. My family and I are staying."

Two days later I met him on Fort Road, pushing a pram packed with everything imaginable on his way with his family to the White Rock to catch the boat to England.

Another two days passed and I again met him, this time in the Jerbourg Road. I was surprised to see him as I thought that he and his family had left the island.

"I thought you had left us." I exclaimed.

"Well" he said, "on the way down to White Rock, we came across a number of people who were coming back and they said that it was no use going down there as there were no more boats. They said that they had heard that the people going to England are having to sleep on the beaches in Weymouth. They advised us to turn around and go back home, so that is what we did and now we are staying."

I was totally confused and uncertain. So, just to keep our options open, I obtained embarkation tickets for Mabs, Mum and myself to travel on the mailboat on the Friday evening, the 28th June. As the time to leave approached I still could not make up my mind, neither could Mabs or Mum. Should we use the tickets or wait for a later boat. I felt that the decision to go or to stay could be put off for a few more days. I convinced myself that by hanging on a just a little longer I would be able to see how the situation developed. I never did make a decision, the Germans made it for us. Mabs still has our three unused boat tickets.

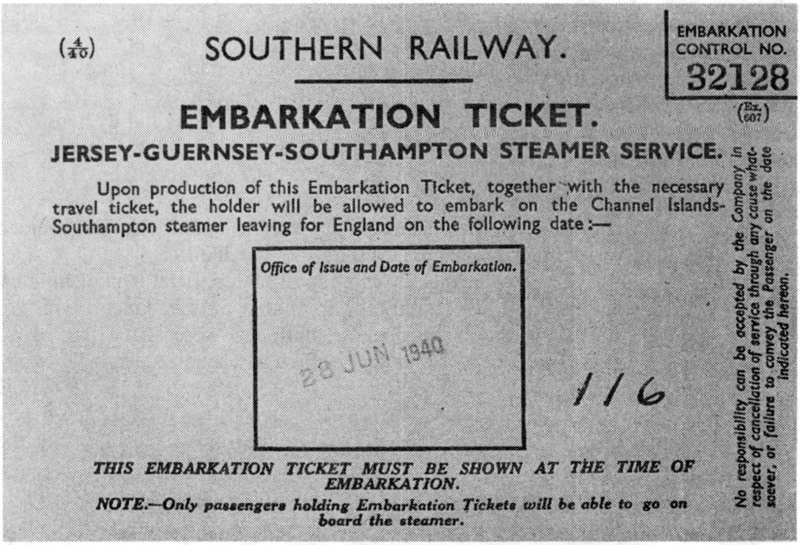
(4/40) SOUTHERN RAILWAY.

EMBARKATION CONTROL NO. 32128

EMBARKATION TICKET. (Ex./607)

JERSEY-GUERNSEY-SOUTHAMPTON STEAMER SERVICE.

Upon production of this Embarkation Ticket, together with the necessary travel ticket, the holder will be allowed to embark on the Channel Islands-Southampton steamer leaving for England on the following date:—

Office of Issue and Date of Embarkation.

28 JUN 1940

1/6

THIS EMBARKATION TICKET MUST BE SHOWN AT THE TIME OF EMBARKATION.

NOTE.—Only passengers holding Embarkation Tickets will be able to go on board the steamer.

No responsibility can be accepted by the Company in respect of cancellation of service through any cause whatsoever, or failure to convey the Passenger on the date indicated hereon.

Unused embarkation ticket for 28th June 1940.

Chapter 9

TRACER BULLETS WERE PATTERING DOWN LIKE RAIN

Whilst I and many others islanders agonised whether to leave or stay, it became painfully clear to everyone in authority that it would only be a matter of time before the island was occupied by the Germans. The Bailiff, leading States Members and officers clearly saw it as their duty to stay and assist the community in any way they could. The Lt. Governor of the island, General Minshull Ford, had been recalled and the Bailiff assumed his duties.

The States of Deliberation, the Guernsey Parliament, met on the 21st June and in order to streamline the government of the island, decided to set up an Emergency Controlling Committee under the Presidency of A.J. Sherwill, His Majesty's Procureur. In practice what was created was a new form of government for Guernsey, with Ambrose Sherwill taking on the role of Prime Minister. He quickly appointed seven members to the Committee, each with responsibility for a particular Department. The island was now run by a Cabinet of eight islanders, with the authority and ability to make quick decisions. In the circumstances which prevailed at that time, speed was of the essence.

Ambrose Sherwill's Cabinet consisted of:

Jurat A.M. Drake	Horticulture
Raymond Falla	Agriculture
Deputy R.H. Johns	Employment
Jurat John Leale	Economics
Dr.A.N. Symons	Medical Services
Deputy Stamford Raffles	Information
Jurat Sir Abraham Laine	Essential Commodities

It was a very strong team which was to serve the island well during the occupation. I regarded Ambrose Sherwill as a man of sound judgement with the ability to make speedy and decisive decisions. Ambrose with his typical legal approach, liked twenty four hours to mull over a matter, before he made a decision, but when made, it was sound and solid. It is often said that the occasion produces the man, certainly Ambrose Sherwill was the man for the occasion.

Commencing on Monday 24th June, one of the members of the new Controlling Committee spoke each evening at 6.15 pm to the crowd outside the Press office. On the Friday evening, the 28th June, the President of the Controlling Committee, Ambrose Sherwill, was due to speak and I wanted to hear what he had to say. There was a large crowd standing outside the Press office in the summer sunshine waiting to hear Ambrose Sherwill, but first we had to listen to Deputy Stamford Raffles who, as Information Officer, read out a procession of statements and notices. I remember him telling us that 500 cattle had been saved and brought over from Alderney, which had been almost totally evacuated. Whilst I did not realise it at the time, those extra cattle must have provided Guernsey with much needed supplies of milk and meat during the occupation.

When Ambrose Sherwill spoke he tried to calm everyone down by saying;

"What ever else is wrong, it has been a beautiful day."

I recall those words so well and I remember later saying to Mabs, how wrong he was!

After the speeches were over, I gave Mum and Aunt Lil, who had also been listening to Ambrose Sherwill, a lift in the car to Belmont Road. I had put my head in the shop and told Artie Selous that I would be back in a few minutes. As I was returning, driving down St James past the prison, I heard a strange noise. It sounded like the clatter of a machine gun and looking up I saw three German aircraft with bright flashes of fire coming from their wings. It was about ten to seven on the 28th June 1940 and Guernsey was experiencing its first air raid. I abandoned my car alongside what was then St Paul's Church, ran for the protection of the buttresses and threw myself on the ground against the wall of the Church. The ground never felt so comfortable.

There were several other people, including Mr W. Frampton, the States Accountant, and his wife, sheltering around the church.

"I don't fancy being out here." said Mr Frampton.

"No, neither do I." I replied.

So I went around to the rear of the church, broke a toilet window, climbed inside and quickly opened a door and let in Mr and Mrs Frampton and about a dozen other people. My thoughts were, as no doubt were everyone else's, to take cover at all costs. We sheltered in the church, and after a while were relieved to realise that we personally, were not the target for the German planes.

It sounded to us as if all hell had been let loose down in the harbour area. First we heard the whistle, then the thud of exploding bombs. Soon it seemed to us that the sea front was under an incessant bombardment. Jerry planes were shrieking overhead, tracer bullets were pattering down like rain, salvo after salvo of bombs were being rained down on our defenceless island. Soon there was a thick pall of smoke drifting slowly across the sky. The reality of war had come to Guernsey.

After what seemed an eternity, although in fact it was probably less than half an hour, there was a lull and as I was getting concerned about Artie and the shop, I jumped cover and ran down to Smith Street. I knew that Artie was normally, of a very nervous disposition.

When I reached the shop, I was amazed to find it was full of people and Artie walking up and down saying;

"Keep calm, everything will be all right, keep calm."

I thought 'good lor, old Artie got more guts than I have!'

Then suddenly the German planes resumed their attack, the whistling and the inevitable thud of the bombs, concentrated everyone's mind on self preservation. The shop was in some ways an exciting place to be, because every time a bomb exploded, all the tools on the bench would bounce up and down and the bikes in the window would jiggle about. None of the bombs fell near enough the shop to cause any damage.

Just after 7.35 pm the last of the German planes headed off back to their bases on the continent. Our first air raid was over, but at the cost of many lives and injuries. A great deal of damage had been caused to the harbour and adjacent areas of the Town.

Guernsey slowly came back to life, everyone was a little apprehensive; was the raid over or was it just another lull. The people who had taken shelter in the shop quickly departed, except for one man who insisted on buying a new bicycle. I didn't want to be bothered with him, but he persisted, so I sold him a five pound bike for £4 and off he went, apparently happily. Very sadly we later learned that he committed suicide soon afterwards by diving down a well. Some weeks later I found that we had a cycle belonging to him, which we had repaired and he had not collected. We thought that it belonged to someone who had left the island but, on checking the registration number, found that it belonged to the chap who had insisted on buying a new bicycle.

Everyone had gone, but there was no sign of Artie. Eventually I heard a strange noise and found him under a desk in my office, drunk as a lord! I then understood where he got his Dutch courage, and now he was 'out cold'. I always kept a bottle of brandy in my office for an emergency and Artie had decided that the German air raid was an emergency ! He finished off the bottle of brandy and, as I learnt years afterwards, supplemented it with a further half bottle he obtained during the raid from the Prince of Wales.

One of his relatives later said to me that Artie was the only person in St Peter Port who 'enjoyed' the raid! Clearly Artie needed assistance to get back to his home, so he could sleep off his over indulgence. I managed to half carry, half drag Artie out of the shop and up Smith Street towards where I had abandoned my car in St James Street.

There is nothing more difficult than trying to carry a drunk man, as I quickly found out. I had with some difficulty reached the War Memorial, with Artie draped around my neck, when a policeman rushed out of the Police Station and took his other arm.

"Where's he hit? Where's he hit ?" he asked.

"He's not hit, he's drunk!"

Whereupon the policeman let go of Artie's arm and we both went arse over head, in the middle of the road. Eventually, however I managed to get Artie into the car and took him home.

During the period when Neville Chamberlain, the then British Prime Minister had been negotiating with Hitler in 1938, Artie became increasingly concerned about the future. He was certain that there was going to be a war, so he started building an air raid shelter at the bottom of his garden in Victoria Road. On Sunday mornings, when he was working on his shelter, it was part of the entertainment for his neighbours to look over the garden wall and pull his leg about it. That did not bother Artie, he just carried on digging his air raid shelter.

The day after the Air raid, Artie was up at the top of his house, still not having fully recovered from his over indulgence, when, at 11 am the air raid siren sounded - the Germans had sent over a reconnaissance plane, to assess the success of their raid. Artie, on hearing the warning, assumed that there was going to be another raid, dived down the stairs as fast as he could go and raced up the garden to his now completed air raid shelter. But when he got there he could not get in because all his neighbours were in the shelter first!

The German air raid, which was concentrated on the White Rock, killed thirty three people and injured many more. Lines of tomato vans and lorries waiting with produce for shipment to the mainland, were left as smouldering wrecks. Forty-nine vehicles were burnt out or seriously damaged. Bomb craters were everywhere. The Weighbridge was extensively damaged and its clock stopped at few minutes before seven. Whenever I had returned to Guernsey from one of my adventures across the water I had always looked up at the Weighbridge clock and said to myself 'Its nice to be home'. That welcoming clock had become the symbol of the island for me. The whole of the front, from the States Offices, where every single window was broken, right along to Les Banques suffered considerable damage, there was hardly an un-broken window to be seen. Well over one hundred windows were broken in the Royal Hotel.

Whilst the main raid was concentrated against the White Rock, the German Heinkel 111's bombers also dropped bombs in other parts of the island. In the country a bomb was dropped near the St Saviour Reservoir and another at the race course at Vazon. A number of houses were damaged by bombs. In the Strand, Strand Villa, an adjoining cottage and another house received considerable structural damage. Two bombs fell, one in the front and another at the rear of this group of properties. At the Guernsey Brewery over one hundred windows were blown out. A house in St Andrews, at La Vassalerie, suffered considerable structural damage, all the windows and doors being blown in. Fortunately none of the occupants were injured as they had taken cover.

The Germans machined-gunned other areas of the town and haymakers in the fields, without causing any serious injuries. The lifeboat, which was at sea during the raid, was machine gunned and Harold Hobbs, the son of the Coxswain, was killed.

When the first bombs fell on White Rock there were a considerable number of people on the quay waiting for the mailboat to leave harbour. Many were about to board the Isle of Sark, others had come down to wave their friends and relations goodbye. Police Constable Fred Short and his colleague 'Snip' Piesing were on duty and quickly directed as many people as possible down below the pier. Fred said afterwards that it was very fortunate that the tide was out because if it had not, the number of casualties would have been far greater.

German air raid damage to arm of Crown Pier June 28th 1940.

Two horses which had recently been rescued from Alderney, were stabled in a shed on the White Rock. As a result of the crescendo of noise from the air raid, the horses stampeded in the shed. The two police constables, during the lull in the raid, decided to try and quieten them down. Both being ex- cavalry men, they knew the value of sugar, so they went into the White Rock Cafe, which was open and deserted, and helped themselves to handfuls of sugar lumps.

Fred and 'Snip' approached the frightened horses, remembering their cavalry training, to 'make much of them'. They soft talked them, saying 'come on my boys' and 'everything is going to be all right my beauties'. The sugar lumps worked wonders and the horses soon settled down. Fred put sacks over their heads to restrict their vision and a rope around each horses neck in the form of a halter. Then they led them out of the shed, down the White Rock and along the sea front to the Terres field at the bottom of Havelet. There they released them before returning to duty at the Weighbridge.

During the raid, P.C. Bob Kimber was in the Watch House at the end of the

German air raid damage at the harbour.

White Rock. While the bombs were dropping all around, he was on the telephone to leading island officials, giving them a commentary of what was happening. Just as he rang off at the end of the raid, a bomb dropped close by in the harbour. The blast blew him out of the Watch House. Fortunately he was uninjured, but it was a narrow escape.

Charlie Froome, was on duty at the St John's Ambulance Brigade Headquarters, when the raid started. He immediately responded to the three calls for assistance he received. With colleague Lionel Taylor, he drove the ambulance down to White Rock and parked it alongside the Weighbridge, facing up the Avenue with its rear doors open.

Joe Way, who ran the small garage next to Stainers in the Pollet, was just about to board the Isle of Sark and leave the island, when the raid started. Joe at one time had been a St John's Ambulance driver and realising that there were casualties, he headed back to the area of the clock tower where the Ambulance was parked.

Joe joined Ambulance men Lionel Taylor and Charlie Froome, in attending the injured. He tried to persuade Charlie to drive the ambulance further down White Rock, saying

"There are many injured down there, who need attention."

"I'm sorry" Charlie said, "we can't be everywhere, there are people here who need attention." and added "It is safer for the ambulance to stay where it is, as many of the tomato lorries are ablaze and if we managed to get down, we probably would not be able to get back again".

As the Heinkel 111's roared in for yet another attack Lionel and Charlie sought cover under the ambulance, while Joe lay flat on the ground. Two bombs exploded between the vehicle and the Weighbridge, causing considerable damage to the ambulance and injuring Lionel in the backside. Charlie was uninjured, but suffered from concussion. Joe was blown, by the force of the blast, into the ambulance and against the partition behind the drivers seat. Sadly Joe Way was seriously injured and died soon afterwards.

Police Constable Frank Le Cocq, who was later to become Chief Inspector, was on White Rock helping the injured, when Deputy Police Inspector Langmead ordered him to drive the ambulance and the casualties to hospital. As the Inspector put it;

"Take all you can out of it, in case the Germans come back again".

One of the ambulance's rear tyres was flat, as was the spare. However Frank managed to drive the damaged ambulance up St Julians as far as the South African War Memorial before the tyre finally came off the rim. Despite that he continued his 'bumpity, bumpity' progress until he reached St James, where he was stopped by Police Sergeant Jack Harper. It was obvious that the ambulance was no longer drivable, so a passing coal lorry belonging to Stan Collings was commandeered. A tarpaulin was laid over the back of the lorry and the injured were transferred from the Ambulance. The coal lorry was turned around and driven by P.C. Le Cocq to the Castel Hospital. The damaged ambulance was abandoned in St James Street, forty or fifty yards down from the junction with Saumarez Street.

When the raid took place, Guernsey had been de-militarised, but no public statement of that fact had been made by the British Government. The island had no defences, but the mailboat, the Isle of Sark, which had been embarking passengers, had an anti aircraft gun on its aft deck. This was in action until the gallant gunner was injured in the arm. A cargo boat, the SS Sheringham was also equipped with a gun which was used against the German attackers.

Another vessel, the SS Courier, was en-route from Alderney to St Peter Port with salvaged stores, two hundred pigs and some of the last inhabitants, when it was attacked off St Sampson's Harbour. She was machine gunned, by the Germans, causing eleven casualties amongst her crew. The aircraft that attacked her also dropped a bomb, which fortunately missed its target. The Captain beached the SS Courier near the entrance to St Sampson's Harbour and many of her crew and passengers managed to make their way ashore. The next day the ship was refloated and immediately set sail for England.

The blast from bombs which were intended for the Isle of Sark, caused a number of fishing boats and yachts to sink in the harbour. Neither the Isle of Sark or the SS Sheringham were hit.

At 10 pm, soon after the air raid was over the Isle of Sark left harbour with 163 passengers and headed for England. That was our last mailboat until after the occupation. Len Rouget's wife Bunty was one of those who managed to get away, she went with her brother, but Len was left behind.

After taking Artie Selous home, I hurried back to Jerbourg to see how Mabs had fared. I had telephoned and knew she was safe. Mabs had seen a formation of three Jerry planes coming in low from the direction of Jersey, and as they circled over the Jerbourg peninsular, she was convinced that they were going to attack our headland. She ran out of the annex and hid in the bracken from where she had a grandstand view of the German planes making attack after attack on the White Rock. When clouds of black smoke appeared over St Peter Port, Mabs realised that considerable damage must have been done. During the lull in the air raid, a neighbour waved for her to go and take shelter with them in their house.

A little later that evening, I received a telephone call from Len Rouget. He had been approached by Reg Blanchford, who was in charge of the St John's Ambulance in those days, to see if he could get the damaged ambulance mobile again. It was felt that it might be needed again before long. Len agreed and wanted me to go down and help him. I saw it as my duty and of course I went. Len and I met in St James Street, where the damaged Ambulance had been abandoned.

One of the two rear tyres, they were the old fashioned balloon type, was totally shredded beyond repair, the other and the spare were in nearly as bad a condition. The rear of the vehicle had been peppered with shrapnel, there were probably in the region of one hundred and fifty holes, both large and small. Most of the windows were shattered, but the engine and cab were almost un-damaged. We decided that we would try to drive the Ambulance round the corner into Saumarez Street to Len's repair workshop, less than a hundred yards away. The engine started easily enough, but the vehicle would not move because the rear wheel, without its tyre, was jammed in the gutter. We fetched a wooden stake from Len's garage and after much effort managed to lever the rim of the wheel out of the gutter and away from the pavement. Len then slowly drove the damaged ambulance to his workshop. We worked all night on the repairs and by dawn had managed to do enough so that the ambulance could go back into service.

Many claims have been made over the years, that the ambulance was machined gunned by the Germans, but we found no evidence to support that allegation. The damage which I saw and helped to repair was, in my view, caused by shrapnel and lumps of road metal.

Whatever is the view in retrospect, at the time we hated the Germans for the raid and for killing and injuring so many islanders, many of whom were our friends. On reflection, however, after over fifty years, the Germans were unaware that the island had been de-militarised and from the air the tomato lorries could well have been mistaken for ammunition waggons. The anti aircraft guns on the mailboat, the Isle of Sark, and on the SS Sheringham, were used in our defence, so from that point of view we were not de-militarised. The Germans may well have launched the air attack in order to ascertain whether we had any defences, and if so, to see just how strong they were.

On the Saturday we realised that there was no hope of getting away from the island by mailboat. The only possible way of leaving was by small boat so Mabs and I went down to the harbour and searched to find a boat that would take us to the safety of the mainland. We pleaded with owners who were getting their boats ready, to let us go with them. We pleaded, we begged, but without success. As I drove around the harbour in search of a means of escape, Mabs spent most of the time with her head out of the car window, being sick, as she was suffering from morning sickness.

Our luck changed when we heard that Reggie Gray, who was a fellow cycle dealer in the Pollet and the owner of quite a large motoryacht, was planning to leave. Reggie was one of the smallest men I have known, tiny even in comparison with me. He had a reputation for being very careful with his pennies and in consequence was a fairly wealthy man. His boat, which he had not used for some time, was lying on the Careening Hard. Reggie decided that if it could be made seaworthy, he and his family would make a run for it before the Germans arrived. Reggie moved the boat from the Careening Hard around to the Old Harbour where, after inspection, it was found that the stern gland needed attention.

I offered to help carry out the necessary repairs, on the condition that Mum, Mabs and I could go with them to England. Reggie agreed and I took my tool kit on board and we worked for most of Saturday night, successfully completing the necessary repairs. At about five o'clock on Sunday morning I went home to fetch Mabs and Mum. We loaded the car with all the essential items we wanted to take with us. We knew we would not be able to take too much aboard the motorboat, as it was already well loaded, probably overloaded and well down in the water. It was about eight in the morning before we had everything we wanted packed up in the car, when we reached the harbour, Reggie and the boat had sailed. That was, I think, the only time in my adult life that I cried. I was totally deflated and felt very aggrieved that Reggie had left without us. To add to my troubles, he went away with my tool kit, which I had left aboard. At the time it did not bother me too much, but later during the occupation when there was a shortage of tools, I could have really done with them.

We went home, feeling forlorn and downhearted. I went to see Len Rouget, who was desperate to get away to join his wife. We discussed the situation and the only hope we saw was for us to 'acquire' a boat in the harbour, one of those left behind by islanders who had been evacuated. Len and I decided that as soon as we could find a suitable boat, we would 'commandeer' it and set sail for England.

On Sunday evening Mabs and I went down to see my cousin Percy Renouf, who lived at the top of the Water Lanes at Moulin Huet, St Martin. While there, we heard the sound of planes; looking up we saw two Dorniers with big black crosses on them, flying low over the house. They were obviously preparing to land at our La Villiaze Airport. After I had taken Mabs home, I drove around the back of the Airport and sure enough there were two or three German troop carriers parked adjacent to the terminal building. I knew then that we were occupied.

Chapter 10

VISITORS

Slowly and wearily I returned home, not knowing what the future held. How would the German Army of occupation treat us, would we be allowed to lead normal lives, would we still be able to live in our home ? Would our womenfolk be safe ? Would there be enough food, would we go hungry ? Would I be able to earn a living, would I be forced to work for the Germans ? Would we be deported ? What facilities would be available for the birth of our baby ? All these questions and many, many, more ran through my mind, none of which I could answer.

Oh how I regretted not having being able to get Mabs and Mum away before the Germans arrived. While almost half the population of the island had chosen to leave, I had brought Mabs, an English girl, who was now expecting our child, to live under the heel of the Germans. What had I done, what were her parents going to think of me!

Mabs reaction when I returned home, was to tell me;

"We must lock all the doors."

"I have never locked my doors and Germans or no Germans, I'm not going to lock them to night."

So we went to bed. I recall lying there, thinking of all the opportunities we had missed to leave the island, thinking of all the problems that could face us, wondering whether we would live to see the end of the war. One thing however, I did know for certain, Len and I would not be going back to Armstrong Siddeley and come to think of it, we never did get paid!

The next morning I was desperate to know what was going on. As the local Press would not be published until later in the day, my inquisitiveness took me down into St Peter Port and to the Royal Hotel, which the Germans had temporarily made their Headquarters and from which the Swastika now fluttered. There, I saw local people handing in guns. Apparently an order had gone out, requiring everyone to surrender them immediately. German soldiers were making a stack of the weapons outside the Hotel. These Germans, in their soon to become all too familiar field grey uniforms, were the first I had seen.

I obtained a copy of the 'Evening Press', which for the first time in living memory was distributed free of charge. I thought at the time that it was a goodwill gesture on behalf of the Press Company, but later learnt that it was on the instructions of the Germans. The whole of the front page was given over to a list of Orders issued by the German Commandant.

'ORDERS OF THE COMMANDANT OF THE GERMAN FORCES IN OCCUPATION OF THE ISLAND OF GUERNSEY'

(1) All inhabitants must be indoors by 11 pm and must not leave their homes before 6 am.

(2) We will respect the population in Guernsey; but, should anyone attempt to cause the least trouble, serious measures will be taken and the town will be bombed.

(3) All orders given by the Military Authority are to be strictly obeyed.

(4) All spirits must be locked up immediately and no spirits may be supplied, obtained or consumed henceforth. This prohibition does not apply to stocks in private houses.

(5) No person shall enter the aerodrome at La Villiaze.

(6) All Rifles, Airguns, Pistols, Revolvers, Sporting Guns, and all other weapons whatsoever, except souvenirs, must, together with all ammunition, be delivered at the Royal Hotel by 12 noon to-day, July 1st.

(7) All British Sailors, Airmen, and Soldiers on leave in this island must report at the Police Station at 9 am today, and must then report at the Royal Hotel.

(8) No boat or vessel of any description, including any Fishing Boat, shall leave the harbour or any other place where the same is moored, without an order from the military authority, to be obtained at the Royal Hotel. All boats arriving from Jersey, from Sark or from Herm, or elsewhere, must remain in harbour until permitted by the military to leave. The crews will remain on board. The Master will report to the Harbourmaster, St Peter Port and will obey his instructions.

(9) The sale of motor spirit is prohibited, except for the use on essential services, such as Doctors' vehicles, the delivery of foodstuffs and sanitary services where such vehicles are in possession of a permit from the military authorities to obtain supplies. These vehicles must be brought to the Royal Hotel by 12 noon today to receive the necessary permission. The use of cars for private purposes is forbidden.

(10) The black-out regulations already in force must be observed as before.

(11) Banks and Shops will open as usual.

(Signed) THE GERMAN COMMANDANT OF THE ISLAND OF GUERNSEY.

July 1st 1940.'

I read the Orders, I re-read them and then I read them again. I took the newspaper home and Mabs read them. Mum read them, we discussed them - what did they all mean ? We understood the curfew, we knew about the blackout. We were glad to learn that the Germans would respect 'The population in Guernsey', but what did it mean when it said that the town will be bombed if there is the least trouble. What did they mean by the 'least trouble'? Oh how I wished that Ambrose Sherwill could explain it all to us.

One thing was certain, I would not be able to use the car, it would have to come off the road. As far as re-opening the shop, that would have to wait until things had settled down, German orders or not.

Len Rouget and I still wanted to get away from the island and escape to England, but as soon as the Germans landed, it became impossible to get away from St Peter Port or St Sampson's harbours. They created harbour defences and security was introduced. The only possibility was to 'acquire' a boat from one of the smaller anchorages around the island. I went down to Bec du Nez, there were two or three boats, but nothing capable of crossing the English Channel. I didn't have very much boating experience, I had motored between St Peter Port, Herm and Sark and that was about the extent of my competence.

The idea of escaping to England by sea quickly faded from my mind, although Len remained determined, as he was on his own. Eventually, however, he reconciled himself to the fact that it was going to be very difficult and dicey, so we decided to put the thought from our minds, at least for the time being.

Whilst I had seen German soldiers in town, the first time Mabs and I saw Germans near Seaplane bungalow, was when two tall young blond Hitler youth types, stopped us in our road and asked;

"Vitch vay London ?"

"Across the sea." Mabs replied.

The answer clearly annoyed them, so Mabs, pointing westward repeated;

"Over there, across the sea."

Eventually they indicated that they understood what she was saying and by their expressions, were not very happy. They were obviously under the impression that they had landed in England and we were delighted to have disillusioned them!

Probably the first casualty of the occupation occurred on the evening the Germans landed in the island. Charlie Froome was on duty at the St John's Ambulance station when an islander, Harry Ingrouille, came in and asked for a wound in his arm to be dressed. Charlie inspected the wound and asked, "Where the hell did you get that from ?"

"Never you mind." replied Harry.

"Come on, that's a bullet wound, where did you get that from ?"

Apparently when the Germans arrived at the airport, Harry had been at the top of the Petit Bot valley. He saw them coming, got scared and ran down the valley. The Germans saw him running away and shot him.

Many of the cattle rescued from Alderney during the days following the evacuation of that island, were put out to graze on our airport runway. When the first Germans arrived by troopcarrier they had difficulty in landing because of the danger created by the presence of the cattle. One of the first orders they issued, required the clearance of the runway, so that further troopcarriers could land.

The Island Police were give the task of organising the removal of the cattle. P.C. Fred Short, who was on night duty, was instructed by Inspector Sculpher, to go to the airport, do whatever was necessary, and to assist the Germans in any way he could. He organised a number of farmers to help remove the cattle and they arrived at the Airport at dawn, around 5.am. Fred and the farmers were debating whether they should drive the cattle across the Route des Landes and into a field on the other side, when three Junkers troopcarriers landed, miraculously missing all the grazing animals.

They disgorged their cargo of fully armed German troops, together with a number of motorcycles and sidecars. The Jerries without transport immediately commandeered all the farmers cars and motorcycles. None of the Germans spoke English, but Fred clearly understood what they wanted when they kept repeating, 'Benzin, Benzin'. He led them, on his police motorcycle, out of the airport and down the road passed the Happy Landings Hotel to Snell's petrol pump at Le Bourg. He broke open the door and started to turn the pump handle, but the tank was dry.

Not knowing quite what to do, he was reminded by a colleague that the force had 'acquired' a supply of petrol from a damaged R.A.F. Spitfire. When the island had been demilitarized, and the R.A.F. evacuated, the police had been put in charge of the airport. It had been guarded by Special Constables. A Spitfire which had crashed landed and was damaged beyond repair, had been left in a hanger. Regular Police Officers on the night shift had discovered that the wings of the aircraft were still filled with fuel. They unofficially collected twenty, 5 gallon cans of high octane petrol, and secreted them in a store next to the Police Garage in Lefebvre Street.

Fred Short decided that there was no alternative but to lead the Germans to that supply of petrol. He led the 'convoy' of German Military motorcycles, with their mounted machine guns, the commandeered farmers cars and motorcycles into St Peter Port, and stopped outside the Police Station. Fred and the Germans had arrived just as the change over from night shift to early shift was taking place. A Nazi Major, motioned all the police to line up against the wall. Fred told me that he and his colleagues did so, only very reluctantly, as they were confronted by fully armed German combat troops. They began to wonder whether they were going to be mown down in cold blood. Instead the Major produced a camera and took a photograph of our Policemen, lined up outside the Guernsey police station.

The Germans then drove into the Police yard in Lefebvre Street, at the end of Court Row, seized the entire stock of petrol cans, and proceeded to fill their vehicles with the high octane fuel. It was perhaps fortunate that the aviation fuel was suitable for the vehicles, otherwise the Germans may have thought that Fred Short had committed an act of sabotage.

Shortly afterwards, Fred was in the station just about to go home when two Germans came in and drew a sketch of a Nazi flag. They indicated that they wanted two large ones made immediately. Because the station Sergeant could not

Police Constable Fred Short on the Police Motorcycle at Jerbourg.

understand that they wanted them by 9 am. that morning, one of the Jerries climbed up on a chair and changed the hands of the clock to indicate their deadline.

Fred, told me that he tried to contact a firm of sailmakers in St Sampson's, only to discover that they had evacuated. Then the station Sergeant contacted the manager of Creasey's who undertook to get his dressmakers to run up the two flags required as quickly as possible. At 9.30 am they were delivered to our 'new masters' at the Royal Hotel. One was immediately hoisted on the hotel flagpole and the other over Castle Cornet.

During the air raid a number of small yachts and fishing boats were sunk in the harbour. One of the yachts, the Olinda, owned by Danny La Farge and packed with nearly all his worldly possessions, was about to sail for England and freedom. It sustained a great hole in its hull when a bomb, which had been aimed at the Isle of Sark, missed and exploded nearby. The Olinda sank and was laying on the bed of the harbour. At low water it was only just below the surface and could be clearly seen. Danny was very keen to recover the two attache cases which were in the forward cabin.

I was approached, not by Danny La Farge, but by one of my swimming pals, who knew my ability to swim for reasonably long distances under water and asked if I would dive down and retrieve the attache cases. Although this was several days after the Germans had arrived, their permission was never sought, we just went ahead and made the attempt.

I was taken out in a boat to where the Olinda was lying adjacent to the old lifeboat slipway. I duck-dived down from the surface, unlocked the engine room door and swam inside. I could see the attache cases near the bow in the forward cabin. Although I attempted to swim through the door to the forward cabin five or six times, coming up for air on each occasion, I failed. Whilst I put my head through the door, I did not have enough courage to go that little bit further, although I wasn't out of air. What frightened me was the fact that once in the forward cabin, I would have to turn around and swim out. The roof of the cabin appeared very low and I felt that I might become stuck as I tried to turn around. It must have been a form of underwater claustrophobia. On reflection it was rather like my approach to motorcycle racing, where I never pushed myself beyond what I believed to be my ability.

The Germans, only days after my abortive attempt at salvage, raised all the boats sunk by them in their raid. Whether the attache cases were returned to Danny La Farge, together with his many other possessions on board the yacht, I do not know. It was not until many years later that I discovered that the attache cases had contained his life savings, thousands of pounds in bank notes and the family silver. It was no wonder that Danny was so keen that they should be recovered.

The Germans were issuing Orders almost on a daily basis. We were told by our occupiers that:

> 'The population is hereby required to retain calmness, order and discipline, and if that was assured, the life and property of the population will be respected and guaranteed.'

A notice appeared in the Evening Press signed by Dr Reffler, the German Feldkommandantur, prohibiting the riding of bicycles two or three abreast. The Order, we were informed was in the interests of road safety. Those who disobeyed would be punished. Another of Dr Reffler's orders was to prohibit the lighting of fires in the open air, at any time of the day or night.

All buses were withdrawn, so it was a choice between cycling and walking. Our island authorities and the Press told us walking would be good for our health - perhaps, but not for our tempers!

Clocks went forward an hour to bring the island into line with German time. The announcement of the change was made only hours before the new time came into operation. The next morning islanders going to work were taken by surprise when they arrived an hour late. My first knowledge of the change, was when I looked up in amazement at the Town Church Clock, as I cycled by on my way to Smith Street.

We were allowed to keep our wireless sets, but the National Anthem was forbidden to be played as a public performance without written permission from the German Commandant. Church services were permitted and we were allowed to say prayers for the Royal Family and the wellbeing of the British Empire.

Within a few days life began to settle down to a new routine. We were being allowed to live our lives to a very great extent unhindered by the Germans. There were in fact, very few Germans on the island. A few hundred, five hundred or so had arrived within the first forty eight hours of the occupation and it was then some time before they were substantially reinforced.

I soon reopened the shop for business and, without cars and buses, there was a tremendous demand for cycles and cycle repairs. Business boomed. I was fortunate to have good stocks, something like three hundred and forty new cycles. I had a substantial overdraft, due to buying out my sister's share of the business after Dad died and because I had being building up my stocks. I saw the demand for bicycles as an opportunity to turnover some of my stock quickly and reduce my overdraft. It was bad enough to be indebted to the bank in normal times, but to have an overdraft now the Germans were here worried me a great deal. I wanted to clear my debt as quickly as possible, so I decided to take full advantage of the situation and inserted a series of advertisements in the Evening Press. Pre war I developed a method of advertising which, while being inexpensive, was at the same time eye catching and highly successful.

I used the reverse block method in which the background was entirely black and the message white. The message I used, was simple but to the point.

'Green's of Smith Street - Guernsey's leading Cycle People'.

The advert was small and therefore inexpensive, but it stood out from the page and 'hit' the eye of the reader. The combination of the advertisements and the sudden upsurge in demand meant that within weeks of the occupation we had sold our entire stock of cycles. I sold them at our normal prices, £4.19s.9d. with a three speed gear and £3.19s.9d. without. I can remember the prices as if it was only yesterday. What I should have done, was to have kept some of them back and obtained a much higher price, since later, new and nearly new machines were changing hands for well in excess of £50.

I did, however keep two cycles, one for Mabs and the other for my own use. Mum was too old to ride a bike, she was seventy three when the occupation started.

Deputy Stamford Raffles, the Controlling Committee's Information Officer, produced a stream of announcements which were always fully reported in the Press. An early message ran:-

> 'Do not consume tinned or dried goods which will keep, eat as many fresh vegetables as you can, as a majority of these will not keep. Most growers will give you tomatoes if you will pick them. Drink milk, which is very good for you, there is an abundant supply. Share houses with your friends, this will save heating and lighting. Pay your tradesman's accounts and rent if you have any

money to do so. If you pay it enables your tradesman and Landlord to pay others, the money circulates for the good of the community. Treat the German troops in occupation with courtesy. Keep yourself informed of any orders issued by the troops in occupation and obey those orders. Such orders will be published in the newspapers. Do not purchase two articles when one will serve your immediate requirements'.

With the population almost halved and people uncertain about the future, many local businesses found it a struggle to keep going. My own business was fortunately one of the exceptions. My old friend Frank Stroobant proved that as a businessman he still had an eye for an opportunity.

As a result of the evacuation, seven town cafe's or restaurants closed down. My favourite meeting place, Stainers, shut up shop for the duration, Reg and Eileen Stainer having evacuated to the mainland. As soon as the evacuation had taken place, even before the Germans arrived, 'Stroo' saw the need for a cafe in town. Within hours of identifying the opportunity he obtained the lease of premises above his shop in the Lower Pollet. Then he and some of his friends spent the whole of the next two days and nights getting it ready. He equipped the cafe with items from other restaurants, which had closed - the Esse cooker came from Stainers and all the cutlery and furniture from other restaurants. This 'lend lease' operation was carried out with the full approval and authority of the Controlling Committee. Within forty eight hours the cafe was open for business.

On Monday the 24th June, the first of many press advertisements appeared. 'Stroo' initially called it the Evacuation Cafe, but quickly changed the name to the 'Home from Home Cafe'. A month later he upgraded the name to the now famous 'Home from Home Restaurant'. The venture was an instant success. Many husbands had sent their wives and families away to England, with the intention of joining them when they could, and 'Stroo' was one of them. Now they were cut off and used the 'Home from Home' both as a meeting place and the source of good cooked meals. 'Stroo' made the Cafe comfortable, provided music and a great variety of food. All in all it was a very successful enterprise.

Within a few days of the German occupation of the island, the problem of the pets which had been left behind by the evacuees became apparent. A great many of the people who left only decided to do so at the very last moment. They had not been able to make any arrangements about the future care of their domestic animals. Many just turned their dogs and cats out to fend for themselves. The result was that these animals, particularly the dogs, quickly became hungry and were hunting for food in packs. They soon became very aggressive, and many of them had to be shot. That could only be done by the Germans, as all locals had been required to hand in their guns.

The carcasses of these pets, many of them beautiful animals, were piled on to high-sided tomato trailers. The Germans went down to see Jackie Upham, the General Manager of the Guernsey Railway Company, which operated an incinerator, or as it was then called, the destructor.

"You will" they instructed "start up the destructor and destroy all these carcases."

Jackie told me that the stench was awful.

Jackie had taken over the management of the Guernsey Railway Company in 1934. Its name, in fact was a misnomer, it operated a bus service, but also ran the destructor. Just before he had taken over the management of the Company, the Guernsey Customs Authorities needed to destroy over one hundred thousand cigarettes, which had little brown spots all over them.

The Custom Officer went down and inspected the destructor to satisfy himself that it would do the job. He arranged that he personally would be on hand, to witness the cigarettes being put into the furnace. Word quickly circulated around the staff of the plans to incinerate the cigarettes and they, not un-naturally, considered their destruction a tragic waste. What the Customs Officer did not know, and was not told about, was that the furnace had two doors. This allowed the rubbish to be put in one door and clinker removed by the other.

The staff quickly devised a plan whereby the cigarettes would apparently be thrown into the furnace through one door and then caught at the other door. A rehearsal was held and it was established that by careful timing and the use of a tarpaulin many of the cigarettes could be 'saved'.

The Customs Officer duly came down and 'stood guard' while the cigarettes were solemnly thrown into the furnace. What of course he did not see was the other door being opened silently at just the right moment and the cigarettes being thrown right through the furnace and into the tarpaulin. The vast majority of the cigarettes were saved and for many months islanders were happily smoking spotted cigarettes.

Just as we were settling down to our new existence, we received a visit from a British Commando raiding party. We of course did not know what was happening until it was all over and even then did not hear the full details until after our liberation. We were all asleep when the raid took place on the Sunday night of July 14th/15th. The British Tommies landed at 1 am and left about two hours later. I was awakened by the barking of dogs and heard what sounded like a rifle shot, which I assumed was fired by the Germans.

The raiding party, consisting of some forty Commandos, landed at Petit Port near our home and climbed the seemingly endless flight of steps, over two hundred, to the main Jerbourg Road. While some of the party searched the peninsula and cut telephone wires, others created a barricade opposite Vue Des Isles, Fred Veal's house, on the corner of the lane which leads down to the Petit Port steps. The stones they used were very large white gneiss rocks removed from

Fred Veale's rockery stones used as a road block by British Commando's. Also Doyle monument demolished by the Germans in June 1944.

Fred's rockery and must have taken some moving. The barricade was erected to prevent the Germans cutting off the raiding party's eventual retreat down to the beach and their boats.

Apparently the Commando raid had the objective of capturing prisoners and ascertaining the strength of the German garrison. The raiding party found that the Jerbourg Barracks were unoccupied and that there was no sign of any German military presence on the peninsula. They started knocking on doors of houses trying to find someone who could give them information about the Germans and details of the occupation.

One of the British party knocked on the door of a modest wooden bungalow, Rockcliff, not far from the Barracks. Bill Crocker, a farmer, lived there. The bungalow, which has long since been demolished, was created from another of the first world war huts from the French seaplane base at the harbour.

Bill had a stammer, even when he was not nervous. However when he was nervous or under pressure he found it almost impossible even to stammer. Bill, in the darkness, thought that the man in battledress, with a blackened face and foliage sticking out of his tin helmet, was a German and attempted to remonstrate with him, stuttering at the top of his voice.

In desperation the British soldier, fearing that any Germans who might be in the vicinity would be awakened by the noise, mouthed:

"Shut up talking so loud and tell me where the bloody Germans are".

Bill apparently kept on stuttering at the top of his voice, so the British soldier, in order not to raise the alarm knocked him out. Mabs and I saw Bill after the raid, - he had two lovely black eyes. It also looked as if he had been struck forcibly under the left eye.

Shortly before 3 am the Commandos withdrew down the steps to Petit Port beach. On retracing their steps, the officer in command tripped and his revolver went off accidentally. That must have been the shot that I heard during the night. Trying to re-embark, one of their two boats hit the rocks and was holed and the other was not able to get close to the shore, due to the heavy swell. The Tommies abandoned their equipment and swam to the boat. The result was that four Commando's who could not swim were left behind and were eventually taken prisoner. What possessed the British military authorities to send Commandos on a raid, without them being able to swim, I still find difficult to fathom.

On the Monday morning, on my way to work, I saw the rockery stones in the road, where they had been placed to create the barricade. Later, as a result of complaints from subscribers, the cut telephone wires were discovered. Surprisingly the Germans did not realise until the Tuesday morning that there had been a Commando raid. On my way home on Tuesday lunch time, I came across Police Inspector Sculpher, Dr Maass, the German Commandant's Chief of Staff and Charlie Mitchell in Jerbourg Road. They were closely inspecting what appeared to be ammunition. I waited until Inspector Sculpher and Dr Maass had driven off in the police car and asked Charlie what it was all about.

Charlie Mitchell, who lived in a States House in St Martin, had been down on Petit Port beach earlier in the morning, where he found some of the equipment and ammunition left by the Commandos. As he was on his way home he had seen the police car approaching and waved it down. He said that he had been surprised to find Dr Maass in the car. He handed over to Dr Maass the twenty rounds of rifle ammunition, in four clips and a quantity of detonators which he had found on the beach.

During the afternoon Mabs and I, being a bit nosey, went for a walk around the top of Petit Port trying to see what was happening on the beach below. Looking down, we could see how the Commandos had misjudged things. The tide had gone out and un-covered some of their weapons and equipment, which had been left behind. There was a party of Germans down on the beach, one of whom looked up and saw us. Suddenly, shots rang out, we were being fired at by the Germans.

It was very frightening though in retrospect they were only shooting to frighten us away. We quickly retraced our steps along the cliff path which passed the top of the steps coming up from Petit Port. As we reached the steps, we met a party of German officers coming up from the beach. It was a very scary moment, but they said nothing. On our way back to Seaplane Bungalow I recalled the old adage - 'That there is nothing more exhilarating in life, than to be shot at - without result!'

The Germans recovered a quantity of military clothing and equipment, from the beach at Petit Port, the Jerbourg parking place and the field opposite Bill Crocker's bungalow.

After the British Commandos' visit the Germans conducted a full inquiry into all aspects of the raid. The boat which was holed and had been deliberately sunk by the withdrawing Commandos later surfaced and was found by the Germans. The British Commando, who had knocked out Bill Crocker was one of those left behind and captured. The Germans took him back to the old man's bungalow and made him apologize to Bill.

The Germans accused Fred Veale of helping to build the barricade with his rockery stones, which he of course denied. They said that at very least he must have heard them doing it, which of course he did, but thought it was the Germans and didn't venture out. They vigorously interrogated old man Veale, so much so that he was almost a nervous wreck for a long time afterwards.

It was after this raid that the Germans began to take a real interest in the Jerbourg Peninsula. It soon became evident to me that the raid had made the Germans very nervous and jumpy. More and more troops appeared in the district, trenches were dug and machine gun posts established, with patrols constantly moving around the area.

It is fair to say that I have always been inquisitive by nature. I have always wanted to know what was going on and be where the action was, to the extent that some people may at times have thought I was nosey. Over the years I spent many hours standing at my shop door in Smith Street, talking to passing friends and acquaintances. It was surprising what you learnt and often it was good for business.

During the occupation it was essential to meet people in the street, in order to know what was going on. The Evening Press and the Star were from the first day of the occupation, required to have their editions passed by the German Censor before they could be printed. We knew that all they were allowed to print was the very basic and often uninteresting local news, together with the German war communiques and articles such as the outpourings of 'Lord Haw-Haw'. The Front page of the two newspapers was solely German contributions which I rarely read. I always turned to the inside of the papers without looking at the front page, unless of course I wanted a laugh at the Germans' expense. If we wanted any local news we obtained it by word of mouth. Meeting people passing my shop, I found, was the best way of keeping informed of both the real news and the latest gossip.

While we had always driven on the left, the Germans were used to driving on the right - this caused confusion. Many of the Germans, from the start of the occupation, insisted on driving on the right. It was not until June 1941 that they issued a proclamation decreeing that we had to drive on their side of the road. In the meantime I enjoyed watching the difficulties that the Jerry traffic managed to get into as they negotiated their way around the plantation at the top of Smith Street.

Soon after the occupation began I was standing outside the shop watching the world go by, when a German soldier on a motorbike rode passed me on his way up the street. As he went around the plantation, a local coal lorry, which had been commandeered by the Germans and driven by one of their drivers, came around the plantation on the wrong side of the road. The German motorcyclist hit the lorry head on and went over the handlebars in a dramatic fashion and was killed outright. He was the first dead German I had seen and I was delighted - that's one less, I thought. A terrible attitude in retrospect, but at the time that's how we looked at life. They had bombed and occupied our island, killed many of our friends and we hated them for what they had done.

The dead German was removed, the lorry driven away, but the motorcycle remained, leaning against Doctor Bostock's wall. After all the Germans had left, I went and looked at the motorcycle which was an almost brand new British Norton, still in khaki, with it's number on the petrol tank. Obviously it had been captured from the British forces in France, probably at Dunkirk. It had six hundred miles on the clock and was in perfect condition except that the front forks were badly bent.

Back in the shop, I said to Artie Selous;

"There's a Norton up there with only six hundred miles on the clock, I think we should take care of it if we can. You know, if it's left there, anyone might get 'interested' in it?"

Artie agreed and after we had ensured that there were no Germans around, we picked up the front end of the Norton and wheeled it down the street and placed it against the wall opposite the shop, where the German Band used to play before the first war. We could keep an eye on it there and no one, particularly the Germans could accuse us of stealing it. Well not just yet. We left it there for a couple of days and no one came to collect it or inspect it, or even to inquire about the motorcycle, so Artie and I moved it across the road and into our passageway.

Each day we moved it a little further up the passageway and when we were reasonably sure that it had not been missed, we turned it into nuts and bolts and spares and carefully stored all the parts in boxes. I felt that we might well be able to get away with a dismantled British motorcycle, but if it had been a German machine it would have been an entirely different matter. We had 'captured' a Norton motorcycle and one German soldier had been accounted for, Artie and I felt that we were playing our part in the fight against Hitler's occupying force.

During the occupation Artie straightened and repaired the forks and when liberation came we were able to re-assemble 'our' British Norton.

The occupation of the island coincided with the peak of the tomato production by our horticultural industry. In 1940 the island produced a bumper crop, but we were cut off from our traditional export market, the British mainland, so hundreds of tons of tomatoes were going to waste. We were urged to eat all the tomatoes we could.

Soon we were eating tomatoes as never before. Ripe tomatoes were available free and farmer's were feeding them to cows, pigs and poultry. Recipes regularly appeared in the Press for the use of tomatoes such as bottling ripe tomatoes, tomato jam, tomato sauce, tomato chutney, green pickled tomatoes and tomato juice, to say nothing of tomato soup. Demonstrations on how to preserve tomatoes were being held at Boots and as supplies continued to increase free distribution of tomatoes was taking place from door to door, both in the Town and St Sampsons.

An 'Eat more tomatoes campaign' was launched, with slogans such as 'A tomato a day keeps famine at bay,' and 'A tomato an hour will add to your power'. There appeared even more recipes, for tomato pie, macaroni with tomatoes, tomato curry, stuffed tomato, tomato casino, tomato toast and tomato pudding. We 'feasted' on tomatoes as we had never done before.

A method of preserving tomatoes which we tried at that time was to cover a layer of green fruit with a deep layer of dry sawdust. Providing the tomatoes were not bruised and the sawdust was perfectly dry, the fruit retained their colour, substance and flavour for several months. Tomatoes stored in this way in July, were, by Christmas, almost as good as freshly picked fruit.

With the arrival of the Germans all my motorcycling activities came to an abrupt halt. My other great interest and sporting activity, swimming, was not interrupted to anything like the same extent, at least in the early days of the occupation. I still swam most days down at the Valette bathing pool, along with many of my friends who had remained in the island.

One afternoon four or five of us were swimming in the pool. We had a water polo ball which we were throwing back and forth across the pool to each other. Another swimmer intercepted the ball and joined in our game. Of course a German in a bathing costume looked very much the same as anybody else. We did not know this fellow, so we assumed that he was a German. We winked at each other and gradually, one by one, came out of the water. We lay on the pool side, sunbathing, 1940 was a beautiful summer and that day was no exception.

By and by this swimmer came over to me and said in broken English;

"Do you not wish to play ball with me?"

"No!" I replied.

"Because I am a German soldier?"

"Yes!"

He spoke reasonably good English and I reluctantly got into conversation. He tried to 'explain' why Germany annexed territory and had gone to war. "You see Germany must have living space."

"Yes" I replied, "your Mr Hitler is trying to breed a pure Arian race, you pay your couples to have babies whether they are married or not and then you scream for living space."

Willie Hesse, a Sergeant in the Wehrmacht, was in fact quite a decent German. He was put in charge of housing Germans troops in our properties. He worked closely with the States Housing Officer, Vernon Le Maitre. If the Germans wanted a house, then they would requisition it and Willie Hesse, in collaboration with Vernon, would make arrangements for the removal and the re-location of the owners or tenants and their furniture.

Willie Hesse and I were to continue our conversation many years later.

The Evening Press organised a number of Swimming Galas at the Valette bathing pool during the occupation. The first took place in August 1940. The original advertisement publicizing the event invited entries from both local and German swimmers. The Press received so much private criticism of their gesture to include our unwelcome visitors that they had to find a way of withdrawing the invitation. How they achieved it I do not know, but the invitation was withdrawn.

The Gala was attended by well over five hundred spectators and proved, for the Evening Press, to be a great success. I won the Men's Plunge, with a dive of 56ft. I came second in the costume race, I could not have done any worse as there were only two entrants! Gerald Sparkes and I, appearing as Billy and Company, provided the comic interlude, with the re-enactment of a dramatic episode in the career of Bluebeard. It provided good entertainment during the early days of the occupation.

Using the top diving board as our stage we gave our performance which concluded by putting a noose around the neck of Bluebeard, who was played by myself. After apparently tying the other end of the rope to the diving board rail, Bluebeard was pushed off the diving board to the consternation of the crowd. The audience was sure that I was going to 'Hang'. No doubt many of the crowd would have welcomed a good hanging, whilst others were aghast at the prospect!

The trick was that there were two ropes, one which was around Bluebeard's neck and the other attached to the rail. The crowd loved our sketch and so did the German Commandant Dr Albrecht Lanz and his Chief of Staff Dr E. Maass, who had regrettably been invited to attend by the Directors of the Guernsey Press. I personally was very unhappy about entertaining the Germans and I only took part very reluctantly as I did not wish to disappoint the large crowd of islanders. However, on reflection, I should have refused to participate, it was an error of judgement on my part.

There were some who were only too happy to welcome the Germans to Guernsey. One such was the Hungarian maid who worked for Mr W.N.Lovell at his home, Kinmount, in Sausmarez Road. He was staunchly pro-British and understandably furious when, shortly after the occupation started, a German officer arrived at his house to take his maid, Elizabeth Kakas, to a dance at St Georges Hall. As the evening wore on he sat at home, progressively becoming more incensed. Finally just after 11.pm, which was well passed curfew time, he telephone the Police Station and left a message for the Inspector:-

"My maid Elizabeth Kakas, was picked up by a German officer at 7.pm and taken to a dance. It is now five minutes past eleven and she has still not returned. I am going to dismiss her."

It was obvious almost from the moment that they landed in the island, that the Germans were trying to create good relations between the island administration, the local population and themselves. Guernsey was the only part of the British Empire that the Germans set foot upon and they were well aware that it was important to their international image that they refrained from the excesses practised in the rest of occupied Europe. The Germans sought to treat Ambrose Sherwill and the Controlling Committee with respect. Within a week of their occupation, their Commandant Dr Lanz, made himself available for interview with any islander who wished to consult him. From 11 am-1 pm, on weekdays at the Channel Islands Hotel, he listened to anyone who wished to talk to him.

In the first few months the Germans were extremely successful in establishing what has been called a 'Model occupation'. In fact they so ingratiated themselves with Ambrose Sherwill that he agreed to record a talk which was broadcast over the German Radio station at Bremen. The text of his broadcast was, on German instructions, published in the Evening Press.

He said:

> 'This is His Britannic Majesty's Procureur in Guernsey, Channel Islands, speaking to the people of the United Kingdom and in particular to those who left Guernsey and Alderney during the evacuation which proceeded the German occupation.
>
> I imagine that many of you must be greatly worried as to how we are getting on. Well let me tell you. Some will fear, I imagine, that I am making this record with a revolver pointed at my head and speaking from a typescript thrust into my hand by a German officer. The actual case is very different.
>
> The Lieutenant Governor and Bailiff, Mr Victor Carey, and every other island official has been and is being, treated with every consideration and with great courtesy by the German Military Authorities. The island Government is functioning. Churches are open for public worship. Banks, shops and places of entertainment are open as usual.
>
> Naturally, the sudden severance of communications with the United Kingdom created innumerable problems with which we

have wrestled and are still wrestling. Perhaps the best indication of the measure of our success will be shown by the latest figures of unemployment, which are as follows:-

Males unemployed, of whom hardly any are fit for manual labour 186. Females unemployed 191. Relief by way of public assistance is not above the normal figure.

The States have set up a Controlling Committee to speed up public business. My friends Sir Abraham Laine, A.M. Drake, R.O. Falla, R.H. Johns, John Leale, Stamford Raffles and Dr A.N. Symons are collaborating with me on this Committee and are working like trojans.

The conduct of the German troops is exemplary.

We have been in German occupation for 4 ½ weeks and I am proud of the way my fellow-islanders have behaved, and grateful for the correct and kindly attitude towards them of the German soldiers.

We have always been and we remain intensely loyal subjects of His Majesty, and this has been made clear to, and is respected by the German Commandant and his staff. On that staff is an officer speaking perfect English - a man of wide experience with whom I am in daily contact. To him I express my grateful thanks for his courtesy and patience.

And now let me end on a more personal note. To Elizabeth College, the Guernsey Ladies College, the Guernsey Intermediate School, the Guernsey Primary and Voluntary schools, to both teachers and scholars, all our love and good wishes.

To all men of military age who left here to join His Majesty's forces, God speed. To all wives and mothers and sweethearts, God bless you. To all Guernsey children in England, God keep you safe. God bless you all till we meet again.

Will the B.B.C. please re-transmit this message and will the daily papers please publish it.'

When I read the text of the speech I was astounded, how could our leader fall into the German trap so easily. For a long time Ambrose Sherwill's speech was the local talking point. Some people thought it was right that he should let our relations and friends in England know how we were making out under the Germans. Others thought that he had played into their hands. The more I thought about it the more I gave Mr Sherwill the benefit of the doubt. Perhaps he was in fact outwitting the Germans and there was a secret message in the text of his speech.

Later it was established that the original idea for a broadcast came from a representative of the Evening Press. He put the suggestion to the Controlling Committee's Information Officer Deputy Stamford Raffles, who passed it on to Ambrose Sherwill. The Germans obviously could not believe their good fortune in obtaining such a propaganda coup.

Now, over half a century later, I can only conclude that Ambrose Sherwill, at best, was well intentioned but naive. Whatever else, I now believe it to have been a serious error of judgement.

Later we learnt that Mrs May Sherwill also recorded a talk for the Germans to broadcast.

There is no doubt in my mind that the Germans were very fortunate in getting both Ambrose and Mrs Sherwill to make those recordings. I understood that they were transmitted over Radio Bremen a number of times and were proceeded by skilful propaganda about the conquering of the 'British Channel Islands'. They also bragged how well the Military authorities were getting on with the local population. It was significant that no one in Jersey volunteered to broadcast in a similar vein.

Chapter 11

A SICKENING PERIOD

The Germans having commandeered all the buses in the island for their own use, old fashioned horse drawn vehicles soon started to reappear on our roads. Landaus, Broughams and Governess cars, which had lain idle for years in barns and sheds, were quickly brought back into use. Horse drawn wagonettes with bench type seats soon reappeared in country parishes, in place of our buses.

While most of us walked or rode bicycles, the Germans drove around in commandeered cars and buses. I soon became concerned that my car, Dad's old car, would be requisitioned by the Germans. One of the decrees that the Germans issued required all owners of motor vehicles, except those used for military purposes, to put their cars into serviceable condition in readiness for inspection by the Military Authorities. Owners were required to ensure that the battery was charged, the tyres, including the spare, were in good condition and the tool kit, complete. The receipted account for the original purchase of the car and any bills for subsequent servicing had to be made available to the German authorities.

The Germans inspected the vehicles at St Peter Port Garage. If they decided that they wished to purchase the car, which they virtually always did, they arbitrarily set a purchase price and gave you a receipt. There were no means of appeal either against their decision to purchase or the price, however low and unreasonable it might be. The owner received a voucher, which he was required to present to the States Treasurer, who paid him in Reichmarks.

I was determined that the Germans were not going to commandeer my car, orders or not ! As I had not bothered to have the registration of ownership changed, the 1938 Morris Series E, was still in Dad's name, and the Germans could not ask him. They were not to know that my sister had not taken it with her when she, her husband and family, left the island shortly before the occupation.

The big question was where was I going to hide the car. Cecil Hardwick lived at Fairmount in the Bouvee Lane and adjacent to his house was a double garage. Or rather a shed with double doors, which opened directly on to the Lane and a lean-to extension, with a large internal window in between. Cecil kept his pride and joy, an immaculate Singer Eight, in the lean-to and had jacked it up, taken off its wheels and generally taken every precaution necessary to keep it in good condition. The shed, however, was empty and Cecil agreed that my car could be hidden there. I did not bother to take the same precautions as Cecil had done, as I still believed that our occupation and the war would soon be over and the car would be back on the road.

Sure enough the Germans came to see me at Seaplane Bungalow, to find out why the car had not been presented for inspection according to their orders. I explained :- "I don't know where the car is, it belonged to my Father, I never found it, perhaps my sister took it with her when she left the island". I told them that I was in Coventry when Daisy left Guernsey."

I managed to satisfy them that the car was not in my possession, although if they had found out that I still had the keys in my pocket when they questioned me, I would have been in real trouble ! I knew that the Germans were hunting around for cars and I soon realised the difficult position in which I had put myself. What would be my answer if the Germans found the car. I was worried that, yet again, I had been too clever by half, so I removed the number plates, the engine and chassis identification plates from the car and took them down to the shop. There was a blocked off fireplace behind the stairs and I hid them in there.

I told Ted Laker, who was in charge of the Civil Transport Depot in the Pollet, of my fears and asked his advice. A couple of days later he came into my office at the shop and presented me with a notice in German, which he said would get me out of my difficulty. It apparently stated that 'This car is reserved for German use'. Ted explained that I should stick the notice on the windscreen. Any German going around looking for cars and finding mine, would leave it alone. Ted told me that he had been issued with six of the notices by the Germans. I was grateful that he 'lost' one in my direction.

Whilst we in Guernsey were not subjected to air raids in the way civilians in England were, the R.A.F. did however keep a close watch on the activities of the Germans, particularly at the harbour and the airport.

R.A.F. reconnaissance planes regularly monitored movements at the airport. On August 9th, forty or fifty German aircraft were spotted on the ground. A single R.A.F. Blenheim, bombed and machinegunned the airport around lunchtime, destroying a troopcarrier. According to a B.B.C. broadcast, which I heard, three further attacks were made later in the afternoon and evening, but by then the German aircraft had departed. The B.B.C. claimed that considerable damage was done to a hanger, which was set on fire and a petrol dump hit.

The Germans did not allow any details of the R.A.F. raids to be published in either of our two newspapers. They did their best to ensure that we were left ignorant of the results of such action. We did learn, however, that the Fire Brigade had been called out by the Germans to help put out the fire caused by the raid. That had to mean that it was a fairly serious fire. Apparently, the R.A.F. dropped a considerable number of incendiary bombs. Regrettably, a number of them failed to explode, and others fell some way away from the airport.

However because the B.B.C. broadcast a report giving details of the raid, the German Commandant, Dr Lanz issued an official statement for publication, which played down the whole attack. We of course believed the British version.

The Germans only admitted that five of their men had been killed, one by British action and four when one of their aircraft crashed near the airport. I learnt that many more had been buried in the island and that other bodies had been flown to the France. I am sure that the number of Germans killed was nearer twenty five. Of course, I rejoiced at that.

After hearing the B.B.C. broadcast, many islanders, including Mabs and I, ventured in the direction of the airport, sight seeing. We wanted to see the damage caused to the airport by the R.A.F. Many church congregations were seriously depleted that Sunday evening!

Around that time a German plane overran the runway at the west end of the airport and careered across the road, before becoming to rest in a field. Surprisingly there weren't any guards, so when Mabs and I went up to have a look, I managed to get into the plane. I tried to remove the compass from the instrument panel, but was not able to without tools. However I did manage to acquire a piece of the fuselage. I certainly wasn't the only Guernseyman crawling about that plane after souvenirs.

Regrettably the Germans put our airport to good use from very early on in the occupation. Early each morning, the Luftwaffe brought their Messerschmitt fighters over from mainland France. They landed and refuelled and when the bombers arrived overhead later, the fighters would escort them as they flew on their deadly missions over southern England. Guernsey was being used as an assembly point.

At times there would be as many as three or four hundred German planes in the skies above Guernsey, far more planes than I had ever seen before or indeed since. The sky was often black with layer upon layer of German aircraft. Mabs and I sometimes cycled up to the airport to see what was going on. There was no airport fence in those days, so we could approach from almost any direction. I remember one day going around the back of the airport and seeing dozens of Messerschmitts fighters on the ground, all around the perimeter, with their crews lolling around in the sunshine. Then suddenly an R.A.F. Spitfire appeared overhead and the crews rushed to their planes.

Guernsey was at about the limit that Spitfires could operate. They came over here having followed the German bombers back from England, attacking them all the way. We saw many dog fights and on a couple of occasions, witnessed German bombers being shot down in flames. Every one we saw shot down was one less to raid England.

It was a sickening period, as we knew that the planes we saw in the air over Guernsey were on their way to rain terror and destruction on our kith and kin in English towns and cities. However we rejoiced at the losses the Luftwaffe suffered during the Battle of Britain. Listening to the tally of the German losses for the day, on the B.B.C. news each night, certainly lifted our spirits.

Rumours were always rife during the occupation. Whenever there was a 'happening' in the island the news spread like wildfire. The only trouble was that it quickly became embellished and distorted.

Around mid September 1940, a party of islanders 'borrowed' a fishing boat from Bordeaux and escaped to England. A week or so later, we received accurate confirmation of what happened when the R.A.F. dropped leaflets over the island during the early hours. Young Herbert Winterflood, who worked for me part time, found one of these leaflets on his way to work, it was soaking wet, so he brought it into the shop to dry it out. The leaflet read.

'ESCAPE FROM GUERNSEY - EIGHT REACH BRITAIN

London September 1940.

A party of eight men have successfully escaped from Guernsey to England in a 20ft boat. The London Press is headlining their adventures.

They left Guernsey under cover of darkness and rowed half a mile before using the motor. When they were about two miles out four flares were dropped by three German planes flying over them. One fell only twenty yards from the boat but they were not seen.

Just after passing the Casquets their engine broke down, but the repairs were finished in four hours and they eventually sighted Start Point, the landmark for which they were making.

The party consisted of Mr Frederick Hockey, 47, a signalman employed by the harbour administration at St Peter Port, three of his sons, Frederick, 25, George, 21 and Harold,16, who were engaged in tomato growing and Messrs William Mahy, Percy du Port, William Dorey, and Herbert Bichard, independent growers.'

We were all delighted to read the news, it gave us a lift and was one in the eye for Jerry. Inevitably the Germans reacted swiftly and vigorously. Ambrose Sherwill was 'required' to insert a 'notice' in the Press which read:-

> The attention of the public is drawn to the fact that leaflets which were dropped on the island by a British plane on the night of the 23rd-24th September 1940, come within the definition of 'enemy propaganda material' contained in the German Proclamation dated 29th July 1940.
>
> It is therefore an offence to hand on such leaflets or to communicate their contents to others and it is the duty of persons in possession of such leaflets to deliver them to the Feldkommandantur, Grange Lodge Hotel.
>
> 25th September 1940 A.J. Sherwill.

Herbert never handed in his copy of the leaflet, in fact he showed it to as many people as possible, subject to them being Guernseymen he knew he could trust.

Mr Sherwill issued a further press notice condemning those who:-

> 'may be considering running away, for that is what it is...,
> an action unworthy of a Guernseyman.'

We realised that he was required by the Germans to make such statements, no doubt against his better judgement. But many of us felt that the choice of words was more than unfortunate, in fact we very much resented his statement.

As a direct result of the escape, the Germans decreed that all boats had to be transferred from wherever they were, both in the water or on land, to St Peter Port Harbour by October 1st. This was a mammoth task for some fishermen, who could only bring them to St Peter Port by road. In the days leading up to the deadline I saw many boats being manhandled along the roads leading to St Peter Port harbour.

This order, of course, very considerably disrupted the already restricted fishing that the Germans allowed. Fishermen living on the West coast had to cycle or walk into town before they could set sail and their time at sea was considerably reduced as they had to return home at night before the curfew. As a result of this 'Decree', our supplies of fish were substantially reduced.

In the early hours of September 4th 1940, two British Officers, both Guernseymen, landed at Petit Port, the same bay as the earlier Commando raid. For Lt Hubert Nicolle it was his second clandestine visit since the occupation. He landed from a submarine a week after the Germans arrived. On that occasion he stayed for three days, during which time he obtained information regarding the Germans, their strength, their whereabouts and the restrictions that they had imposed on the local population.

Now he was returning with Lt James Symes, their mission was to obtain information, particularly in regard to how the Civil government under Ambrose Sherwill was getting on with the Germans. This time they came in civilian clothes and knew that, under international law, if they were caught they would be treated as spies. They contacted relatives and friends and obtained all the information they required to make their mission a success. In the middle of the following night they retraced their steps to Petit Port, expecting to be picked up by the Royal Navy. There was no sign of a boat, they waited at the pick up point for the next two nights but no rescue boat appeared. They realised that they were stranded. We of course knew nothing of their activities. The only islanders to know were their relatives and one or two friends.

Both men fully appreciated just how dangerous a situation they were in, only having civilian clothes, and the perilous position in which they had placed their friends and relations. Inevitably, as time went on, more and more people knew that two British Officers were on the island. Ambrose Sherwill was most certainly aware of their presence and realised that in time, they would have to surrender.

The Germans were suspicious that there were still some members of the British Armed forces who had not given themselves up when the island was occupied. There may have been as many as a dozen, not including Nicolle and Symes.

It was suggested to Ambrose Sherwill, by the Germans that there might still be some military personnel hiding in the island illegally, and that it would be a good idea if the matter could be cleared up. The Germans told him that they intended to publish a notice in the newspapers suggesting an amnesty and a deadline for surrender. Ambrose saw this as an opportunity for Symes and Nicolle to give themselves up. He told the Germans that if that is what they wanted to do, it might be a good idea if he was to see the notice before it was published, because in all due respect their english was not all that good, and if there were any minor corrections needed, he could make them.

The result was that on the 12th October 1940, there appeared in the Evening Press an exchange of letters between Mr Sherwill, the President of the Controlling Committee and Major Bandelow, the new German Commandant. By this time I was aware that there were two British Officers in the island and I realised that the significant part of the letter from the German Commandant was:-

> '....Furthermore, there exists the possibility of British soldiers still being on the island in hiding with the assistance of the inhabitants. These may be soldiers who stayed behind at the time of the evacuation or have since entered the island. ...... I intend to arrange with you a certain date by which all members of the British Armed Forces still in hiding here will have to report. Those reporting up to that date will be treated as prisoners of war, also no measures will be taken against their relatives who have assisted in hiding them.'

Mr Sherwill's published reply, included the statement:-

> '.... I have noted that you intend to arrange with me a time limit within which any personnel of the British Armed Forces in hiding in this island (if such there be) must surrender and that, if this condition is complied with, such personnel will be treated as prisoners of war and no measures will be taken against any of their relatives who may have given them assistance. This, Herr Commandant is a generous offer on your part. I appreciate, that thereafter you will be unable to afford such immunity.'

Clearly Ambrose Sherwill manipulated the exchange of letters to cover Symes and Nicolle. They could now surrender without fear of being treated as spies, or any of their relatives or friends being implicated.

In due course a statement signed by the Feldkommandantur appeared in the Press giving a deadline for surrender, of 6 pm on the 21st October and stating that no action would be taken against anyone who had assisted any British personnel.

At 4.15 pm on the 21st October, Mr Emile W. Nicolle and Louis Symes went to the Police Station and reported that their sons were at their homes. They said that in view of what had appeared in the newspaper, they thought it was their duty to report their sons' presence in the island. Deputy Police Inspector A.J.Langmead, accompanied by Police Sergeant C. Le Lievre, went first to Rouge Huis Avenue and collected Lt Hubert Nicolle, and then to Clarke's Estate, Grand Bouet and collected Lt James Symes. Both men, wearing uniforms that Nicolle's uncle had obtained from stocks left behind in Alderney by the British Military Machine Gun School, were taken to the Police Station. At 5.30 pm, half an hour before the deadline the police officially informed Ambrose Sherwill of their surrender.

The Germans did not honour their undertaking, which had been so well publicised. Hubert Nicolle and James Symes were taken to Fort George and interrogated for long periods before being brought before a court martial. They were found guilty of being spies.

Their relatives including Nicolle's parents, his aunt and uncle, his fiancee, Symes parents, girl friend and some of her relatives were all arrested. Ambrose Sherwill, His Majesty's Procureur and President of the Controlling Committee and the States Supervisor, H.E.Marquand were arrested and relieved of their Offices. Mr Marquand, like Mr Sherwill had known of the presence in the island of the two British officers. All those arrested were shipped to France where they were imprisoned in the Cherche Midi prison, in Paris.

Chapter 12

PROUD PARENTS

In the matter of a year my life and my world had changed dramatically. Gone were the days when I could turn to Dad for support and advice. Now I was the head of our little family. Mabs and I were happily married and we were about to have an addition to the family. Our unwanted and unwelcome visitors issued decrees and orders which inevitability controlled, curtailed and restricted us as individuals. Permits began to regulate all aspects of our daily lives. They had put a stop to my motorcycling activities, no longer could I travel to the mainland and enjoy the freedom that I had so much taken for granted. The curfew curtailed my social life, we had to be indoors by 10 pm, later reduced to 9 pm.

Mabs and I settled down to family life and we quickly became very domesticated. It was all a new way of life for me. We were happy despite the occupation. Perhaps we did not realise just how happy we were, we told ourselves we were miserable because the Germans were here, but looking back now I think we were really very happy and contented. Mabs and I did a lot of things together, just like any newly weds, we went for walks, gathered wood together and shared our lives.

We had both been looking forward to the birth of our baby. Mabs did not have an easy pregnancy, she suffered from morning sickness for long periods. There were considerable difficulties in obtaining an ambulance at night, as the Germans did not like them travelling around during the curfew, so we booked a bed for Mabs at the Castel Emergency Hospital. The baby was due in early December, but our daughter was born prematurely on the 11th November 1940. We named her Margaret Vera and were very proud parents, as we still are today.

Margaret was very jaundiced and needed a blood transfusion. Mabs gave blood, which was then given to Margaret. While most new mothers were spending only a few days in hospital, Mabs was there for three weeks. I do not believe that at the time I realised just how ill Margaret and Mabs were.

I regularly visited Mabs and the baby in hospital. I rode there on my bicycle in the failing early evening light and after spending almost an hour with them I returned home in the dark. I had a dynamo lighting set on my bicycle, the type that the light only comes on when you are moving. One evening I came out of the Hospital and into the pitch darkness of the night. The blackout was total and I could not see a thing. As it normally takes about ten minutes for my eyes to acclimatise to the dark, I groped around, finally found my bicycle, mounted and set off for home.

Alongside the Castel Emergency Hospital, there was a little lane leading to the entrance and the main road. I rode down this lane towards the road. Unknown to me, across the road from the hospital, was a tennis court enclosed by wire netting. I must have ridden straight across the road, through a gap in the surrounding netting and on to the tennis court. The first I knew of my difficulty was when I saw the wire netting in the beam of my headlight. Of course as soon as I stopped, the light went out.

Holding on to the handlebars of my cycle in one hand and groping my way along the netting with my other hand, I spent a considerable time trying to find my way back to the road. I remember thinking, as I was fumbling around the wire netting, that this was some bloody German trap. I was puzzled and could not understand where I was, I certainly did not realise that I was on a tennis court. After spending some time picking up the back wheel of my bike and spinning it to get some light, I finally found the gap through which I must have entered the tennis court and got back on to the road.

I was in the 'cage' for some time before I escaped, it really was a very strange experience. The next day when I went to visit Mabs and baby Margaret at the Hospital, I went early so that I could see just how and where I had been trapped. Only then did I realise that I had accidentally ridden on to a tennis court. When I told the nurses at the hospital of my adventure no one believed me, they all suggested that I had been over indulgent in 'wetting the Baby's head'

Our baby daughter was very precious. Mabs was a marvellous mother and we were a very happy family. I remember pushing Margaret in her pram to St Martin's Parish Church, where she was christened by the Rev R.Coulthard. Dora Johns was Margaret's Godmother.

On the 14th of November a Notice appeared in the Evening Press, requisitioning all civilian wireless sets, as a punishment for 'the favouring of espionage'. This was another twist in the Nicolle, Symes saga. We were required to stick labels on the sets with our name and address, in order that they could be returned to us at some future date. I had two sets and decided that they could have Dad's old Alba Radio, but I kept the other, a Philco Pilot. I was not going to be deprived of the B.B.C. news, despite the advertised penalty of six months in jail and a fine of 30,000 Reichmarks, which at the time was the equivalent of over £3,000.

The Germans soon took over the Barracks at Jerbourg, above Telegraph Bay and one or two of the empty homes on the Jerbourg peninsular, including my Sister's bungalow Sen-Sook, next door to Seaplane Bungalow. I tried to move out all her furniture, but only succeeded in rescuing part of it. 'Old Joe', the grandfather clock was one of the pieces which I failed to save. It was never seen again, no doubt it was sent 'Home' by one of our German visitors. A few years after the occupation ended, I heard that someone had seen a large number of grandfather clocks packed up for shipment to Germany, perhaps 'Old Joe' was part of that consignment.

Before the island had been demilitarized, Jerbourg Barracks had been occupied by the British. They always stationed a sentry outside the Barracks, whom we had to pass to get to the private lane leading to Seaplane Bungalow. Whenever we approached the sentry post, the Tommies used to shout.

"Halt, who goes there ?"

We always had to explain that we lived at Jerbourg Point and after suitably identifying ourselves were allowed through. When the Germans occupied the Barracks they also had an armed sentry, who merely shouted out; "Guten Nacht" as we went by. There was a considerable difference between the German attitude, which was helpful and polite, and the British attitude which was surprisingly bureaucratic. The British always wanted to see our identification, but the Germans accepted that you wanted to go home. This was another example of the Germans attempt to create a good impression and a model occupation.

However, on one occasion, the German guard wouldn't allow me to pass. It was the middle of the day and, try as I might to reason with this sentry, he would not let me past. After a time I gave up trying to argue and talk my way past the German and went down to the States Office and saw Louis Guillemette, the Secretary to the States Controlling Committee. I explained my problem and asked him if he could help. He took me to see Dr Maass, the German Commandant's Chief of Staff, who got in touch with the German guard Commander. After that we were issued with passes and there was no further problem.

Cycling towards home, just before Christmas 1940, I met the German guard outside the Barracks. We must both have been in a reasonable convivial mood, because he offered me a mince pie, which I accepted. Normally I was not that 'friendly' towards the Germans that I would accept a gift from them.

One day when I was at the shop and Mabs was at home by herself a troop of German soldiers marched along our private lane and halted outside Seaplane Bungalow. They fell out and two of them went into our garage and helped themselves to a pick and shovel, and started digging in our front garden. Mabs went and asked them what they thought they were doing. They just ignored her and went on digging, what turned out to be a gun pit in our lawn. Later the Germans planted land mines along the cliffs in front of our home, right up to the wire fence. Across the lane opposite our garden they erected a sign;-

'Danger to Life
MINES!
Lebensgefahr !'

Also at the entrance to our private lane, they placed their standard warning, 'Achtung Minen'.

One of the Germans who came to dig a gun pit in the lawn at Seaplane Bungalow.

On Christmas Eve 1940 the Germans issued a Proclamation announcing that all persons concerned with the Nicolle - Symes affair would be 'exempt' from punishment. The two British officers, Hubert Nicolle and James Symes were sent to a prisoner of war camp and the other islanders who had been arrested and imprisoned in France, were allowed to return to Guernsey. Mr Sherwill, the Proclamation added:

German sign opposite Seaplane Bungalow.

'Will be released from his Office, as further co-operation with the German authorities is no longer possible.'

Our wireless sets, all thirteen thousand of them were returned to us by the next day, Christmas Day. The States organised the distribution of the sets back to the owners, a superhuman task, with great efficiency. It was an excellent Christmas 'Present' to those who had surrendered their only sets. I was happy to have my Alba Radio back, which was delivered to Seaplane Bungalow on Christmas morning, but I had not missed a single B.B.C. Home Service evening news broadcast.

During the first winter we had to accustom ourselves to the German curfew and their alignment with continental time. By the middle of December it was dark until almost 9.30 in the morning, the sun did not rise until after 10 am and lightning up time in the evening was before 6.30 pm. This caused considerable problems for cyclists, because there were no replacement batteries for cycle lamps and street lights were no longer in use.

At the start of the occupation we had large stocks of torch batteries, but there was such a run on them that they were completely exhausted by the middle of October. Cyclists with dynamo lightning had no problems, but there were comparatively few of these sets in use.

In the shop we had a constant stream of cyclists wanting batteries or dynamo sets which we could not supply. Cycles were the only form of personnel transport available and lights were essential to get to work in the mornings. In the evening it was often dark by the time people were on their way home. Many cyclists who had no lights ignored the legal requirement and travelled to and fro without them. Islanders were incensed when the Evening Press advocated in one their leading articles that cycling without lights in the dark must be stopped and that they would welcome a few exemplary convictions in the Police Court.

That statement and others of a similar tone really enraged cyclists. They were constantly bending my ear on the subject, so I decided to write a letter to the Evening Press expressing their and my point of view. It was published on Christmas Eve 1940, under the heading:-

'Cyclists' Lightning Difficulties'

'Sir, With reference to your many leaders on the subject of cyclists and lights, the latest of which appeared in your paper on the 23rd December, may I put forward the following:-

Are you aware that the unfortunate cyclist through no fault of his own is completely unable to provide lights for his cycle. Guernsey is out of lamp batteries, Guernsey has plenty of carbide but NO carbide lamps in which to burn it; dynamo lighting sets are sold out in the shops and those that have them are very few. The States Purchasing Committee are unable to assist in these matters. What then do you suggest the poor cyclist should do?

He has to be at work before lighting up time, he cannot walk there as he cannot start until seven am, he does not finish until six and he has to be home before nine, collecting his bread, his groceries, his washing from the depots on the way. He cannot do it by walking. He MUST cycle; yet he cannot light his cycle as you are insisting he should do. The Guernsey cyclist is keeping Guernsey going. His lot is hard, help him, don't hinder him.

At a time when all Europe is taking risks, I suggest Guernsey must take them also in this small matter of road danger.

W. Green,
Green's, Smith Street'.

I did not have long to wait for the broadside reply by the Editor of the Evening Press. On the 27th December a leading article on the subject appeared.

'Those Cyclists'.

'Our recent leading article on cyclists' responsibilities called forth a spirited reply from that well-known champion of cycling and its adherents, Mr W. Green, the receipt of which we acknowledge with pleasure.

With the contents of Mr Green's letter, however, we must entirely disagree in so far as they are advanced as an excuse for breaking the law. We admit the shortage of carbide, oil and other illuminants at present, but we cannot concede that their absence should entitle cyclist to use the roads without any lighting at all on their machines. If the matter resolves itself down to a case of absolute destitution as regards cycle illuminants, then the cyclist must do as people do in other things and go without.

We admit this is hard in cases where a man must be at work early in the morning or remain out until after dark, but it is better for him and for everyone else on the island that he should walk, than that he should risk riding on the roads without a light. Mr Green's argument that many people now have to do their shopping and similar errands on their cycles cannot, we submit, be applicable, as such journeys can only be undertaken during the hours when the shops are open, namely between 10 am - 4 pm when it is broad daylight.

> But as criticism to be of value at all should be constructive, we would suggest that in view of the shortage of cycle luminants, a properly constituted deputation of those concerned in the trade and practice of cycling, should approach the authorities through the recognized channels and after explaining the position, appeal for help in procuring supplies'.
>
> 'If however it should prove impossible to supply these, with what is necessary, then we can only harden our hearts and say that the alternative must be faced - the cyclist without a light must walk until it is light enough for him to see where he is going and, what is even more important, until other people can see where he is coming from'.

I took the view that while the Germans were imposing restrictions which were having a major impact on our daily lives, it was unnecessary for the Editor of the Evening Press to make things worse by calling for Police prosecutions. It was very noticeable that in the weeks and months which followed the publication of my letter a large number of prosecutions for riding without lights were reported in the columns of the Evening Press. It seemed to me that the Editor was taking every opportunity to ram home his view. Dozens of cyclists were being fined five shillings for each offence, when they had no means of equipping their bikes with lights.

It was all the more ridiculous because we were only allowed to show the smallest of lights. Cyclists brought their lamps into the shop to have them converted to comply with the German regulations. We smoked the whole inside area of the glass and then rubbed out a small circle of not more than half an inch in diameter in the middle. It was virtually impossible to see your way with such an apology for a light, its only possible purpose was for you to be seen by other road users.

During the occupation bicycles became very precious possessions, they represented the sole means of transport for the average Guernseyman. Islanders relied upon them as never before and if their bicycles were stolen it was a major disaster. It was virtually impossible to obtain a replacement. If a bicycle had a good tyre on it, there was always a danger that it would be missing when the owner returned after work or shopping. There were no locks and chains available. Cyclists were not prepared to take the risk of loosing their bicycles, so when they came into town we stored their bikes for them in the shop. They paid 2d. or later 5 Pfennigs in German money so they could leave their bicycles with us, in safety.

The storage of cycles became quite a profitable sideline, on Saturday's there were often up to one hundred and fifty stacked in our shop. In fact we tried not to stack them, because if you did the owner who came in for his bike wanted 'that one over there' and we would have to shift all the others, which usually was quite a major task. The first cycle in was often the first one collected by its owner, and I can only too well remember having to lift them over all the other bikes which had come in later. However it provided me with a nice little income, although we had to work hard for our money.

Mabs came and gave a hand on Saturdays, which was still market day. People continued to came to town although there was virtually nothing to buy in the shops.

The Germans had bicycles with detachable handlebars, they would park their bikes and go off carrying their handlebars. Cycles without handlebars, parked around the town became a common sight.

Throughout my life I have been interested in the Courts and many of the trials have caught my imagination. Working close to the Royal Court, I found it easy to 'pop in' from time to time, often for something to pass the time. Over the years I got to know the public gallery well! Early in 1941 business was slack and it was cold outside, so I went in for a 'warm and a listen'.

The case being heard was that of a twelve year old boy, accused of stealing 4/- from a gas meter and damaging the meter at his home in Victoria Road, close to where Artie Selous lived. He was found guilty and his mother, who was also in court, was ordered to re-pay the 4/- and 7/6 damages to the Gas Company by the weekend, at the latest. The boy promised the Court to behave himself in future. His Majesty's Comptroller, Mr G.J.P. Ridgeway suggested the boy be conducted over the prison where he could be shown the birch, so that he would see for himself what to expect if he again came within the arm of the law.

The Court agreed and the boy was handed over to His Majesty's Sheriff, Mr H.A. Blampied, who was instructed to conduct him around the prison taking care to show him amongst other things the birch.

Looking back I find that case and how it was handled by the Court typifies the change that has taken place over the last fifty years in the attitude of the community to wrongdoers. I regret the influence that the 'dogooders' have had, in putting the emphasis on finding excuses for those who commit crimes. The Courts of yesteryear sought to make an example of the criminal in order to deter others from crime. The change in my lifetime has been so great that we have now almost reached the position of 'encouraging' criminals.

I regret the passing of the birch. Perhaps the approach that the Court took in those days, in instructing that the twelve year old boy be shown what was in store for him if he continued to misbehave was going a bit far, but it was a very adroit way of deterring future offenders.

At the beginning of 1941 we learnt of the death of one of the island's characters, Ben Harry. Ben was known as the 'Hermit of L'Ancresse'. Over the years I had seen him many times. He looked a typical hermit, tall and gaunt, white haired, with a long flowing beard and stooping shoulders. On the only occasion that I ever spoke to him, I was struck by his quavering voice. It was very distinctive and in a way, attractive.

Ben, aged 78 when he died, was at that time, Guernsey's only hermit. He had lived in a Martello Tower, number 6, at L'Ancresse for over thirty years. The tower had two foot thick walls and a doorway that was so low that you had to stoop to avoid hitting your head on the lintel. There were two rooms in the tower, one above the other. I remember reading in the Evening Press that he paid 1/2d a week rent for his unusual home. Although he lived less than a stone's throw from L'Ancresse Bay, he hardly ever went on the beach and had no interest in the sea. He never married, could not read or write, but thoroughly enjoyed his chosen way of life.

During the first year the Germans were in the island, they built up their defences around our coasts. The Jerbourg peninsula became one of their major strong points. It provided a commanding position to control the waters around the south east of the island. Also they considered it necessary to ensure that it was sufficiently well protected against any repetition of the British Commando raid in the early days of the occupation

Progressively the Germans were taking over more and more of the houses in the area. We realised that it was inevitable that we were going to be turned out of Seaplane Bungalow, so it came as no surprise when, in the early part of March 1941, we were given forty eight hours notice to move out. We were the last residents on Jerbourg Point to be evicted. In some ways it was a relief to be required to move as all our neighbours were now Germans. Mabs was particularly happy, as while I was at work, she and Margaret were isolated in Seaplane Bungalow, surrounded by German soldiers.

The Germans notified the States Housing Officer that they wanted both

Seaplane Bungalow and the Annexe. Vernon Le Maitre, the Housing Officer, duly gave us notice and helped us to find alternative accommodation. We were given the choice of a number of houses in the Jerbourg Road. I went and looked at them all and decided that we would move to La Croix, near Bouvee Lane. I chose La Croix mainly because it had a bay type window in the roof from which there was a panoramic view of the islands, the Little Russel, St Peter Port Harbour and much of the Jerbourg peninsular. I was able to climb out of the window on to the roof from where I obtained a marvellous view, north, south, east and west. Mabs and I spent many hours during the occupation looking out of that attic window watching the activities of both the Germans and the Allies.

La Croix was the home of Charles Hodder, who was later to become a Jurat. He was out of the island, serving with the Army Pay Corps. Before we moved in, all the Hodder family furniture with the exception of the lounge carpet and the kitchen stove, was removed by his mother.

The Housing Authority sent transport, in the form of a coal lorry and a horse and cart from Lovell's, to move our furniture and possessions from Seaplane Bungalow to our new home. The move was less than three quarters of a mile down the road. Because Seaplane Annex had been used as a Boarding House there was a lot of surplus furniture, such as beds and bedding. What was not needed at our new

Moving out of Seaplane Bungalow, March 1941. Note horse and cart, and coal lorry.

home I took down to Smith Street and stored in the top flat which was empty during the occupation.

On the day we moved I remember spending a great deal of time climbing up and down the stairs at Smith Street, storing the surplus furniture in the flat. Mabs was left to sort out our new home at La Croix. One of the removal men from Lovell's must have felt sorry for Mabs, because he came back in the evening and gave a hand putting up Margaret's cot, our bed and generally helping get the house into some order.

Mabs and I were lucky that we were only moved once during the occupation by the Germans and spent the rest of the war in Charles Hodder's house. There were occasions when a family who had been turned out and had settled into a new home, were then required to 'up sticks' again because that house was required by the Germans. Some people were moved three or four times.

After we moved out of Seaplane Bungalow, the Germans sealed off the peninsula and Mabs and I did not go down there again until after the liberation. Jerbourg Point was a no-go area as far as islanders were concerned. The Germans set up a barricade and entry gate to the peninsula at Monument Tavern, which became their Guard House, and no one was allowed past other than a few civilians who worked for the Germans. The Mitchell family lived in the family quarters at Jerbourg Barracks, until they were turned out by the Germans. They moved, with their two daughters, further down the Jerbourg road, to Jerbourg House. The two girls were employed by the Germans as domestics and we used to see them making their way up to the barrier every morning. Len, Bill Crocker's son was also allowed beyond the barrier as he carried on farming some of his father's land on the point. Otherwise it was a totally restricted area.

One day when Cecil Hardwick came home from work, he found two or three Germans, accompanied by Stan Noel, the St Peter Port Garage owner, trying to force open the doors to his garage with a large tyre lever. Cecil was absolutely livid and shouted at the Germans :-

"What the hell do you think you are doing ?"

"Mister - your barrack ?"

"Yes my barrack." replied Cecil.

"You will fetch the keys and open the doors."

They had come to inspect Cecil's prized Singer Eight. Stan's presence was required by the Germans to help with the valuation of any car they acquired. They saw my Morris car, looked at the notice on the windscreen and merely said that it should be jacked up and the wheels removed, but otherwise ignored it. They looked carefully at Cecil's car, inspected the mileometer, which he had adjusted to read forty thousand more miles than the car had actually done. Cecil hoped that if the car had covered a large mileage the Germans might lose interest. One of the Jerries, picked up a pot of paint and painted a number on the car. Cecil turned to Stan Noel,

"What have they done that for ?"

"They have just bought your car."

"Don't I have a say in the matter Stan ?"

"No, they have bought your car and you have to accept what they offer."

Stan Noel valued it at seventy five pounds, no doubt a low valuation due to the large mileage !

Cecil was infuriated that his car was to be taken by the Germans while mine had apparently been ignored. Later I explained to Cecil that Ted Laker had obtained the notice for me at great personnel risk.

"Why the blazes didn't you get another one for me." exclaimed Cecil.

Cecil was so incensed by the Germans action of commandeering his car that, before they towed it away, he stripped the seat covers out of the car and kept the spare tyre. Later during the occupation with the help of his brother, who was a trained shoemaker, he used the leather and the rubber to make shoes for his children.

Later, still fearing that the Germans might take another look in the shed, I disconnected the battery, jacked the car up on bricks, removed the tyres and greased all the parts I thought necessary. Then I placed bales of hay, which I obtained from Bert Crocker at Bouvee Farm, in such a way that the shed appeared to be a hay store.

That was one car the Germans did not commandeer and it was still in Cecil's garage at the end of the occupation.

Chapter 13

KENNY'S DISCOVERY

The Guernsey Aero Club in the early thirties purchased an Avro Avian MK IV two seater bi-plane, type 594B. It was regularly used by members of the Club and hired out to other flyers. At their L'Eree Aerodrome, the Club constructed a hanger in which the Avro Avian was usually kept.

On a November day in 1935, a member of the Club flew the plane on a trip to England and when he returned late in the evening, parked it out in the open. That night there was a great gale, which tore the hanger to ribbons and a gust of wind picked up the Club's Avro and hurled it onto its back. The plane, with its back broken, was so badly damaged that it was not considered worth repairing. Cecil Noel who was one of the Directors of the Flying Club, as a result of Harold Le Parmentier's cajoling, had carefully collected all the parts of the Avro Avian and dumped them in a heap outside his house, La Retraite, Les Adams.

The Avro Avian at L'Eree in 1935.

A couple of years later Cecil wanted a cheap second hand car. He went to 'Parmy' at the Motor House Garage, who provided him with one in exchange for all the parts of the Avro Avian. The plane was still just a heap of pieces outside Cecil's House. The deal that 'Parmy' made with Cecil Noel included all the drawings, the plans and the right to use the registration letters, G-AACF.

All the parts and pieces of the plane were taken up to the loft at the top of the Motor House Building on the corner of St Julien's Avenue and Ann's Place. 'Parmy' set about rebuilding and reconditioning the Avro Avian and spent practically every evening and weekend working on it. The fuselage was totally rebuilt with the help of Sam Cook who was a master carpenter. Working closely from the plans and diagrams, they recreated the whole of the planes' wooden frame. The engine was also fully reconditioned and tested.

After more than two years work, the plane was fully restored and ready to fly. However 'Parmy' never managed to fly his plane before he left the island just prior to the arrival of the Germans. The loft in which the assembled plane was stored was locked up and the keys entrusted to his petrol pump attendant, William Gilson. 'Parmy's' instructions to William were to keep the plane clean and well oiled.

After the Germans arrived in the island they requisitioned the Motor House Garage for the repair of their military vehicles. Kenny Bell, who previously worked for Bougourd Brothers at Les Banques, was put in charge of the garage by the Germans. Kenny for a long time was unaware there was a plane in the loft. The door was locked and he didn't bother to investigate as he did not need the space. One day William Gilson broke the news of the planes existence to Kenny and even then he took the view that the plane was not his responsibility.

The Germans issued an order that all inflammable material stored in the upper floors of property in the town was to be removed. Kenny Bell who by now knew of the plane's existence, was concerned. He knew that if he reported its presence to a States Official, they could become implicated. After thinking it over for some days he decided that he would personally declare it to the Germans. So early in March 1941, he went up to the German Police Headquarters at Grange Lodge and reported the plane's existence.

The Germans immediately arrested Kenny. He was taken back to the Motor House Garage, where the plane was inspected by the officers of the Luftwaffe, and photographed from every possible angle. Kenny was questioned by the Feldkommandant, Rittmeister Fuerst Prince Von Oettingen, who was known to locals as 'the Prince'. The Germans noticed that the engine had been freshly oiled and said that proved that Kenny had repaired the plane and was planning to escape. The fact was that in keeping the engine oiled, William Gilson had only been carrying out 'Parmy' instructions.

Kenny was made to hand over the keys of the garage and two fully armed soldiers were placed on guard at each entrance. Kenny was taken to Fort George and imprisoned on the second floor of the original Royal Engineers Office. The windows were barred and the room was permanently blacked out. The only furniture was a bed, a chair and a chest of drawers. He was held there in solitary confinement for nine days, during which time he did not see daylight or have any physical exercise. Then he was transferred to the old military detention room attached to the guard room just inside the main entrance to Fort George.

When I saw the two armed Germans guards on the doors of the Motor House Garage I enquired the reason and learnt for the first time of the plane's existence. Kenny Bell had only been put in charge of the garage by the Germans some weeks after 'Parmy' had left the island, therefore I knew that he could not have been involved in the repair of the plane. The Germans, however, were not convinced. They felt that if a Avro Avian plane could been hidden from them for so long, it was almost certain that other weapons were still un-detected and in the hands of islanders !

On the 5th March there appeared in the Evening Press a proclamation from the German Commandant.

> 'There is occasion to again call attention of the population to the fact that the retention of weapons, including hunting guns, or of implements of war of every description is punishable according to martial law.
>
> The population is herewith requested to search every nook and corner of their premises for weapons and implements of war. They are to be delivered to the Controlling Committee at once.'

The proclamation was accompanied by a notice from the Bailiff, saying that 'Aeroplanes and parts of aeroplanes were included in the term 'implements of war'. As far as I know no further aeroplanes were handed in to the Germans !

The Motor House Garage was guarded for almost a month, first by armed German soldiers and later, after the Germans had removed the plane's propeller so that it was immobilised, by our island Police.

Kenny Bell, a long time friend of mine, was held at Fort George all this time. I was so concerned at his plight that I went to see Louis Guillemette, the Secretary to the Controlling Committee who was in regular contact with the Germans. He telephoned and made an appointment for both of us to go and see Prince Von Oettingen. We were allowed to put our case on behalf of Kenny Bell. I at that time was under the mistaken impression that the plane in the Motor House Garage, was the remains of the Wee Mite. That was the story I told the Germans and explained that it was a very small plane which had crashed years before, that it had never flown any real distance and was totally unsuitable for a sustained flight to the mainland.

Whether we did any good or not I really do not know, but shortly afterwards Kenny, who had been held for three weeks without any charge being made against him, was released. The Germans allowed him to return to his job as manager of the Motor House Garage.

The Avro Avian was put on board a transporter by the Germans and taken to the airport. Some time later it was taken down to the White Rock and shipped to the continent. That was the last anyone saw of 'Parmy's' Avro Avian aeroplane.

After the war 'Parmy' returned to the island and tried to get compensation for the loss of his plane. He claimed £1,800, but it was never forthcoming. Everyone who had their car requisitioned by the Germans was paid some compensation, but poor old 'Parmy' never received any for his aeroplane.

A few years ago when the States were turning out the archives down in the cellars of the old Town Hospital, reference was found to this plane. 'Parmy' heard about this discovery and went down to investigate. Sure enough there was an entry regarding his Avro Avian. So again, he raised the matter of compensation with the States, but regrettably without success.

The Germans who had ordered the surrender of all radios in November 1940, as an island punishment for the help given to Lt's Nicolle and Symes and then returned them as a goodwill gesture the following Christmas, now confiscated them again. This time for 'military reasons'.

They were becoming very concerned about B.B.C. broadcasts, being fully aware that messages were being transmitted to the resistance movement in France and other occupied countries. They no doubt felt that the same might happen in Guernsey. In early June 1942 they issued an order that all sets had to be surrendered by the 17th June. I handed in my Alba set to the local receiving depot, which was a house in the Jerbourg Road called 'Changsha', but again kept my Philco Pilot Radio.

I was of course concerned that the Germans might search La Croix for some reason and find the set. There was no doubt in my mind what would happen to me - I would be locked up, probably for a long time. I was not concerned for myself, but was worried what would happen to Mabs and Margaret. The Germans told us it was a grave offence to possess or listen to a radio set. Heavy penalties, they said, would be exacted on those who failed to comply with their order.

I decided that my set would have to be well hidden. I gave a lot of thought to the problem. It had to be somewhere I could listen to the B.B.C. news after curfew. That, of course, meant that it had to be inside the house. The attic was a good place, but I suspected that would be the first place the Germans would look. Under the floor was another possibility, so was the chimney. Finally I decided to hide the set in one of our armchairs.

I removed the radio from its case and inserted it in between the springs of the chair. Fortunately it was a very neat little valve set, which was unusual at that time. Once the radio was fixed into position, I reassembled the chair. Initially the power connecting lead was tucked down into the side of the cushion, but this arrangement could be spotted by anyone sitting in the chair. It was also difficult to remove the lead from the socket and stuff it down the side of the chair quickly enough if someone suddenly interrupted you. After some thought, I put connectors in the two front castors of the armchair, so all I had to do was to attach the mains supply wires to the castors. The set was preset, both from the point of view of the station and the volume. I would lie on the floor with my head leaning on the chair and listen to the B.B.C. news. The volume on the set was turned down very low and all I dare do was listen to the news.

There were many islanders with radio sets, but we kept the fact very much to ourselves. We were never quite sure whom we could trust, or indeed who was listening to our conservations. On one occasion when Winston Churchill was going to broadcast, I invited Cecil Hardwick, a good friend and near neighbour, to come over and listen on my set.

We were about to turn my set on when Dick Gardiner arrived and sat himself down in my 'radio' chair. Although he was an islander, I dare not use my set while he was there. He was probably all right, but we could not take the risk, we had to be so very careful. Cecil and I were desperate to hear Churchill's broadcast, so I said to Cecil:

"When are you going to repair my chair for me Skipper ?"

I often called him 'Skipper'.

"I don't know, any time, tonight if you like" replied Cecil.

"Well Skipper, lets do it now."

So I asked Dick to sit in another chair, which he did. We picked up my armchair and carried it down to Cecil's house, passing several Germans on the way. We connected the power to the castors and listened to Winston Churchill.

When I was at the shop in Smith Street, I was keen to listen to the news programmes, so I fitted another un-surrendered radio set into an oil drum. I cut the bottom out of the drum and put the radio set on a cork float. Then I re-sealed the drum by soldering the bottom back on. It was a very difficult job as I had to hold the radio in position with a broom stick, which I inserted into the drum through the pump housing aperture. Then I laid the oil drum on its side and soldered the bottom back on. When I had completed that operation, I stood the drum upright and half filled it with oil, so the radio was floating in the middle of the drum. I fixed the lead wires just below the rim of the drum, so I could get hold of them by inserting two fingers into the pump housing aperture. I attached the lead to the power supply and like my set at home, the radio was preset for the news. I had these two secret radio sets, so I kept pretty well up to date with the news from the B.B.C.

Edgar Stacey, one of Guernseys' most successful small growers, had been forced by the Germans to move out of his home in La Vallee Road. However they allowed him to continue to work his vinery, which was alongside his house. Edgar, his wife Jane, and their young son John, moved into Lyndel, the bungalow next door to us. Although our families became very friendly, it was some months before I let on to Edgar that I had a radio set.

From then on, Edgar would regularly come in and listen to the news with me. Despite this, it was some time before he disclosed to me that he too had retained one of his radio sets. It was hidden in his vinery packing shed, right under the nose of the Germans billeted in his house.

"I would like to bring it home", said Edgar "but I don't know where to hide it, so it won't be discovered."

"Bring it home Edgar. I will help you hide it in your house somewhere"

"O.K. Bill" he said, "I will try and bring it home tomorrow evening. I think I can rescue it from its hiding place without Jerry finding out."

The next evening Edgar came home from his day's work at the vinery riding his carrier bike. The radio was in the carrier covered by a great mound of carpet. He untied the knots, removed the rope and the various pieces of carpet and there was this huge radio with its set of accumulators. I would never have had the nerve to ride through St Martin's with a wireless set that size under the nose of the Germans.

"Where on earth are we going to hide that, Edgar ?"

"Well, you told me to bring it home!" he replied, "I am not going to take it back. The ruddy Huns might spot me! I have taken a chance to bring it here, so you have got to help me do something with it."

I thought there was only one place for that size of set and that was under the floorboards. So in Edgar's front room we lifted the carpet and took up some floorboards. There was no way we were going to fit this Bush Push Button radio in between the floorboard joists, it was far too big.

"There is not enough room to get it down there." Edgar declared.

"No" I said, "Then we will have to saw through a joist".

"We can't do that it is not my house".

"I can't help that we have to get this radio hidden!"

So we cut through two or three cross joists and then a main joist. We removed a number of concrete blocks from the foundations, still it would not go in. So we dug a deep trench below the joists, lined it with a sheet of rubberiod and lowered the radio into it, together with the accumulators. We fitted two contact points and a switch so we could turn the set on and off. We pre-tuned it and fitted a socket, so that we could plug in a set of headphones or loudspeaker. When the accumulators went flat we were able to lift the floorboards and take them out and recharged them.

Despite having pre-tuned the radio it gave trouble from time to time, due to dust and grit getting into the set. Then we would lift the floorboards, recover the radio and clean it up. One evening we could not get the B.B.C. so we retrieved the set and placed it on the dinning room table. I was adjusting the radio with my back to the window and Edgar was watching me when there came a rap tat tat on the window. I turned around and saw the faces of two Germans beckoning through the window for us to go and talk to them! Edgar and I were both scared stiff and we must have shown it.

"Crumbs, that's torn it!" Edgar exclaimed.

I went and opened the front door, I was shaking like a leaf. We had been caught red-handed with a forbidden radio set. As I went out to where these two German soldiers were standing, I was thinking of the almost certain six months in prison on the continent. I just stood there and Edgar, who by this time was as white as a sheet, joined me. We must have looked a pathetic pair.

One of the German soldiers asked in broken English:

"We are lost, can you please tell us where we can find the house of Betty Osborne!"

Edgar pointed to the house next door where she lived and the two soldiers went on their way with a:

"Thank you very much."

Within seconds we had replaced the radio, the floorboards and the carpet, just in case the Germans came back for further directions. I find it incredible that they did not see the radio, it was certainly a large set. Perhaps they, as soldiers, were more interested in the company of Betty Osborne than trouble at that particular time of the day. Whatever the reason, I am convinced today, as I was then, that they saw the radio and did nothing about it. Edgar and I were both extremely fortunate.

There was however one snag in what we did in hiding Edgar's set under the joists. After the occupation ended I purchased Lyndel, the house that Edgar was living in, and it cost me over £150 to repair all the damage we did to the foundations and joists. The trench we excavated for the radio, is still there to this day.

Later when our electricity started to run out, I heard a broadcast by Colonel Britton from Start Point, the British station which was beamed to occupied Europe. He instructed his listeners how to make crystal sets. That was just the information I had been hoping for, so I got to work constructing a crystal set so that I could keep up with the B.B.C. news after our electricity finally ran out. Crystal sets, of course, operate without electricity. To construct a set I needed assistance, so I enlisted the help of my near neighbour, Cecil Hardwick. He was a great character, who always had a smile on his face. He had no technical or mechanical knowledge, but was very keen to help.

La Croix had an attic which was boarded out with loose lengths of timber. I decided this would be the ideal place to construct our crystal set, away from prying eyes. The first and most important task was the creation of the crystal. Colonel Britton explained that what was needed was a piece of coal with a gold vein in it, this would act as the crystal. The Cat's Whisker, a pointed piece of wire, was used to make contact with the crystal and the use of a coil, in theory, turned the crystal into a crystal radio receiver.

The search for coal with a gold vein was like looking for a needle in a haystack, almost an impossibility. Coal itself was like gold dust, there were virtually no stocks left in the island. We went to one or two people we could trust and looked in their coal bunkers for a suitable piece of coal, but without success. After all our searching, Cecil Hardwick found a small piece of coal in his own coal shed and by good fortune it had a gold vein in it. We were in luck. The one piece of information we did not have was the size of coil required. Colonel Britton had given all the other details needed to construct a crystal set, he explained how to wind the coil, but did not tell us the coil size that was needed or, if he did, I had missed it. So we had to experiment with various sizes of coil.

We carefully followed Colonel Britton's instructions and all that was required was that we get the right size coil. Cecil put on old set of A.J.S. headphones, which had belonged to Dad from his wireless dealership days and listened for any sound, while I jiggled with the coil. I remember Cecil walking up and down on the loose planks of wood which formed the floor of the attic, making a clatter, clatter, clatter noise. This gradually got on my nerves and the fact that I could not get our newly built crystal set to work put me in a bad temper. Mabs remembers me getting mad and as my swearing reached a peak, constantly asking Cecil:

"Can you hear anything Skipper ?"

Cecil replying "Not a bloody sausage!"

This apparently went on for hours, with my temper getting shorter and shorter and still not being able to get any life out of the crystal set.

Just before curfew time Cecil, who was still walking up and down, threw his hands in the air, jumped up and down and shouted:

"Bloody music!"

The loose planks went in all directions, everything was sent flying, including our now prized and working crystal set.

After that success, Cecil and I were prepared to carry on all night. That of course would have been a complete waste of time, as the broadcasts were almost finished for the night. Mabs was insistent that we left off and tried again another time.

The next evening we had another session of trying to get our crystal set to work. We knew we were nearly there, Cecil had heard music and now it was only a matter of repeating our success without repeating the wrecking celebrations! This time Cecil was stationed at the top of the ladder to the loft, with the headphones and strict instructions not to get carried away if he heard anything. If he did, the worst that could happen was that he would fall off the ladder.

I was carefully adjusting the coil, now knowing what size was required, suddenly and this time quietly, Cecil, with that inevitable shine on his face, said:

"I can hear the news."

Success - I had made my first, but not my last, Crystal Set.

Initially I hid the set in the rafters by the attic window. Later I kept it in our bedside cupboard. When it was in the attic, the aerial was hidden along and under the lining of the eaves. In our bedroom the wire for the earth was led along the passageway to the bathroom and attached to a tap. That arrangement gave excellent reception.

Many people who surrendered their radio sets to the Germans later bitterly regretted it. Dr Rose was one. As a Doctor he was allowed to keep his car on the road for much of the occupation. He knew that I had a radio, as I had told him on one of his calls to see Margaret, so he would often pop in to listen to the news. In fact he came so often that he parked his car outside other people's houses, as if he were attending them in order that he did not arouse the suspicion of the Germans.

I only possessed one set of headphones, the old A.J.S. set of Dad's, and that caused a problem. We would hold the headphones between us and both try to listen in but it was not the most successful way of hearing the news. Doctor Rose solved the problem when he 'raided' the store room at the Castel Emergency Hospital, where the surplus radio equipment had been stored after the Germans had collected all the radios. On one of his regular visits to listen to my radio he, with a flourish, produced a set of headphones from his medical bag.

Dr Rose said it was obvious that he was not the first person to have helped themselves to a set of headphones, as all the wires were in a terrible tangle. The fact that the stock of headphones was rapidly disappearing, day by day, was a clear indication that I was not the only one who had a illegal radio.

The importance that we attached to hearing the B.B.C. news during the occupation is, I suppose, difficult for anyone to understand who was not in the island during that time. Our local Press could only print the German 'version' of the news, which we totally distrusted. The B.B.C. was our sole source of genuine and truthful news that we could rely upon. Even if it was bad news, and it often was, we wanted to know the truth. There must have been scores, if not hundreds, of illegal radio sets in the island, all being tuned to the B.B.C. for the news. Most people who had a set would pass on the main points of the news to other islanders whom they could trust.

On one occasion Mabs picked up the telephone and found herself listening to the B.B.C. news. She did not understand why, but she took the opportunity of listening to the latest news. It never happened to Mabs again. A German officer went into a packing shed to use a telephone and when he picked up the receiver he also heard the B.B.C. news. There was a hell of a row about that. Apparently this happened when someone using their crystal set, earthed it to a telephone cable.

Ted Laker, one of my many friends, lived not far away at Cliffways in the Calais Road. It was just across the fields at the rear of La Croix. Sometimes after curfew, I would creep along the hedges and make my way to his house for a chat. Ted was, by trade a radio engineer and electrician. A short while before the war Ted started his own electrical business. When the Germans arrived, his business virtually folded overnight. Ted needing to find some other means of supporting himself, took on the job as Manager of the Civil Transport Depot in the Pollet. One evening we were discussing what could be done to keep islanders informed on how the war was progressing. We decided we could help by producing crystal sets.

Someone discovered, I believe it was Mat Angell of Boots the Chemist, that with a small quantity of sulphur, a silver sixpence and a rifle bullet case, a suitable crystal could be produced. The method was to file down a silver sixpence, put the filings and the sulphur in the bullet case, of which there were thousands about because the Germans were always firing at something or another, clamp the end in the vice and put it in the fire. For self protection we ran like hell for cover before it exploded with a loud bang. If you could find any of the resulting bits, that was crystal. Ted Laker found out how to wind the coils to get the right balance. So he and I were making crystal sets semi-commercially, but secretly of course. I turned out lovely little bull's eye cats whiskers on my lathe, they operated beautifully, not the hit and miss job that I made with Cecil Hardwick.

Ted Laker also attempted to manufacture headphones, but he ran into trouble with the magnets. We had however to rely on headsets we 'obtained' from the hospitals and telephone hand sets, although there was a lot of competition for these. We were certainly not the only people making crystal sets.

The Start Point broadcasts came over loud and clear on our crystal sets. We produced quite a few sets, some we gave away and a few we sold. We quickly achieved a reputation for making them, but I was scared stiff in case the Germans were to hear of our activities. Fortunately they never did.

What the Germans did not realise was that the average Guernseyman was an amateur radio enthusiast. There were quite a number of islanders who quickly acquired the knowledge and ability to sketch out a rough circuit on a cigarette packet and pass it on to a friend. Guernseymen have always been very adaptive and inventive and as a result many crystal sets were made and in use by the end of the occupation. People found the most ingenious places to hide their sets, in watches and clocks and in electrical plugs and often the headphones were stitched into cushions.

Jackie Upham, who was a very skilled engineer, made a one valve radio and fitted it into a tomato chip. He laid the valve on its side, inserted a false bottom and filled the chip with broad beans. Everyone, even the Germans, were walking around with tomato chips, they were everywhere, so Jackie could leave his radio set around without attracting attention. That tomato chip, complete with the secret radio, was put on display at the German occupation Museum. as part of a wartime Guernsey kitchen.

Chapter 14

WONDERFUL MR. RENOUF

Many of my business competitors left the island prior to the occupation. Reggie Gray, who sailed away without me, Theo Millard, the Giles family, Salmon's from Tower Works and Wilf Denning all evacuated. The trade during the occupation consisted of West's of St Sampson's, Herbie Tostevin in Grande Rue St Martin, Reg Moullin St Georges Esplanade, Stan Taylor in St Martin, Domaille and Sons in the Bordage and myself.

Those dealers who evacuated had their stocks taken over by the Essential Commodities Committee. John Loveridge, who was the Secretary of that Committee, approached me and asked if I would help to value their stock, which I willingly did. The stock of cycles and accessories were then sold to other dealers and the proceeds credited to the absent owners. They were paid in full on their return to the island after the war.

Millards and Dennings had a considerable number of new cycles in stock, I bought them all. Reg Moullin took over Reggie Gray's stock. It certainly helped in keeping us going for a while. The system worked very well and very fairly, not only in my line of business but right across the retail trade.

After the re-distribution of the stock from traders who had left the island, I realised that it was going to be impossible to obtain any further replacement stock of spares and accessories. Ash's Garage, at the top of the Grange, were wholesalers of cycle parts. I went up to see Mr Winterflood, who was in charge as the owner had evacuated. I bought as much of his stock as he would let me have, including all his dynamo sets. I vividly remember Stan Taylor complaining bitterly that I should not have been allowed to buy so much stock. He felt, probably rightly, that it should have been shared amongst the trade.

As the Germans had ordered all cars and motorcycles, with only a few exceptions, off the road, business boomed. Although we soon sold all our new bicycles, there was a lot of repairs required. Now that the bicycle was virtually the only form of transport available to islanders, they needed to keep them in working order. Repair, repair, repair was the order of the day. In a census taken early in the occupation, it was found that there were 14,452 cycles registered in the island, which provided plenty of work for the few cycle dealers still in business.

Because of the volume of work I was in need of additional help. George Cave, who had worked for Theo Millard until he evacuated to England, came to see me enquiring if I could find him a job. He was a skilled motorcycle and bicycle mechanic, so I was only too pleased to employ him.

George was a very serious character, I don't think I ever remember seeing him smile. He was a slow thinker, but a very good and trustworthy employee. George was renowned for his ravenous appetite.

Cooking fat was in extremely short supply. One day I said to George:

"You know, I reckon we could cook chips in motor oil."

"Do you reckon?"

"Yes" I said, "It's good stuff, Castrol 'R' oil, it should be all right."

We managed to obtain a few potatoes and one lunch time chopped them up and cooked them in motor oil. The chips were excellent providing you kept eating, but when you stopped you certainly could taste the motor oil. George Cave was, as ever, ravenously hungry and enjoyed a good feed of these beautiful looking brown chips. Regrettably his enjoyment did not last long and we did not see him again for about two weeks. He was pretty ill. Castrol Oil did not feature in our diet after that, however hungry we became - and later we were to get very hungry.

I can remember just how hungry George became. On one occasion Harry Broughton came in to have a puncture mended and decided to wait while George carried out the repair. Harry took an apple out of one of his pockets and a penknife out of another and proceeded to peel it. I could see George enviously watching Harry eating this apple - I could see the hunger in his face. What he would not have given for that apple ! He finished mending the puncture and Harry Broughton left. Immediately George grabbed the apple peel that had been left behind and devoured it ravenously.

Whilst George's craving was for food, Artie Selous's was for cigarettes. Artie, who was one of life's loveable characters, missed his smoke much more than his food.

Bicycle tyres and tubes were issued on a permit system by the States Essential Commodities Committee. From time to time the island received very limited supplies of spares from France. The procedure was that if a cyclist needed a new tyre or inner tube, he applied to the Committee and attempted to prove to them that his need was essential, such as carrying vegetables to market. Then, if a sufficient case had been made, the cyclist would be given a permit for a tyre or a tube.

The cyclist would then nominate the dealer he wished to deal with and they would be issued with that tyre or tube. Dealers would only be allowed to draw the exact number of tyres for which permits had been issued. Herbie Tostevin would be allocated six tyres, Domaille four and we might get eight. I don't suppose it was only Greens, but Greens were always a tyre or two short. If ever we had an allocation of tyres it wasn't very long before Artie could be seen contentedly puffing away. He would have fiddled a tyre to someone who was able to supply him with cigarettes, or he would 'suggest' to a customer who already had a permit that it would be easier for him to find the tyre if he had a smoke. This approach generally prevailed throughout the island, money didn't matter, bartering was the way of life.

That was fine until the last applicant with a permit came in and no tyre was available. Nevertheless, Artie did superb work, brazing up broken frames, pedals and forks, rebuilding wheels and later when there were no further supplies available, he even managed to create tandems out of two bicycles. By this means a husband and wife could still remain mobile, even though their two bikes had only one set of usable tyres between them.

Artie regularly went around the island visiting quarries to find old cycle frames and wheels. He would then re-build the wheels, replacing some of the spokes and, where possible, polishing them to make them look like new. Some wheels were very rusty and he would paint those with silver paint. The frames would also be repainted. I had a large supply of paint in stock, mostly a horrid green, but also some other violent colours. Artie sold many of these 'reconditioned' and often gaudily painted bikes to foreign workers subject, of course, to them having sufficient cigarettes!

One particular 'reconditioned' cycle was sold to a Spanish worker, Giurnez Antonio Maraton, who was quartered at Frie Baton Camp. Shopkeepers were required by law to give a receipt for each sale and affix to each receipt, occupation sales tax stamps to the correct value. A few days after the 'reconditioned' cycle had been sold, P.C.Sebire came knocking on my door at home and showed me the receipt without any sales tax stamps.

I admitted that I had clearly broken the law by not sticking on the required sales tax stamps. P.C.Sebire said that I would be charged and what had I got to say for myself. He took out his note book and pencil, and waited for my reply:

"You have got me cold, book me, put down what you like in your book. It was an omission on my part. I hope that Quertier Le Pelley, the magistrate, is in a good mood when I attend Court."

I had to pay three times the value of the sales tax stamps I had omitted to affix, that was the normal requirement. I paid that sum before I appeared in Court. I thought it might mitigate in my favour. In Court, Police Constable Sebire read out from his note book the remarks I had made, including my hope that the magistrate would be in a good mood. When my sentence was announced, Jurat Quertier Le Pelley, looked at me and said;

"Mr Green, you can now judge whether I am in a good mood or not, you are fined five pounds."

Sprucing up rebuilt bicycles was not the only painting that Artie did, he was a very fine artist. He really enjoyed sitting at his easel, painting one of his favourite scenes. He spent hours at his easel, in his attic, painting and looking out across the roof tops of St Peter Port. At other times he would go up to the empty flat above the shop and sit for hours painting various views of the harbour.

Not long after the occupation started, a German soldier brought a motorcycle into our shop with a repair order from the German H.K.P., their Transport Office. I certainly did not want to help the Germans by repairing their motorcycles so I went up to Maison Allaire at the top of the street where the Controlling Committee had established their offices and saw Deputy Stamford Raffles.

"There is a German motorcycle in my shop which they have asked me to repair. I don't want to do it, that's collaboration!"

"Now look Mr Green, we had instructions from the Home Office, just before the Germans arrived, that we were to look after ourselves the best we can and I am going to ask you to mend that motorbike for the benefit of the rest of us. If you refuse it is going to mean a lot of trouble."

"That is a German motorcycle, Sir, I won't repair it".

John Leale, who was later to become the President of the Controlling Committee, was also there and chipped in;

"Bill, I think the best thing to do, is for you to repair their motorcycles for the time being."

I had immense respect for John Leale, so of course I reluctantly took his 'advice' and repaired that particular motorbike. However, I mixed up some grinding paste and oil and put it into the gear box of this German machine. I regretted doing that like blazes later on, when I ran short of grinding paste. What happened to that motorbike I don't know, but I suspect that the gearbox soon had to be replaced. In consequence of accepting that one motorcycle for repair, before very long we had a shop full of work. In no time at all we became the main motorcycle repairers for the German army locally.

I complained that I did not have enough room in my shop to repair all their machines, so the Germans took over Doctor Bostock's garage at the top of Smith Street and allowed me to establish additional workshop facilities there. Dr Bostock was out of the island during the occupation.

In order to cope with all this additional work I took on another employee, Gordon Stabb. He was a wonderful mechanic and did not care what work he did as long as it involved motorcycles. There were no other opportunities around in Guernsey in those wartime days to work on his beloved motorbikes, so of course he was keen to have the job. He worked with George Cave on the German machines, in Dr Bostock's garage.

Having been 'instructed' to repair German motorcycles, I did as little as possible. In fact, I and other members of my staff deliberately damaged parts and then indented for replacements from the H.K.P. Transport Office, which was situated in a house in the Grange, near the junction with Brock Road. We quickly learnt which were the parts in short supply, so these components would regularly 'fail' and we would report that they needed replacing.

By this ruse we managed to get quite a few of their military motorcycles written off, never to be used again. Other machines were only partially repaired and we were sure that they would soon be off the road again for further repairs, not necessarily with the original fault. We damaged a link in a chain so that it would snap after a few more miles use. We would remove half the plates from a clutch, so that it was not long before the clutch failed.

The H.K.P, was the only German department with which I really had any regular contact during the occupation. When we needed spare parts for their motorcycles, I went there to order them. They had comprehensive parts lists and referred to these to identify the particular item required. The Germans always created a mass of paper work for every replacement part we required. They were sticklers for procedure. Many of the components had to be ordered from Germany and despite all their paperwork, which I think they loved, the parts seldom materialised.

The German clerk I dealt with could not speak any English and my German was non existent. When I tried to sketch or draw the part I needed, the German would get very ratty. There was a Guernsey lady I knew, a Mrs Stephan who had married a German before the war and in consequence spoke excellent German. She worked at the H.K.P. Office and often acted as my interpreter.

It was surprising how many replacement parts were 'needed' to keep their motorcycles on the road. Sometimes on closer inspection we found there were a few teeth sheared off cogs and suchlike, which had not been apparent when they were first brought in for repair. Gordon Stabb was an excellent mechanic, but he had one fault, he was a perfectionist. All his repairs had to be the best possible job he could do, even with the German machines. I often had to point out to him damaged parts which he had 'missed'. However, under my guidance he quickly learnt and soon got the hang of the 'system'.

With his skill as a mechanic, Gordon soon became an absolute master in devising 'future' breakdowns of German military motorcycles. He spent a great deal of time carefully fraying a brake or clutch cable, so that with a few more miles running it would snap. He would put a high current through a light bulb so that one of the two filaments would blow. The headlamp would function until the full beam was turned on and then there would be total darkness. Gordon and George Cave were always discussing ways they could subtly sabotage German machines. There was one German Under Officer who they could not stand, so whenever he brought his motorcycle in for repair, it never travelled very far afterwards.

The Germans captured or commandeered a large number of French Army motorcycles and equipment. They brought to the island some of the Nome Rhone machines with their huge sidecars. All the motorcycles and sidecars I had previously worked on had their sidecars on the left but these were, of course, on the right. Some of the machines had shaft drives to the sidecar wheel and others had a reverse gear. They really were wonderful pieces of engineering, which I found fascinating. Neither I, nor any of my staff, had seen generator fly wheels up to that time. At first we couldn't understand where the generator was located. Some of the machines had excellent electric equipment, so there had to be a generator, but for a long time we couldn't find it.

Gordon finally stripped down one of the fly wheels.

"There's the generator!" he exclaimed.

"Cor hang! That's very ingenious!" I exclaimed.

The generator was built into the fly wheel. Villiers copied that many years afterwards, but until that time none of us had seen that arrangement. It was a beautiful piece of engineering.

In one way I was happy to be repairing the German's motorcycles since it gave me a chance to ride them, a pleasure which I otherwise greatly missed. I made a point of test riding every machine before returning it to the Germans. One day I was stopped by the German Police and asked for my permit to ride the motorcycle. Of course I had no permit, so I was hauled up to their Police Headquarters at Grange Lodge. I produced my H.K.P. work order paper, but they said;

"This doesn't give you permission to ride the machines."

"It's no use, you can't repair a machine if you can't test ride it to see if you have done the job properly."

After that they gave me a permit to ride and test their motorcycles and I made full use of it.

Len Rouget, with whom I had spent a few days working in Coventry just prior to the occupation, found that with no cars and very few lorries on the road, he was no longer able to keep his motor repair business going. My workshop was very busy, so I was only too happy to give him a job, particularly as he was a very good mechanic.

One day a German brought his motorcycle in for repair and Len dealt with him. Trying to find out what work they wanted carried out when they could not speak very much English was not the simplest of situations. This particular German removed the cap off the petrol tank, took a stick and dipped it in the petrol. He then cut a notch on the stick, which was the measurement of the petrol in the tank. The German showed Len Rouget the stick and the cut he had made. He put the stick in his pocket and off he went leaving Len to repair his motorcycle. Obviously he had been to Greens previously to get his motorcycle repaired and had lost some petrol.

Len Rouget, for sheer devilment, spent all afternoon removing the petrol tank, cutting a hole in the bottom and soldering a pint can inside, near the back where it couldn't be seen. Then he soldiered it all up again, painted the solder to match the rest of the paintwork, with grey paint which the Germans had previously supplied for use when we were working on their motorcycles, and fixed the tank back in position. Len refilled the petrol in the tank to the level it was when the German brought the machine in for repair and kept the spare pint. The German returned later, took the stick out of his pocket, and checked the petrol level. His measure was fine, everybody was happy, especially Len with his hard won pint of petrol.

Herbert Winterflood, who after he left Vauxbelets College worked for us full time, often managed to help himself to some petrol from German motorcycles parked around the town. On one occasion he was caught in the act of syphoning petrol by an 'American' speaking German N.C.O. This Jerry had left his machine at the top of Smith Street. Herbert went across with a can and a length of hose, and was just in the act of draining the petrol from the tank when the German returned. Herbert was threatened with the most horrible punishments, but fortunately the German went off without taking any further action.

The idea of putting sugar or a lump of rubber into the petrol tanks of German vehicles was always very tempting, but sugar was scarce and precious. You had of course to bear in mind that the German driver might discover what you had done and come back and confront you.

One day in May 1941, I was standing outside my shop in Smith Street, looking up and down, when I noticed two German sailors coming up the street on a motorbike. As they reached me, all of a sudden they turned left and shot up the passageway past me and into the rear of my shop. I thought that was a dangerous thing to do, so I went to remonstrate with them, not to violently of course, you had to be careful not to overstep the mark with our German 'visitors'. One of them said, very agitatedly, in his best broken English:

"Mr, Mr, Gendarmerie."

Apparently as they were riding up Smith Street, they saw two German policemen coming around the corner near the Plantation, at the top of the street. They had 'borrowed' the motorbike from their ship and had no right to be using it, so as soon as they spotted their Police, they drove into the first passageway they saw. It was now my turn to be agitated, I did not want the German Police coming down into the rear of my shop, they might start searching the place. I thought of the hidden radio in the oil drum, which I certainly did not want found.

Fortunately the two German Police had not had their suspicions aroused and walked on down the street, past the shop. The two very relieved German sailors eventually rode off on their motorbike, no doubt they went straight back to their ship.

The next day these two sailors came back into the shop, this time on foot, with a bag of sugar which they presented to me as a way of saying thank you for not letting them down. I am quite sure that they had 'borrowed' the sugar from their ship, just in the same way they had 'borrowed' the motorbike. I accepted the gift gratefully, sugar was nearly as valuable as petrol. We struck up a conversation and they told me how they had seen London burning from their ship as they were sailing down the English Channel. I said it would take a lot of burning, as there was still an awful lot of London left.

A few days later, these two Germans were back in the shop bragging that the Bismarck had sunk H.M.S Hood. Regretfully I already knew, as I had heard the sad news on my 'oil drum' radio, but of course I expressed surprise. Within forty-eight hours the Royal Navy had sunk the Bismarck. I had just heard the good news on my radio and was busy telling Artie Selous, when these two German sailors came in again and I could not resist tormenting them by asking;

"Did you hear that we have sunk the Bismark?"

"No - really!"

"Yes," I said with great glee. "Yes, the pride of your navy is kaput!"

That made me feel good. Fortunately they did not ask me how I knew.

All sorts of inventiveness was required to keep motorbikes and cycles on the road. I acquired a small lathe just before the war and this proved invaluable. I received a certain amount of lathe training as part of my apprenticeship with Bassett Lowkes, but certainly not enough to make full use of the lathe. Jackie Upham, the General Manager of the Guernsey Railway Company, was a very experienced lathe operator and did a lot of the type of work that I wanted to do with my lathe. I often went and worked with Jackie, copying what he was doing. I learn a great deal from him and as a result put my lathe to better use.

As I became more experienced, the number of requests I received for help increased. The Guernsey Press lads often came around to see if I could 'turn' them a piece to replace a worn out component on one of their machines. I like to think that in a small way I helped to keep the presses rolling. Bill Pitchford, who ran the Singer Sewing Machine shop, regularly came over to see if I would 'turn' him up a connecting rod or some other essential piece to keep a sewing machine going. Eventually I became quite proficient and was turning up pistons, which had first been rough cast in old alloy by Jackie Upham on his forge. I also produced other essential items, like piston rings out of cast iron pipe, which were otherwise unobtainable.

'Greens' were also responsible to the Controlling Committee for keeping serviceable the few civilian motorcycles that the Germans allowed to remain on the road. The island doctors were allocated two motorcycles, the Water Board one, the Housing Officer, who's job it was to rehouse civilians turned out of their houses by the Germans, was allowed one. Somehow we kept them all going, my lathe turning out many of the bits and pieces that needed replacing.

During the later stages of the occupation, when the electricity supply failed, I fixed up a pedal unit with a gearing to keep my lathe operating. I would inveigle my staff, customers or friends who just popped in for a chat, to take turns at pedalling. By one means or another I kept my lathe going throughout the occupation.

When the electricity supply ran out, Ted Laker fixed up a little petrol motor so that he could recharge batteries down at the Civil Transport Depot. My lathe had a 24 volt motor so, as an alternative to the pedal unit, I used two 12 volt batteries. Ted, many times swapped one of my discharged batteries with a battery from a Civil Transport lorry. I remember that when I wanted to recharge or exchange a battery I took them down to the Depot workshop on a greenhouse trolley. Taking the trolley down Forest Lane was easy enough, but bringing them back up the steep hill was another matter. However Ted was a good friend to me and provided me with an excellent 'Battery service'.

Ted Laker's assistant, was Ken Gould, the carter and docker. It was a job where they came into daily contact with the Germans, but they were both totally anti-German. Ken, whose function it was to allocate lorries, would make it as difficult as possible for the Germans. He would refuse to supply a lorry, saying that none were available, when in fact there were. He led them a merry dance and surprisingly managed to get away with it without ever being rumbled.

One day I was in the office at the Civil Transport Depot, in the Lower Pollet, when the telephone rang. Ken answered, it was obviously a German on the other end. I can hear him now, repeating out loud what the German was saying:

"Have you got a tarpaulin for the lorry?"

"Oh yes, if it rains we have got a tarpaulin and if the sun shines we have got a bloody sun shade!"

I sat there listening to this conversation hoping that the German's command of the English language was limited.

Mrs Hollis, the optician next door to my shop, had a spectacle grinding machine for grinding lenses to fit frames. I used my lathe to make parts for her machine which helped to keep her going. I spent quite a lot of time in Mrs Hollis's shop because she also possessed a hidden radio. Her's was a very small set and was built into the drawer of her safe. She would pull the draw out and string up her aerial and we would listen to the news together. Mrs Hollis was the Channel Islands Chess champion and we often played a game of chess during working hours, although I never beat her.

When cycle supplies started running low, we began cannibalising old bicycles. Eventually the island ran out of tyres and other spares. In the summer of 1942 I was instructed by the States Commodities Committee, to prepare a list of cycle requirements. The Guernsey Purchasing Commission, under Raymond Falla, promised to try and obtain whatever cycle supplies were available in France. I literally told Raymond to bring back anything to do with bicycles and, bless him, he did just that.

He brought back problems too, none of the 'metric' French supplies fitted our 'imperial' British bicycles, but we adapted. The tyres, tubes, ball bearings, everything French was metric, but the trade surmounted the problem with creditable ingenuity. We would cut a tyre in half, overlap it and stitch it up again. You felt a bit of a bump, but so what, it went round and you were mobile. We encountered the same problems with inner tubes, so we cut and spliced them to make them fit British bicycles.

We also often spliced two old tubes, that were individually beyond repair, together to make one serviceable one. We used a broom handle to splice tubes. The tube was cut in half and then one end was pushed on to the broom handle and peeled back. The peeled back portion was covered with repair solution and the other end of the tube pushed over it. It sounds tricky and complicated, it was, but it worked and kept many islanders mobile.

Raymond Falla managed to import six complete Peugeot bicycles from France in 1942. Greens were allocated two, one of which I sold to Mr H. M. Lihou who worked for the Post Office, the other to Mr A. Le Mole, who was involved in printing the Star newspaper. The retail price was £8.17s.6d. plus the sales tax of 14s.9 1/2d.

The Central Commodities Committee were responsible for distributing supplies to retailers in the island. This included supplies of cycles spares and accessories. I was asked to help with the allocation and distribution, which I willingly did on an entirely voluntary basis. The Committee had its offices in the Ladies College and I liked going up there because they employed some very nice young ladies. Two in particular I can remember were sisters by the name of Johns, who emigrated to Australia after the war. They were really good looking girls.

Very soon the cycle repair trade was in real trouble, simple items such as solution to stick patches on tubes had run out. Matt Angell, a chemist with Boots, found a way of making a solution which proved to be an adequate substitute. It was amazing how inventive people became during the occupation. Brake blocks replacements were made of wood, which didn't stop you very well, so we inserted rubber strips from old tyres into the wood. That gave a slightly better braking performance. Some things like valve rubbers became non existent. However we found that by stripping the insulating rubber from certain types of electric cable we could provide a reasonable substitute. But tyres and tubes were the real problem

When supplies became totally non existent, many people tried using garden hose pipe, or anything that provided a cushion between the bicycle and the road. I however found a better solution, he was a wonderful little man called Renouf.

Mr A.G. Renouf worked as a boot repairer for Beghin's in the High Street. One day I was talking to him about the problems of trying to repair cycle tyres when they were really worn out. He suggested that I purchase some canvas and a boot stitching machine. His idea was to cover the outside of an old tyre with canvas, overlap it on the inside, then stitch the canvas onto the inside of the worn tyre and so give it an extended life. Acting upon his advice I bought a boot stitching machine from the premises of a boot repairer who had evacuated. It was in effect a heavy duty sewing machine which was man enough to stitch through the soles of shoes. We were very fortunate to get a large supply of needles with the machine and these lasted us right throughout the occupation.

I bought a number of old hose pipes from the Guernsey Fire Brigade, canvas hoses that leaked and were redundant. Our one problem was the supply of strong enough thread. Raymond Falla came to our rescue when he located and obtained a supply of suitable thread on one of his buying trips to the continent.

Mr Renouf, who worked part time for me, from his home in the evenings and weekends, used the boot repairing machine and the canvas from the fire hoses to such good effect that we built quite a reputation for Green's occupation repaired tyres. But it was Mr Renouf's reputation really, although Greens took the credit. He was a incredible little man, who did a yeoman job and kept the people of Guernsey cycling.

Our wonderful Mr Renouf repaired many hundreds of cycle tyres with lengths of old fire hose, in fact we were so successful that the news spread throughout the island and were inundated with work. Our Mr Renouf died soon after the war and if ever a man deserved recognition for his efforts, he most certainly did.

Before I discovered the supply of redundant fire hose, Raymond Falla obtained a huge roll of good quality heavy navy linen in France. Mr Renouf tried to use this linen to repair tyres, but found that it was unsuitable. Mabs had the idea of making shopping bags out of it and this proved a winner. She took the roll of linen home and made hundreds of shopping bags, which sold for 2/6 each.

As time went on repairs to cycles became more urgent, but more difficult. What had taken only a few minutes to repair before the war was now taking hours. Previously we had fitted a new part from our stock, now there were no new parts, so we had to cannibalise, repair or adapt. It all took time. Because their bicycles were so essential to them, our customers would spend long periods talking to my staff about their machines. My lads were getting frustrated because they could not get on with their work. After a time I decided that there was only one solution, to close one day a week so that we could get on with our work behind closed doors. In May 1943, I put an advertisement in the Evening Press.

'Greens' Smith Street,
Guernsey's Leading Cycle People.
Telephone 688

> Owing to extreme pressure on our Cycle Repairs Dept., and the fact that all materials, solution, etc have either to be sought after, or made on the Firm, we have decided to remain CLOSED all day on MONDAYS, enabling our staff, to work behind closed doors, thus keeping pace with weekend-work. We trust that this arrangement will enable us to give you a better service, and ask you to believe us, that repairing your cycle is becoming more and more difficult, and we ask your tolerance and help in our efforts to keep you on the road.

My advertisement caused considerable interest and as a result I received a visit from an Evening Press reporter. Later an article appeared.

> 'I walked into Mr Bill Green's shop in Smith Street and he told me "It is truly remarkable how things have been kept going. All cycle traders have accomplished a grand job of work. Credit must go to the mechanics who have stood up to the definite strain. How they have done it is certainly remarkable. All the cycle mechanic does these days is mend tyres and punctures - and then more punctures. For instance, I know of two mechanics who suffered a nervous breakdown only due to the concentration required in mending tyres and punctures. Some extraordinary jobs we have had, amongst them converting gents cycles into ladies cycles. Tyres have been reduced in size and practically every part of a cycle has been manufactured in the island, even to the extent of making chain wheels. Everything that is humanly possible has been done to tyres, and the lathe that we have is almost in constant use."

> 'As I left Mr Green's shop there was a terrific bang. The mechanics looked at one another. An inner tube they had mended not long before had exploded. I expected them to pour forth what Jack Warner would call 'blue pencils' but this was an every day occurrence and they got on with the job of mending the puncture once again without a murmur.'

> 'So a big thankyou to the lads throughout the island who keep us a- wheel.'

It was not only islanders who relied on their bicycles, the Germans were also great cyclists. Their machines, just like ours, broke down and needed repairing. One of our problems was that members of the occupying forces would bring their bikes into our shop, upend them and start to repair them using our tools and materials. This caused great resentment, but as they were our occupiers, there was no way to refuse.

One day I was in the Motor House Garage, talking to Kenny Bell, when I noticed a large sign in German in a very prominent position on his garage forecourt. I asked him:

"What's all that about Kenny ?"

"That's a great sign", he said, "We had a lot of trouble with the German soldiers coming down here repairing their own vehicles and using our tools and equipment. I complained to the H.K.P. Office and they gave me this notice. Now the Germans are forbidden to come and repair their own vehicles, only my mechanics can do it."

"Oh!" I said, "I've got the same problem. That is just the type of notice I need."

So I sat down and copied out the wording. Later I laboriously reproduced the notice with my hand printing set, onto a large card.

One day when I came back from one of my walkabouts around Town, there was a German in our shop with his bike in bits, using our precious solution and patches. I asked Artie:

"What's all this ?" pointing at the German.

"He's mending his own bike"

I had been waiting for one of these so-in-so's, so fetching the notice, I tapped the German on the shoulder and showed it to him. He looked at it and I don't know what it said to this day, but it must have been dynamite, because he hurriedly picked up his bike and all his bits and went out on the pavement. I never had the nerve to use that notice again.

Chapter 15

HANS THE COMMUNIST

During the occupation, if we could 'acquire' anything from the Germans we did, and we did not consider it stealing, rather we looked upon it as our duty in helping the war effort. Colonel Britton, who broadcast to occupied Europe, encouraged us to do everything in our power to harass the Germans, in every possible way. His message was:- 'Do something anti-Nazi every day'. While major acts of sabotage were not possible in our small island, it was however possible to 'relieve' our occupiers of small quantities of food and other supplies. German property was far from sacrosanct in our view. The Germans however took a different view and so too, at least in public did some of our leading citizens.

At that time, St Paul's Church stood where the St James sunken garden is today and right around the church were railings. During the autumn of 1941, there was great activity around the Church. The Germans cut down a considerable number of trees as fuel for their own use. Large teams of men were regularly employed stacking logs between the buttresses of the Church. The mountain of wood became so high that when walking by, I could hardly see the windows of the Church.

The Police station, which was just across the road from the Church, was heated by a stove. The station sergeant would from time to time, send a policeman across to fetch a few logs for their stove. One day I heard that the Germans had caught one of our policemen in the act of collecting wood. According to the Germans it was stealing from their Military wood yard, according to our Police it was Guernsey wood and belonged to them anyway. The Police station was not the only establishment that benefited from the wood store, the Prison was also kept well supplied

As a result of the 'log' and other incidents the Germans set a trap at their Organisation Todt store in the Truchot on the night of the 4-5th March 1942. They caught P.C.'s Frank Tuck and Ken Bailey, entering the store and helping themselves to German food.

The Germans took this incident, and the 'log stealing', very seriously. They saw it, I am sure, as an opportunity of discrediting the 'British' Police. They set their 'Feldgendarmerie' loose trying to drum up a case against as many of our policemen as possible.

The next morning, an officer of the Feldgendarmerie arrived at the Police Station and ordered Inspector Sculpher, the Chief Officer to close the Station and accompany him, together with all available police to the Feldgendarmerie Headquarters at Grange Lodge. There Inspector Sculpher was informed that a quantity of butter, sausages and tins of tomatoes had been stolen from the German forces by PC's. Tuck and Bailey, who were in their custody.

In consequence every remaining member of the twenty nine strong Guernsey Police Force was rounded up and taken to Grange Lodge. During the afternoon each police officer was taken in turn, to his home where upon it was searched by the Germans. At 4.30 pm the Germans announced that they were detaining PC's

Friend, Burton, Tuck, Smith and Bailey, but the rest of the force were, as the Germans put it, 'provisionally allowed their freedom' and could resume their duties. Inspector Sculpher was, however required to remain behind.

At six forty five that evening Deputy Inspector Langmead received a telephone call from Jurat John Leale, President of the Controlling Committee, notifying him that Inspector Sculpher had been suspended from duty by the Germans. He told Deputy Inspector Langmead that his name had been submitted to Grange Lodge to take over the responsibilities as Inspector of Police. A quarter of an hour later his telephone rang again, this time it was the Germans, who told Mr Langmead to report to Grange Lodge the next morning.

As Mr Langmead left the Police Station later that evening, he met Inspector Sculpher, who was understandably dejected. Mr Sculpher handed over the keys of his desk, his notebook and informed Mr Langmead of some of the outstanding cases.

The next morning Mr Langmead duly reported to the Feldgendarmerie at Grange Lodge and was instructed by the Germans to carry on as Inspector of Police.

Deputy Inspector A.J. Langmead was promoted Acting Inspector by the Police Committee and became the first locally born officer to take command of the Island Police force. Sergeant Bert Lamy became acting Deputy Inspector.

The Germans set about interrogating the rest of our Police force. One by one, they were arrested and incarcerated at Fort George. By the middle of April 1942 eighteen Officers had been charged by the Feldgendarmerie with various offences, mainly of stealing German supplies and were held in custody.

Besides the eighteen Police officers, a number of civilians were later charged with receiving the 'stolen' goods. The officers charged were:

Police Sergeant Fred Duquemin,
Detective Sergeant Ted Pill
Police Sergeant Jack Harper,
Police Sergeant Alf Howlett,
Police Constables' Ken Bailey,
Frank Tuck,
Charlie Friend,
Bill Burton,
Bert Smith,
Bill Quin,
Fred Short,
Frank Whare,
Tom Gaudion,
Archie Tardif,
Eugene Le Lievre,
Alf Le Gallez,
Harold 'Snip' Piesing,
Peter Bretel.

All were 'tried' before a German Military Tribunal, accused of stealing and receiving goods from German stores, except Detective Sergeant Ted Pill, who was only charged with being aware that the wood was being stolen. Ambrose Sherwill, now back in private practice, acted as the defence advocate. The German Military Judges were Doctor Biel, Rittmeister Furst Oettingen- Wallerstein and Uffz Kraft. The prosecution was handled by German Doctor Graut Trauttmansdorff.

The 'Trial' was held in the our Police Court, with a Nazi flag draped over the Royal Coat of Arms. I went early on the first day, around 8 am., to listen to the case and to give our policemen some moral support. The only crime that they had committed, in my view, was that they had been found out doing their patriotic duty in support of the British Crown and in harassing our German occupiers!

The proceedings were started with a whole series of questions being put to the eighteen policemen, such as how long they had been in the Force, had they served in the Great War, had they ever before been charged before a court, what was their salary. I was surprised to learn that a Sergeant only received £2.19s.10d. a week. They were asked if they owned their own homes and if they had any outstanding debts. Such questions, in my limited experience of Court practice, were never put to the accused before the case had been heard.

The Germans' accusations included entering and stealing from five German stores, the military wood store, the Provision Stores at Market Halls, the Market meat stalls, the Grain Stores in Hospital Lane and the Organisation Todt Food Supply Stores.

Police Sergeant Jack Harper was accused of being the instigator of the various raids on German Military and Organisation Todt food supplies. He was likened to being the 'Managing Director' of the operation to systematically plunder large quantities of German Army foodstuffs. From the civilian populations point of view, of course he and the rest of our Policemen were heroes.

Apparently they regularly broke into the Organisation Todt Food store during the hours of curfew. They used either a car key, a piece of metal, or a penknife to pick the lock. They helped themselves to tins of meat, boxes of butter, lard, sausages and bones. On a number of occasions they used the Police car to carry away their 'booty!' Some of the proceeds of the raids were shared out amongst themselves and other colleagues and some was taken to Sergeant Harper's flat in the High Street. A lot was passed on to Steve Duquemin who owned the Victoria Hotel. Any surplus was buried in the garden of Sergeant Harper's aunt.

The Germans had 'thoughtfully' provided the Police Station with a key to their cold store at the Market Halls and this was used on several occasions. Considerable quantities of meat and butter had been obtained from these 'raids'.

The grain store in Hospital Lane, was broken into on several occasions and each time the lock expertly forced. On one visit a sack of grain was 'acquired' and Sergeant Fred Duquemin transported it back to the Police Station in the police car.

Inevitably the Germans found all the police officers, with the exception of Ted Pill, guilty. Guilty in my view, of doing their duty as Colonel Britton urged them, of sabotaging the German army of occupation by any means possible. Jack Harper was sentenced by their Military Tribunal to four and a half years hard labour. The other police officers were sentenced to terms of imprisonment from four years down to four weeks, some with hard labour.

To add to the injustice, ten of those found guilty by the Military Tribunal were, on German instructions, brought before our Police Court on charges relating to the original convictions. The Germans provided twenty seven pages of statements which the Feldgendarmerie had 'extracted' from the ex- police officers.

When the case against the police officers was opened, the Court was cleared and the evidence heard in camera. The ten men were remitted for trial by the Royal Court, where they were all convicted, with the exception of Police Constable Bill Burton, and sentenced to further terms of imprisonment with hard labour. The proprietor of the Victoria Hotel, Steve Duquemin was also jailed for nine months with hard labour, although he was over seventy.

The Royal Court was presided over by the Bailiff, Victor Carey. I felt sad that the dignity of our Court, which in the past we had all held in such high regard, could be besmirched in this way and that the Bailiff, our first citizen, could be part of the travesty. No doubt the Germans insisted that the trial be held and so add credibility to their puppet military tribunal. I did not attempt to attend the Royal Court hearings as I did not wish to be part of the farce.

Inspector Sculpher who had been arrested in March, soon after he was dismissed as Inspector of Police, was held at Fort George until the end of the Royal Court 'trial' in early June, before being released. He was not charged with any crime by either the German or the Island Authorities. He and his wife were later deported to Germany and spent the rest of the war in captivity.

On the 30th July 1942, a letter was received by the President of the Police Committee, from the German Authorities stating that Penal Proceedings were pending against Inspector Langmead and that he was to be immediately relieved of his duties. So barely five months after he had been appointed to take charge of the Island Police Force, Inspector Langmead was dismissed. He was convicted by the Germans of receiving and sentenced to one month's imprisonment. Acting Deputy Inspector Lamy, who had only a short time before, been a Sergeant, was appointed Acting Inspector and took charge of the Force. There can never have been such rapid promotion !

During the occupation of the island by the Germans, I did everything I could to distance myself from them, their rules and their regulations. I was totally against any form of collaboration, we were at war and there was nothing that I was going to do to help them if it could be avoided.

We were all issued with Identity Cards and required to carry them at all times. I deliberately left mine at home and from time to time was in trouble as a consequence. When they came to our home, either officially or unofficially, I would never invite them in. Indeed both Mabs and I were very firm and short with them in order to protect our privacy. As far as business was concerned it was impossible to avoid them. They brought their cycles into the Smith Street shop for repair. I did what I had to do, certainly no more and as often as possible, nothing at all if I could get away with it. I had been 'instructed' by the President of the Controlling Committee, John Leale to repair their motorcycles. This I did, but very unwillingly.

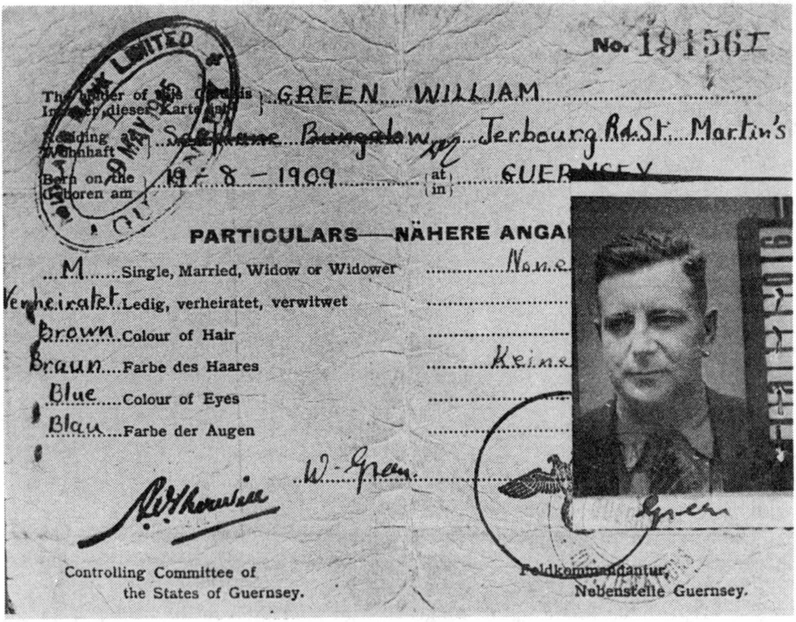
No. 19156I

The holder of this Card is / Inhaber dieser Karte ist: GREEN WILLIAM

Residing at / Wohnhaft: ~~Sea... Bungalow~~ Jerbourg Rd St. Martin's

Born on the / Geboren am: 19-8-1909 (at / in) GUERNSEY

PARTICULARS—NÄHERE ANGA...

M ... Single, Married, Widow or Widower ... None

Verheiratet ... Ledig, verheiratet, verwitwet

Brown ... Colour of Hair

Braun ... Farbe des Haares ... Keine

Blue ... Colour of Eyes

Blau ... Farbe der Augen

W. Green

Controlling Committee of the States of Guernsey.

Feldkommandantur, Nebenstelle Guernsey.

Occupation Identity Card. The Midland Bank stamp was added when Reichmarks were exchanged for Guernsey currency on liberation day.

There was an officious little German soldier from their H.K.P. Transport office who often came to inspect the work we were carrying out to their motorcycles. He would walk into Dr Bostock's garage, or the shop and say 'Heil Hitler' and we would respond by saying 'Heil Churchill'. That was my and my staff's way of showing dissent and, in fairness to our little German bureaucrat, he took it in good part.

A namesake of mine, but not related, was not so fortunate. Mrs Winifred Green worked at the Royal Hotel and a feud developed between her and and the Swiss chef, who was very pro German. He would greet her with;

"Good morning Mrs Green, Heil Hitler."

"Good morning Chef, Heil Churchill" was the response.

Eventually the Swiss Chef reported Mrs Green to the German authorities and she was arrested for insulting the Fuhrer. She was tried and sentenced to six months in prison. She served her sentence in Caen jail, on the continent, before returning to the island. When the news spread that Mrs Green had been been jailed, a considerable number of people came and sympathised with me because they thought it was Mabs.

Germans would come into the shop and demand that their bicycles be repaired. They would get into a frightful tizzy if they did not get what they wanted.

I remember young Herbert Winterflood working on a puncture, while the German, who had brought it in waited. Herbert was taking the tube out so that he could repair it when it tore. The German soldier almost went blue with rage. One of our Guernsey policemen, Sergeant Ted Pill, happened to be in the shop at the time and he quickly stepped in to defend our young mechanic. The German was really letting rip and threatening all sorts of dire punishments.

Ted Pill stood up to him,

"I am from the local police" he said. "It was an accident, so don't start going on about it. If you want to make anything of it, go and report it to your own German Authorities."

Fortunately the German calmed down, but I was never quite sure what was going to happen next. That was just one of many examples of how well our police protected their own islanders.

During the early months of the occupation a number of Germans officers came to me trying to buy my little bike that hung over the shop. That was the bike that Dad had made for me before the first war and which had become a landmark in Smith Street. One or two Germans become very insistent that I take it down and sell it to them. Fortunately I was able to fob them off, but I realised that I might not always be so lucky. There was no way that I was going to part with my little bike. So I removed it and hid it in the back store, amongst the oil drums. That little bike was of great sentimental value to me then and still is today.

Some of the 'Germans' who came into the shop were not in fact Germans, they were other nationals who had been forced to join Hitler's army and wear its uniform. I can remember one such soldier, he was a Georgian and was openly anti German. He would occasionally come into the shop, pick up a piece of chalk and indicate by drawing on the bench where the various armies were and what was happening. His English was very limited, but he did an excellent job with the piece of chalk.

Two German soldiers came into the shop one day and announced,

"We have orders to take you down to the Albion Hotel."

"What for ?" I enquired.

"We have instructions that you have to come with us."

I was escorted by these two armed Germans through the streets of St Peter Port. Anyone who saw me must have thought that I had been arrested, as indeed I believed. When we reached the hotel, I was marched upstairs and shown into a room, where sitting behind a large desk was a well decorated German officer. He was a pretty heftily built man, whom I recognised immediately. He dismissed the two henchmen and said:

"You, Mr Green, are the premier motor racing man of Guernsey?

"No I am not, I am the motorcycle racing man."

"Ah," he said, "I have the wrong man, who then is the most important motor racing person in Guernsey ?"

"He has left the island for the war."

Mr Green, you don't know who I am?"

"Yes I do," I said

"You do? Who am I?"

"You are Hans Von Stuck, Germany's leading racing driver."

"How do you know that ?"

"I was at Donington Park in 1937 when you crashed into a wild deer. You got out of your Auto Union car and stood right alongside me."

Although I had not been involved in motor racing, it had always fascinated me. I think that I would have recognised most of the racing drivers of the day.

"Well I never." he said, and offered to shake hands with me.

"I am sorry Sir, I can't shake hands with you."

"I respect that," he said, "is there anything you want, is there anything I can do for you, please accept this as being genuine."

"There is nothing you can do for me, thank you".

"You don't want anything?"

"No Sir." I was dismissed.

I was in the shop one day when a German soldier came in and asked me if I wanted some petrol. Well of course I wanted petrol, by that time it was totally unobtainable as far as the civilian population were concerned. When we repaired German motorcycles we always took the opportunity, where possible, of helping ourselves to some of the petrol in the tanks. You couldn't, you dare not take very much, perhaps half a cup full. Any petrol I 'won' was used to run a primus stove we had at home for cooking.

This German explained that he was in charge of a petrol pump, at Guernsey Motors, which was adjacent to the Picquet House in those days. He said that if I would like to go there during the lunch hour, he would sell me half a gallon of petrol. He emphasised that I would have to keep a sharp eye open, in case there were any German officers, or indeed other soldiers around. I was a bit cautious of this offer, although I was desperate for any petrol that I could lay my hands on.

I soon discovered that my little German, he was called Hans, was a communist and very anti Hitler. He took the view,- down with the British army,- down with the German army, down with the American army,- down with any army except the Russians. Hans was hoping that they were going to win the war, in fact he was longing for the day. But for the present he would do anything he could to bring down the German army.

I took him up on his offer and went down to the Picquet House about once a week to collect some of Hans illegal petrol. When it came to paying for the petrol I found that he was a Communist with capitalist ideas about its price. However the price to me did not matter too much, as the petrol was so valuable.

I enquired how he 'obtained' the petrol he was selling me. He explained that the pump was hand cranked and instead of turning the handle right over, he would turn it back and save a drop of petrol out of every gallon. As all the 'Official' petrol was supplied against paperwork, he had no difficulty in accounting for his stock. From that explanation I suspected that I was not his only Black Market customer.

It was during the summer when I started 'dealing' with Hans and I noticed he always had his electric fire switched on in his little office. This was at a time when islanders were allowed little or no electricity.

"What's the fire on for, Hans ?" I asked.

"Use up the oil, make the war finish."

"Good idea." I said.

I went down there in the winter, Hans had no fire and he was wearing his overcoat, buttoned right up to the neck.

"Where's the fire, Hans ?' I enquired.

"The bloody thing burnt out!" and added "and there isn't a replacement element to be found anywhere in Europe".

Hans went back to Germany on leave and my supply of petrol was interrupted. When he returned to the island he came up to the shop.

"No petrol, no more petrol." he said regretfully.

"No ?" I commented.

"No, my wife has gone off with another man and I am in trouble."

"Oh well, you know Hans, there are plenty more fish in the sea."

"Oh yes, but that is not the point, my wife knows I am a Communist."

He was petrified, but that was his worry, not mine. However, I think his worry was justified, because it turned out that his wife had gone off with a Nazi. She must have spilt the beans, because it wasn't long afterwards that Hans disappeared and so did my supply of petrol. The Germans did not like Communists any better than Jews.

As the shortage of fuel of all descriptions became apparent, the interest in possible deposits of peat at Grande Mare, Vazon, increased. It was known that islanders had dug and used peat for fuel in earlier days, so it was not very long before a trial digging took place on Steve Duquemin's race course near Vazon beach.

Exploratory digging started during September 1940 and at one time there was a gang of nearly twenty men employed. They dug through the surface, which was sand and shale and at a depth of about three feet found a mixture of peat and clay. Further excavation revelled pure Peat at a depth of about ten feet.

I cycled down to see what was happening and found that a number of pits had been dug and a considerable quantity of peat excavated. Workmen were carving out the peat into blocks about ten inches square by six inches deep. Each block was transferred to a wheelbarrow with what looked like a hay fork. The peat was then wheeled away and stacked in pyramid fashion, so that it could dry by exposure to the sun and the wind. There were several large mounds of peat which had already been dug.

Newly dug peat resembled and smelt like rich manure, very dark in colour with a fibre consistency. Some of the blocks appeared to contain small parts of a tree trunk or branches - it is miraculous how nature preserves these prehistoric trees for so long.

After the peat had been dried sufficiently, it proved to be an excellent fuel, providing the large lumps were broken up before they were placed on a wood or a coal fire. The pieces of peat I burnt soon started to glow red and threw out a good heat. I found that burning peat had a very pleasant aroma.

Peat was widely used, particularly in schools and other States establishments. The Intermediate School was always desperately short of fuel, and it was only with the addition of a fairly generous supply of peat from the Grande Mare that they managed to remain open.

In the winter of 1941 dried peat went on sale at Helman's Brickfield and they were literally besieged by potential customers. Islanders with sacks and every form of carrier purchased, in two days, the total supply that was planned to last for months.

The German police, the Feldgendarmerie used to wear a plate across their chests, a huge big plate with a chain, to identify themselves. Inevitably they were often refereed to as the chain gang. One day a German policeman brought one of these plates into the Smith Street shop and asked me to shorten the chain for him. I suggested that he leave it with me and call back for it later in the day. Quite surprisingly he left it, his symbol of office and badge of authority.

After he left the shop, I put his plate on and went out into Smith Street. Opposite was the German bookshop, called Frontbuchhandlung, and two sailors were looking into the window where there was displayed a Nazi sign and a huge portrait of Hitler.

I stood on the pavement outside my shop and shouted:

"Nein Verbieten".

The two sailors turned around and just stood and looked at me, so I tapped the plate vigorously with my finger. I did it as a joke and thought that they would also see the funny side. But no, they smartly performed the heil Hitler salute and marched off up the street. It made me chuckle to see these two Germans obey my command. Even during the occupation, I never lost my sense of fun and devilment.

In all occupied countries, the Black Market flourished and Guernsey was no exception. With the introduction of rationing and price control it was inevitable that a Black Market would result. Farmers and others with surplus items, such as butter or eggs easily fell to the temptations of a better financial return, by selling to islanders who wanted more than the meagre ration provided.

There were two main sources of supply for the Black Market, the farmers and the French sailors who crewed the boats from France and brought with them quantities of butter, eggs and saccharine. Wealthy islanders and those at work, obtained additional supplies on the black market. It was the unfortunate people who lived on retirement pay, often on their own, who had few friends and who were not strong enough to stand in queues or walk long distances, who found it difficult to obtain extra food on the black market.

I readily admit that I obtained extra supplies, whenever the opportunity occurred, subject of course to being able to afford the price. In the shop I would get a lot of offers, sometimes to buy goods, but often in return for services we were able to offer our customers. I recall the time when one of the foreign workers came into the shop and haggled over the price of a repair we had carried out to his cycle. He wanted to barter, and pulled a string of sausages out of his trousers. We never bothered in those days where the food came from, as long as it was edible.

For a time we received a supply of butter from one of the Under Officers attached to the HKP Transport. Fritz, as we called him, came to check that we were carrying out the repairs to the motorcycles satisfactorily. Often he brought us some butter, which no doubt was his way of rewarding us for the work we were doing.

I can remember one occasion, there was one small pack of butter over after every member of the staff had received a share of Fritz's latest supply. George Cave, Gordon Stabb and I were standing outside the entrance to Dr Bostock's garage with this packet of butter, discussing how we were going to share it between us. Just then a little old lady appeared, walking up Forest Lane carrying her almost empty shopping basket. I walked towards her and as we passed, I dropped the packet of butter into her basket. She did not even notice what I had done and continued walking on up Ann's Place. I have often wondered what were her thoughts and reaction when she reached home and found that packet of butter. I hope that she enjoyed it because butter was very scarce at the time.

A chap came into to my shop one day and inquired;

"Bill, do you want some meat?"

"Yes sure." It was the automatic answer to that sort of question.

"Tonight after four o'clock, keep the shop door open."

The Germans decreed that all shops in town had to shut at 4 pm.

"Hang on a bit tonight boys" I said to my staff "I'm supposed to be getting some meat."

We shared everything, life was like that, there was no selfishness amongst the local population. We would do the Germans down if we possibly could, but as islanders we stuck together.

So just after closing time, along comes this chap with a hand cart and almost half a cow, all covered over with sheeting. He ran up the passageway and into our workshop. We closed the door behind him. Where he obtained this cow and how he had managed to transport it through the streets, in broad daylight, under the noses of the Germans, I had no idea and I certainly did not want to know.

We all set to with hacksaws, chisels and God knows what, to carve up the carcass. We were mechanics not butchers and the results clearly showed our lack of butchering skills. The mess was unbelievable, but we all acquired some precious meat. The rest of the meat was put back on the hand cart, suitably covered and our benefactor set off to visit his next customer.

My share was a nice big chunk of meat which I took home to Mabs. We thoroughly enjoyed it. After a week or so the cow was missed and our benefactor was hauled up before the German Police. He confessed that he had killed the cow and told the Germans how he had shared out the prized animal. He admitted that he supplied me with some of the meat, but fortunately did not involve my staff.

It was not long, before I was ordered to report to the German Police Headquarters at Grange Lodge. With some considerable trepidation I presented myself at the prescribed time. I was immediately locked up in a room with all the other known recipients of the meat. One by one we were taken out for interrogation. What mystified me was that no one returned. As I sat there waiting my turn all sorts of possibilities went through my mind. Were we going to be sent to prison on the continent without being able to tell our families, were we being put in cells to await sentence ?

The Germans threatened the most severe punishments for Black Marketeers, and without doubt, we were Black Marketeers. Whatever my fate, the Germans had me worried. The long wait, was no doubt, all part of their psychological approach and it certainly worked on me.

My turn for interrogation came. I was marched into an office where a German, who spoke excellent English, was sitting behind a typewriter. He asked the questions and with one finger, typed my answers onto the form in the typewriter. He wanted to know everything about me, my family, my mother's name, my father's name, their ages, my uncles and aunts, how old I was, where I lived, the colour of my eyes, every last detail. All this information was typed onto the form as fast as his one finger typing would allow. No wonder we had been keep locked up for so long! The wheels of German justice ground exceedingly slow.

Finally he gets around to asking about the meat.

"How much meat did you have ?"

"Two or three pounds, I suppose."

"Only two or three pounds ?"

"Yes, about that."

"You are sure that is all ?" he said.

"Yes."

"Well then, what did you do with it, Mr Green ?"

"Well I had a bit of bad luck."

He inquired "What do you mean, bad luck ?"

I explained "I tied it on the back of my bicycle and when I got home I had lost it."

My German inquisitor burst out laughing. What he typed on his form I do not know, but he enjoyed my story.

I said to him, "Well what's going to happen?"

"This report will go to Paris for your sentence. You may go. You can go down that way."

I was directed out, not by the door I had entered, but by a rear door which exited out at the back of the building. That was why none of my fellow 'Black Marketeers' had reappeared.

Teddie Zabiela who had also been interrogated about the missing cow, came to see me. Normally he was a very nervous person, and this episode had really scared him.

"What's going to happen to us, Bill ?" he asked anxiously.

"Well Teddie" I said, "The papers have been sent to Paris and god knows what will happen."

"We are going to get sent away, I know it." said a petrified Teddie

After about two months, during which time I think we all sweated a bit more than usual, we were called back to Grange Court to hear our sentences. This time we had to report at about quarter of an hour intervals, in alphabetical order. This German, the one with the one finger typing ability, was there and referred to his papers and said;

"Mr Green, you are fined twenty Reichmarks, please pay now."

I nearly said, 'Thank you very much, I would like some more at that price'! Two pounds five shillings, I had expected a much bigger fine. I was given my change in half crowns, coins which I had not handled for a considerable time. Our coinage had rapidly disappeared and we were trading in Reichmarks and Pfennigs.

On my way back to the shop, I met Teddie Zabiela going to keep his appointment - with his name he was inevitably the last. He was extremely worried and apprehensive.

"No worry." I said "Twenty marks fine."

"Thank Christ." he said, and brightened up.

I next saw Teddie in the Town a few days later,

"How did it go ?" I asked.

"Forty five bloody quid." he said.

"But why so much Teddie ?"

"Well," he said " they added up all the bits of cow you chaps said you had, and as I was the last person, I was charged for all the missing portions."

Teddie apparently had to sit there while the German added up all the fines he had collected from other recipients of the meat. Then he deducted that total from what he was required to collect by way of fines and that was what poor Teddie had to pay. Teddie was the last man in and paid for every bit of the cow that was missing. Life was like that during the German occupation.

Early in 1942 the German Authorities notified the Controlling Committee that they required one hundred and fifty mens cycles in full working order. Jurat John Leale accepted that under the Hague convention the Germans were entitled to requisition cycles. I was asked to help in organising the collection of the cycles and to do so in a way which would cause the minimum inconvenience to the civilian population.

With the help of the staff of the Civil Transport Department, I set about collecting the cycles. Some bikes left behind by the evacuating islanders were collected from houses, others were provided by traders. The police also had a number of unclaimed machines and altogether we got hold of ninety seven bicycles. The Germans were prepared to pay for them and I was given the task of valuing them jointly with a German officer.

This officer, I discovered, was in civilian life a cycle dealer in Frankfurt. We recorded details of the cycles, their registration plate number and the price agreed. The owners were eventually paid the value we set. When we couldn't agree about a machines value, that machine was put aside and the German officer suggested that I could bring in one of my staff to settle the matter. Artie Selous became the arbitrator, mainly agreeing with my valuations. The officer accepted Artie's decisions without hesitation.

Later in the week the German officer came into the shop and presented Artie and me, with a kilo of French sugar each. Our only payment for the work we had done at the request of the States Controlling Committee.

On another occasion I was requested by the Controlling Committee to requisition thirty civilian motor bikes. I was given a list of registration numbers and the addresses of the owners. The requisitioned machines went to the Germans. The Germans paid for any machines they 'acquired', so I had to agree a value with their owners.

I set about this task with Artie Selous. We went to each owner on the list and tried to reach agreement with them for the purchase of the motorcycle. The fact that all the machines were laid up and off the road meant that, by and large, the owners were only too pleased to sell them. The money I was able to offer was good. For a machine that was worth £40 before the war, I offered £50. As most of the owners could do with the money, Artie and I had little difficulty in agreeing terms.

When we approached Eddie Robins about selling his motorcycle, he said;

"I don't want my blessed bike going to those bastards, what is more I am surprised you are doing this job for the Germans, Bill."

"Well perhaps you are right Eddie, but I have had instructions from the States, so I suppose I had better do it. But if you don't want your motor bike going to the Germans, do the same as I have done with my car".

"What's that?" inquired Eddie.

"I have stuck it under bales of hay in a barn."

"Can I do that ?"

"Well I can report that I have been to your place and you have told me that your son took it away with him when he left the island."

"If you are prepared to say that Bill, I'm prepared to stick to the story."

So that was one motorcycle the Germans didn't get, Eddie Robins still had his machine at the end of the war and rode it regularly after the liberation. One or two of the motorcycles on the list were missing, because they belonged to people who had been evacuated. I tried to deal with relatives who were still in the island, but not always successfully. However I am very proud that all the motorcycles that were requisitioned were obtained by agreement and none by compulsion.

Chapter 16

ARRESTED

As the occupation progressed, spares of every description became very scarce. Walter Renouf, from the Bouvee Farm, owned an old Morris coupé car which had seen better days and was nothing more than a wreck, which should have long since been sent to the scrap yard. Walter never got around to having it removed and now, with the shortage of spares, it was valuable if only for the nuts and bolts. I bought this wreck from Walter and parked it in the field opposite La Croix, alongside a hedge where I hoped it would be out of sight.

I gradually dismantled the car and took the parts, a few at a time, down to the shop. Anything and everything was of value. The tyres on the Morris were in reasonably good condition and as I had no immediate use for them, I just left the them leaning against the body of the car. The Germans issued an order that all tyres had to be handed over to the Civil Transport Depot by a certain date. I ignored as many German orders as I could, including that one. I didn't bother to report these tyres, as I thought that they would not be noticed anyway.

Herbert Quevatre, who lived across from us at Les Faitieres and cultivated the field in which my old car was parked, met Mabs one afternoon when she returned form her daily walk with Margaret. Herbert told her that he had seen a German help himself to two of the old car tyres and walk off with them down past the military barrier at the Monument Tavern. Mabs who would never let the Germans get away with anything without a fight, went up to the barrier and demanded that the guard fetch someone who could speak English. The guard picked up the telephone and after a brief conservation in German, which she did not understand, Mabs and little Margaret were marched up Monument Hill to the German Command Post at Les Divettes. This was a large house, later to be renamed the Dolphins, which the German used to control all their activities on the Jerbourg Peninsular.

Mabs was shown into the hall where she explained, most forceably, to an English speaking officer that her husband's tyres had been stolen by one of his men. The officer listened to her complaint and then went off to made some telephone calls. While Mabs and Margaret waited, German heads appeared around opened doors. Clearly they wanted to see who she was and what she wanted. Other people would have been scared, but not Mabs. When the German officer returned he apologised, but said it couldn't possibly be one of his men, they wouldn't do a thing like that. But if he found that someone had taken them, he would ensure that the tyres were returned. He told Mabs that if he did find them, they would be left at the barrier. She could come back next day to see if they were there.

When I came home from the shop, Mabs told me the whole story. I was proud of the way she had stood up to the Germans. It took some courage, but that was typical of Mabs.

A short while later a German, a nasty little man from the Feldgendarmerie at Grange Lodge, appeared at our door, pushed past us and sat down in our 'radio' armchair. Normally we avoided using that chair so I was alarmed to see this Jerry sitting in it. I reckoned that I was probably in enough trouble with the tyres, without the possibility of the radio being found. The German said that the tyres had been found and returned. He then asked, in perfect English, if they were my tyres. There was no alternative but to admit that they belonged to me. Then he gleefully enquired why had they not been handed in to the Civil Transport Depot, as had been decreed.

I attempted to brazen it out, saying that I had reported their existence to the Depot and that they had been recorded but not collected. He said that he would check up and no doubt that I would be hearing more about the matter. I was, of course worried, once again I was in trouble as a result of ignoring a German order.

After curfew, when it was dark, I nipped across the fields to see Ted Laker and told him of my problem. He promised to do what he could to help. He went to his office early the next morning and tore up two or three tyre lists and rewrote new ones, with my entry included. The list now showed that I had reported the tyres but, as I had no transport, they had not been delivered to the depot. Civil Transport had not been able to collect them, so it was their mistake.

The nasty little German returned the next evening, walked in and again sat down in our 'radio' armchair. He said;

"I would like to forget all about the tyres, but I can't."

Mabs felt that he was trying to blackmail us, possibly to make friends with us, or that he wanted payment. Now that I knew that Ted had 'modified' the official records, I felt in a much stronger position.

I said; "Why don't you go down to the Civil Transport Depot and check the records ?"

Inevitably this German went down to check the lists. Ted Laker was expecting him and asked what authority he had to inspect the records and insisted on telephoning the Feldgendarmerie Headquarters at Grange Lodge. Whilst Ted was on the phone, the German disappeared and never came back. I heard no more. Dear old Ted Laker had got me out of trouble, bless him.

One day two soldiers came to our home and tried to 'borrow' Mabs bicycle. The Germans had acquired a lot of cycles by this brazen approach. I was sitting on the toilet when they approached Mabs and I heard her say;

"No - I am British, you are German, please go."

I rushed out just in time to see the Germans bowing and one of them said, "Thank you." They clicked their heels and off they went. If you stood up to them, the average German respected you for it. Mabs always stood up to the Germans, perhaps even more than I did. Several other attempts were made to 'borrow' her bicycle, all unsuccessful.

During the occupation, Mabs and I had many skirmishes with Germans who came to the house. Mabs, because I was at work or off on one of my many activities, would often have to deal with them on her own.

Early one evening around Christmas time, Mabs was alone in the house with Margaret when she heard the sound of jack boots coming up the path. There were two Germans who were obviously drunk. Her immediate inclination was to lock the door, but realised that when she had earlier returned from her walk, she had left the key on the outside of the door. She went out and confronted these two Germans and surreptitiously took the key from the outside of the door and transferred it, to the inside. Her action was seen by one of the drunken Germans who, reacted by aiming the bottle he was carrying, at Mabs. She luckily managed to dodge the bottle and succeeded in getting the door between herself and her attacker. The German again smashed down the bottle, this time it shattered the glass in the door.

Fortunately the Germans went away and didn't cause any further trouble, but Mabs was scared.

On another occasion, when it was pitch black outside, we heard noises around the rear of the house. I went to the back door and slowly opened it to see if I could see anything. A drunken German soldier, carrying a live rabbit by it's ears, pushed past me and staggered into the kitchen. He slowly progressed through the kitchen, into the hallway and was apparently making for our sitting room. When he had almost reached the sitting room, I opened the front door, put my foot behind him, gave him a push and he sailed out into the front garden. I slammed the door and that was the last we saw of that German. Our uninvited visitor had, however, dropped his rabbit when I booted him out the front door. We thoroughly enjoyed it!

One evening we were having our evening meal in the kitchen, when we heard what we thought was a German voice coming from Margaret's bedroom. I went to investigate and sure enough there was a German leaning over her cot giving Margaret chocolate. Apparently this German spotted Margaret through her bedroom window, standing up in her cot. He came into the house and gave her some of his chocolate ration. Obviously he was very fond of children.

I enticed him out of her bedroom and as I ushered him towards the front door he looked longingly into the lounge. I could read his mind, he just wanted to sit down and be friendly - the temptation was for me to weaken. He was probably a married man, missing his own children and family back home in Germany.

"I am sorry," I said, "this is war and you are German, please don't give my child chocolate. Thank you for the kindness." I don't know how much he understood, but I ushered him out.

Mabs and I refused to entertain Germans in our home, but some islanders did.

A near neighbour, Betty Osborne, regularly entertained Germans in her home. They in their turn provided her with entertainment. Late one evening there was a piano accordion being played by a Jerry in the road outside the front of her house. It was after curfew and was just getting dark. I put my head out of the window to see if I could discover what all the noise was about. What I saw was Edgar Stacey's head sticking out of his window. His house was between mine and Betty Osborne's.

I enquired; "What's this all about Edgar ?"

"I don't know," he replied "All I know is, it will wake up my son."

"It will wake up Margaret as well if it goes on like this, I'll slip over."

So I went over to Edgar's house and we could see this Jerry playing his accordion just over the hedge. I picked up a sod of turf from Edgar's lawn and I threw it high up into the air and over the hedge. It must have landed right on the piano accordion, because one moment it was producing its terrible sound and the next it was silent. There were some German swear words, which by this time I had learnt to recognise, and then two or three Germans started running up and down the road, looking for the culprit.

It was to our advantage that they did not know from which direction the sod of turf had come. Clearly we had to make ourselves scarce, so Edgar and I ran down the back of our gardens and hid amongst Cecil Hardwick's greenhouses. In our haste to depart the scene, Edgar and I became separated. For a considerable time I heard the tramp of German boots, obviously looking for us. Eventually everything went quiet so I started to venture towards home. As I slowly and silently crept around corners, I realized that somebody else doing the same thing. For a long time I could not decide whether it was a Jerry looking for me, or Edgar. Finally I recognised Edgar and together we crept back home. Fortunately we heard no more of that little episode.

Germans troops were continually holding manoeuvres of one sort or another.

They regularly held exercises in the Jerbourg area. A machine gun post would be set up in our front garden, outside the lounge window. That position provided them with a commanding view of the field opposite. German troops advancing across the field would be fired upon by the machine gunner, using blanks. Unbeknown to the Germans there was the remains of an old fence wire, largely hidden by long grass, at about ankle height, across the gap in the hedge where they entered the field. Mabs took great delight in watching Germans trip and fall flat on their faces as they set off to race across the field. After they had completed their exercise Mabs always ensured that the 'trip wire' was properly replaced. Mabs regarded this as free live entertainment and always looked forward to the encore.

The noise of the machine gun was very frightening for Margaret, so Mabs tried to keep her out of the way when the gun was being fired. However, Margaret, who was by this time a toddler, enjoyed collecting the empty cartridge cases which were scattered all over the path and garden.

Secret photograph of German troops marching past La Croix in the Jerbourg Road.

Many of the German Military activities were more than mere exercises or manoeuvres. Large quantities of mines and roll bombs were laid all around the island and Jerbourg was no exception. They sought to make the headland impregnable, as they feared the possibility of another seaborne landing. The garden of the house opposite us, Les Faitieres, where the Quevatre's lived during the early part of the occupation, was mined. The mines were planted to within a few feet of the terrace steps. After the Quevatre's left, Mabs and I would often go and sit on their terrace and enjoy the magnificent view over the south coast cliffs, which were out of bounds to all civilians.

On one occasion Mabs had gone over to sit on the terrace and enjoy the sun while Margaret played with her ball. There was a wire along the edge of the terrace, which indicated the extent of the minefield. Margaret threw the ball over the wire and it bounced into the fish pond which was within the minefield. Margaret started yelling for her ball, as children have a habit of doing, and Mabs was understandably very reluctant to retrieve it. Then she noticed the overgrown brick path leading to the fish pond, which she assumed was not mined. Mabs very gingerly tip toed down the path and recovered Margaret's ball, much to her delight!

The Vauroufs field, which lies between Gipsy Lane and the cliffs, was divided into two by the Germans. The area nearest the cliffs was heavily mined. One Good Friday morning we were having breakfast, when we heard a series of explosions. They came from the direction of Bouvee Farm and the Vauroufs field. Soon military vehicles were dashing back and forth to the area.

A German, who was part of a team planting mines in the field, had apparently dropped one and was killed, when it exploded. Other soldiers who were injured, panicked and ran through the mine field trying to escape. Inevitably they set off more mines, and more Germans were killed. Later a party of high ranking officers visited the scene and made a detailed inspection of the area. As soon as they had left, Mabs and I went to see the devastation that the exploding mines had caused.

In a field just up the road from La Croix the Germans established a cemetery and mortuary. The concrete access road to the cemetery is now the Le Baugy Estate Road. About one third of the way into the field, they constructed a mortuary, with big double glazed doors. If there had been an air raid, or some other incident, I would take an evening walk up to the mortuary and on tip toe, look through the windows to see how many coffins there were.

It was part of our wartime entertainment to see these German cheap plywood coffins all draped with Nazi flags and on occasions some even appeared to have blood dripping from them. The floor was covered with sawdust, which clearly showed signs of blood.

As islanders, we were delighted to see the mortuary full of dead Germans, that meant that there were fewer German soldiers to fight the allies. We were also happy to hear the sound of rifle volleys, when they fired three shots over the graves, at funerals. Sadly at the time, that is the effect the German occupation of our island had upon us. After the war all the remains were cleared from the Cemetery, many of them being repatriated to Germany.

Mabs had a regular walk, that she took Margaret - along the Jerbourg Road, down the lane adjacent to the cemetery, which now leads to the house called Gulls Green and then back along Gipsy Lane to the Bouvee and home. Sometimes when they walked along the hedge bounding the cemetery they could see and hear the funerals taking place. Margaret loved to listen to the band, which played the music for the short service.

On one occasion Mabs and Margaret witnessed the funeral of nine Georgians, who had died as a result of eating poisonous berries. First the service was held in German and then it was translated into Russian. The Georgians volunteered for service in the German Army and many of them came to the island. They wore distinctive flashes on the shoulders of their uniforms, but we learnt to recognise them in other ways as well. A column of marching Germans would often pass our house and they could be heard singing in their guttural way. A column of marching Georgians would sing in a much more jolly, merry fashion, there was no way of mistaking them.

As a family we were extremely fortunate right throughout the occupation. There were many times when we thought we were going to starve, particularly near the end. But looking back now, I think it is fair to say that in fact we were probably a long way from starvation. For a number of reasons, we were certainly luckier than a great many of our fellow islanders. I had a number of friends in the country parishes and cycled out occasionally at weekends to see some of them, sometimes collecting milk here and an egg there. We had a small garden so we were able to grow some vegetables and for part of the occupation, Cecil Hardwick allowed me to grow potatoes in one of his glasshouses. Also, being in an essential trade, the cycle trade, meant that I was sometimes paid in kind of some sort. If I repaired a farmers cycle he would, as often as not, bring me root vegetables or something edible.

A kindly man who lived on the Jerbourg Road kept hens and sometimes he would send an egg down for Margaret. The island authorities ensured that every child had a ration of full cream milk each day throughout most of the occupation. Adults were only allowed skimmed milk.

Despite all the shortages and what must have been a totally unbalanced diet, our general health during that period, was surprisingly good. We acclimatised ourselves to eating less and that in itself was good for our health. Islanders didn't become ill nearly so often or as easily as we had done pre-war, or indeed since. Diseases such as measles or mumps were almost unheard of during the occupation. Our lack of contact with the outside world meant that the common illnesses from which we normally suffered, just like any other community, were no longer imported.

I lost a stone or so in weight, which was a lot less than many islanders. In many ways our wellbeing was due to Mabs ingenuity and foresight. Prior to and during the early months of the occupation Mabs had built up a reasonable stock of tinned food and this stood us in good stead for some time. There wasn't, however, much hoarding by anyone because no one had much left after a while.

Fred Veale, who lived in the house at the junction of Jerbourg Road with the path that leads to the Petit Port steps, had a reasonable stock of tinned food at the start of the occupation. In order that it was not requisitioned or stolen, he decided to hide a considerable part of his reserve. So he buried it behind some outbuildings in his garden. When the Germans installed the Strassburg Gun adjacent to the Doyle Monument, they built some big underground bunkers. The excavated soil from the bunkers was tipped to form a mound in Fred's garden, right on top of where he had buried his precious tinned food. The mound and no doubt Fred's precious tinned food, is there to this day.

Fred Veale's house, Vue des Isles, before having first floor permanently removed to provide clear line of fire for Strassburg gun, seen on skyline.

But the food was not the only possession that Fred lost. His house, Vue de Iles, commanded magnificent views of the surrounding area and the neighbouring islands. From his upstairs windows Fred could see for miles and the view gave him many hours of enjoyment. Because of the need for a clear field of fire for their Strassburg Gun, the Germans demolished the first floor of Fred Veale's house. Today it is a one storey bungalow and it is still called Vue de Iles, although its former magnificent view no longer exists.

As food and many other items became scarce, Mabs like every other housewife spent long hours in queues - it became a way of life. Fish was one of the last items of food to be rationed and to stand a chance of getting any, Mabs queued for hours in the Fish Market. There were occasions when having stood in a queue half the morning she came away with nothing.

It was not only food that quickly became scarce, non food shops had virtually no means of replacing the stock they sold. In 1940 the Germans came with their Reichmarks by the barrow load and bought up all the goods in the shops so that before long there was nothing left for islanders. Mabs, with her usual foresight, anticipated this happening and had bought up as much cloth and other material as she could. She made clothes for Margaret and herself right throughout the war. Mabs was a very good seamstress and as a result Margaret was one of the best dressed children in the island during the occupation years. She made Margaret a beautiful white linen dress with red smocking on it. She looked a picture in it, but Margaret hated the dress, she was happier dressed as a tomboy.

Many retailers virtually ceased to carry on their normal business and instead set themselves up as exchange or barter shops. People with items which they no longer needed, or didn't have a use for at that time, exchanged them for goods they urgently needed. The result was that these shops appeared to be well stocked, but the goods were only for exchange and not for sale. Tickets on the goods usually indicated the item for which they could be exchanged, but they were not priced. This system of bartering worked well, particularly as this exchange of goods prevented the Germans from acquiring items, which would have inevitably been send straight back to Germany.

One of the first shops to set up as a 'Barter Mart' was at 33 The Pollet, in the autumn of 1941. The Evening Press announcement said:-

> 'Bring us anything you have for exchange our charge 4d. per item for an exchange, window display 3d. extra.'

Another of the exchange shops was in the Arcade. Mabs made considerable use of this shop, doing many deals, but particularly exchanging toys for Margaret. After a time Barter Marts were turning up everywhere, at 16 Fountain Street, the Trinity Barter Mart, next to Britannia Pub, and a Barter Mart at 25 Mill Street.

The Barter shops were not the only way we found of exchanging some of our less wanted goods for items we desperately required. The Evening Press ran a special column for exchanges. It was a very popular feature, and exchanges sought included:-

> 1 cwt sugar beet for a cycle dynamo.
> 1lb tea for 16lb fresh flour.
> Duck eggs for cycle tyre and tube size 26x1.3/8".
> English cigarettes in good condition for cycle tyre 28x1.1/2".
> 1 gallon paraffin for tyre 28x1.1/2".
> 50 Bucktrouts' Specials (cigarettes) for 1lb tea.
> 100lb table carrots for 1 new outer tube 28x1.1/2".
> 28lb shallots for 14lb sugar.

Barter marts which had been so successful when they were introduced were, by the autumn of 1942, being criticised by the Police and States officials. They were described as a growing evil and an incentive to thieving. The Police said that:-

> 'In nine out of ten recent robberies some of the goods involved have been traced to barter shops'.

At the end of 1942 the States Controlling Committee published an Ordinance prohibiting transactions in barter shops, auctions and in the Exchange columns of the press, of goods listed in a long schedule. Included were, meat, sugar, margarine, potatoes, bread, tea, coffee, clothing, baby wear, shoes, cigarettes, tobacco, leather, cycles, cycle tyres and soap.

That spelt the demise of the barter shops. One or two managed to stay in business, but most just closed their doors. Auctioneers who had included many of these items in their auctions, also suffered a considerable reduction in trade. At the last auction to be held at the Bordage Auction Room, before the Price Restriction Ordinance came into force on the 15th January 1943, a half pound packet of Orange Pekoe tea fetched £7.7s.6d. Before the war it could have been purchased for 1s 5d. The man who bought it said that he had not tasted a cup of real tea since a month after the occupation began.

With the demise of the barter marts, the Black Market prospered and prices soared. Tea was to cost as much as £22 a pound before the end of the war. A pound of sugar cost £3.17.0 and butter almost £5 a pound. Eggs in 1944 were fetching 7/- each.

As fuel supplies dwindled so the task of cooking the family meals became more and more difficult. Mabs became very adept with the use of a haybox, or as some called it, a fireless cooker. The principal was that the food was brought to the boil by normal heating and then placed in the haybox to complete the cooking. By this means the minimum amount of fuel was used to cook food.

A haybox was basically a wooden box, lined with newspaper and packed with hay. The one that I made and which I believe Mabs kept hidden away in the attic of Lyndel for many years, had a hinged lid which was padded with a cushion filled with more hay. The haybox contained two cooking pots, which when the lid was closed, were totally surrounded by tightly packed hay.

Mabs brought the food she was cooking to the boil on the stove and then placed the pot in the haybox, put the cover on and replace the lid. Food placed in the haybox in the morning was cooked by supper time, but only lukewarm. We found that full cooking pots cooked better than only partially filled ones and that it was important to eat the food as soon as it was taken out of the haybox.

During the occupation coal soon became unobtainable. Electricity was cut off for part of the day and later all together. Gas was severely rationed and then totally cut off to our part of the island. The gas supply in town, however continued for a time. Mabs obtained a supply of sugar beet and brought it down to the shop where, after first cutting it up into small pieces, she boiled it to form a syrup. It took a lot of boiling but made a worthwhile quality of quite a pleasant sweet syrup which we all enjoyed.

Once or twice I managed to obtain from the Gas Company a supply of tar and charcoal which I mixed together. This concoction helped to keep our fire going and provide some heat when other fuel became almost unobtainable. Through repairing German motorcycles, I was able to 'acquire' small quantities of petrol, which was of a very low grade. This, we used in the primus stove for cooking. That of course was highly dangerous, but we had to take chances or go hungry. As the occupation progressed wood become more and more our mainstay for cooking and heating.

Fortunately we had water right through the occupation, albeit towards the end for only an hour or so each day. One of our great assets during that period was the islands' magnificent herd of Guernsey cattle. They provided the milk which was essential to our diet, although in limited quantities and as often as not only skimmed. Real coffee and tea quickly became non existent, although substitutes such as acorn coffee, were sometimes available.

Mr Pitchford who ran the Singer Sewing machine shop, produced a most acceptable substitute for tea, dried blackberry leaves. During the occupation he found it impossible to earn a living from the repair of sewing machines and his sales of new ones were non existent. He went out in the countryside and picked great quantities of blackberry leaves. He perfected a way of drying them, so that they could be used to make a substitute tea. I became used to the taste and really found it quite drinkable.

Raymond Falla and his purchasing team in France obtained considerable quantities of food, although most was rationed and the variety extremely limited. I enjoyed the Camembert cheese, which almost always was in a very ripe condition. Often we didn't have any bread to eat with it, so I ate it with potato or anything that was available. Macaroni was imported from the continent and while I ate it then, I have never touched any since.

While we went short of many things during the occupation, I find it difficult to recall what I missed most. I often dreamed about Kunzel cakes and longed for the day when they were again available in the shops. However when I eventually managed to obtain some after the liberation, I didn't like them any more, either the cakes or my taste had changed.

The Germans generally took hygiene very seriously and did everything possible to prevent the outbreak and spread of disease. Even though there were a considerable number of Todt and other foreign workers in the island, there wasn't any major illness among them. There was a scare at one time when a case of typhus was detected amongst the foreign workers. They were billeted in the Allez Street and George Street area of the town. During the typhus scare considerable quantities of lime was spread around the streets. I remember George Street being white with lime. In fairness to them, the Germans took every precaution to ensure that the disease did not spread.

An axe during that period was a very prized and valuable piece of equipment as we were chopping up all the wood we could lay our hands on. Cecil Hardwick was a carpenter by trade. One day, when I went to see him in his shed, he had just finished making an axe handle. He made a beautiful job of this handle, it was shaped and curved and had a very professional finish. Cecil fitted the handle into the head of the axe, split the end and put a wedge in to finish it off. I said to him:-

"By jove Cecil that's wonderful, that is going to be very useful."

He said, "Would you like to borrow it?"

"Yes I would, thank you."

I took the axe home, there was some wood that I wanted to chop up and set to work immediately. I placed a log on my chopping block, took a swing with Cecil's new axe and missed. The handle hit the chopping block and the head of the axe flew off. I had broken Cecil's new axe, even before he had a chance to use it himself. I went back down to Cecil's with the axe head in one hand and the handle in the other, and confessed. I will never forget his reaction, he took the axe head from me looked at it, then he took the handle and looked at that. He did not say a word. Cecil was really hurt. I would have sooner he had lost his temper and shouted at me, but he didn't, that was typical of Cecil

My love of swimming was undiminished during the occupation, although at times I was prevented by the Germans from bathing at my favourite spots. Early on, we swam in the Ladies Pool, but after a time the Germans erected a barrier at the big rock near the swimming pools, so we could only use the Gentlemen's Pool.

During the summer of 1941 I often went for a swim at lunch time. Mabs brought Margaret and we would enjoyed a picnic lunch together by the pool. Mabs pushed Margaret in her pram all the way down from Jerbourg and all the way back home again after lunch. That was some feat. When Margaret was a little older Mabs brought her down on her cycle, to which I had fitted a child's seat. Almost before she could walk, I encouraged Margaret to swim. When she was only about two, I recall swimming around the pool with her on my shoulders while she had her arms around my neck. Margaret exclaimed :-

"Don't sunk Dad! Don't sunk!"

In those days I liked to swim under water, so she probably thought that I was going to submerge with her on my shoulders. Perhaps I tried to push Margaret to learn to swim too quickly, because for a time she claimed to be terrified of the water. Later however, she became and has remained, an enthusiastic and excellent swimmer.

One of my favourite times for swimming was Sunday mornings. There was a regular band of us who swam summer and winter. This band also turned out on Christmas Day. I particularly remember my swim on Christmas morning 1941 and the events which followed. The Evening Press ran a small story headed:

XMAS DAY BATHERS.

Nine take plunge.

> 'Although the weather was mild on Xmas Day the temperature of the sea water did not rise correspondingly. Nevertheless there were nine Xmas bathers on view at the Gent's Bathing Pool, La Valette.
>
> This morning's bathe has become a regular institution, and it was enjoyed by all. Among the swimmers were two young ladies.'

After the swim I was on my way home for my Christmas dinner. Three or four of our little band, including the two girls, had reached the top of Hauteville and were finishing off a bottle Cream de Cacao, and saying our goodbyes before we went our different ways. I was leaning on the saddle of my bicycle, when somebody nudged me in the ribs. I looked up, it was a German officer, and he gestured me to move my bike out of his way. It would have only taken him a stride or two extra to walk around me. Any other person, a Guernseyman or German would have done that and there would have been no difficulty. I assumed that this officer, as he had not said anything, could not speak or understand English.

No doubt, happily imbibed with the Christmas spirit, I responded;

"What's up with you, do you think you've bought the bloody place." And added, "Your Commandant has decreed that we all keep to the right of the road, so you get off the pavement!"

It was just my luck that he in fact spoke perfect English and understood every word I said. He had two henchmen with him and I was immediately arrested for being rude to a German officer.

I was frog marched to a house in Hauteville, called Maytrees. It was then and still remains, an imposing house set back from the road. I was taken down to the cellar and locked up in a cell, with a German guard stationed outside the door. After a while I was brought up before the German officer who had arrested me. He questioned me about the war and was obviously very upset about the fact that the Americans had recently entered the war. As he was clearly trying to goad me, I refused to say very much at all.

I responded to his continual verbal provocation by saying;

"I am a British citizen, you are obviously a Nazi officer and there is nothing I can say to you."

He was very angry and there was no doubt in my mind that the war had ruined his Christmas and he was going to ruin somebody else's and it looked as if it was going to be mine. After a while I was taken back down to the cell.

Meanwhile Mabs was at home cooking the Christmas dinner which was parsnip pie. For Margaret, this was her first Christmas, in the sense that she was now thirteen months old and sitting up and taking notice. Mabs had spent a lot of time making and putting up decorations and creating the Christmas atmosphere. Mum was there, no doubt fussing around in her own inimitable way, all that was missing was yours truly. Everyone was beginning to get a bit concerned, they were accustomed to me being missing, but not on Christmas Day. There was a knock on the window, it was Margaret Carey, who said to Mabs:

"Bill won't be home for Christmas this year!"

Margaret, one of the girls to whom I had been talking when I was arrested, also brought my bicycle home. The other girl, lived at that time in Hauteville, just up the road from where I was arrested. Later in the day she came down to Maytrees with a packet of sandwiches for me. She managed to talk her way past the German guard at the front door of the house and gave the sandwiches to the guard outside my cell, who passed them to me.

Some hours later that evening, a German policeman came and asked me what the incident was all about.

I explained, "I wasn't in this Officer's way, as he only had to walk around my bike. I objected to being shoved in the ribs and gestured to move. Quite frankly I would have said the same to a Guernseyman."

"Ah!" said the German policeman, "Just a lot of rubbish."

Off he went and it was not long before I heard these two Germans, the policeman and the officer who had arrested me, having a row. Oh boy did they have a humdinger of a row, shouting at each other and making a tremendous noise. Finally it ended and the German policeman came down and said,

"Ah!, your imprisonment is at an end, you can go home now, good Christmas."

"Excuse me", I said, "there is a curfew, I can't go home."

"Ah," he said, "I will take you home in my car."

And so he did, I was driven back home to Mabs, whose Christmas dinner of parsnip pie was, by the time I arrived, not in the best of condition. So that was Christmas Day 1941.

One of the reasons that I said to the German officer to get off the pavement was that earlier in the year, the Germans had decreed that we drive on the right of the road. Even wheelbarrows had to conform to the new rule of the road! Farm horses didn't understand why all of a sudden they had to go onto the other side of the road and of course they wouldn't, it caused all sorts of fun, it really did. The Germans had also taken away our right to ride our bicycles two abreast and many islanders were being fined for disobeying that law.

During the occupation I acquired an Excelsior moped for next to nothing as the owner could not use it without petrol. I very occasionally used it when I managed to obtain some petrol from 'Hans the Communist'. On one of my trips out on this moped I was riding it alongside a friend of mine who was on his bicycle, when we were stopped by a German officer.

My first thoughts were, 'God strewth, I have lost this thing now and I'm going to be in trouble again'.

"Riding two abreast!" the German Officer said.

He fined us two Reichmarks each on the spot. The moped was the type which you could also pedal. Fortunately he did not notice the engine, so after paying my fine, I pedalled away as quickly as possible.

The Germans imposed speed limits of 25 mph. in town, 50 mph. in the country during the hours of daylight and an all island limit of 12.5 mph at night. This did not worry many islanders as our bicycles were our only means of transport. At road junctions, they decreed that the main road always had priority. The main roads were distinguished by means of a red diamond on a white background, minor roads junctioning with main roads were distinguished by a red triangle standing on it's point on a white background. German vehicles however, always had to be given priority at any junction, regardless of any other rules of the road. Their vehicles were usually painted an iron grey colour, so they were easy to identify and generally were the only vehicles on the road.

This was another set of rules I attempted to ignore if possible, I certainly did when I was testing their motorcycles. The trouble was that a cycle was no match for a military vehicle, so as far as those regulations were concerned the Germans tended to get their way.

Doctor A.W. Rose, who could swim the breast stroke, was keen to learn the crawl so I agreed to teach him. The two of us went down to the pool at La Valette most afternoons, after the shop shut at 4 pm. Despite all my efforts he never actually managed to master the crawl. I spent many hours trying to help him perfect the leg kick action. Whenever he tried to do what I was attempting to teach him, he appeared to go backwards, rather than forwards. Finally he became so disheartened that he gave up trying to learn.

His wife, who managed to get away before the arrival of the Germans, had given him a gold signet ring which he always wore on his little finger. It was a valuable ring, both in monetary and sentimental terms. One day when swimming down at La Valette, he lost the ring from his finger. Dr Rose was very upset and over a period of days we spent many hours under water, groping around the bottom of the pool searching for his ring. Anxious for its return the Doctor offered a £25 reward, which was a great deal of money in those days. Finally, when all else failed, we drained the pool and continued our search. He was extremely pleased and incredible lucky when the ring was found by a young schoolboy called Roger. Dr Rose happily paid him the reward.

The Germans put all the bays around the island out of bounds to the civilian population, the only place on the coast we were allowed to swim was at La Valette Pool. Periodically even the La Valette would be put out of bounds to islanders as a punishment for escapes or attempted escapes to the mainland.

On one occasion, when we were banned from the pools, Dr Rose came to me and asked:-

"What are we going to do about it Bill ?"

"To hell with the so and so Germans, it's our Island, not theirs. I have swum in the bathing pools all my life, it is going to take more than the bloody German army to stop me, I am going down for a swim!"

"Right Bill" he said, "I will come with you."

So we went for a swim and of course there was a German officer with a couple of henchman looking for a couple of blokes like us. When we came out of the water, we were duly arrested, Doctor Rose had his identity card with him, so they took the details from that and allowed him to go home. I didn't have my identity card. They had been issued to all islanders in the autumn of 1940 and as a matter of principle, I made a point of not carrying it, so I was arrested. I was bundled into the back of a military car, with a fully armed German soldier either side of me. The officer who had arrested me sat in the front with the driver. I was driven up through the town to their Feldgendarmerie Headquarters at Grange Lodge.

On arrival, I was ordered out of the car and with the officer in front and the two armed guards behind me, marched up to the entrance where we met another officer coming out. The two officers had a conversation, which I did not understand. The outcome was that the officer who had arrested me, turned to me and said:

"You follow him", pointing at the other officer.

I was taken into a room which overlooked the forecourt and the car that had just brought me from the bathing pool. This German officer just stood there looking out of the window. He said nothing. I stood behind him, now regretting that I had swum in a restricted area and had not carried my identity card. What sort of punishment would I receive ? He stood there looking out on to the forecourt, watching the other officer for a long while and then suddenly turned around and looked at me and said in perfect English:

"Thank Christ he has gone, you can go home now." He was an officer called Liptner and I was very grateful to him, that is probably why I have remembered his name!

I went home.

When we were prevented from swimming at La Valette Bathing Pools, we transferred our activities to various flooded quarries. One which we swam in fairly regularly was Guillotin quarry, in the Vale near Bordeaux, which at that time belonged to the Hubert family. I remember the water tasted foul and there seemed to be little buoyancy. We rigged up a pulley, which ran from one side of the quarry to the other. Using that we could get up quite a speed before jumping off and plunging into the water. There was an added incentive to swimming in Guillotin Quarry, you could, if you were lucky, catch a trout or two.

During the occupation the Germans were very keen on propaganda, and the Evening Press and The Star had to print their reports detailing all their so called victories and successes. The front page of both papers carried the latest communiques from the German Supreme Command, or from the Fuhrer's Headquarters. The British Traitor, who was hanged after the war, William Joyce, had his regular column under the title of 'Lord Haw-Haw's Platform', or 'William Joyce says'. We all knew that these were being published on the direct instructions of the Germans and took little notice of the gloom and doom they purveyed. Often when the Germans had misspelt words in their 'copy', the item was deliberated printed with the spelling mistake uncorrected, such as 'William Joyce sees'. The Germans were made to look foolish and it was their own mistake - we loved that !

The communiques from the German Supreme Command continually claimed massive sinking of Allied shipping. In February 1941 the Press recorded the daily theoretical losses of British shipping as

February 11th 24,000 tons sunk
" 12th Two ships in the Suez Canal sunk
" 13th 58,000 tons sunk
" 14th 13 armed Merchant ships sunk.
" 15th 82,000 tons sunk
" 17th 19,000 tons sunk
" 18th 150,000 tons sunk
" 19th 4,000 tons sunk.

The headlines blazoned the German claims of the shipping their U-Boats had sunk. They must have 'sunk' a minimum of six Ark Royals and the whole of the British Merchant Navy at least twice. Fortunately it became so laughable that no one believed any of their daily communiques.

On one of my regular visits to the bathing pools at La Valette, I was experimenting swimming under water, breathing through a rubber tube, what was later to be called a snorkel. In the course of the experiment I came up at the side of the pool at the feet of a young German officer, who enquired:

"How did you get on down there ?"

In jest, I said. "Fine, I've have just sunk the usual two hundred and fifty thousand tons of allied shipping and a couple of British battleships."

This response provoked a laugh at the officer's expense, in fact any skit at the expense of the Germans and their propaganda, was always likely to produce a laugh! This young officer, if he understood what I said, must have had a sense of humour because he took it in good part.

That story somehow found its way to England and was published in the wartime Channel Islands Monthly Review, the magazine that was specially produced for Channel Islanders who had been evacuated. The headline was 'Bill Green pulls the German's leg'. I saw the publication after the war and it took me years to realise how the magazine obtained the story.

Alf Bougourd, of Belgrave Motors, who I knew well from our morning coffee days at Stainer's, had escaped with some other islanders in his motor launch in early 1942. It was his escape that resulted in the closure of the bathing pools for a time. Later that year he had by chance, met my great friend, Ralph Palmer, when he was walking down the main street in Oxford. While they were swapping news, Ralph asked how his old playmate Bill Green was coping with the Germans. Alf told him, amongst other things, the story of my underwater swimming and my remark to the German officer.

I read the account of the Oxford meeting in the book that Ralph wrote after the war. It was only then that I realised that it must have been Ralph Palmer who passed the story on to the magazine- typical Ralph.

One of the reasons that I chose Charles Hodder's house, La Croix, when we were forced out of Seaplane Bungalow, was the window in the loft. It was from there that I observed all that went on in the waters between St Peter Port Harbour and the islands of Herm and Sark. I spent a great deal of time up there, watching what was going on. On the night of the 12th February 1942, I was intrigued that the lighthouses were lit. I could see the Casquets and the Sark light from my elevated vantage point. I was very puzzled about the lights being on during wartime. Clearly it was not for the benefit of the Allies, so I assumed that the Germans were providing safety markers for some of their shipping.

Later I learnt that the German battleships, Scharnhorst and Gneisenau, together with the Cruiser Prinz Eugen, had slipped out of the French port of Brest at night, sailed up the big Russel behind Sark and made a dash through the Straits of Dover to the greater safety of a German port. The Allies must have been slow off the mark, because the warships successfully arrived at their destination, apparently unharmed and undamaged.

In the early autumn of 1942, my neighbour Edgar Stacey was offered the opportunity of taking over the running of Les Nicolles Farm in the Forest, by the owner, Motor Agent Stan Noel. Edgar jumped at the chance, it was much better for him and his family, they would be assured of an adequate supply of food. It was also to benefit Mabs, Margaret and myself because we were regularly invited to the farm and well fed when we were there. Les Nicolles Farm was somewhat primitive, but very picturesque. Margaret loved the farmyard atmosphere and all its activities.

Edgar had a couple of cows so, of course, on our visits we were fed on butter and good rich Guernsey milk. He also grew a variety of crops on the farm. Edgar and his family were very good to us and I think their generosity did much to see us through those difficult wartime days. We were never as hungry as we might have been.

Mabs, with Margaret on her carrier seat and I would cycle out to Les Nicolles Farm on a Sunday afternoon, have tea with Edgar and his family and then go to the early evening service at the Forest Church afterwards. On many occasions Mabs and I would cycle over to the farm on Saturday evening and not return until the

Monday morning and then as often as not with a pint of full cream milk and whatever vegetables were available. In return I would repair Edgar's bicycles and help in any way I could.

When Edgar and his wife Jane moved to Les Nicolles Farm they took with them the radio set which we had hidden underneath the dinning room floor at Lyndel. This time it was hidden in a barrel under a weeping willow tree in their garden. When they wanted to listen to the news they manhandled the barrel into the House. They dare not keep the set hidden in the farmhouse because the Germans regularly searched the place for food. Edgar and his wife continued to use the set until there was no electricity available to charge the accumulators.

In order to defend the island, the Germans carried out a vast programme of military construction. The Organisation Todt brought in a considerable number of slave workers to work on the vast labyrinth of defence fortifications. Hundreds of thousands of tons of cement were imported into Guernsey and I am glad to say that not all of it was used for the purpose the Germans intended. A great number of renovations and improvements to local properties, by islanders, took place quietly and unobtrusively. How we mysteriously managed to share in the imports of German cement is no secret. The Germans were sticklers for rules and systems. A rule would be decreed and the German rank and file blindly obeyed.

A number of local men were employed by the Germans to drive their lorries between the docks and various depots and construction sites. The imported cement was loaded on to a lorry straight off the boat. An armed soldier would sit alongside the driver while the lorry was driven to its particular destination. The rule was that when the lorry and its guard had passed through the barrier, the German soldier got off and another German counted all the sacks of cement on the vehicle. Once the lorry and its load had been checked and all the rules complied with, the Germans ceased to have any further interest.

The Guernsey driver would be left to unload the bags of cement, before driving out through the barrier, often with a number of the bags of cement still aboard and on some occasions with the whole lorry load. Nobody noticed! The German rules did not require the 'empty' lorries to be checked on the way out. The driver then delivered the supply of cement he had 'won' to one of his pals. It would be quickly unloaded and the driver then returned to the harbour, to collect his next load and a new guard. Numerous drives were concreted and many wartime improvements achieved from supplies which were diverted from the Hitler's Atlantic Wall.

Reg Moulin, who owned Lyndel and lived there almost up to the time Edgar Stacey moved in, wanted a new drive and some steps laid in concrete. He approached a builder who agreed to do the work.

"What about the cement ?" Reg asked the builder.

"I will get that for you, no questions asked."

"How are you going to do that?" asked Reg.

"If you don't say anything, I will tell you. It comes, courtesy of Hitler's building supplies."

Edgar was a very hardworking chap, not only did he look after the farm, he also continued to work his vinery. He wanted to make some improvements and required a few bags of cement. So he came to an 'arrangement' with one of the local drivers of a German cement lorry, an arrangement which did not involve payment. The driver was happy to divert as much cement from the German war effort as he could, that was satisfaction enough. One day a lorry arrived at the farm with his 'order'. The driver had 'captured' a full load of eighty bags of British 'Portland' cement. Where the Germans had obtained that no one knew, but as the driver said to Edgar:

"It wasn't theirs in the first place!"

Edgar had only wanted five or six bags, but much to his consternation the driver unloaded the whole lot and drove off. Edgar hid it in the stables and hoped that the Germans would not find it. He used his carrier bike to transport the few bags of cement he required for the job at his vinery. The things that Edgar transported on that carrier bike, under the very nose of the Germans, makes me shudder at the thought.

At the end of the war Edgar still had most of his 'captured' cement. When I purchased Lyndel from Reg Moulin after the war, I needed a couple of bags of cement to patch the drive where I removed the steps Reg Moulin had built, so that I could drive my car in off the road. I naturally turned to Edgar for my supply of cement. This time two bags of 'Portland' cement were transported openly to Jerbourg Road. Edgar's carrier bike had gone into retirement.

Edgar, the farmer, was very un-cooperative as far as the Germans were concerned. He never complied with their edicts in regard to accounting for his produce or registering his animals. He kept a pig in the yard near the farm house. The pig of course wasn't registered, if it had been, he would have needed permission to slaughter it.

Edgar learnt that the Germans were checking up on pigs. Feeling that his pig would be easily found, he decided to move it to a safer place. There was pigsty hidden away amongst an overgrown area on high ground, a little way from the farm. Edgar thought that would be the ideal place to hide the pig, so enlisted the services of his wife, Jane, Mabs and myself to help in the move. Together we drove the pig up the hill and tried to encourage it into its new home. The pigsty was so overgrown and the pig so big that it would not go through the entrance. Edgar hacked away some of the foliage to make the entrance wide enough to get the pig through. The pig had a mind of its own, which did not include going through that entrance. After many attempts we finally managed to get the wayward pig into its new home.

Jerry did not discover the existence of Edgar's pig and in due course it was slaughtered by a friendly butcher and the proceeds distributed. The only problem was that for some reason Edgar did not get his share. I remember him complaining bitterly that he had done all the work, taken all the risk in rearing the animal and received none of the benefit !

Another occasion when he obtained no benefit for all his hard work was when he planted a field with seed potatoes. Edgar set them in rows at a standard distance apart but did not ridge them, so as not to give any indication that the field was cultivated. He knew that if the Georgians on the nearby gun site were aware that he had planted the potatoes he would loose the lot. After a time when the shoots should have been appearing and there was no signs of life, he realised that he had lost his crop. Apparently the Georgians used poles, which had nails on the end, to jab the ground and spike the seed potatoes. The potatoes were then extracted without noticeably disturbing the earth. They realised that the potatoes were in rows, so far apart and once they had found two potatoes, they had located them all.

In order that he had some feed for his animals during the winter Edgar grew a crop of grass, which he intended to cut as hay. With the use of some irreplaceable chemicals he produced a bumper crop. One morning he found about fifteen Germans scything his hay for themselves. The officer in charge looked, with his monocle, a real Nazi. Edgar did not think he understood English and started calling him some choice names.

The officer interrupted Edgar's flow:

"What did you say?"

"Crumbs!", which was his standard answer to such a situation.

Edgar explained that they were taking the hay he needed to feed his animals in the winter. The officer retorted that a considerable number of horses had been imported from France and they too needed the hay. If Edgar wanted to do anything about it, he had better go to the Military Office at the top of Petit Bot and make his complaint.

The only thing Edgar could do was to make a complaint. At the office, the Germans took not the slightest notice of what he had to say. While he was there he was taken into a room festooned with portraits of Hitler. Edgar was expected to salute and show his respect to Fuhrer, which of course he refused to do. After holding him for three or four hours he was allowed to go back to the farm, by which time all the hay had been harvested and removed. That monocled Nazi officer, a really nasty bit of work, who had crossed his path, was now, as Edgar put it, "On my hit list!"

The Germans commandeered a greenhouse on the farm, in which they planted cabbage plants. One day Edgar caught them watering their plants with his water, which he required for his cattle. There was a windmill that drew the water up from the well into a five hundred gallon storage tank. On this particular day there wasn't any wind, so it was important that he conserved as much water as possible for his cattle. When he found them watering their cabbages with his precious water, Edgar, as only he could do, complained bitterly. They took no notice and continued watering the cabbage plants.

A few days later a German came and complained to Edgar that the cabbages had all died and suggested that he was responsible. He was taken to see the cabbages and clearly they had all been pulled out of the ground and died. Then he noticed that there were a lot of little foot marks. It was obvious what had happened, his son John, who was still only a toddler, had been around when Edgar was complaining to the Germans about using his precious water. John had heard his father and obviously returned later and pulled up every single cabbage plant. Unfortunately he had left the tell tale marks of his foot prints.

Edgar said later that the German officer was very threatening and that if anything had been done to harm John, he would have taken the law into his own hands. This was another German who went on Edgar's hit list.

Local people were not alone in keeping pigs and other animals for their own consumption. A number of German officers were billeted at Bon Air, a big house in large grounds, on the Sausmarez Road. I passed it each day on my way to and from town. They reared a pig, which they wanted killed and prepared for their table. They apparently asked around and found out that a fellow by the name of Le Page was the local pig butcher. He used to go around slaughtering pigs for farmers and other butchers. The Germans engaged Le Page to kill and prepare their pig for them.

He slaughtered the pig and hung the carcase from a branch of a tree in the garden of Bon Air. Then he opened the pig up and gutted it. After finishing he was invited into the house and offered a drink. German officers always had a good supply of schnaps and other spirits. When they came out of the house, low and behold the pig had disappeared. I must have cycled past just as the Germans realised that their pig had been stolen from right under their noses. One German officer was absolutely furious, he was shouting and ordering junior officers and men around. I quickly realised that it was not the place for me to be and swiftly peddled away towards home.

I heard later that this officer had personally visited all the gun sites in the neighbourhood, Fermain, Fort Road, Jerbourg, everywhere hunting for the missing pig.

It appears one of our local lads who was driving for the Germans, drove into Bon Air with some items for the Jerry officers. He saw the pig hanging from the tree, so he backed his lorry in underneath, quickly cut the pig down and drove home to St. Sampsons like the wind. He dumped the pig and rapidly returned to his delivery round. Two or three days later the local pig butcher, Mr Le Page, had a call from someone in St Sampsons asking him if he would go and cut up a pig. When he arrived, he recognised it as the pig he had killed at Bon Air. The German officers never did find their pig, somebody else, however, benefited.

Chapter 17

PEPPERY COLONEL FORTY

The whole population of the island and virtually all the German Army of occupation were mystified when, on Tuesday the 15th September 1942, a Notice signed by Colonel Knackfuss, of the Feldkommandantur, appeared in the Star newspaper. It read:-

> 'By order of higher authorities the following British subjects will be evacuated and transferred to Germany.
>
> a. Persons who have their permanent residence not on the Channel Islands, for instance, those who have been caught here by the outbreak of the war.
>
> b All those men not born in the Channel Islands and 16 to 70 years of age who belong to the English people, together with their families.'

There was no explanation given, no reason for the enforced evacuation of so many people. As I had been born in Guernsey, I would not be one of those to be caught by the Order, but I knew many who would. Every one covered by the order had to fill in a form and return it to the Greffe Office by the following Friday.

The approaching deportation of what was to turn out to be over eight hundred islanders was a great shock and a matter of major concern to us all. No one could explain why it was happening, even the Germans were questioning the action. We had been living under Germans rule for over two years and no serious acts of sabotage had occurred. The official Notice stated that it was on the orders of 'Higher Authorities'. Did this mean Hitler had decreed the deportation as a reprisal for the Dieppe Raid by the Allies. We did not know, but what we did know was that many of our friends and their families were going.

On the day after the order was issued I went to see Bill Pitchford, the manager of the Singer Sewing Machine shop, who as an Englishman was due to be deported. He was a deeply religious man, who preached regularly at the Bordage Hall.

"Hello Pitch, how are you feeling ?"

"Well, as a person terrified, but as a Christian, fine." He replied,

Pitch had developed his little sideline of drying bramble leaves as a substitute tea into quite a flourishing enterprise. So, with his Singer Sewing machines repairs and his bramble tea, he had become quite essential to the community. In the event he wasn't deported, because the Controlling Committee, who had some influence with the Germans, persuaded them that he would be impossible to replace.

The German rules did allow for persons they considered essential to the island to be exempted. 'Higher authorities' had set the rules and the 'local officialdom' stuck to them to the letter, however bizarre their decision might appear.

Freddy Priaulx, although he could speak very little English, his mother tongue being Guernsey Patois, was one of those caught in their net. His father was wounded in the first world war and while he was convalescing in the Isle of Wight, Freddy's mother went to visit him. During her stay, she gave birth to Freddy so, according to their rules, the Germans categorized him as English and he was duly deported.

Their rigid adherence to rules, however, saved others from going. Allan Grut's father-in-law was born in Malta. So when the order came out that everybody born in England had to go, Allan went to the German Authorities and said:

"You say everybody born in England has to go to an internment camp, my father-in-law was born in Malta."

"Where's that?" they inquired.

Allan retorted "Well, you jolly well should know, your airforce is bombing it like mad."

"Our order says England, right, it is only those born in England, that have to go."

Allan Grut's father-in-law was born whilst his father was serving in Malta and was as much an Englishman as anyone. But the rigid application of their rules meant that he was not deported.

Cecil Hardwick, who was born in England, realised that he and his family were likely to be deported. He was very worried and came and talked to me about his position. At the time they were daily expecting an addition to the family and I suggested that this might be a sufficient reason to be excused deportation. Cecil went to see the Germans and was told to write a letter explaining his family's situation. They were granted a deferment, until six weeks after the baby was born. Their daughter Mary was born soon after, but Cecil never heard anything more about being deported.

Our former neighbour and now 'Farmer' Stacey, was born in Devon and was clearly caught by the deportation rules. He was a very worried man and hated the prospect of him and his family being forceably transported to Germany. Edgar went to see Raymond Falla, a member of the Controlling Committee, whose responsibilities included agriculture. Raymond backdated, in the official records, the date that Edgar had taken over responsibility for Les Nicolles Farm and obtained his exemption from deportation. Edgar's continued presence, as a farmer, was considered essential to the wellbeing of the community. Wasn't he pleased that he had accepted Stan Noel's offer to take over the care and running of the farm. But for that he and his family would have been on their way to Germany and my family and I would have lost a very good friend and a source of precious food.

My old friend 'Stroo', Frank Stroobant, was caught in the deportation net. He had continued to run his 'Home from Home' Restaurant despite the almost non existence of food supplies. 'Stroo' had worked miracle after miracle in order to keep the place going.

The States did a marvellous job, giving all the deportees a good sendoff. They were provided with warm clothes for the oncoming winter and food for the journey. 'Stroo' decided that their rations should be supplemented, so he set about organising supplies in his own inimitable way. A large advertisement appeared in both the Evening Press and the Star, saying:-

1,000 Eggs wanted immediately.
8/- a dozen offered.
Stroobant, Home from Home Restaurant.

The need is VITAL.

'Stroo' soon had all the eggs he required, many of them being donated by willing islanders, only too pleased to be helping in some small way their departing friends. He then persuaded the Germans to lend him two field kitchens, fully staffed, to cook last minute meals for the deportee's. The meals were served at the White Rock and consisted of hot meat stew, ham sandwiches and a hard boiled egg for each person. Only 'Stroo' had the ability to organise such a feast in a time of famine. When the deportees who were imprisoned at Laufen came to elect a Camp Senior, it was not surprising that they chose 'Stroo'.

The first party of deportees were due to depart on the 21st September 1942, but rough weather delayed the sailing until the 26th, when the M.V. Minotaur took them to St Malo. The rest of the deportees left two days later.

Amongst the second party was 'Stroo'. The German order was that deportees could take with them only what they could carry. 'Stroo' had clearly understood the order and interpreted it to the last pot and pan. I was down on the quay, helping with the distribution of the food, when along he came rattling as he walked. It was a wonderful sight, 'Stroo' had tied to himself everything imaginable, everything that he thought could possibly be useful. At the time I was very sad to see him go, as he was a wonderful character who I had known most of my life and I felt that it was possible I would never see him again.

I called out "Cheerio 'Stroo', God bless." Thank God he came back.

As the M.V. Minotaur slowly edged away from the dockside, I heard the deportees singing, 'There'll always be an England' and 'Rule Britannia'. It was a very moving and sad moment.

It was some time after the war before we discovered the reason for the deportation of almost eight hundred islanders. In the late summer of 1941, Hitler learnt that Iran was contemplating interning Germans in that country, at the request of the British Government. Looking for means of reprisal the Germans realised that there were a considerable number of British born civilians living in the Channel Islands. Hitler gave an order that for every German detained in Iran, ten British subjects should be deported from the Channel Islands. For some reason this order was not implemented in the autumn of 1941 and it was only when Hitler, almost a year later, queried whether his order had been carried out, that the deportations actually took place.

In January 1943, as a result of a British Commando raid on Sark, further deportations were ordered. This time the deportees were largely former British Army officers. They were required to report at the Regal Cinema for a medical examination. The standard of examination varied very considerably, no doubt depending on which German doctor carried it out. Many of the older men were thoroughly examined and some were rejected as being unfit. On the other hand the medical examination by one German doctor was very cursory. He simply enquired;

"You well?"

If the person being examined said anything to the effect of;

"Very well indeed," the answer was "You are passed, that is all."

In the end some one hundred and twenty more islanders were deported, including Ambrose Sherwill, who had been a Major in the first war.

One Guernseyman who escaped deportation was Colonel S.Heber Forty, who lived in a Regency House in Cambridge Park. He was a very tough old peppery Colonel, who walked around in shorts, summer and winter. He swam all the year round. I got to know him well, because pre-war he always visited his family in Siam for Christmas and brought his bicycle to the shop for us to store while he was away.

The Germans requisitioned all the houses in Cambridge Park and billeted troops in them. That is all the houses except Colonel Forty's. He went to see the

German Commandant and told him that, as he was a Colonel, under the Hague Convention they could not turn him out of his house. He saluted and marched out. He was never turned out and continued to live in his house in Cambridge Park, surrounded by Germans, throughout the occupation.

The Colonel was one of those almost extinct breed of big game hunters. When he returned to the island to retire, he carried on shooting duck and quail, but when the Germans arrived they confiscated his guns. Not to be deprived of his favourite sport he took up the catapult and became very proficient in it use. He still managed to get a good 'bag' of birds, except in very cold weather when, as he put it;

"My hands became too cold for anything like accurate shooting."

When called to attend the medical, at the Regal, to judge his fitness, he successfully evaded deportation. He managed to obtain a supply of a doctor's notepaper and, with his quite considerable knowledge of medicine, concocted a medical certificate and forged the doctor's signature. He reported for the medical and was examined by three doctors who, after reading the certificate, came to the conclusion that he was unfit to travel.

The Colonel, being a big man, became extremely hungry during the later part of the occupation and resorted to some unusual concoctions to satisfy his appetite. He once described to me how he ate garden snails boiled in cabbage. Another of his 'recipes' involved blood which he obtained from the slaughterhouse. He made pies out of vegetables, flour and blood, which he baked in the oven. He said he quite enjoyed them.

When the Germans put the beaches and the swimming pools out of bounds, the Colonel was prevented from enjoying his daily dip. Instead he used to go out early in the morning, even in the depths of winter, about 6 am, absolutely starkers, walk across Cambridge Park to the pump and take a shower. He was a real tough old character, who used to frighten me, so what effect he had on the Germans I hate to think ! He stood up to the Germans and never let them think that they were the 'masters.' As he walked around Cambridge Park the Germans would salute him and he would return their salute. I suspect that Colonel Forty did more for the war effort than many serving soldiers.

One of the earliest acts of the Germans, was to prohibit meetings of every description. This included meetings of the Chamber of Commerce.

Pre war I joined the Guernsey Chamber of Commerce, mainly because Dad was a member, but also being in business I felt it right to be involved and have a voice in matters which affected my livelihood. Dad had been a very active member of Chamber almost since he started in business and for many years was a member of their Council.

When I became active in the affairs of the Chamber, Reg Luxon was our President. Reg, who was Manager of the Gas Company, was a very forthright, able and respected man. He was first elected as President in 1935 and served right through the occupation. Later, like so many former Presidents of the Chamber, he was elected a People's Deputy.

The effect of the Germans prohibiting meetings of the Chamber of Commerce, was to stultify its activities. As a consequence Chamber had no effective voice with which to raise opposition to changes which were forced upon the business community during the occupation. There was no opportunity to make representations regarding the orders issued from time to time by various States Committees.

Many of us felt that if the Chamber had been given the opportunity to meet the Committees, we would have been able to make available to them the wealth of experience within Chamber membership. The expert advice that we might have been able to offer could well have materially assisted the working of those committees. It appeared to be the official view that businessmen who had successfully spent their lives in a particular trade were, for some reason or other, incapable of being of service to the community and their trade in a time of need. There were many offers from individual local businessmen who were prepared to assist the island by helping with the additional administration necessary during the occupation. Others offered, at their own expense, to go and represent Guernsey in France or elsewhere, in order to secure urgently needed supplies for the local population. I found it surprising that all these offers of help were not entertained in any serious way at all.

The various States Committees, however, did a good job and were well led. But as traders we believed that their thankless task could have been a lot easier if they had consulted with Chamber members and listened to their advice.

The States were very keen that we continued to employ as many members of our staffs as possible. Some companies found the inadequate profit margins that were allowed by the Prices Determination Committee on goods imported from France, insufficient to pay the wages of their staff. During the early part of the occupation, States policy directly contributed to the sacking of a considerable number of long serving employees.

The ban placed on the Chamber of Commerce meetings by the Germans was temporarily lifted at the end of August 1940, when the first occupation meeting of members was held. One of the items on the agenda was the need to obtain supplies from France or elsewhere. Mr Raymond Falla, Agricultural Officer and member of the Controlling Committee, was already making regular visits to France. He went equipped with lists of our needs and firms on whom he could call. Members felt that it would be desirable for the States to appoint permanent agents in various occupied countries, whose job would be, to arrange purchases on behalf of the island.

Later the Controlling Committee appointed a Chamber member, George M. Vaudin, as its Agent in Granville. He spent most of the rest of the occupation in France obtaining food and other much needed supplies for the island. George, who was Managing Director of Vaudin and Keates, the general produce dealers of the Bordage, had a intimate knowledge of trading between France and Guernsey. He did a magnificent job on the islands behalf. In retrospect I believe that George received very little recognition and thanks for his work.

Some members were concerned at the debts that had been left by evacuees, particularly some teachers, who had left in a hurry and there was no prospect of them being paid. It was suggested that the States should arrange that the assets of evacuees should be realised and distributed amongst their creditors.

At about that time the Controlling Committee had set an example by reducing States House rents by a third. The Chamber supported the move and many rents of business premises and commercial property were reduced. The Chamber of Commerce office was in the High Street, above Midland Bank. As our landlord they reduced our rent to forty pounds per annum, on the condition that our sub-tenants rent was also reduced proportionally.

No permission could be obtained for further meetings until the middle of 1941, when Chamber was granted a permit, subject to the approval of the place of the meeting and the agenda, by the German Feldkommandant. A letter was sent to Herr Dr Reffler, the head of the Feldgendarmerie at his Headquarters at Grange Lodge. It read:

> Dear Sir,
>
> Under the terms of the permit you kindly granted us, I have to inform you that a meeting of the Chamber of Commerce has been called for Tuesday the 13 May 1941, in the Chamber Room, High Street, at 4.15 pm when the following agenda will be dealt with:

1. Prevention of unemployment amongst shop assistants.
2. Indenting for supplies of commodities ex-France.
3. To consider the appointment of a permanent buyer in Jersey.
4. To discuss the retail price of fish and the control of supplies.
5. To read a letter from Mr Leale re permits for German forces.
6. Rent of premises, an application for reduction.
7. Subscriptions for 1941, 15/- a year.
8. Remuneration of secretary.

Signed by R.G.Luxon, President.

Dr Reffler approved the agenda with two letters, one in English and the other in German. The meeting attracted so many members that it was transferred to the lower Central Halls. Permission had to be obtained from the German authorities for the change of venue.

Some eighty members of the Chamber attended. It was thought wise to record, in the minutes, the thanks of the Chamber to Herr Dr Reffler for giving members the opportunity to meet as a Chamber of Commerce. Our President, Reg Luxon, explained that Dr Reffler had contacted Channel Islands Feldkommandantur, Colonel F.Schumacher, in Jersey on two occasions in order to get permission from the Colonel for the meeting to be held.

It was over two years before the Germans allowed another meeting of the Chamber of Commerce. That meeting, in June 1943, was to give consideration to the financial position of Chamber, which had become precarious. Income had been considerably reduced, many members having been evacuated and other members found it difficult to make ends meet. Chamber costs had been cut down in every possible way, the rent had been reduced, the electricity cut off, as had the telephone. The caretaker had been put on a reduced salary and the Secretary had become Honorary Secretary and his salary saved.

A further year was to pass before another meeting was held, this time in the board room of Le Riche's stores in the High Street. Our own office had been badly damaged by bomb blast. At that meeting the balance sheet showed a surplus for the first time since 1935, the profit being seven pound six shillings and ten pence, obviously cost cutting had had it's effect ! That was the last meeting of the Chamber of Commerce held during the occupation.

Chapter 18

THOUGHTS OF SABOTAGE

Without doubt the great contribution the Channel Islands made to the Allied war effort was the tying down of considerable numbers of German troops, who otherwise would have been available on mainland France when the Allied second front was launched.

Had von Rundstedt, the German Commander in the West, had available the 30,000 troops who were stationed in Guernsey, Alderney and Jersey just after D-Day, it would have made the Allied task of holding their bridgehead considerably more difficult.

Also many thousands of tons of reinforced concrete and steel were used in the islands, building fortifications which Hitler looked upon as part of his Atlantic Wall. Had those materials and the many thousands of construction workers been used to strengthen the costal defences on mainland France, the Allies would have certainly had a tougher task when they invaded.

The Organisation Todt, which was used to build the vast network of defence fortifications around our coast, employed many foreign workers. They were mainly French and Russians, but there were also other nationals, including Spaniards. Many of these Spaniards were Communists who fought on the loosing side in the Spanish Civil war and fled across the border to France. There they were interned in camps and when France fell the Germans 'recruited' them into the Organisation Todt.

In the summer of 1943 there were almost 7,000 of these workers in Guernsey, but by the time the Normandy landings took place, almost all had returned to mainland Europe.

From the day the Germans arrived in our island I was concerned that we should not collaborate with them more than was absolutely necessary. I felt that it was our duty to try and take such action as we could to disrupt and sabotage our occupiers. What I found difficult was, where to draw the line, between sabotage which was acceptable to the local community and sabotage which brought about unnecessary reprisals against islanders.

From the first days of the occupation, Ambrose Sherwill advised against any form of resistance. He was reported in the press as saying that:

"No one should put the liberty of the people at risk, without furthering the Allied cause."

He took the view that there was virtually nothing we could do which would materially help the Allies. Any acts of resistance or sabotage were looked upon with the utmost disfavour by Ambrose Sherwill, as he felt that they tended to negate the efforts which he and the Controlling Committee were making to create good and courteous relations with the German Authorities.

Jurat John Leale once pointed out to me that there were more Germans per square mile in Guernsey than there were in Germany, and therefore he thought that the temptation to commit acts of hostility was not as great as it would have been if they had been more thinly spread. That fact, in his view, made the island a most unsuitable place to indulge in acts of sabotage.

However, despite all that good and no doubt sound advice, I did not share their view. I thought that we should take every opportunity to cause disruption without getting caught as individuals and without bringing undue reprisals down upon our fellow islanders. I was determined that I would do whatever I could to 'annoy' our visitors.

When they issued regulations or decrees, I sought to ignore, or disobey them. When they made it compulsory to carry Identity Cards, I left mine at home. When they forbade us to swim at the Valette Pools, I swam there. Whatever they required me to do, I tried to do the opposite. I enjoyed being bloody minded, in fairness I think it came naturally! However, many of my actions caused me a great deal more trouble than they caused the Germans.

I always thought it possible that the British would repeat their Commando raid on the Jerbourg peninsula. If they did, I realised that their reception by the Germans would be very different next time. The area was now bristling with defences and any raiding party would inevitably suffer heavy losses. Persons escaping from the island would, I felt, only be able to give general information about the strength of the German garrison in the island. I was not convinced, however, that any of them would know what the situation was on the Jerbourg peninsular.

After a time my sister, Daisy and I were communicating with each other through Red Cross messages. One message I sent her, was an attempt to warn the British authorities that Jerbourg was now heavily fortified. The Red Cross message read:

> 'Mr J. Point, very strong in the arms now, tell Vic Oliver's father-in-law'

Vic Oliver was the well known comedian who was married, at that time, to Winston Churchill's daughter Sarah. My sister cottoned on to the meaning and passed the message to the War Office in London. Daisy eventually received a letter thanking her for the information and saying 'Message understood'.

There were some early acts of sabotage. In the middle of March 1941, a telephone cable in Les Moulipieds, near the airport, was cut in two places. The Germans reacted violently. The Feldkommandant, Colonel Schumacher, issued an Order further restricting the curfew from 9 pm until 7 am and requiring the States to supply sixty men between the ages of eighteen and forty-five for patrol and guard duties every night.

The Bailiff called an emergency meeting of the States to hear details of the act of sabotage. He said that:

> "A few days ago an ill disposed person or persons deliberately and maliciously cut a telephone cable in two places, in the neighbourhood of the Airport, which belonged to German Military Authorities and thus performed an act of grave sabotage. Such an act was not only stupid but criminal, as it involved those who were participating in it with the death penalty and it also brought the population of the whole island under grave displeasure of the German Authorities and in danger of the loss of their liberties.
>
> Since the occupation the German Authorities, both Military and Civil, have treated us with humanity and consideration and have gone out of their way on several occasions to help us in these difficult times. It is our duty and obligation to co-operate with them in carrying out their Orders and Regulations.

> It is the duty of any individual who has any information with regard to the perpetration of this act of sabotage to inform the Police immediately, as unless the culprit is brought to justice, we do not know what further penalties the population may incur."

The Bailiff's words were, in my view, yet another example of his over reaction to events. I have no doubt that the Germans required him to react adversely to such acts of sabotage, but was it necessary for him to go so far in praising their courtesy and consideration. At the time, his remarks were more than I could stomach and had the effect of making me more convinced than ever that I and other islanders should be doing everything possible to assist the Allied war effort by disrupting the Germans.

A few days later the Upper Division of the Royal Court was summoned and the Bailiff and ten Jurats passed the 'Compulsory Civil Duties Law'. In those days the Royal Court had the power to approve legislation.

The new Law empowered that any man, who was eighteen or over, could be called upon by the States to do guard or other duties. Every night sixty men from the five parishes closest to the Airport had to perform guard duty from 8.30 pm until 8.30 am the next morning. The Constables of each Parish were required to supply the States Labour Office with a list of men from their parish who were able to perform the guard duties. I received my notice from the Labour Officer, Deputy R.H. Johns, requiring me to report for duty at 8.15 pm on Friday 28th March 1941, at Ashmore, a vinery opposite the water tower in Forest Road. We patrolled in pairs, two hours on and four hours off. Police Constable Kimber was, that night, in charge of the operation and escorted us to our place of duty and collected us again when we were finished.

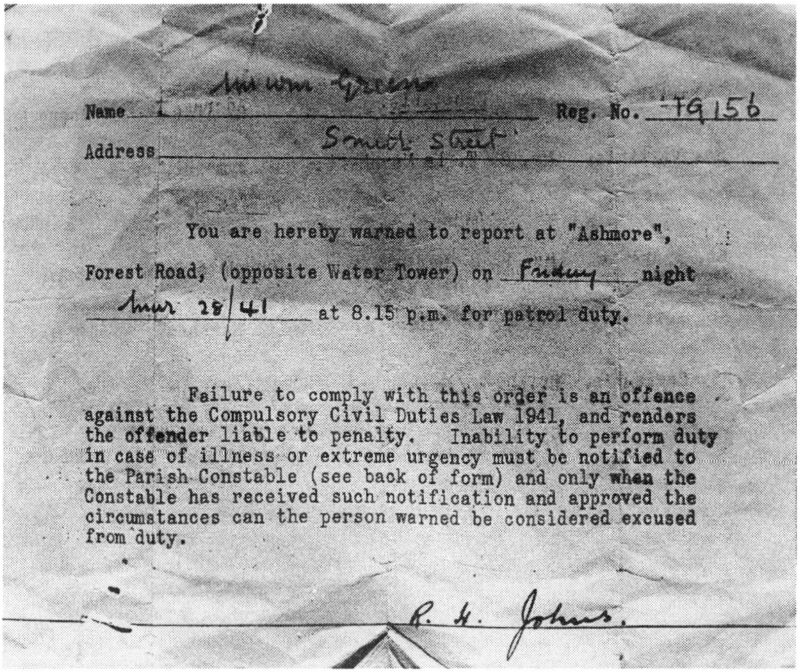
Name ________ Reg. No. ________

Address ________

You are hereby warned to report at "Ashmore", Forest Road, (opposite Water Tower) on Friday night Mar 28/41 at 8.15 p.m. for patrol duty.

Failure to comply with this order is an offence against the Compulsory Civil Duties Law 1941, and renders the offender liable to penalty. Inability to perform duty in case of illness or extreme urgency must be notified to the Parish Constable (see back of form) and only when the Constable has received such notification and approved the circumstances can the person warned be considered excused from duty.

R. H. Johns.

Notice to report to 'Ashmore' in the Forest Road for patrol duty on March 28th 1941.

I was stationed at the La Vilette, Les Cornus junction, with a wonderful character, Stan Workman, known to us all as 'Workie' Workman. He could speak passable German. When Germans came along the road and asked directions to the airport or elsewhere, 'Workie' gave them the most wonderful instructions - so much so that they must have taken weeks to arrive at their destination! Our guard duty required us to patrol a stretch of road. 'Workie' and I marched off in opposite directions, about-turned and met up again. Then off we would go again. After one of his marches into the darkness 'Workie' turned up with half a sack of cabbages! He always took advantage of any situation in which he found himself.

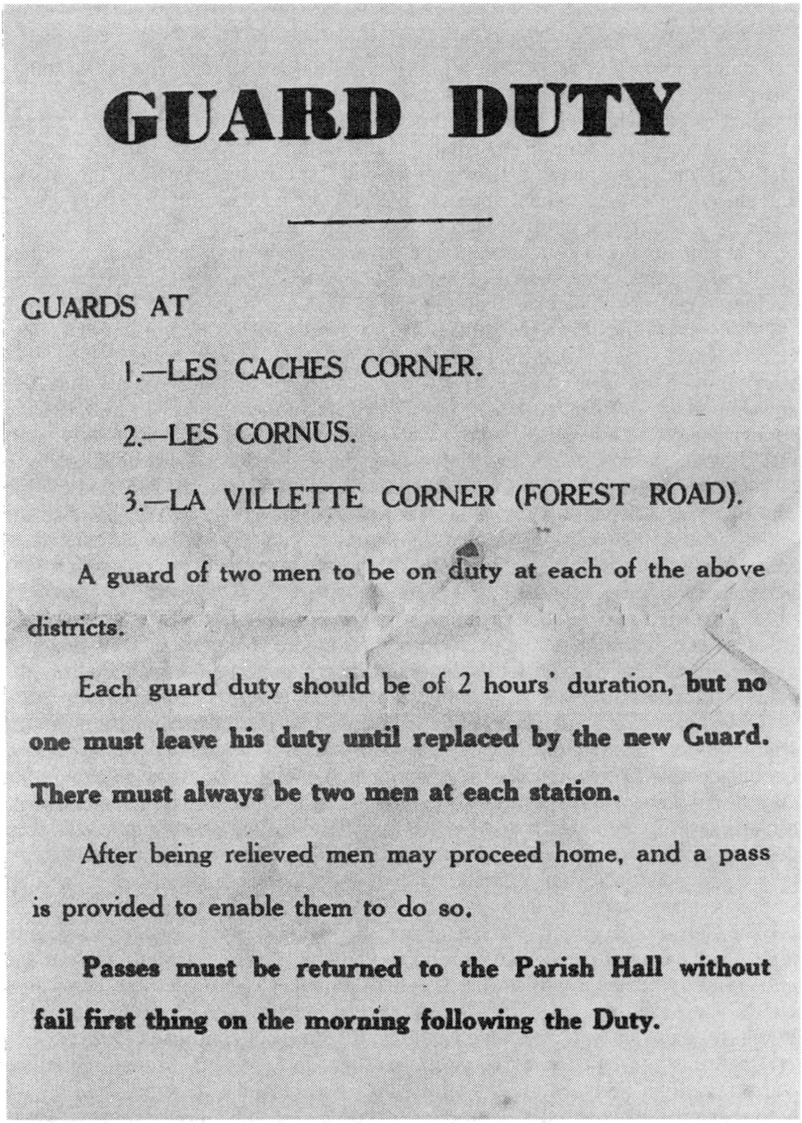

GUARD DUTY

GUARDS AT

1.—LES CACHES CORNER.

2.—LES CORNUS.

3.—LA VILLETTE CORNER (FOREST ROAD).

A guard of two men to be on duty at each of the above districts.

Each guard duty should be of 2 hours' duration, **but no one must leave his duty until replaced by the new Guard. There must always be two men at each station.**

After being relieved men may proceed home, and a pass is provided to enable them to do so.

Passes must be returned to the Parish Hall without fail first thing on the morning following the Duty.

Guard Duty instructions, under the Civil Duties Law 1941.

'Workie' used his limited German to good effect. When we were on stand down for four hours, we sat in the Ashmore Vinery and chatted amongst ourselves. Every now and again a German officer came in to check on us. 'Workie' bragged to us that next time the officer came in he would ask him for a cigarette. He came back and 'Workie' duly asked, using his best German, for a cigarette. The officer produced a packet of British Westminster Cigarettes, and 'Workie' was given two. I have often wondered how and where the German obtained those cigarettes.

After three weeks, guard duties were cancelled and the curfew restored to 10 pm. I had only been called upon once to do guard duty, which rather disappointed me as I really quite enjoyed being out after curfew. Further opportunities were, however, to occur. The Germans had made their point, it was their way of making you pay for your own acts of sabotage and irresponsibility

Later that summer the B.B.C. broadcast announcements of a new campaign on mainland Europe to use 'V' for Victory signs as part of the general resistance movement. Guernsey was not included in this campaign, but many people heard it on their radios, which up to then had not been confiscated by the Germans. Soon 'V' signs were appearing in the island. The Bailiff, Victor Carey, no doubt again on the German's instructions, issued a notice in 'La Gazette Officielle', the official announcement column which appeared in the Evening Press, to the effect that to write a 'V' sign in a public place was an act of sabotage. He warned that the punishment for those caught would be severe. A few days later another notice appeared over his name, offering a reward of £25 to anyone who gave information leading to the conviction of a 'Signwriter'.

Many islanders thought that offering a reward for turning in a fellow Guernseyman was 'beyond the pale'. I am proud to say that no reward money was ever claimed and the number of 'V' signs multiplied. I heard that some had appeared near the Beaulieu Hotel, so I cycled down there to see for myself. Sure enough there was a large 'V' on the wall in front of the Hotel. About sixty yards further down the road the letters 'EV' were painted on the road surface. I noticed a 'V' on one of the pillars of Chertsey House, and another at the junction of Rue Maze and Les Caches. A German signpost now displayed the letters 'EV'. All the letters were written in black tar and bitumen and were fairly crudely done. They looked to me as if the signwriter had written them in a hurry, which was understandable in view of the possible consequences.

The Germans inevitably reacted to this act of defiance and confiscated all wireless sets within a radius of 1000 meters of the Beaulieu Hotel. They also required men from St Martin to stand guard over signposts in the area during the hours of darkness.

I was again called upon by Deputy R.H. Johns to report on the night of August 13/14th to the Les Caches, Rue Maze junction, to perform three hours guard duty. On this occasion I was issued with a pass, which allowed me to cycle there during curfew and home again afterwards. The night prior to doing my turn at guard duty, a German military vehicle had been damaged with 'malicious intent', as they described it. This act of sabotage had clearly annoyed them and the Germans were very active and touchy during my three hour period of duty. After another week or so the Germans cancelled the guards.

The Germans, in an effort to detect any unauthorised movement on the roads at night, laid sheets of corrugated iron on the ground. Any one travelling along the unlit roads, whether it was in the St John's ambulance, on a bicycle or on foot would scare themselves to death and reveal their presence to the Germans. Whenever there was a scare, down would go the sheets of corrugated iron.

I had this constant feeling of guilt about not doing enough to help the Allied war effort. John Ferbrache was a young man with whom I became friendly - we both regularly swam at the Valette Pool during our lunch hours. Afterwards, as we strolled back to town, we often chatted about what we could do to 'upset Jerry'.

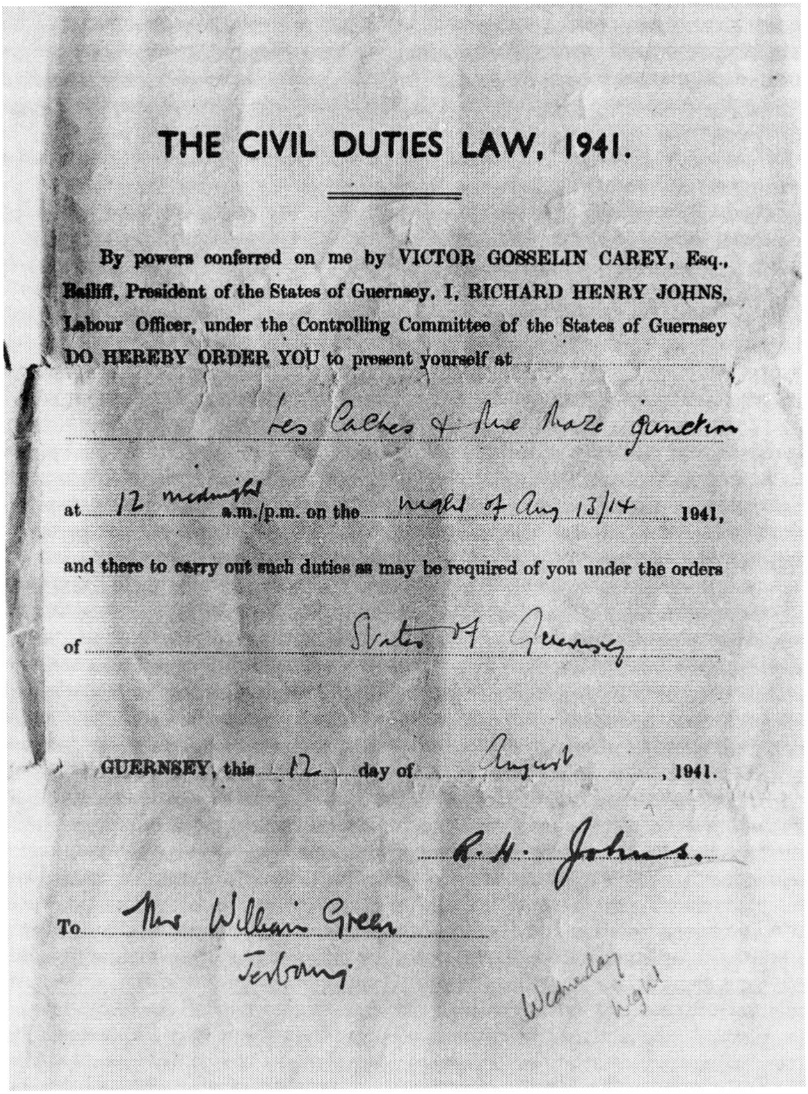

THE CIVIL DUTIES LAW, 1941.

By powers conferred on me by VICTOR GOSSELIN CAREY, Esq., Bailiff, President of the States of Guernsey, I, RICHARD HENRY JOHNS, Labour Officer, under the Controlling Committee of the States of Guernsey DO HEREBY ORDER YOU to present yourself at........................

Les Caches & Rue Maze junction

at 12 midnight a.m./p.m. on the night of Aug 13/14 1941,

and there to carry out such duties as may be required of you under the orders

of States of Guernsey

GUERNSEY, this 12 day of August, 1941.

R. H. Johns.

To Mrs William Green
Torteval

Wednesday night

The Civil Duties Law 1941. Notice to report to Rue Maze, Les Caches junction at midnight on 13/14th August 1941.

The Germans installed a number of gun positions down at the Valette, on the approach to the Bathing Pools. We noticed that their crews always went to their lunch at a set time and the guns were left unattended. The Germans were very methodical, to such an extent that you could safely rely on the fact that if their lunch hour was from 12 to 1 pm. they would not be on duty. John and I thought that this presented the ideal opportunity to, as he aptly put it, “Have a bit of fun with the Hun”.

We poured spirits of salt into the breach of one of the guns. What harm it did I do not know, but we thought that spirits of salt would eat away at the metal. At least we felt that we were doing something to make the Germans' life and their war effort just a little more difficult.

In the early summer of 1944, the Germans installed two guns on the South Esplanade between the Brewery and the slaughter house. The guns were apparently situated there in order to protect Havelet Bay from seaborne assault. I think it is unlikely that those guns were ever fired, other than in practice. Because of the need to have the crews on constant call, they were billeted close by in the Strand area. As always, the Germans could be relied upon to be missing during their lunch hour.

This was a situation which John and I both felt could be used to our advantage. One lunch hour, John stood guard while I nipped into their gun emplacements and removed the wing nuts from the gun mounts.

We hoped that the Germans, in the flurry of the moment, would not realise that the wing nuts were missing, so when the gun was fired it would jump off its base. I managed to throw three or four sets of wing nuts into Havelet Bay. Because the guns were protected by sandbag stockades, which restricted our view of them, we never knew if we had been successful in our attempt at sabotage.

Bill Pitchford occasionally brought over some of his bramble tea and we would go up into the empty flat above my shop and brew up. Sometimes I invited other business friends to come up and join us. We would have a mug of 'Pitch's' tea and a chat. One day I invited Harry Chapple, the Acting Head Postmaster, whose office was in Smith Street, to come over and join us.

When Harry came in and saw the empty flat, the old cast-iron kettle and the gas ring, he quietly said to me that was just what he was looking for, as he needed a place to steam open letters! Harry explained, that he and his staff handled a lot of letters which were addressed to the German Feldkommandant at Grange Lodge and he tried to 'vet' them before they were delivered. I was only too happy that Harry used my flat and the kettle. I gave him a key so that he could use the private door. He often went up there, without anybody knowing, to 'inspect' the suspect mail.

I personally did not get involved in the actual steaming open process, but I know that he managed to minimize the amount of information getting through to the Germans by vetting many of the considerable number of suspicious letters addressed to them. The bone-fide ones were re-sealed and delivered, but over two hundred letters were intercepted and destroyed. Many of them were anonymous tip offs, probably from neighbours letting the Germans know about hidden radios, illicit food, or other information which, if it had reached its destination, would have put many people in prison or worse. Apparently, according to Harry, the vast majority of these letter were from women, who wrote them out of spite or jealousy.

Harry, quite rightly, believed that he was only doing his duty in intercepting these letters and his action saved many islanders their freedom and possibly their lives. Unfortunately, when the gas supply ran out at the end of 1944, so did his ability to 'inspect' the suspicious mail. Knowing Harry, I suspect he found another way of intercepting the treacherous mail. By the end of the occupation there were very many Guernseymen and women who owed Harry a great debt of gratitude but, perhaps fortunately, they never knew it. Harry Chapple was, without doubt, one of our unsung heroes.

One Monday morning as I cycled along the Forest Road, on my way from Les Nicolles Farm to the shop, I noticed that there were some newly erected small posts carrying telephone wires. The poles were set in the earth bank of a field almost opposite the water tower and the telephone wire was strung between the posts in such a way that they hung down, almost touching the top of the earth bank. In the field there was a small herd of Guernsey cows. It occurred to me as I cycled past, that the cows could easily sever some of the wires as they grazed off the grass on the earth bank.

I thought about this and, after one or two more trips past the spot, I decided that it would be possible to cut the cable without being seen and quickly get away from the area. I noticed that there was a German guard positioned on the top of the water tower, but I calculated that there was a small section of the earth bank which was out of his sight. Further down the road, almost opposite the St Elmo Private Hotel, which was being used as a residence for senior German officers, there was a gun emplacement. It was nicknamed 'Big Bertha' by the locals. On one of my journeys I stopped to pick some wild flowers from the bank and made sure that the gun crew were not able to see the telephone wires from their emplacement.

I was convinced that here was an opportunity to cause the Germans some aggravation, I looked upon it as my duty to cut the wire. In readiness to carry out my act of sabotage, I put a pair of wire cutters in my cycle carrier bag.

Two or three times I cycled past the site early on Monday mornings on my way back from the Les Nicolles Farm and on each occasion there was something or someone which prevented me from carrying out my plan. On one occasion, just as I reached the site, a German on a bicycle peddling in the opposite direction appeared.

This was not just an opportunist act of sabotage, it was well thought out and planned. I tried not to take too much risk as I knew the consequences of being caught carrying out sabotage - a firing squad!

It was a bright early autumn morning as I cycled along the road towards town, everything was quite and peaceful. As I reached the site there was no one in sight and the cows were all at the far end of the field. I crossed the road, mounted the pavement, put one foot on the earth bank and, taking the wire cutters from my saddle bag, leant over and quickly snipped the wire. Thrusting the cutters back in my saddle bag, head down over the handlebars, I peddled away like mad down the road, which was slightly downhill. I soon passed 'Big Bertha', where there was no sign of life. I was very relieved when I reached the the turning down to town at Rue des Caches. Fortunately I had not seen another soul. Relief quickly turned to elation and as I peddled towards town I really felt pleased with myself. Now I rode bolt upright, with my head held high, sure that my little act of sabotage had been a success.

The German Authorities, of course took a different view. The cable, it turned out, was a telephone line between a high ranking officer's residence at St Elmo and his Headquarters. All hell was let loose. The local community was threatened with the most dire consequences if the culprit was not found, which I am glad to say he wasn't! The Germans immediately brought forward the curfew from 10 pm to 9 pm and the opening hours for public houses and taverns were also cut, as a community punishment.

Looking back on the telephone cable cutting incident after fifty years, I now wonder what I achieved. I caused many of my fellow islanders quite a considerable amount of inconvenience. They were punished for my act of sabotage. The Germans were only very slightly inconvenienced, the cable being repaired within a few hours. I certainly put myself and Mabs at risk.

At that time during the occupation I felt very strongly that I and my fellow islanders should be doing something positive to help the war effort, and an act of sabotage, as this was, I felt was fully justified. If I had cut a communications cable at a time when the Allies were about to carry out a raid or a full scale invasion of the island, there would have been no doubt in mine or anyone else's mind that my act of sabotage was fully justified. Certainly it caused the Germans to increase their guards and their vigilance and to that extent it was certainly worth the effort.

I don't think that I ever contemplated any act of sabotage which would have caused me to kill a German, although I always rejoiced when one was killed. I took the view that every German accounted for was a further nail in Hitler's coffin.

Mabs, however, was very worried during the occupation because she though that she might have to help dispose of the body of a German that I might kill. She thought that I might run into a German on one of my escapades and be forced to kill him for some reason or other. She, recalled later how, she often lay awake at night planning how she would get rid of the body. After the war, Mabs told me, "You activities scared me more than the whole German army put together.

John Ferbrache was another person who, long after the occupation ended, confided to me that he thought it inevitable that it would only be a matter of time before I was caught by the Germans. He told me that my anti-German activities were so blatant, that he was seriously concerned for my safety, in view of the penalties they proscribed. He said that it was a great relief to him that I was never caught.

One of the options which was not open to me was escape to the mainland by boat. I had seriously considered it when the Germans first arrived, but I was not prepared to leave Mabs, Margaret and Mum behind. However there were a few islanders who did manage to escape by boat to England and, after D Day, to France.

In August 1943 Alf Bougourd and four others managed to slip away successfully and, as a consequence, swimming pools were put out of bounds to islanders. The relatives of the escapee's were arrested, as was Stan Noel who had helped overhaul the boat prior to departure. Stan was due to go with them but somehow missed the rendezvous. He was sentenced by the Germans to a term of imprisonment and sent to an internment camp in Germany for the rest of the war. Fishing was again stopped, this time for almost five weeks. When the fishing ban was relaxed, only those fishermen who did not have relatives in England were given permits to fish. Almost half of our fishermen were barred from fishing and as a result there was a considerable loss of catches and food.

However all escapees took with them a great deal useful information, not only in regard to the German defences, but also in respect of the food situation and the condition of islanders.

At the beginning of November 1944, Captain Fred Noyon and Bill Enticott, managed to get away in 'Old Fred's' boat the Littlewood. They went, I believe, at the request of the Controlling Committee. The two escapees took with them important information regarding German fortifications and details of the serious state of our food supplies. It was not long after their escape that we heard that the British Government had agreed to allow Red Cross food parcels be sent to the island.

Both escapers went to extraordinary lengths to cover their intentions. Fred didn't tell his nephew of his plans, in fact he had made arrangements to go out fishing with him the next day. Tom Ounsworth, with whom Bill lodged in Vale Road, St Sampson's, told me that all he said when he left home that morning, was that he would be back about 7 pm.

Ralph Palmer, who had been given command of the small motor vessel,'The Oma', was stationed down at Plymouth awaiting the liberation of the Channel Islands. He and his ship remained at Plymouth from Christmas 1944, until the surrender of the Germans the following May. Ralph spent many hours in Plymouth being briefed on the German defences in the island. One of the charts he studied showed all the German fortifications, gun sites, and other 'Concrete Works of Art'. It had been brought over by Captain Noyon,

The last escape by sea that I was aware of, was made in early 1945 by the two Le Page brothers. Tom and Jack were accompanied by a French electrical engineer who had worked on a number of installations, including the long range battery at Frie Baton. It was very much an 'official' escape and had the approval of the Controlling Committee. Monsieur L.V. Lambert, Vic to everyone, who was the

French Consulate Agent in the island, approached the brothers and suggested that they escape with the Frenchman. The Le Page brothers were selected because they had no other relatives in the island. The Frenchman, because it was considered that an engineer who had been involved in the construction of the fortifications could provide the allies with details, which no plan could adequately supply.

Tom and Jack obtained permission for the Frenchman to accompany them fishing. Vic arranged with the Controlling Committee for the brothers to be supplied with plans of the German fortifications and details of the deteriorating food position. All these plans and information were packed, together with a brick, into a tin, so it could be thrown overboard if necessary.

When they left St Peter Port harbour they sailed around behind Herm, and only then did they set course for the French coast. They arrived there four and a half hours later and were picked up by the Americans.

Vic Lambert was a short tubby Frenchman, with white hair and shiny bright eyes. I often saw him furiously peddling his bicycle around the town, no doubt off to assist one of his fellow countrymen who had been forced to work for the Germans. He would always give me a cheery wave. After the occupation Vic and I became firm friends.

Some of the Frenchmen, brought to the island by the Organisation Todt, were used as labourers in the installation and commissioning of a new Electricity Power Plant in the Bouet. These Frenchmen were sufficiently successful in their acts of sabotage to prevent the plant ever being used by the Germans.

Any thoughts of an underground movement, such as the 'Maquis' in occupied France, was clearly out of the question. We had no bridges to blow up, there was no railway lines to sabotage. The B.B.C. never broadcast any messages of encouragement for us to form a resistance movement. No secret agents had landed equipped with radio transmitters. We had no arms or explosives, in fact from a resistance point of view there was very little we could do. However there were certainly a number of islanders who were constantly trying to find something that could be done that would be a real contribution to the Allied war effort.

One day in the autumn of 1943, Frank Falla the journalist came into the shop to talk to me. He had resigned his position with the Star newspaper and was working temporarily as a clerk for the Medical Services Officer. Frank was clearly bored and, like myself, was looking for some way of harassing the Germans. Unbeknown to me at the time, he was involved, with four former 'Star' colleagues, in the production and distribution of an underground news sheet, called G.U.N.S., the Guernsey Underground News Service.

Frank was a very patriotic fellow and, like a number of us, had not surrendered his radio. He regularly listened to the B.B.C. evening news, taking the main details down in shorthand. He typed out a master copy, averaging over five hundred words a day. Sometimes he added a postscript when the morning news included details of overnight R.A.F. raids on Germany. Copies were made by colleagues and surreptitiously distributed on a daily basis to those they believed could be trusted.

Distribution points included a bakery, a tobacconist, a barter mart, and a copy was even smuggled to Sark. Each copy was widely read and passed on from reader to reader. I regularly saw a copy, but it was sometime before I was aware where it had come from or who had produced it. G.U.N.S. was first 'published' in June 1942 by Charles Machon, who's original idea it was when the Germans confiscated our radios. At one time it became so successful that some members of the G.U.N.S. team wanted to make a charge for the news-sheet - typical newspapermen !

Circulation continued until February 1944, when the Germans discovered its existence. An Irishman, Paddy Doyle, who lived in Victoria Road, informed the

Germans that G.U.N.S. was being produced and supplied them with copies he had collected. He worked at the bakery in Victoria Road and had apparently enjoyed reading the copies of G.U.N.S, that were supplied to the proprietor. Paddy was seen directing the Germans to Charles Machon's house in Victoria Road just before he was arrested. Later Frank and his other colleagues were also arrested. They were all sentenced to terms in jail and deported to Germany only hours before the D Day landings. Regrettably Charles Machon and another colleague, Joe Gillingham, both failed to survive their imprisonment.

Frank and I talked over our desire to be more active in 'fighting' the German war machine. He suggested that I organise a meeting of some people whom we could trust, with the possibility of forming a resistance group in Guernsey. I jumped at the idea and it was decided to hold the meeting in the empty flat above my shop. Who were we going to invite?

Young John Ferbrache, with whom I had often discussed my thoughts of sabotage, was an obvious choice. Others who were invited included Jackie Upham, who ran the Guernsey Railway engineering workshop and foundry at Les Banques, Lloyd Warry, the island's leading baker and of course Edgar Stacey. Alf Mauger, who pre war had been a growers Commission Agent and 'Chipper' Bougourd, who worked as a linesman for the States Electricity Board, were both included. Frank Falla and I completed our little band of potential saboteurs.

The first meeting to form a Resistance Committee was held one evening, when we all secretly met in the flat above my shop. I laid the room out for a formal meeting, with a Union Jack draped over the table and another hanging on the wall.

Frank and I had planned such a wonderful meeting, but it did not turn out that way. We talked a lot, the subject was serious, but the comments were certainly not. We were going to do such terrible things to the Germans. Had we carried out many of the ideas suggested we should have all found ourselves in deep trouble.

Edgar said that the only reason that he had attended was to obtain a revolver so that he could settle a score with a couple of Germans. He told us how he had it all worked out and what he was going to do with their bodies once he had killed them. They were going into the farm cesspool tank, weighted down. He was confident that once in there they would never be found, no dog would be able to sniff them out. Edgar was most disappointed when he realised that no one was going to provide him with a revolver. He was serious - these two Nazi's had crossed his path and if Edgar had had the means they would have died.

Lloyd Warry was very wise and cooled us down, squashing all our big ideas about sabotage. As he pointed out, it would have little effect on the German war machine, but a great effect on the civil population. When it was realised that we were not going to get very far talking about sabotage, our thoughts turned to political conspiracy. Someone wanted the Controlling Committee sacked, another went further saying the whole system of government in the island should be changed. Alf Mauger suggested that he would make a good Bailiff. The meeting was totally out of hand and Jackie Upham urged that we should put the brakes on.

With that, Lloyd Warry stood up - I can see him standing there, with his spats and rolled umbrella - and said:

"This has gone far enough, you are all out of your tiny minds, all this will do is cause trouble for the rest of us. All I am concerned about is my business when this war is over. I am after all the bakeries in the island." and with that he left.

We all went home totally disillusioned and that was the only meeting of the Resistance Committee. However a number of us kindred spirits did get together from time to time. We would talk and scheme, but nothing ever came of any of our meetings - perhaps the Germans were luckier than they realised !

Chapter 19

FOR MILITARY REASONS

After we were evicted from Seaplane Bungalow, the Germans sealed off the Jerbourg peninsula. It was to be over four years before Mabs and I were again to set foot on our own property.

All over the peninsula the Germans created strong points, trenches and gunsites. One of the first coastal artillery units the Germans installed in the island was the Tarbour Strassburg battery, just south of the Doyle monument. The battery consisted of four 22.0 centimetre French guns which the Germans captured during the early part of the war. They spent a great deal of time and effort installing this battery, together with concrete bunkers, ammunition stores, control points and crew quarters, many of them underground.

When the Strassburg battery was assembled and ready to be test fired, the Germans came around warning householders to open their windows to prevent them from being shattered by the blast. The Germans weren't altogether inconsiderate to the civil population. Mum and I went out into the Vauroufs field which was a little further away from the battery. They test-fired one gun, which it turned out had been sabotaged by the French before it was brought to the island. It blew the breach out and killed a couple of Germans. A piece of the breach was carried by the force of the explosion right over our heads and landed in the field not far away from where Mum and I were standing. Despite the sabotage, the gun was quickly repaired and used fairly frequently against allied warships. It had a range of about 21 miles.

Whilst the Germans built many miles of railway track around the north and the west of the island, initially to facilitate the construction of their countless military fortifications, they never extended it to our part of the island. There were plans at

A German column marching along Jerbourg Road passed Bouvee Lane.

one stage to continue it as far as the Jerbourg Hotel, opposite the Barracks. The line would have serviced the Strassburg Artillery Battery, but for some reason it was not constructed. I remember seeing the pegs that the German engineers set out along the proposed route, all down the Bouvee and right through the front garden of the Nook.

On the night of the Normandy invasion we couldn't sleep because of the sound of hundreds of aircraft going over in wave after wave. Margaret was by that time too big for a cot and was sleeping in a bed in a room of her own. The drone of the Allied planes woke her up and she cried. Mabs said to me as we lay in bed listening to both Margaret and the aircraft:

"This is it, the invasion!"

In the morning we listened to the news on our crystal set and the start of the long awaited Second Front in Europe was confirmed.

At 3.20 am. on D Day a German officer rushed into the Police Station, and announced a 'general alarm'. He ordered that all police officers were to be called out and report to the Feldgendarmerie. There was no doubt that the opening of the Second Front made the Germans very jumpy and not before time.

The Germans were terrified that Guernsey would also be invaded by Allied forces. Guards and patrols were doubled and all German troops were in constant readiness for a landing. When I went down into town, German soldiers appeared everywhere in full battle order, carrying rifles and hand grenades, their helmets camouflaged with twigs and green leaves. All telephones went dead, the Germans had taken over the telephone exchanges and temporarily disconnected the lines.

A few day later, the entire Island Police Force was confined to the police station. They were quartered on the top floor and supplied with mattresses and bedding. Bill Sebire, one of the island's Special Constables was brought in and acted as cook. Two policemen were allowed out, under guard, to collect rations. The Force was kept in its special quarters for a fortnight before it was released and allowed to resume its normal duties.

The Germans at one time had planned to use the island as a U-Boat base. Whilst a great deal of work was carried out, they never came near to completing its construction. Two dredger ships which they brought to our waters were used to suction sand and shingle from Petit Port and then transport it to Havelet Bay. These two vessels took turns to tie up alongside Albert Pier and then, by means of a pipe of very considerable diameter, almost three feet, would discharge the sand and shingle into Havelet Bay. The delivery pipe ran along the Albert Pier, the South Esplanade and down the slipway to Havelet Bay.

The Germans were constantly dismantling and re-assembling the pipe line. It was bolted together with a considerable number of very large nuts and bolts. When they were adjusting the pipe the nuts and bolts were usually left lying on the quayside. A friend and I would go down during the lunch hour, when there were never any Germans around, and walk along the quay, kicking these nuts and bolts into the water. We became quite adept at appearing to saunter along enjoying the sunshine, whilst doing our little bit to sabotage the creation of a submarine base.

The sand, gravel and rocks, some as big as a mans head, which were pumped into the bay, converted Havelet into a lovely beach. The Germans did a considerable amount of blasting and excavating into the cliffs adjacent to the Valette swimming pools. A huge oil storage tank was installed in one of the tunnels which they created. That tank is still there and forms part of the Military Museum which is now based in the old German tunnels. The Germans were going to construct submarine pens in the bay, but that plan was never proceeded with for one reason or another. Havelet Bay kept its sandy beach for a long time, but eventually the sea returned it to its original state. It is incredible how nature will always win in the end.

Whilst the Germans did not succeed in constructing a U-Boat base in Havelet Bay, they did from time to time bring submarines into St Peter Port Harbour. Just before D Day a U-boat appeared and it was not long before the R.A.F. located it with their regular aerial reconnaissance. Clearly a U- boat would be a threat to the cross channel invasion and Allied planes paid regular visits to attack the submarine. The Germans moved it, almost daily, around the harbour and sometimes even took it to Petit Port to try to put the R.A.F. off the scent. What the Allies did not know was that the U-Boat had been damaged and could not submerge.

The Germans tried to hide the location of the submarine by sandwiching it between another larger vessel and the quay. On one occasion it was protected in this way by a German Naval Patrol boat, the Franz Westerman. The R.A.F., however, spotted it and launched another air attack, sinking the Franz Westerman, although not damaging the submarine.

Every time the Germans moved the submarine, the R.A.F. reconnaissance planes spotted it and another attack would be launched. I don't think the Germans were always aware of the Allied reconnaissance and photographic planes, probably because they flew so high. They suspected that there was an islander with a secret radio transmitter, giving the Allies a fix on the submarine.

Pop Travers, from the Prince of Wales Hotel, had a lookout at the top of his premises from which you could see right over the harbour and observe everything that was happening. I often went up there with him, because I liked seeing what was going on in the area to which we were forbidden to go. The Germans apparently had men positioned in Castle Cornet, scanning the town with binoculars, looking for anyone spying on the harbour. One day, Old Pop Travers was spotted in his lookout and was arrested on the suspicion of being a spy.

The Germans searched his premises, looking for transmitting equipment, but of course found none. Pop Travers liked the view and was inquisitive, but otherwise totally harmless as far as the Germans were concerned. He was a good story teller and for years afterwards enjoyed telling everyone about his 'spying activities!'

Soon after D Day, on 19th June 1944, Typhoon fighter bombers of the Royal Canadian Air Force raided St Peter Port Harbour, without doubt trying to destroy the elusive U-boat. As people were on the way to work at about twenty to nine in the morning, five or six R.C.A.F. aircraft came roaring in to attack the harbour. Young Herbert Winterflood was cycling along the front and dived into the small petrol station by the Crown Hotel for shelter.

One bomb which the Canadians dropped in the raid caused more damage to St Peter Port than any other bomb throughout the war. Normally bombs hitting the water exploded underwater, but this one exploded just above the surface of the harbour. Instead of blowing all the glass of windows into the buildings, there was a vacuum action. The glass from windows was sucked out and scattered in the streets. The suction action, caused the door of the Midland Bank safe to spring open. It was still locked, but must have had it's sides blown out enough to open the door. The lock was undamaged, but had to be unlocked in order to shut the safe again.

When Herbert emerged from his hiding place, the streets were literally covered in glass. He could not push his bicycle, far less ride it, for the fear of getting a puncture. I can still, in my mind's-eye, see Herbert arriving for work carrying his bicycle on his shoulder.

The bomb exploded in the middle of the Old Harbour directly opposite Creasey's and the damage had not only occurred in the High Street, the Pollet and Smith Street, but extended to Market Street, the lower part of the Bordage as well as Mansell Street and Mill Street.

After finding that our only damage was to a window in our workshop, I went for a walk around town to see the extent of the devastation. Shopkeepers were collecting some of their very limited and precious stock from the streets outside their shops. There was women's clothing, mens suits, all secondhand, in the streets, awaiting rescue by shopkeepers. In the High Street there was the very distinctive aroma of perfume. Lloyds Bank's beautifully engraved windows, which carried the crest and name of Capital and Counties Bank were miraculously undamaged. The windows of the Town Church were not so fortunate. As I cycled home that evening I noticed that the damage had extended as far as Victor Hugo's house in Hauteville.

Whilst it was fortunate that there were no casualties amongst islanders, the Town took a long time to recover from that raid. Sheet glass to repair shop windows was non existent, all that was available was small greenhouse glass. Carpenters did a great job by adapting many shop fronts to take small panes. In some ways it created a new character which was not un- pleasing.

German shipping and naval vessels in St Peter Port Harbour were not only attacked from the air, the Royal Navy shelled them from time to time. One night, under the cover of darkness, the Royal Navy shelled targets in the harbour. One of the shells landed on Boots the Chemists, but failed to explode, although it severed a water pipe and flooded the premises. Dickie Butterworth, the manager of Boots, who served in the Royal Navy during the first war, recognised the un-exploded shell as a type he had handled during his service. Being shelled by his own shells didn't strike Dickie as being funny! He was never quite sure whether he should be happy, or embarrassed that the shell had failed to explode. Another shell from that night's engagement landed at the junction of Lower Vauvert and Victoria Road and exploded, doing considerable damage.

The Doyle Monument, which had been used by the Germans in the early stages of the occupation for observation purposes, was demolished on 23 June 1944. The German authorities said 'For military reasons'. The monument being less than one hundred yards away from the Strassburg battery, clearly interrupted their field of fire, particularly as its likely targets were now almost certainly in the direction of Alderney and the French coast. Frankly I was surprised that the column had not been removed before as it provided the Allies with a good landmark for Naval use, since it appeared on all their charts. It also provided pilots with a easily identified feature to home in on for quick identification of targets. The Delancey Monument had previously been demolished for just those reasons.

The Doyle Monument was one hundred and six feet high and had an observation platform that was reached by climbing one hundred and thirty three steps. I can safely vouch for that number as I counted them many times as I climbed the stairs to enjoy the magnificent view. All the way around the observation platform was a safety rail. Many years ago, long before the war, I saw a British sailor walk around that rail.

To gain access to the Monument, the key had to be obtained from Susie Osborne, at the nearby Monument Tavern. On that occasion I had picked up the key and opened up the stairway when the sailor and a number of his friends followed me up to the observation platform. Once up there, this Jack Tar, who was completely sober, climbed up on the parapet and proceeded to walk around the rail, with his arms outstretched in the manner of a tight rope walker. He scared me stiff. Fortunately he completed the full circuit without mishap. I shudder to think about it even today!

When the Germans were about to demolish the Monument they came around and warned local residents that it was going to be blown up. They feared that there might be some bits of masonry flying about and that the local population had better move further away for their own protection. Mum took Margaret, who was three and threequarters at the time, down near the German Cemetery and they watched the demolition of the monument from there. Margaret claims that she can remember standing on the Cemetery wall, wearing a jumper knitted by Mabs, holding her Gran's hand and seeing the column wobble and crumble before disappearing in a cloud of dust.

I came home from the shop, to find the skyline without the familiar Doyle Monument. It was a very sad day for Guernsey. While the Monument was replaced after the war with a granite column, the observation platform and the magnificent panoramic view it provided have regrettably gone for ever.

During the occupation, my only view was from the window in the roof of La Croix. I spent a lot of time watching what was going on and it was from there, one Saturday lunch time in August 1944, I watched a long series of explosions on Alderney. They lasted almost two hours from the time that I first noticed the explosions. At that time, two months after D Day, I was not aware what was causing them, whether they were allied action, or the Germans blowing up their own fortifications.

Later I learnt that the Germans had installed a number of 150mm Guns in Alderney, with a range of over 15 miles. After the Americans liberated the Cherbourg peninsular, the Germans used these guns, the Blucher Battery, to bombarded Allies supply routes.

The explosions that I had seen were caused by the battleship H.M.S. Rodney shelling the battery, which was situated adjacent to the Longy Road. The Rodney's sixteen inch guns, which fired shells weighing almost a ton, blasted the battery for almost two and a half hours. The Rodney's gunners had a reputation for accuracy and I believe, that the eighty or so shells they fired did considerable damage. This was confirmed when one of the damaged guns was shipped over to St Peter Port for repair. A German soldier told me that when the Rodney started shelling, the Jerry gun crews were mystified because they did not know whether they were being bombed or shelled. The Germans never saw the Rodney because it was positioned so that the Cherbourg peninsula came between it and the island of Alderney.

Regrettably, the Blucher Battery continued to do considerable damage to Allied supplies and positions in and around Cherbourg. I was surprised that more effective efforts were not made by the Allies to knock out the German long range guns, including the Strassburg Battery.

The shelling of Alderney by H.M.S. Rodney, was not only intended to put out of action some of the guns of the Blucher battery, but also to encourage Germans in the island to surrender. To that extent the action was a failure.

From my vantage point in the attic window, I saw a great deal of activity in the air during the occupation. On the morning of D Day the sky was black with planes towing gliders, all destined for Normandy. They came in from the south and headed north just beyond Sark. While many of the German anti- aircraft guns inevitably opened up, I did not see any aircraft or glider shot down. By this time the allies most certainly had total command of the air and that day there was no sign of any Jerry aircraft.

On many occasions I watched R.A.F. planes attacking the harbour and shipping in the Little Russel. There were many dog fights between the Allied aircraft and the Luftwaffe. Once I saw a Spitfire shot down - the pilot came ashore at Petit Port and safely walked up the cliffs through the mine field.

One day four planes in formation flew in from the direction of Sark going along the coast towards St Peter Port. The anti-aircraft guns on the Jerbourg peninsula let fly at these planes and hit one of them. I watched as it lost height and crashed into the sea near the Brehon Tower in the Little Russel. I remember the jubilation, shouting and cheering by the German gun crews as the plane went down. Then they found out that they had shot down one of their own planes !

The Luftwaffe planes had come in from the wrong direction. Apparently there was a requirement that all friendly planes approached the island from a particular direction and if they didn't come from that direction, then they were assumed to be enemy aircraft. We heard that the German gun-crew was severely reprimanded, particularly as the plane and the pilot were both lost.

Another time, I saw a British aircraft shot down and the pilot was drifting in a boat off Sark. Another British aircraft was trying to save him, but the Germans prevented his rescue. Eventually the Germans picked up the R.A.F. pilot and took him ashore at the harbour. Later he was taken to the Happy Landings Hotel, near the Airport. Mabs and I cycled out there and saw him at a window of the Hotel. We waved to him as we went past.

Towards the end of the occupation the Germans cut off all our power, so we had no electricity at all. They drew the mains fuse from the houses all the way down the Jerbourg Road. I was puzzled about this because I thought that if there was no power then none of the German equipment in their billets and administrative buildings would be working. To my certain knowledge, some of the German electrical equipment was working. So, with a couple of pins with lengths of wire attached to them and wearing rubber gloves, I pierced the cables on the supply side of the meter. I found that, as I suspected, it was live. With the pins in position, I managed to pick up enough current to run my set, but I dare not turn on our lights. As a result of that discovery I was able to use my Philco Pilot set, which I had built into the armchair, right up to the end of the occupation, thankfully without being discovered.

One of my great delights during the occupation was sitting on the wall outside Maison Allaire, talking to John Leale and other members of the Controlling Committee. I had a great respect for the whole Committee, they did an outstanding job on behalf of the island. As one of them said one day:

"None of us are trained diplomats, but we have been pitchforked into the task of representing the island in our daily confrontations with the Germans".

During the occupation the Hague Convention almost became the Controlling Committee's 'Bible'. John Leale's conversations with me, often turned to the subject of the Convention and International Law. Clearly he had made a very detailed study of the convention and held very firm views of how it should apply to our situation in Guernsey.

It was very near the end of the occupation when he let on to me that the Controlling Committee had taken almost a year to locate a copy of the Hague Convention and its accompanying commentary. The Convention itself was a comparatively short document, but the accompanying commentary, an interpretation of the Law written by British lawyers, was much longer and very much more helpful. Each country apparently produced its own commentary and John Leale was particularly pleased when the Germans gave him a copy of their interpretation. He said that it made his job a lot easier. The Jersey Authorities, he told me, could not find any trace of the Hague Convention in their island, so he supplied them with a copy.

The Convention gave the German occupying forces rights and obligations, as it did islanders. John Leale often emphasised to me that we as islanders must carry out our responsibilities if we were to expect the Germans to honour the Convention. John Leale looked upon the Hague Convention as an ally and as he later said:

"When you have it on your side, you feel less alone."

He was a man of the highest integrity and if he felt the Convention allowed the Germans to do something, such as commandeer motor vehicles, he did not object, but if it said that, as it did, they could not make Guernseymen work on fortifications, then there was no moving him.

Chapter 20

THE VEGA – GOD BLESS HER

In June 1944, the Allied invasion of Normandy quickly cut off both the Germans and ourselves from further supplies of food and fuel. Within a matter of weeks we were completely isolated from the European mainland and survival became our overriding objective in life. Food progressively became more important in both our thoughts and conversations. Our meagre rations were constantly being cut and the prospect was that the island food supplies would run out altogether, in early 1945.

Throughout the occupation the island's efforts to produce food were severely hampered by the Germans. They created prohibited zones, which prevented hundreds of vergees from being cultivated. Numerous glasshouses were commandeered, many more demolished. They deported many able-bodied workers and evicted hundreds of Guernseymen from their growing properties. Master plans were produced for the cultivation of land which bore no relation to reality. Our island authorities, within the restraints placed upon them, did a marvellous job and managed to produce considerable quantities of food. The Germans, however, regularly commandeered much of our locally produced food for their own consumption.

Looking back on that last winter of the occupation, I now realise just how near the island came to starvation. If everyone had remained in the island in 1940, there would have been a further 20,000 people to feed. That would have been impossible - almost certainly we would have starved. In retrospect it was fortunate that so many people chose to evacuate.

D Day, brought with it the great hope that our subjugation would soon be at an end. At first, we hourly expected the Allies to land and liberate us. Then we daily waited for the Germans to withdraw. It appeared entirely logical to us that their presence in France would be of more military value than sitting occupying non-strategic Guernsey.

Slowly we realised that it was not to be, slowly we realised that the Allies were going to leave the Germans 'to rot', as Winston Churchill put it. Although we didn't like it at the time and would have perhaps wished the Allies to invade, they very wisely left us until the Germans finally surrendered. It was the right strategy and looking back after all this time, there is no doubt about that at all. The lives that would have been lost, the damage that might have been inflicted to our island would, without doubt, have been far greater and more lasting than any of the privations we had to suffer during the last winter and spring of the occupation.

As the autumn of 1944 turned to winter, we realised that the islands' food situation was getting extremely serious. All talk inevitability turned to the prospects of help from the International Red Cross. On the 11th November 1944 we were encouraged by a Notice in the Evening Press signed by the Bailiff, Victor Carey stating:

> 'The German Authorities have allowed me to send a radio message to the International Red Cross at Geneva, stating the present serious shortage of many essentials in the island, and asking for immediate help and a visit from a Red Cross representative without delay.
>
> I am informed that the message was despatched last Monday morning, the 6th November.
>
> Victor G. Carey. Bailiff.'

Whether I was at home or in the shop, all conversations were inevitably about the possibility of the Red Cross sending us food, but when, no one knew. So rumours abounded and were readily believed. We heard repeatedly that the Red Cross ship had sailed and would arrive in a few days. Then rumour had it that the vessel had been seen off the Casquets, then off the Hanois lighthouse. Another report said it was in the Little Russel. Then on 8th December the headline in the Evening Press said:

'Red Cross ship sails for C.I.'

> 'The Evening Press is authorised by Victor G. Carey Esq, the Bailiff of Guernsey, to announce that he has been informed by the German authorities that an International Red Cross ship was due to sail from Portugal for the Channel Islands yesterday, loaded with 750 tons of stores.'

That had to be true, because at the Bailiff's request, Intermediate School children had been given the following Monday off, so they could go and look for the ship, that he said, would be arriving from a south westerly direction, that day. It failed to materialize. Our hopes were raised and then dashed so many times that Mabs and I almost gave up hope of ever receiving any food from the Red Cross.

Then listening to the evening news on my crystal set, the B.B.C. reported that 'The Ship' was due to leave Lisbon the next week. That was no rumour, that was fact, the B.B.C. was always accurate and could be relied upon. The Swedish ship, the B.B.C. said, would bring food, soap and medical supplies. The only question left in my mind was whether it would arrive in time for Christmas. If it did it would be the best possible Christmas present islanders could ever receive.

As Christmas drew near, there was still no definite news of the arrival of the Red Cross ship or relief food supplies, although I was sure that the B.B.C. would not have misled us. Many people in the island were desperately short of food. The bread ration was now less than half a pound a day and that was often stale. Pre-war we had eaten an average of two pounds of bread a day and that had been of a much better quality. Men who were engaged in heavy manual work just could not exist on our meagre ration.

Meagre as it was, there was no prospect of any bread ration at all after the end of January. Supplies of cheese, sugar and fat would also come to an end during January. The supply of meat would probably last a little longer, largely due, I suspect, to the fact that there were a lot of horses on the island. I don't know if we ever ate any horse meat, but I expect that we did - we just ate, without question, any meat which we were lucky enough to obtain.

Christmas day arrived, but the ship did not. Mabs with her usual ingenuity managed to conjure up a Christmas dinner, composed almost entirely of root vegetables. As we ate our meagre dinner, I reflected that if the Red Cross supplies did not arrive very soon, islanders would be dying of starvation by early February.

The day after Boxing day, Wednesday 27th December 1944, the long hoped for news flashed around the Island, the International Red Cross ship had been sighted off the south coast. Mabs and I and other local residents went into the Vauroufs Field to get a glimpse of the ship which was going to be our salvation. The field was still divided in two by a wire fence, beyond which mines were laid. We were all leaning over the fence as far as we could, straining to be the first to see the ship coming around St Martin's point.

It was just before noon when I first saw the 'S.S. Vega' coming through the mist. She was a long, low ship, painted a blue grey, with little superstructure other than the bridge. She had large Red Crosses painted on her bow and stern. Amidships in very large letters was C.INTERNATIONAL.

We watched as the Vega sailed majestically on, and then dropped anchor outside the harbour. There she stayed tantalisingly throughout the afternoon, until just after five thirty, when she at last weighed anchor and eased her way into St Peter Port Harbour. Ever since the news of the first sighting, early in the morning, islanders had been gathering on the Esplanade. Every window, every roof which had sight of the London berth where the Vega was due to dock, was packed with people. Every available vantage point was filled with islanders who wanted to welcome the Vega. No one was allowed on to the White Rock, it was restricted to Germans and permit-holders only.

As the S.S. Vega slowly entered the harbour on that moonlit winter's evening, all eyes were strained to catch a glimpse of the boat that was going to save the island from starvation. The Vega turned towards the London berth, where she tied up. Suddenly cheering broke out from the thousands of joyful islanders who wanted to witness and be part of that historic moment. Ask any Guernseyman who was in the island during the occupation where they were when the S.S. Vega arrived with its precious cargo of Red Cross parcels and they will tell you precisely. It was one of those moments in our lives that we will never forget, not even the slightest detail!

While the S.S. Vega was being unloaded, virtually every islander went down to the Esplanade to stand and admire and, indeed, to pay homage to the ship that had brought us our next meal and our next and our next..., the ship that had brought us hope, the ship that had brought us life. I stood on the Esplanade and admired the ship, with its Swedish Flag proudly flying from its stern and proposed a silent 'toast', "The S.S. Vega - God bless her!".

Unloading of the Red Cross parcels, together with sacks of salt, cases of soap, cartons of medical supplies and nine cases of cigarettes, was commenced at lunch time on the Thursday, under the watchful eyes of many islanders.

German soldiers and foreign workers manhandled the crates of parcels from the Vega and loaded them on to trucks of the German light railway, which transported them to St George's Hall. Gradually the task of stacking the 42,500 food parcels in the hall proceeded, until it was completed on the Saturday morning. The Vega left for Jersey at lunch time. There were no crowds to see her leave, all eyes and thoughts were now on St George's Hall.

Many of us were very concerned that the Germans might decide to 'acquire' some or all of the Red Cross parcels for their own consumption, as they were as hungry as we were and had no prospect of receiving additional supplies. The administration for the distribution of the parcels was under the control of a senior States official, John Loveridge. All credit, the distribution was very quickly and efficiently carried out, but there was concern regarding possible pilfering.

Jurat John Leale, the president of the Controlling Committee and Louis Guillemette, the Secretary to the Committee, expressed concern regarding the number of people who were being admitted to St Georges Hall. The Police were asked to take control of the situation and only allow persons with a pass issued by Louis Guillemette and signed by John Leale, into the Hall. Police Constable Frank

Le Cocq, known to many of us as 'Ginge', was sent down with specific instructions to 'only admit persons with Official Passes'.

He positioned himself at the entrance and was inspecting every pass and only letting those in with the necessary authority. John Leale appeared at the door of St Georges Hall with Louis Guillemette.

"Your pass please Sir." requested P.C.Le Cocq.

John Leale, swallowed hard, obviously trying to control himself, turned to Louis and said:

"You had better go back to the office and get two passes for us."

Louis Guillemette quickly returned with two passes he had made out and handed them to John Leale for him to sign. Then he turned and presented them to Frank, who said:

"Thank you Sir." and stood aside and let them in.

Other police officers were allocated the St Georges Hall duty from then on. Frank Le Cocq said that it was just pure cussedness on his part, as they were the ones who had originally complained.

During Saturday, sufficient numbers of the parcels were transferred to retail shops throughout the island to enable every islander to collect one on Sunday the 31st December. Everyone received a Red Cross parcel, babies, the sick, hospital patients and even those unfortunates who were in prison. The biggest distribution was at Le Riche's High Street shop, where over three thousand parcels were handed out. It was a very happy end to 1944.

There were certain conditions imposed by the International Red Cross. The food parcels were provided for the benefit of each member of the civilian population, no German could receive one or even some of the contents. They were to be given out free of charge and no one was allowed to sell any of the contents.

Mabs and I went up to Luff's, which later became Manor Stores, to collect our three parcels and one for Mum. I can remember sitting in the kitchen, with Mabs and Margaret, unpacking our parcels. We were all tremendously excited as we very carefully examined the contents. My parcel, which was beautifully packed in a cardboard carton, contained all sorts of wonderful goodies, some of which were new to me. There was a tin of ham which they called Spam. I read and re-read the labels, they fascinated me. I can remember spending hours just sitting studying the contents of my parcel.

Some of the parcels, such as ours, came from Canada and others came from New Zealand. We were soon able to tell the difference because the Canadian food came in a square box while the New Zealand one, was oblong.

Our first Red Cross parcels from Canada contained:

6oz chocolate,
20oz biscuits,
5oz sardines,
20oz milk powder,
6oz prunes,
10oz salmon,
14oz corned beef,
8oz raisins,
8oz sugar,
4oz tea,
4oz cheese,
16oz marmalade,
20oz butter,
13oz spam,
3oz soap,
1oz pepper and salt.

Later we received parcels from New Zealand and they contained:

6oz tea,
19oz corned mutton,
15oz lamb and green peas,
8oz chocolate,
20oz butter,
15oz coffee and milk,
10oz sugar,
9oz peas,
16oz jam,
16oz condensed milk,
15oz cheese
6oz raisins.

There is little doubt that the provision of Red Cross Parcels to islanders allowed the Germans to hold out longer than they might otherwise have done. Certainly it prevented the possibility of large numbers of islanders dying from starvation in the spring of 1945.

Today there are paintings of the 'Vega' proudly hanging on the walls of many Guernsey homes. For years, many of us kept a tin of food which we had saved from one of those precious Red Cross parcels. It was a prized possession. Even after all this time I would not be surprised if an odd tin is still not tucked away at the back of a cupboard!

While the arrival of the Vega brought relief for islanders, no further supplies of food reached the Germans. They at one time planned to bring in food by submarine, but nothing ever came of that scheme. Their plight rapidly worsened, even though they were requisitioning locally produced food which had been intended for islanders.

During November and December 1944 the Germans requisitioned five hundred tons of potatoes, virtually all the stocks at the States Depots, despite the fact that these were needed to supply islanders for the rest of the winter. The Controlling Committee, in turn, was forced to require all growers to hand over their total stocks, with the exception of 90 lb, so that the civilian potato ration could be maintained, albeit at a much reduced level.

The rumours which circulated in the island regarding the requisitioning by the Germans of our potato stocks caused the Bailiff to issue a statement in La Gazette Officielle. He said that he had received personal assurances from the German Commandant that their demands would not exceed five hundred tons. 'Personal assurances' from a German. How gullible could he get! That was another one of his 'mistakes'. Despite that assurance, the Germans continued to help themselves to our limited supplies, both States and private.

The German Feldgendarmerie searched private houses and commercial premises and took away any food or drink that they found, that they considered excessive. Many of their police took the view that now we had Red Cross parcels, any other stocks were excessive. Very few people had any reserve of food, it had all been eaten. The food seized was not handed back to the Essential Commodities Committee for distribution amongst islanders, it was kept by the Germans for their own use.

There was a lot of thieving taking place at that time by foreign workers and starving Germans. The Feldgendarmerie searches were looked upon by islanders as legalized armed robbery.

Towards the end of the occupation we had all become only too familiar with the activities of thieves. Red Cross parcels, bicycles, potatoes, chickens and even cats and dogs were all targets of petty thieving. Sometimes the Germans and the foreign workers would offer to buy a cat or dog and only if you refused, did they steal them. By the time of our liberation, the cat population of the island had virtually been wiped out.

During the last winter of the occupation a new line of thieving was taking place - gate snatching. We were warned to keep a very close eye on our wooden gates and fences, because if we didn't, they would disappear and be used as fuel. Many people removed their front gates themselves and hid them away, otherwise they would have disappeared over night. During the last Christmas of the war, Mrs Emma Best, who lived in Les Cornus, lost part of her garden fence. I met her in the street on New Year's Day and she was almost in tears. She took me to see where the thieves had stolen a section of the fence at the rear of her garden. I could see the new saw marks on what was left of the fence. A ten foot by five foot section was missing.

From time to time, people found that their telephones were dead. It was not a fault at the exchange, it was because yet another telephone pole had been cut down by islanders who were desperate for fuel. Every now and again we would read of a court case concerning the stealing of a telephone pole and as often as not the culprit would be sent to prison for fourteen days.

Thieving apart, the fuel shortage was causing many islanders to destroy their own property. Familiar old tables and chairs were being sawn up to provide wood for cooking and warmth. Sheds were being pulled down, to vanish for ever in flames.

Bonamy Martel found that his cows were being milked at night, he suspected, by Germans or foreign workers. He complained to the German authorities, who agreed to provide him with an armed guard. Bonamy and the guard sat in the cow shed all night waiting for the intruders. Sure enough just before dawn, two figures appeared and prepared to milk one of his cows. Bonamy grappled with one of the intruders and a scuffle developed. Bonamy's throat was cut, but despite his injury, he managed to get one of the intruders, who was in German uniform, down on the floor. Bonamy yelled to his wife, who had come out to see what was going on:

"Hit him! Hit him !"

His wife grabbed a wooden stake, swung it in the air and smashed it down, missing the German, but hitting Bonamy, knocking him out. The intruder escaped. The German guard chased the other man, but failed to catch him. A few days later Bonamy came into the shop with his throat heavily bandaged, it was by all accounts, a very nasty wound.

By the spring of 1945 the Germans were very hungry and in poor physical condition. They had always kept the foreign workers short of food and in a very pitiful state and now they were suffering in the same way. I watched their soldiers, who looked pale and under nourished, coming up Smith Street, which is not all that steep. They would stagger and rest on their way up the street. Many of them were just shrunken ghosts of their former selves. Hunger, of course, saps the mind and their faces expressed the certainty of defeat. German officers, however, always seemed to be better fed than the Wehrmacht soldiers.

Mabs watched a German in the field opposite La Croix using a bayonet to scratch around in the soil looking for roots which had been missed when the previous crop had been cleared. He found a root of some sort and Mabs watched him cut it up and eat it on the spot - he must have been hungry.

Cecil Hardwick worked four greenhouses, which were adjacent to his house. Like all growers, Cecil was told what crops he was required to plant. At one time he had potatoes, carrots, lettuce and broccoli growing under glass. One morning he went out to find his crop of carrots had been pulled up, and all that was left were their tops in a heap on the path. Every potato root had been pulled up by the stalk.

Cecil reported the theft to the Police, who came and inspected the damage with a German policeman. The Germans declared the crops a write-off and agreed that any carrots or potatoes that were left in the ground could be kept by Cecil, for his own use. Bert Crocker and I gave him a hand to dig out the remaining potatoes and we were both rewarded with a basket full for ourselves.

Whilst we were digging out the remains of the crop, in came two Germans, who said to Cecil:

"Ah potatoes ! Mister, potatoes for me and my comrade."

Cecil said; "Nein potatoes for you and your comrade, you want potatoes, you speak to Hitler, he give you potatoes. These potatoes are for civilians." and he indicated the looseness of his trousers around his waist.

The Germans would not take 'No' for an answer and persisted with their demand. After a time Cecil lost his cool and, with the business end of his five pronged fork, pushed one of the Germans out of the greenhouse. As the German was ejected through the door, he tripped and went head over heels. Everyone started laughing, which probably saved Cecil. I don't think he realised the serious trouble he could have been in for threatening a Jerry with a five pronged fork.

The thieves came back that night when everyone was in bed and finished the job, by picking every lettuce Cecil had growing in his greenhouse. The next morning the Crocker's dog was found with its throat cut, no doubt to keep it quiet whilst the greenhouses were raided.

The fact that we had Red Cross parcels and the Germans and their foreign workers had none substantially increased the likelihood of thieving. Islanders guarded their food parcel with their life. Some would not go out of the house, because of the fear of a burglary and others would take their precious food with them wherever they went. Most people, if the truth were known, took their parcels, or what was left of them, to bed with them.

One of the great tragedies to occur towards the end of the occupation was the death of Bill Pitchford's wife's parents. Mr and Mrs George Robins, of Sunnyside Cottage, Ruette Braye were murdered by an intruder raiding their house for food. It was one of the few really serious atrocities that took place locally. Both were found with their throats cut. Bill and his wife were shattered

The Germans were on the whole very correct in the handling of the Red Cross parcels. They unloaded the Vega and transported the cargo to St Georges Hall and as far as I know, not a single parcel went astray. They made no attempt to divert any of the Red Cross supplies for their own use.

The German army was without doubt a well disciplined military force and, in the main, respected the local population and their property. There were however, individual German soldiers and foreign workers who caused tremendous problems. The Germans were very tough on any of their troops who were caught stealing, particularly food.

John Ferbrache, who was still in his teens, had a particularly harrowing experience in the spring of 1945. Early one morning he was cycling to work at Bucktrouts. As he rounded the bend in the Coutanchez, near where the College of Further Education is now established, he was stopped by an armed German and made to dismount. John was taken into a field opposite the present College site, where the Germans had built a series of potato clamps. The German's were stopping men and women on their way to work and they were all herded into the field and compelled to witness the execution of a German soldier, whose crime was stealing a piece of fruit from the cook house.

The Germans had erected a pole, about nine inches in diameter and seven or eight feet in height, and the unfortunate German was trussed up to it. John Ferbrache and the young girls that were there found the whole incident very distressing, particularly one girl who, he remembers, was a seamstress at Creasey.

First the charge sheet was read out, then the firing party, on the command of an officer, carried out the execution. When the shots rang out, the only movement John saw was the condemned man's head drop two or three inches. The German discipline was, in many ways, much tougher in respect of their own troops, than it was with the local population.

Whilst the 'Vega' was in port two lengthy conferences took place between representatives of the International Red Cross, the German Military Authorities and the Controlling Committee. The Bailiff of Jersey, Alexander Coutanche, came over to Guernsey to attend the conferences. It was agreed that the 'Vega' would continue making trips to the islands with Red Cross supplies. The Swedish vessel could only make six knots, so it would take four weeks at least to complete the round trip. In view of the deteriorating bread situation, our Controlling Committee requested that priority be given to the supply of flour.

The possibility of the 'Vega' transporting sick and infirm people from the island was also considered. The Germans were keen that islanders, who could no longer be treated in Guernsey should be evacuated to Lisbon. Notices appeared in the Press regarding the possible evacuation of invalids and their next of kin. The classes of invalids included:

Eye cases requiring operations.
Cases of Phthisis and other classes of tuberculosis where benefit might be expected.
Cases that might receive treatment not available in the island, such as Radium or deep X.Ray treatment.
Persons suffering from old age, with decrepitude.
Mental Cases.

It was added that men of military age between 16 and 50 could not expect permission to depart with their next of kin. The lack of response to the proposed evacuation of the sick showed that the general situation and the hopes of islanders had significantly improved and that it was believed that liberation was just around the corner. The Germans, however, were still talking as late as May 7th - only hours before the liberation - of their intention to evacuate sick and infirm islanders in a Swedish Hospital ship. This time, however, it was to be the turn of the Germans to be evacuated.

After the 'Vega' had left St Peter Port on her way to Jersey at the end of December 1944, we knew that it would be over a month before it brought us any further life-saving supplies. She returned on February 7th, again with a large supply of food parcels but no flour, which by then was desperately needed.

We received our last ration of bread on Tuesday 13th February 1945. I realise that this was the point during the German occupation when, had it not been for the Red Cross parcels, many Islanders would have most certainly starved.

We had been warned by the Bailiff in a newspaper announcement, on February 10th, that supplies of flour were about to become exhausted.

'OUR FLOUR

IMPORTANT ANNOUNCEMENT.

To the People of Guernsey.

To my deep regret I have to inform you that the supply of flour will be exhausted after next Tuesday's bread issue, but I have received a letter form Colonel Iselin, the International Red Cross representative in Lisbon who visited us six weeks ago, in which he states that on her next trip the 'Vega' will bring flour. This has been confirmed by Mr Callias the International Red Cross representative now in the island. The Vega is expected back about the fifth of March.

The position has been considered in all its aspects and in order to alleviate suffering as far as possible, arrangements are being made for the distribution of the Red Cross parcels on the 15th February and on the 1st of March.

For the week commencing the 18th February we hope to issue increased rations as far as our resources allow.

Victor G.Carey, Bailiff'.

When the 'Vega' arrived for the third time on March 6th she brought almost three thousand sacks of flour, pure white Manitoba No 1 flour, of the highest quality.

Two doors down from our home, on the corner with Bouvee Lane, Miss Wilson ran a small shop and this became one of the distribution points for the newly baked 'Vega' bread. Mabs went down to collect our first loaf of bread and on her way back she passed a German soldier. She still remembers how proud and triumphant she felt with her big loaf of new white bread. The Germans did not have much food and certainly no bread. After so many years, of our occupiers lording it over us, the boot was now on the other foot.

That was our first bread for over three weeks. The pure white bread was too rich for our digestive systems after being used to the small ration of rough German rye bread for so long. Although we were warned, it was very difficult not to over indulge. Our stomachs were just not up to digesting the pure white bread and it made some of us ill.

The end of February brought further bad news. Major-General Graf von Schmettow was replaced as German Commander-in-Chief in the Channel Islands by Vice-Admiral Huffmeier, a former Captain of the battleship Scharnhorst. General von Schmettow had ruled Guernsey and Jersey with reasonable benevolence and certainly without the excesses which had been seen in parts of occupied Europe. Admiral Huffmeier, on the other hand, was a dedicated Nazi whose declared intention was not to surrender, but fight to the death. However, in the event of surrender, it was believed that he would order the destruction of all German arms and ammunition supplies. I realised that if they were blown up, it would cause massive damage to the harbour and other parts of the island. Huffmeier's appointment made me very apprehensive, because I thought it inevitably meant that we could only be liberated by Allied military action. That would be pretty disastrous for all of us.

Chapter 21

LIBERATION

It was now becoming clear to everyone, with the possible exception of Admiral Huffmeier, the German Commander, that the war in Europe was rapidly coming to an end and our liberation could not be long delayed.

In the months leading up to the end of the occupation, our situation dramatically improved with the arrival of the Red Cross food parcels and other supplies. The morale of the Germans, however, was steadily falling. They knew that as far as they were concerned, the war was lost. They were totally cut off from their homeland and no supplies or mail arrived. Attempts to fly in mail and desperately needed supplies were thwarted by the Allied Air Force, who shot down any plane that attempted to run the blockade.

Prior to D Day, German troops were able, on occasions, to travel to the mainland of Europe for their leave. Now they had to remain on the island. A house on the cliffs, Les Faitieres, opposite where we were living, was converted into rest quarters for their men. It was where the Quevatre's lived earlier in the occupation. The house was large enough to provide facilities for a troop of soldiers at a time. I found out, by careful observation, that one troop would arrive and spend a few days in the house, and when they left it was some hours before the next contingent arrived.

On a number of occasions, I took advantage of this 'gap' and went foraging in and around Les Faitieres for anything of value, particularly items that could be used as fuel. I did manage to 'acquire' a number of small army tables and folding stools and on one visit two bottles of wine. Mabs kept one of the tables for many years, in fact it is probably still hidden away in the attic, the rest I chopped up for fire wood.

The days were very long waiting for our liberation, but the air of expectancy was high. Ever since D Day we had known that liberation was almost at hand, but nothing ever seemed to bring it nearer to reality. There was, however, a considerable relaxation of the implementation of rules and regulations on the part of the Germans. They didn't aggravate us nearly as much as they had done earlier in the occupation. Clearly they realised that the day of reckoning was approaching when they would be our prisoners and they were becoming wary of what might happen.

Whereas earlier, I had been very careful about what I said to Germans, particularly their officers, now I was getting a bit cocky. During the last few months of the occupation, I was only too happy to take the Germans on verbally. One morning I was in Rabey's bookshop, when a German officer came in with his almost obligatory two henchmen. This officer spoke English with a broad American accent, which I suspect, could only have been obtained by spending a number of years in America. I had previously seen him in the shop, at a time when I was still being very careful as to what I said to the Germans. Then he had commented:

"Things are going well for your lot."

I had merely said "Oh."

I hadn't taken him up, because you never knew where you were really with them.

"Don't you know?"

He apparently was referring to a battle we had won and he added:

"We made a balls of that don't you know, your pals did very well."

Now he was again in Mr Rabey's bookshop and dropped a few Reichmarks notes on the floor. One of his henchman dived down to pick them up, but he turned around and said in his broad American accent;

"Ah, leave them there, they are only pictures!" and he winked at me.

"What are you going to do when you have lost the war and the British turn up?" I asked provocatively.

"Get out of this uniform and disappear into the woodwork. Yes it is time I got out of this uniform, don't you think?"

"You will be out of it sooner than you think." I prophesied.

"I might be out of it sooner than you think," came the reply. And I think he probably did disappear into the woodwork. I feel sure I recognised him in civilian clothes soon after that, but I never knew exactly what happened to him.

As time went by and there was still no sign of getting rid of our German occupiers, I became progressively more frustrated. I had to ride every where on my bicycle - how I wanted to jump on a motorbike and go for a burn up - how I wanted to get Dad's car back on the road. The Germans had a lot to answer for as far as I was concerned. The Germans were preventing me from enjoying one of my favourite pastimes.

My impatience finally got the better of me and I decided that I would put the car in roadworthy order and start rebuilding the Norton motorcycle which I 'captured' early in the occupation. Artie Selous had straightened the accident damaged front forks, so Gordon Stabb and I set to re-assembling the motorcycle. Gradually the machine took shape. We assembled everything except the petrol tank, which was still painted in British khaki. I felt that, even at that late stage of the war, it would be a complete give-away if the Germans found it. Anyway it would only take us a matter of minutes to fix it when the time came.

The car, my Dad's old Morris 'E', was still under bales of hay in Cecil Hardwick's shed. It being so close to where we were living, I had taken the opportunity, from time to time to check it over. The temptation to take it out for a run was always there. Finally, I succumbed and removed the bales of hay, pumped up the tyres, charged the battery with Ted Laker's assistance, replaced the number plates and managed to get her running.

I collected Mabs and announced that we were off to the Lyric Theatre. A short way along the Jerbourg Road we were stopped by two German soldiers. I immediately regretted my foolishness in getting the car out of its hiding place. I had successfully kept it for so long and now, due to my impatience I was going to loose it, probably for ever. One of the soldiers asked if we were going into Town and when I meekly replied "Yes", he asked if we would give them a lift. When we arrived in Town, they got out, thanked us for the lift and threw some money into the car. I just drove on as if nothing unusual had happened. We managed to get back home without further mishap. When I had successfully put the car back in its hiding place and re-covered it with bales of hay, I heaved a great sigh of relief.

In the middle of April we heard of the death of Mr Franklin Roosevelt, the President of the United States of America. This was very sad and distressing news. He was, without doubt the leader of the free world and his life had been snatched away at the very moment of victory. Mabs and I were very shocked and we both felt that we should find a way of paying our respects to the great man.

I went up to see Mr Fisher, who ran a general shop in Cambridge Park and asked him if he would make up a big wreath, which he did. I managed to get it down to the shop without attracting too much attention. I wrote an anonymous dedication to President Roosevelt, attaching it to the wreath. During the lunch hour, when the streets in Town were dead and there was nobody around, I took the wreath up to the War Memorial at the top of Smith Street. I laid it against the plinth with the roll of names of Guernsey soldiers and sailors who had fallen during the First War. As I placed it in position there was a German lying on the adjacent seat sound asleep. He certainly did not see me place the wreath on the War Memorial and there was no one else in sight. Regrettably the wreath was only there a very short time before the Germans removed it, but I felt happy and satisfied that I had paid my respects to one of our great war leaders.

As April 1945 drew to a close we knew that the war in Europe was rapidly coming to an end. Whether Admiral Huffmeier would surrender, or continue to hold out, was a question we could not answer. The Germans still operated armed patrols, their gun emplacements were fully manned and the Strassburg gun near La Croix was in action as late as the 29th April. With its twenty one mile range, it had been in regular use against targets towards the French coast. The Germans fired at any Allied naval vessels which came within range.

On May 2nd we were delighted to learn of Hitler's death in Berlin. I heard the news first on my crystal set and it was then confirmed in the Evening Press later in the day. Normally we chose not to believe what was printed on the front page of the Press, as it was 'the news' that the Germans required to be published. This time, however, I was quite willing to accept the authenticity of the short, but wonderfully informative news item, which read:

DEATH OF THE FUHRER.

> 'The Fuhrer, Adolf Hitler has fallen in the capital of the Reich in the battle against Bolshevism. His successor is Gross-Admiral Doenitz.'

The news of Hitler's death and Doenitz's appointment as his successor would, we hoped, have a salutary effect on Admiral Huffmeier. The Admiral's threat to blow up all the arms and ammunition was still a possibility, but would his new Commander-in-Chief take the same attitude. I spent much of my time listening to the B.B.C. news, praying for the German surrender and our liberation. Hour by hour excitement mounted and on Saturday May 5th the B.B.C. said that the war would be over in a day or two.

By Sunday, the long wait for our liberation was beginning to get on my nerves. I knew that it could only be a matter of a few hours away, but still there was no sign of it really happening. Fully armed Germans were still to be seen around the island. Then just after six pm I heard on the B.B.C. news, that peace was imminent.

Monday again found me glued to my crystal set, listening for any news which would remove the uncertainty and confirm our liberation. It was an endless day, waiting and waiting. I dare not move far from the radio in case I missed any news. Then all the waiting suddenly seemed worthwhile, I heard the announcement on the B.B.C. that tomorrow, Tuesday the 8th May was to be V.E. Day, Victory in Europe day. But what about Guernsey, when were we going to be liberated ?

When we got up that Tuesday morning, we knew that in Britain everyone was celebrating and rejoicing, but we were still occupied. It was a most miserable morning, and then at noon the Star issued a small 'Special Edition' that brought us the news for which we had all been waiting:

THE WAR IS OVER FOR GUERNSEY

German Officers Inform Bailiff of Surrender

HISTORIC STATES MEETING AT MID-DAY TO-DAY

> At 10.30 this morning 'The Star' was officially informed by Mr Louis Guillemette, Secretary to Jurat John Leale, President to the Controlling Committee of the States of Guernsey, that the war, so far as Guernsey was concerned had ended.
>
> People of Guernsey can to-day at 3 o'clock, if they are able to do so, listen to the speech made over the British Radio by Prime Minister Winston Churchill. Immediately after that hour flags can be flown in Guernsey as a sign of rejoicing.
>
> At 10 am to-day Korvetten Kapitan Reich and Baron von Aufsess called on the Bailiff at his Chambers at the Royal Court House. Jurat John Leale, President of the Controlling Committee and his Secretary, Mr Louis Guillemette, were also present. Kapitan Reich said that the war was over in the Channel Islands as well as elsewhere. He said that Mr Churchill, the British Prime Minister, was making a speech at 3 o'clock this afternoon and that the German authorities had no objection to the hoisting of flags after the speech.
>
> On receipt of this news the Bailiff convened an extra-special States Meeting to be held at mid-day today where the full details of this momentous news was conveyed to members of the States'.

Von Aufsess, one of the two German officers who called on the Bailiff, said, speaking in English:

"The war is over, we herewith hand back the islands to you"

So ended four years, ten months and seven days of German occupation. At last we were free again.

Winston Churchill was due to broadcast at 3 pm, so like everyone else who had access to a radio, Mabs and I were tuned in on our crystal set. We heard our victorious leader say:

> "Hostilities will end officially at one minute past midnight to-night, Tuesday the 8th May, but in the interest of saving lives, the 'Cease Fire' began yesterday to be sounded all along the fronts, and our dear Channel Islands are also to be freed today."

'Our dear Channel Islands are also to be freed to day.' There is not a Channel Islander, alive today, who listened to Churchill's broadcast, who cannot tell you of the excitement and pride that they felt when they heard those never to be forgotten words.

As we listened to Winston Churchill, telling us that we would be freed today, I looked out of the window and saw the German who was in charge of their military cemetery nearby and who we had seen almost every day for the last three or four years, walking past armed to the teeth. I turned to Mabs and said, with a considerable degree of frustration:-

"It doesn't jolly well look like it, the German Army is still on patrol. The war is not over for me yet, I am not free."

Earlier that day the destroyers, H.M.S. Bulldog and H.M.S. Beagle, had sailed from Plymouth and made a rendezvous at 2 pm with a German minesweeper off the south coast of Guernsey.

Mabs and I were up on the roof when we saw H.M.S Bulldog come in close to shore, directly south from Petit Port. We rushed downstairs and across the road to the terrace of La Faitieres, to get a better view. Through binoculars, which we had kept hidden, I made out the figure of a German officer going aboard the Royal Navy vessel. As we watched we became terribly excited, this really was the end of the war. We were sure that this must be the act of German surrender. Then the German officer left the British destroyer and returned to his own ship. H.M.S. Bulldog retired southward, whilst the German vessel sailed around the Pea Stacks, and back into St Peter Port harbour. Was it the German surrender or was it going to be a yet another false dawn ? We did not know.

We later learnt that Admiral Huffmeier had sent as his envoy a young and junior naval officer, Lieutenant-Commander Zimmermann, to make the first contact. Zimmermann, who went aboard the Bulldog, had no powers to sign the surrender but was only authorized to discuss armistice terms. He greeted the British with a Hitler salute and, on leaving, announced that as the German surrender did not officially take effect until one minute past midnight, the presence of Allied ships would be looked upon as an hostile act by Admiral Huffmeier. He warned that if the Royal Navy did not withdraw, they would be fired upon by the German long range artillery batteries.

This arrogant twenty seven year old German officer, who probably earned himself a place in history by his performance, was sent packing with the message that the surrender was to be unconditional and that a properly accredited representative, with full powers, must attend a further rendezvous at midnight.

In the meantime, as Mabs and I had seen, the Royal Navy retired to a safe distance to await the time of the second rendezvous. When Major General Heine arrived aboard H.M.S. Bulldog at midnight, the two British warships sailed into the Little Russel. At 7.14 am, on the 9th of May 1945, the unconditional surrender of the German garrison in Guernsey was signed on the quarter-deck of H.M.S. Bulldog and our occupation was officially over.

Almost twelve years later, in 1957, the arrogant young Nazi Naval Officer, Lieutenant-Commander Zimmermann, was appointed Germany's Senior Naval Attache at their Embassy in London. One can only hope that his approach to international diplomacy had improved.

Britain celebrates May 8th as Victory over Germany in the second world war, while we in Guernsey have designated May 9th as our Liberation Day.

Chapter 22

WELCOME VISITORS

After Winston Churchill's broadcast, there was a great air of expectancy throughout the island. The big question was, when will the British arrive? Many people immediately set off for town to ensure that they missed nothing. Quite a number of islanders did not go home at all that night. By early Wednesday morning people from all parts of the island were making their way down to St Peter Port Harbour, by bicycle, by foot, by farm cart and some even by cars, that had been successfully hidden away from the Germans during the occupation. The Town was alive with expectation, Guernsey was celebrating even before the British arrived. Union Jacks and red, white and blue decorations were everywhere. Everyone was ready to rejoice as soon as the British arrived. People were smiling, people were laughing, people were happy, in a way they had not been for over four years.

Edgar Stacey came and asked me to go and help him to get his car, a Morris eight, started. It was hidden in Cecil Duquemin's barn at Les Baissieres. Edgar had felt that the Germans would not look for his car there, as Cecil's own car had previously been requisitioned. The Morris had been there for almost the whole of the occupation and remained undetected. He naturally wanted to get it back on the road again as soon as possible. Previously, I had taken the car's battery down to the Central Transport depot, where Ted Laker had surreptitiously managed to get it charged. The battery was now at my shop, so we set off to collect it. Edgar brought his son John, who was four and a half and was dying to see the car. His father said that he should not have brought him, but as John had heard him talk about it so often, felt he could not disappoint him.

Having collected the battery, which I was carrying in my cycle carrier, we set off for Les Baissieres. Edgar had his son on the back of his bike. We had just ridden along Rouge Huis and crossed over into Coronation Road, when young John turned round to see if I was still following and caught his foot in the spokes of the wheel. Edgar, his son and the cycle went base over apex and landed in a heap in the road. We both thought that young John had broken his foot, but thankfully that was not the case. It was lucky that the spokes were rusty, otherwise it would have caused a far worse injury. A car came around the corner with a couple of Germans, so I flagged them down and demanded that they take young John to a doctor. The Germans knew that the war was as good as over and were consequently most obliging. We lifted John into the car and we were all taken by the Germans to Dr Gibson's house on the corner of Grange Road and Doyle Road.

At the doctor's we met Ossie Le Lacheur of Doyle Motors who already had his car back on the road. He gave Edgar and John a lift home. I walked back, collected my bike and the battery, and cycled out to Les Baissieres. I fitted the battery and, after a number attempts, successfully managed to get Edgar's car started. Later that evening he went back and collected his car and made good use of it the next day, Liberation day. It was not taxed or insured, but that was not going to prevent Edgar using his car after it had been off the road for so long.

When I returned home after fitting the battery, I went up and looked out of our loft window, but there was nothing to be seen. I periodically kept watch and soon after midnight it was obvious that there were ships in the Little Russel. At first light I could see that Royal Navy vessels were at anchor just outside St Peter Port Harbour. They were H.M.S. Beagle and H.M.S. Bulldog. I set off for Town almost immediately and when I arrived at the Weighbridge, there were already vast crowds there, singing and cheering. At 8 am a small party of British troops, two officers and twenty men, came ashore at the New Jetty, White Rock. They were met by Inspector Bert Lamy and other police officers. Colonel Power who was in command of the first party ashore, set off immediately in the police car, with Police Sergeant Bull, to call upon Jurat John Leale at his home in Bulwer Avenue.

It took some time for the police car, with its welcome guest, to get through the crowd at the Weighbridge. Colonel Power was the first British officer anyone had seen for almost five years and we wanted to give him a welcome he would remember for the rest of his life. The crowd repeatedly cheered our welcome visitor. Islanders shook his hand, kissed him, insisted that he made a speech and only then was he allowed to go to meet Jurat John Leale. Colonel Power arrived to find John Leale was still in his pyjamas. He didn't care how he was dressed, he was just overjoyed to meet a British officer.

The rest of the British contingent marched up to the Royal Hotel, which they made their headquarters. On their way there, they were mobbed by the vast crowd. The British tommies brought gifts with them of chocolate and cigarettes, which they gave away to delighted islanders. The huge crowds, who were now celebrating our newly regained freedom, virtually besieged the Hotel and when the German Swastika was lowered and the Union Jack hoisted in its place, there was a great roar of approval.

Later that morning Colonel Power, Lt Colonel Stoneham and about a dozen men marched up to the Royal Court to meet the Bailiff and members of the Controlling Committee. On their way through the streets, newly bedecked with flags and lined with wildly cheering islanders, they received a tremendous reception. Guernsey was delirious with joy. As they marched up Smith Street, I was standing at my shop door with a very attractive and pretty young girl, Doreen Mallet, who worked for Mrs Hollis the optician. When I pushed my way through the crowd and shook two or three of our Tommies by the hand, Doreen rushed forward and started kissing them. Together we followed the contingent, with hundreds of others islanders, up to the Royal Court House and stood on the steps cheering. The British tommies signed autographs on anything available, particularly islanders' Identity cards.

I went up on to the roof above the Prince of Wales Hotel to get a better view. Almost as soon as I reached the roof, I looked down and saw Mabs, Margaret and Jane Stacey arriving, so I went down to join them. At about 10.15 am the Bailiff, the members of the Controlling Committee and the two British officers came out on to the terrace. The Union Jack was unfurled from the Royal Court flagpole and the vast crowd instantaneously broke into 'God Save the King'. As the singing ended, I shouted:

"Three cheers for Winston Churchill."

The response was deafening.

As we followed the tommies back down Smith Street to the Royal Hotel, Mabs remarked how healthy and full of life they looked. I had to agree, there was a marked comparison between islanders and our liberators. Almost five years of occupation had certainly taken its toll and in many ways to a far greater extent than I thought possible. Later in the day, at noon, a further two hundred British troops landed, again to a tumultuous welcome.

Edgar was unable to go into Town to see the British troops arrive as he had to milk his cows and attend to the animals at Les Nicolles Farm. So his wife Jane collected Mabs and Margaret and together they cycled down to Town to join in the celebrations. Edgar had been left with strict instructions by his wife, to hoist on their vinery chimney stack, the large Union Jack that she obtained 'under the counter' from Creasey's.

Edgar climbed up the extension ladder and hoisted the flag. While he was up there the ladder fell to the ground and was left hanging onto the chimney waving to everyone who passed, hoping that they would come and rescue him. With the Union Jack flying and Edgar waving and shouting, all his 'would be' rescuers assumed that he was just another islander celebrating the end of the occupation. Eventually a neighbour came to his rescue, replaced the ladder and Edgar climbed down.

At lunch time I went home and just after 1 pm heard the sound of planes. I rushed up to the attic window and saw a formation of R.A.F. Mustangs roaring over Jerbourg in an unofficial air display. Mabs and I climbed out onto the roof and waved to them as they repeatedly flew back and forth between Jerbourg and St Sampson's. As they flew over the harbour, I noticed that they dipped their wings in salute.

Mabs and I were both keen to see what fate had befallen Seaplane Bungalow and the Annex, and indeed what had happened to the Jerbourg Peninsula, which we had not visited since we were turned out in March 1941. Before the occupation, Jerbourg had been one of the loveliest and healthiest spots on the island, unrivalled for its sea view and diversity of scenery. My parents loved living at Jerbourg because of it's tranquillity.

Mabs and I walked down to have a look. We passed the barrier at the Monument Tavern and walked up towards the site of the now demolished Doyle Monument - everything was different. A rash of concrete constructions and new earth mounds had appeared and there were far fewer trees. The barracks were as we remembered them, although with some additions. The road, or track, leading to Jerbourg Point was still as unmade and potholed as ever.

As we approached Seaplane Bungalow, we saw the gun pit which the Germans had built while we were still living there. The bungalow was open and deserted but it had obviously been used as their Gunnery Command Headquarters. In the lounge where my Father's funeral had taken place, the Germans had built a large scale model of the Jerbourg headland in sand. They had recreated every gun emplacement and every detail of the landscape. It was beautifully made. From Seaplane Bungalow the Germans had been able to instruct each battery on the point to fire as required. There was a large swastika and a portrait of Hitler hanging on the wall. I now regret not having taken that German flag, in fact there were a lot of items, to which, I now wish I had helped myself.

Mabs and I then ventured into the Annexe, where we immediately noticed that two of the bedrooms had been knocked into one. The enlarged room was fitted out with shelving and there were stocks of German uniforms, sheets, hand grenades, rifles, revolvers, ammunition and even one or two bicycles. It was a veritable arsenal. There was the inevitable photograph of Hitler on the wall. In one corner was a bed and sitting on the edge of it was a German soldier, literarily shivering with fear. We left him to his thoughts - what a change from the arrogant attitude of the Germans when they first arrived to conquer our island!

I now wish that I had found some way of photographing the sand model of the peninsula before it was destroyed. I did not realise at the time the importance of recording the scene for future generations. All I wanted to do, was wipe clean as quickly and as thoroughly as possible, all the evidence of the German occupation. In fact on our next visit to Seaplane Bungalow we took Margaret with us and allowed her to play sandcastles with the model, which of course totally wrecked it.

Both Seaplane Bungalow and the Annex stank of Germans and were in a pretty rough state. Clearly it was going to be a major job to rehabilitate them so that they could be lived in again. There was speculation that we would receive some compensation to help us with the repairs. My first inclination was to leave them both as they were until they had been assessed. Seaplane Bungalow was in a terrible mess and if anything the Annex was even worse.

We walked further down the track towards the point, carefully keeping to the well trodden path as we realised that the Germans had mined the cliffs. They had also placed a considerable number of roll type bombs at strategic points on the cliffs. These bombs could be released by cables, so that they would roll down the high cliffs and explode at the potential landing places. For many years after the end of the occupation, an odd one of these bombs were still being discovered on the cliffs.

The field in which Bassett Lowkes had built his holiday home was now covered with a series of small metal pyramids made from railway rails, to prevent gliders landing. Other fields on the headland were also desecrated in the same way.

There was seemingly endless miles of barbed wire. Gun emplacements, bunkers and flak batteries had sprouted up all over the headland, the Germans had totally changed the landscape. They had left ruin and ugliness everywhere and dug deep into the gorse clad slopes to make bunkers which offered some protection from the attacks by the R.A.F. Nearly 100 Germans had been killed and wounded in the area as a result of bombing and machine gun raids by Allied aircraft.

Some weeks later I found, in one of the cliff top bunkers, our bath which had been ripped out of Seaplane Bungalow. It was one of the cast iron variety, which weighed a ton. I rescued it with considerable difficulty and it was eventually restored to its former place and use.

As we walked back towards our 'occupation home' at La Croix, I found a twenty litre German petrol can in a bunker near the barracks. It was full of petrol and was just what I needed. Whilst I soon used the petrol, I still have the can, though it now leaks like a sieve and it is years since it was capable of containing any petrol.

Some of the German troops we met on the way home seemed rather solemn and downcast, but others were smiling and happy. One Jerry soldier, who shot past us on his cycle shouted in perfect English :

"Better for both of us this way, now your friends will came back, and I will be able to go back to my family in Germany"

That evening, Liberation night, Edgar Stacey and his brother-in-law, organised a dance in the barn at his parent's farm, in Capelles. Les Canus Farm, has in recent years become better known as Aladdin's Cave. It was not possible to get a piano up into the loft above cattle stalls, so the music and song was provided by the Brache sisters. One played the piano accordion, while her sister sang. The sisters were Guernsey's occupation sweethearts, they appeared in countless shows both during and after the war. Apparently they were friends of Edgar's brother-in-law and were only too happy to help celebrate our liberation.

Edgar drove Mabs and I out to the farm in his car. When we arrived, I made the suggestion;

"Wouldn't it be nice if we could get hold of a few British soldiers to join in the fun?"

"Well let's go and see what we can find," was the response. We drove into Town and saw two Tommies outside the Royal Hotel. We asked them if they were off duty? They said that officially they were never off duty, but they were free at that time. Edgar told them that we were organising a dance and would they like to be our guests.

"Yes, that's a great idea!"

They said that they would go and ask their sergeant for permission. Edgar and I never really thought they actually asked permission, but they said they had it, so we took them back to the dance.

They really enjoyed themselves and so did we, but after a time things began to get out of hand. As Edgar put it:

"We have picked up a couple of right roughs."

It was with some considerable difficulty that we persuaded them to let us take them back to Town. When we were approaching the Royal Hotel one of them said;

"Don't drop us outside the hotel, drop us up the road a bit."

So much for them getting permission.

After all the years of German restrictions and curfew, we thoroughly enjoyed the dance. Gone for ever were the days when we had to be indoors at 9 pm, gone were the days when dances were forbidden, gone were the days when we had to watch what we said, gone were the days when we had to ensure that we were properly blacked out. Now we had the freedom to do what we liked, when we liked, the freedom to be ourselves, the freedom to enjoy ourselves, the freedom to entertain British tommies, the freedom to make whoopee! That night we made whoopee, and then went home and slept 'free people'.

For the next few days I spent much of my time down at the Harbour and indeed anywhere where there were British soldiers. Mabs and I were outside the Royal Hotel when a British sergeant rushed up, flung his arms around me and enthusiastically hugged me.

"I am so glad to see you Bill, how have you been getting on ?"

I just did not recognise him at all. It was very sad to be greeted so warmly by someone you cannot remember. I tried to cover up my lack of recognition, how successful I was, I do not know, but Mabs told me that I was totally unconvincing!

It was 'Nobby' Hamon, who had left the island in June 1940 to join up. Now he was a sergeant in the Hampshire Regiment. When I finally realised who he was, I could see that he had put on a fair bit of weight. Before the war he and I were in the same water polo team. He had also been a well known local footballer who played outside right for the Rangers. He worked for Purdy's in the Pollet and lived in George Street.

As we celebrated our freedom, I noticed that some islanders were going out to visit H.M.S. Beagle. There was a punt tied up in the Old Harbour, so I decided that I would 'commandeer' it and row out to personally greet the Royal Navy. When I came along side I was invited aboard. On deck I was greeted by Rex Ferbrache, the former manager of W.H. de la Mere, who now was a Lieutenant in the Royal Navy. Rex was looking extremely fit and well, although he, like 'Nobby' Hamon had put on a bit of weight. We shook hands and enjoyed a good chat about the past, the present and the future.

Later I used the same punt to take Mabs and Margaret out to a motor torpedo boat which was lying in the outer harbour. As we pulled alongside a sailor, leaned over the side, and on seeing Mabs, exclaimed in a broad scottish accent;

"Hello Hen".

Apparently that is a term of endearment used by people in the Dumfries area, where Mabs came from, so she was able to respond suitably. We all went aboard, Margaret was given chocolate which she quickly devoured, and Mabs some butter.

The second invasion of Guernsey took place on the Saturday following liberation, when over three thousand British troops landed to reinforce the small advance party that arrived the previous Wednesday. Once again there were tremendous crowds to greet them as they came ashore. The throng was so thick that a number of people fainted in the heat, but the St John Ambulance Brigade were at hand to deal with the casualties. The tommies were mobbed and kissed by happy islanders, and I remember asking one of them to kiss my daughter. Margaret had been born during the occupation and now, like the rest of us, was free. That kiss was symbolic of our new found freedom.

Perhaps the greatest ovation was reserved for the band of the Duke of Cornwall's Light Infantry which paraded around the Town, playing heart stirring music. Nothing stirs my heart like a good British Regimental band, particularly when you had not seen or heard one for five years.

The second liberation force had been transported across from Plymouth by a fleet of Naval vessels. They arrived in the Little Russel just as dawn was breaking. The fleet was led into St Peter Port Harbour by my great friend and best man at my wedding, Ralph Palmer, in the motor vessel 'Oma'. This was a small thirty eight foot motor launch which had been requisitioned for the duration of the war from a member of the Guinness family. The 'Oma' was capable of twenty-three knots. Ralph, who had left the island on a Dorey coal boat, came back in command of the 'Oma', with its two man crew !

Ralph had been stationed at Plymouth for some time, preparing for the liberation of the Channel Islands. When it came to the time for them to set sail, Admiral Boon, who was in charge of the operation called all the ships' captains together for a briefing. He asked:

"Who is the Commanding officer of the Oma?"

Ralph responded "I am Sir."

The Admiral nearly spoiled the whole war for Ralph when he said:

"We have been worrying about your vessel, its very small I think she should go over as deck cargo."

In absolute horror at the thought of this indignity, Ralph Palmer almost screamed;

"Good God, you can't do that, I am going home to Guernsey - Sir!"

Apparently an awful silence followed, the Admiral turned a delicate shade of purple, then took a deep breath, swallowed and said;

"Oh can't I ?" and after a moments thought, added: "Very well, you can try."

Ralph later claimed that was the first time anyone had told the Admiral what he couldn't do and lived to tell the tale !

Knowing that he was coming home, Ralph wanted to decorate his boat in Guernsey colours for his triumphant return into St Peter Port Harbour. He went shopping in Plymouth for green and white ribbon, but only white was available. So he and his two man crew set to and painted half the ribbon with engineers heat resistant green enamel.

As they rounded St Martin's point, the crew dressed the 'Oma' overall with the green and white ribbon. Ralph and the 'Oma' were allowed to enter the harbour first as he was coming home. The 'Oma' sailed into the harbour and made for Number 6 berth. Ralph expected to see a crowd of cheering islanders to welcome him home. But unbeknown to him, the harbour area was closed to the public and no one ever noticed or appreciated the significance of his display of green and white ribbon.

However, news soon got around that Ralph was back. So Edgar and I drove down to the Weighbridge to look for him. Suddenly we spotted Ralph, dressed up like an Admiral looking very smart, he was walking the length of the White Rock. I shouted to him, when he saw us he ran over and vigorously kissed and hugged both of us, then he went down on his hands and knees and kissed the ground. As Ralph stood up he announced to the crowd, that was by now watching his performance;

"I've been around a lot of places, but I haven't seen anything better than this island. I am glad to be back home."

The Evening Press reporter who had witnessed Ralph's antics, reported that, 'It was apparent that Ralph Palmer had lost none of his famous good humour.' They also mentioned that in 1944, while he had been away he married a Liverpool lady.

So Ralph was married - how I regretted that I had not been around to return the compliment, by being his best man. However I was glad to hear that my old friend Jack Hessel had been his best man when he married Marjorie.

A few days before he was due to sail for Guernsey, Ralph met Fred Renouf, a Jerseyman, in a Plymouth pub. Ralph said that he was soon to come to Guernsey but that it was top secret. Fred asked Ralph if he knew a friend of his, Bill Green. Ralph said;

"Of course I know Bill, he is my old playmate and I was best man at his wedding."

Fred said "If you are going to Guernsey I will get some motor books for Bill Green and, by jove, I would think that he won't half be pleased to have them."

Ralph brought over a pile of Motor and Motorcycling magazines, which surprisingly had been published right throughout the war, and presented them to me. I was delighted to have them, particularly as in them were all the addresses I needed to get started in business again, well ahead of my competitors. Some years later I lost track of Fred when he emigrated to South Africa, but I never forgot that marvellous gesture which did so much to help me get back on to my business feet after the occupation.

Quite recently, in conversation with my old Jersey friend, Ernie Bouchet, who was a member of the Jersey Motor Cycle Club I said:

"I would dearly like to find Fred Renouf."

"Oh," he said, "I've got his address in South Africa."

I wrote to Fred and reminded him how valuable the books had been to me. I received a very nice letter in reply.

The final chapter of Ralph Palmer's association with the 'Oma' remained unwritten until 1982. The then owner of the 'Oma' contacted Ralph and he and I went over to Bristol to see his old wartime ship, still afloat in the City's floating harbour. Ralph was presented with the name plaque from her stern and for a long time it adorned his house in Mount Row.

Within an hour of landing in Guernsey on the Saturday morning, British troops surrounded 'La Porte', an imposing house at the junction of Elm Grove and St Jacques and Vize Admiral Huffmeier the German Commander in the Channel Islands was taken prisoner. He was speedily conveyed to the Crown Hotel.

I was amongst the great crowd on the Esplanade watching all the activity taking place in and around the harbour. At about 10.30 am, Admiral Huffmeier was unceremoniously escorted out of the Crown Hotel under armed guard. As he descended the steps, a cheer went up. The crowd had at first thought it was a British Naval officer, but they soon realised their mistake and the cheering quickly turned to total silence. This was the first time that I had seen the Admiral, who was reputed to have declared his intention to fight to the death, and I am glad to say also the last.

This tall, slim, arrogant Nazi Admiral, dressed in his long top coat with very wide lapels, refused to return the salute from the British officer who met him at the bottom of the steps. However, the German Naval officer who accompanied Huffmeier returned the salute by touching his peaked cap. Gone was the Heil Hitler salute, to which we had become so accustomed.

The now, former German Commandant of the Channel Islands was briskly marched to the White Rock, where he awaited the arrival of Brigadier Snow, the British Commander in the Channel Islands.

At 10.45 am Brigadier Snow landed and received Huffmeier's surrender. The Admiral again refused to salute and, after making an ignominious surrender, was handed over to the Commander of H.M.S. Faulkner as a prisoner of war. The once most feared German in the Channel Islands stepped into a waiting launch and was shipped to Plymouth. His departure was the seal on our Liberation. We were thankful to see him go, it was a symbol of our newly regained freedom.

Later that day, Brigadier Snow read the King's message and the Royal Proclamation to well over two thousand islanders packed into the forecourt at Elizabeth College. It was a moving and historic occasion, with weather to match. The Band of the Duke of Cornwall's Light Infantry, some thirty strong, played the Old Comrades march and when the Union Jack was broken at the flag breaking ceremony, the General salute,

In his message, His Majesty referred to us as 'The oldest possession of the Crown'. It was a great moment for me to be 'reunited' with our own Duke, the Duke of Normandy. All the pride that I have possessed since a very small boy, that had been instilled into me by my Father and my school masters, came flooding back to such an extent that I found myself wiping tears from my eyes.

On that Saturday, English newspapers arrived from the mainland for the first time in almost five years, and oh how we had missed them. It was uniquely fitting that in those first newspapers, the news of our Liberation was making the headlines.

During liberation day and the momentous days which followed, Artie Selous celebrated by sitting at one of the attic windows above the Smith Street shop, looking out over the harbour, painting the scene in oil. That picture of the harbour and the newly arrived British Fleet, hung for many years above the fireplace in our dinning room at Lyndel. I have enjoyed Artie's painting over the years and still do today.

In the convoy of almost fifty ships that arrived in St Peter Port, the one that caught my eye was the American L.S.T. (Landing Ship Tanker). The massive vessel, slowly manoeuvred into the Old Harbour, now the Victoria Marina, between the north and south piers and at low tide, came to rest only yards from the Quay. As the bows of the ship split open and swung apart, an exit ramp was positioned and a stream of vehicles poured forth. Lorries laden with relief supplies of food and military equipment drove off the ship, up slipway and onto the Quay.

St Peter Port and St Sampson's Harbours were soon working to capacity, L'Ancresse Bay and Common were also used to bring in urgently needed supplies. Three L.S.T. vessels landed their cargo at L'Ancresse and parts of the Common were used to stack the stores until they were transported to more permanent storage. L'Ancresse looked more like a warehouse than a golf course.

Only five days after we were liberated the Home Secretary, the Rt Hon. Herbert Morrison M.P., arrived in the island to learn at first-hand how we had coped with the occupation, to witness the rounding up of the Germans and to address the States.

I had the privilege of being in the public gallery when the Home Secretary addressed the States. I recall nothing of his speech, but I do remember that when the roll was taken and the Greffier, in French called;

"Deputy W.H. Arnold"

There was the traditional response of "Present", pronounced 'pray-zahn'. The members of the States spontaneously applauded. Prior to the occupation Advocate Arnold had been elected as a Peoples Deputy, but left the island to join the Army just before the Germans arrived. He came back with the British forces as Colonel W.H. Arnold. He was destined to become Sir William Arnold, the Bailiff of Guernsey.

After the States Meeting was over, Herbert Morrison went out on to the Court Terrace, where he addressed the large crowd that had assembled. When he said:

"Winston Churchill, the Prime Minister, asked me to convey to the people of Guernsey, his greetings, his admiration and his good wishes."

The crowd went mad with joy and cheered him to the echo.

At the end of his short speech, as he came down the steps, I yelled out "Three cheers for the Home Secretary!"

The crowd gave three of the heartiest cheers that I have ever heard. Sometime later that day I met John Leale in the street. He thanked me for leading the cheering and said it was greatly appreciated by Herbert Morrison.

Looking back, I remember the period after our Liberation as stupendous days, we were walking on air, our lives had been transformed. We were outrageously happy and looking forward to the future. Everyone was carefree, it was a time of tremendous enjoyment. Liberation had changed everything. People again smiled and had a spring in their step. Islanders stopped guarding their pets and livestock, fearing that they would end up as food for the starving Germans. Dogs went for walks without their leads and were free to visit any lamp post they fancied. We could talk to each other without the fear of being overheard saying things we might regret. We again drove on the left of the road. The church bells rang out. The blackout and blackout curtains were ignored. The curfew was a restriction of the past. Our long nightmare was at last over, we were free and we loved it!

After seeing German soldiers being dowsed with liberal doses of delousing powder before being bustled aboard ships to take them to prisoner of war camps, Colonel Forty summed up our feelings, when he observed;

"The very air seems cleaner."

Chapter 23

MY HERO

When the British liberation forces arrived, German troops were ordered to move to the west of the island. They literally dropped and abandoned all their equipment and moved away with only their personal belongings.

Within days, thousands of German prisoners of war were shipped out of the island. The L.S.T.s which brought men and supplies were now transporting our uninvited visitors away to P.O.W. camps in Britain. Twelve thousand Germans were removed within two weeks but the remaining fifteen hundred were held back to help with the immense task of clearing up Guernsey after almost five years of occupation.

One morning, soon after our liberation, I was walking past the Town Church, when I saw a British sergeant and three armed soldiers escorting a company of P.O.W. German officers down to their embarkation point on the Castle Emplacement. These obviously arrogant Nazis started singing the German marching song,'We're marching against England'. The sergeant was clearly annoyed, halted the squad and made them put out their cigarettes. Then he ordered them to pick up their baggage and marched them, at the double, down to their embarkation point. I was so intrigued that I stood and watched their progress all the way to the model yacht pond.

As soon as the British landed and the German occupation was over, Gordon Stabb and I completed the re-assembly of the Norton motorcycle. The petrol tank was fitted and filled with some of the precious petrol I acquired on my visit to Jerbourg. I could hardly wait to road test the machine. Whilst I had road tested German military machines during the occupation, I had not been able to have a really good burn up.

I still recall my excitement when Gordon Stabb and I wheeled the newly reassembled Norton out into Smith Street. I kicked the starter and away she went, it was a gorgeous sound, music to my ears. I rode, or perhaps more accurately, raced up the Grange, down the Rohais, past Castel Church to Bailiff's Cross. I really let it go as I went up the Vauquiedor, along Queens Road and back to the shop. It went like a dream.

When I put the Norton through its paces, none of the old thrill was missing, it was a marvellously exhilarating feeling. It was sheer joy, as I sped along, to have the wind whistling through my hair again. I have never enjoyed motorcycling as much with a crash helmet as I did without one. I always wore one when I was racing, but most of my non competitive motorcycling, has been without a helmet.

Then Gordon Stabb, whose face had lit up with a smile from ear to ear when the engine first burst into life, took the machine for a ride during his lunch hour. If anything he enjoyed his burn up even more than I did, if that were possible.

The Norton was in perfect working order, virtually a new machine, with only six hundred miles on the clock. It was still in British khaki with its number on the petrol tank. The motorcycle, I now felt, should be returned to its rightful owners, the British Army.

Artie Selous, Gordon Stabb and I spent a considerable time polishing the motorcycle, so that when I rode it up the Val des Terres to Fort George, it was in immaculate condition. I felt really proud and was sure that, at very least, I would get a medal for capturing and returning the machine to the British Army. I rode up to the North Barrier Gate at Fort George and was challenged by the sentry. I explained that I was returning the motorcycle and was directed to the Citadel.

An officer was called, I think it was Colonel Wilkinson, who asked me how he could be of assistance. As I explained how I acquired the motorcycle, he listened intently. I told him about the crash, how Artie and I had stripped the machine down for the duration of the occupation, how the front forks had been repaired and how we had reassembled it during the last days before liberation. As he listened, he closely inspected the motorcycle, he was clearly very impressed.

I explained that I was now proudly returning the Norton motorcycle to the British Army. He walked around it once or twice, looked at me and said: "Congratulations young man." I was thirty five at the time. "Now take the bloody thing away, because if you knew the paper work that I would be involved in if I took it from you. I don't want to know about it!"

He took another look at the Norton and added: "Good luck, you have got yourself a motorbike."

I did not receive a medal, but I did have an almost brand new Norton motorcycle. I registered it with the Motor Tax Department - the number was 776 - fitted a sidecar and used it for a very long time before it was eventually sold.

It was almost a week before I could get Dad's car back on the road. One of the tyres was punctured and the spare was beyond repair. I had to take the wheel down to the shop so that I could repair the puncture. As I was enjoying using the Norton, and had many other inviting things to do, repairing the puncture did not rate a high priority.

It was surprising how many cars quickly reappeared on the road after the occupation ended. A number had successfully been hidden from the Germans since 1940. Some owners, whose cars had been requisitioned, successfully kept track of their vehicles and 'liberated' them at the first opportunity. The number of cars on the roads was soon almost reminiscent of pre war, particularly on Sundays.

When the Germans requisitioned civilian cars, some had been retained for use in the island while others were shipped to the continent. Nearly all the Wolseley's on the island were taken over by German officers, who looked upon them as a kind of status symbol. They were a nice, comfortable, reliable car and I had often seen senior ranking German officers being chauffeured around in them. Many Wolseleys left the island when officers were posted elsewhere.

After the occupation ended, a large compound of recovered cars was created at St Sampson's and the task of restoring them to their rightful owners, was given to Kenny Bell. He was appointed Requisitioned Transport Officer. It was his job to identify the owner and see that the vehicle was returned. He dealt with over eight hundred cars and was able to identify and return all but eight to their original owners. Some cars were found on the continent, others were recovered in Jersey and Alderney. An Alvis belonging to Mr Cockraine, the Managing Director of Holmes and Son, was found in Alderney and was returned to him.

I noticed an Aston Martin with a Jersey registration number being driven around island and wrote to my old motorcycling adversary, Sid Logan, inquiring if it could possibly be his car. He wrote back saying 'Yes, that is my car, get hold of it.' By the time he had replied the car had apparently been shipped to England. We tried to trace it but never succeeded, that one got away. Whether Sid ever managed to get compensation for it, I don't know.

A month after our liberation, King George VI and Queen Elizabeth came to the island for a whistle stop visit. It must have been the shortest Royal Visit on record, but it was certainly one of the most appreciated. They were due to arrive on June 6th but bad weather prevented them from making the journey from Jersey until the next day. They travelled by air in a silver Dakota, escorted by twenty one Mustang aircraft of the Royal Air Force. The King and Queen arrived at 3.30 pm and left three hours later. They were greeted by a twenty one gun salute, fired on seven captured 100mm German field howitzers, with ammunition especially produced by German prisoners of war.

The King and Queen were driven to Candie Gardens where the Bailiff read the Loyal Address and the King responded. They toured the island and, after having tea at Government House with the Bailiff and senior Army officers, returned to the airport, where they were again greeted by a twenty one gun salute before they left the island.

The King and Queen were driven by Harold Kendall, from Way's Garage, during their tour of the island. When they left Harold was given a pound note as a gift from the King and Queen. He treasured that note and I don't think he ever spent it.

By the time the Royal visit took place, I had fitted a sidecar to the Norton, and together with Mabs and Margaret, was able to follow the King and Queen around the island. Our daughter was four and a half at that time and I tried to get her to see everything that was going on. I carried her on my shoulders at various points, so that she could get a good view. I always tried to instil in her the same degree of loyalty to the Crown that has been part of my life, I think with some success.

The Royal Couple were given a tremendous and deafening welcome. Guernseymen have always been very loyal to the Royal Family. The loyalty the people of this island have given to the Royal family, to Britain and its traditions over the centuries, has always been absolute. I think that the overwhelming majority of islanders still display that loyalty, although, I regret there are today a few exceptions. The vast majority of the population are totally loyal, in fact I would go as far as to say that in many ways, a Guernseyman is more British than the British.

One of the first actions of the Island Authorities on liberation was the declaration that German notes and coins were no longer legal tender. The States, however agreed to purchase notes, at the rate of two shillings per Reichmark. We were only given three days to effect the exchange, the Wednesday, Thursday and Friday of liberation week. I went down to Midland Bank and exchanged the few Reichmarks I had in my possession, it took a long time as there were queues of islanders waiting their turn to get rid of the detestable occupation money. Mabs went up to the St Martin's Mission Hall at Carmel and changed hers there.

Without the Germans being aware of what was taking place, Jurat John Leale and his Controlling Committee had made careful plans for the replacement of the German currency with our own money. In the autumn of 1944 plans were made to use the entire stock of French water-marked paper, which still existed in the island, to print bank notes. It was found that over £400,000 worth of ten shilling, pound and five pound notes could be printed. Whilst this was less than the 'value' of the Reichmarks known to be in circulation, it was felt that it would be enough to cover the immediate civilian requirements.

The Guernsey Press co-operated, by secretly printing the specially designed paper money under the very noses of the Germans. Press staff worked all sorts of odd hours when the Germans, who also used the printing presses, were not about, and completed the job without being found out. These newly printed Guernsey notes were exchanged for the Reichmarks, but only up to a limit of twenty pounds.

Any excess was credited to your bank account. Only people with Guernsey identity cards were allowed to exchange Reichmarks, which meant that none of the money held by the German troops was legally exchanged. Any person exchanging large quantities of Reichmarks, was identified for further investigation. Later there were fervent calls for action to be taken against people who had profiteered out of the Germans at the community's expense.

It was not long after liberation that I received a very imposing looking letter from America. It was from Mrs Eleanor Roosevelt, thanking me for placing the wreath at the War Memorial in memory of her late husband, President Roosevelt.

No one, other than Mabs and one or two of my own staff, knew that I placed the wreath on the memorial. No one had seen me as the Street was deserted. Certainly the German sleeping on the bench could have had no idea of who was responsible for the wreath. It remains a mystery to me as to how the information reached Mrs Roosevelt. I enquired at the Police Station and with Mr Fisher, who made up the wreath, but no one was able to tell me how she learnt that I was responsible for the wreath. I suspect that it was probably a policeman who saw me out of a Police Station window. It was, however, a great thrill to receive such a delightful letter from such a great lady.

Getting back to normal was everybody's aim and great progress was quickly achieved. Electricity and gas supplies were very speedily restored and water which had only been available for very short periods at the end of the occupation, was soon back to normal. It was nice to have water in the tap whenever you turned it on. Telephone and postal services, which had only been maintained as island services, quickly became international again. When the first post arrived from England, the postman had no need to knock on any door, as everyone, in hopeful anticipation, was out in the road to meet him.

Within a few weeks of the end of the occupation, buses started running again. On Saturday June the 9th, the service between the Town and St Sampsons was re-started. Soon five local Bus Companies, The Guernsey Railway Company, Guernsey Motors Limited, Wayfarer, Western Buses and Falla Brother's Paragon and Blue Bird Services, were running regular services. All the island buses had been requisitioned by the Germans and when they were recovered, they were in such poor condition that it was necessary for considerable repairs to be carried out, before they were suitable to carry passengers again.

Supplies of food quickly arrived and from then on we received the same rations that were available to people in England. Within a few weeks sufficient supplies of cigarettes and tobacco arrived, so they were derationed. Smokers could buy as many as they wanted and from any tobacconist of their choice, without having to join long queues. The joy that derationing brought to thousands of men and women who so often during the years of occupation craved for a smoke, was incredible. For years they had been compelled to smoke very inferior substitutes, dried coltsfoot, rose leaves, vine leaves and brambles. Whilst I did not smoke during the occupation, the derationing gave me great hope and encouragement for the future.

Simultaneously with the derationing of cigarettes and tobacco, paraffin also came off ration. Within weeks potatoes were also freed. Things were certainly looking up.

As soon as Guernsey had been liberated, our 'Exiles' were clamouring to return. Our evacuees on the mainland, deported islanders in German internment camps and Guernseymen in the forces, in all at least twenty thousand people, wanted to come home. It was however, to be some months before sufficient transport could be arranged and the long dreamed of homecoming could become reality.

One of the first islanders to return, on the 21st June, was Ambrose Sherwill, who arrived by air. He was accompanied by Mr R.W. Hathaway, the husband of the La Dame de Sark, who had also been deported by the Germans. Ambrose immediately resumed his duties as Procureur and was welcomed in the Royal Court the next day by the Bailiff.

A loud speaker was set up outside Boots and messages recorded by school children, who had been evacuated to England, were broadcast. Mabs was in Smith Street when a message from Cecil Hardwick's son Richard was broadcast. Mabs recalls that Richard started off by saying that he was speaking on behalf of all the evacuated children of St Martin's School.

"Everyone," he said, "is in good health and happy, and we are looking forward to returning home to Guernsey".

Hearing Richard's message made Mabs cry. She also heard a message from John Ogier, head boy of the Intermediate School. The messages had been recorded by the B.B.C at their Manchester studios.

When Richard Hardwick eventually returned, Mabs and I went to welcome him home. He was sitting at their dining room table, looking like a total stranger, rather than a member of the family. Very sad, but it was typical of what was happening to many families who had been separated for so long by the occupation.

It was not until the 26th June that the first mailboat returned to service. At 7 pm the Isle of Guernsey arrived from Jersey and docked at the Great Western berth on the New Jetty. An hour later she left for Portsmouth with passengers and mail, thus resuming the service and link with the mainland after almost five years.

The first contingent of our evacuees returned at the end of June 1945. They were as elated to be home, back in their island, as we were to welcome them. There were the inevitable embraces, tears, laughter and smiles. Once the flow of evacuees started, the rest came back very rapidly. A fair number were never to return, as they had either found themselves good employment, or had established mainland roots for themselves with homes and families. Before the end of 1945, almost eighteen thousand islanders, men, women and children, were back in the island.

Before the occupation we had a well known character in the island, a coloured gentleman of great charm, Charlie Duncombe. His wife and three children were evacuated but Charlie, a docker, had remained in the island. He became very lonely, so he started a second family and by the time of our liberation, had three more children. When it came time for his wife and original family to return to the island, Charlie was obviously in a little difficulty. I was down at the harbour to welcome back one of my many friends and Charlie was there to welcome his family. His wife had apparently also been lonely, as she returned to the island with a young baby. Charlie stood there holding up the baby for all the crowd to see, and yelled;

"Look at that, look at that, she only went out with him twice."

Despite the apparent difficulties, his two families got on very well.

A short time after our liberation, the States was summoned to hear a report on the five years of German occupation from the President of the Controlling Committee, Jurat John Leale. I had a great regard for John Leale and managed to obtain a seat in the public gallery.

What was to prove to be one of the finest speeches I have ever heard was also probably the longest - it lasted well over two hours. His speech was not only a masterly exposition of the history of the occupation, but also an explanation of the activities and work of the Controlling Committee. It was a great privilege to have listened to such an historic speech, one that will never be forgotten by anyone present that day.

He concluded by saying;

> "From the occupation of this island by the German Forces, grim though the experience has been, we have all doubtless learned salutary lessons. But there is one I think we have been taught above all others and it is this; never in the past have we valued liberty as we shall value it in the future. If that thought dominates our political, social and industrial lives then good may yet come out of evil. If because of our trials we realise, as we have never realised before, the meaning of freedom to the human spirit, then those cruel years from 1940-1945 will not after all have been wasted, but, on the contrary out of the wreckage of the weary and seemingly useless years, we shall have rescued and indeed refined that conception of life which alone entitles us to bear the name of men."

At times of crisis every nation produces leaders, Britain produced Winston Churchill and Guernsey John Leale. He was a tall, slim, white haired man, with a reputation of total honesty and integrity. A modest man who rarely, if ever, raised his soft voice. He had an inner strength, which together with his quiet persistence, made him a formidable and effective negotiator. He was a very open man, who was always approachable. During the occupation he and I became firm friends as a result of the discussions we had sitting on the wall outside the Controlling Committee's offices at Maison Allaire. We spent many lunch times putting the world to rights. I quickly learned to respect his views and judgement although, in political terms, he was without doubt a radical. It was John Leale, who did so much to stimulate my interest in island affairs. Over the years that were to follow he encouraged me to become involved in the work of States Committees and eventually to become a member of the States.

Sir John Leale, as he became in the occupation Honours announced on December 12th 1945, was appointed a Jurat in 1934 and in 1940 was President of the Finance Committee. It was he who recommended the States to create the Controlling Committee, of which he eventually became President, after Ambrose Sherwill had fallen foul of the Germans. John Leale had been a Methodist minister in England before re-entering the family business of Leale's, on the Bridge.

It was he who, for most of the occupation, dealt with the Germans and sought to temper their unreasonable demands. His quiet approach contrasted sharply with the Germans' usually brusque manner. He described the Germans as a meddlesome people who did not understand our way of life, our agriculture or our fishing. They meddled and interfered and invented systems which could not possibly work. But, as he said, they had to be obeyed.

After the war ended, John Leale said to me one day:

"You know Bill, we have been very lucky, we have had an occupation with kid gloves on."

That in many ways, even after all these years, sums up the German occupation.

Immediately upon the Liberation of the island, John Leale tendered his resignation as President of the Controlling Committee, but this was wisely and emphatically rejected by the States.

Whilst there was considerable criticism of the Bailiff, Mr Victor Carey and Ambrose Sherwill, both during and after the occupation, I cannot remember any of Sir John Leale. He served his island well and I am proud to have been counted amongst his friends. He was my hero and indeed, I believe the island's hero. He was a wonderful man.

All in all the German occupation was not as bad, or as damaging to the island or its population, as some had feared. Our apprehension of possible excesses by the Germans, particularly against our womenfolk, were thankfully not realized. We were spared the calamities which befell many other Nazi occupied countries.

Whilst we experienced a few air raids, we had slept comfortably in our beds, unlike our evacuees in Britain who had spent many long nights in air raid shelters.

Whilst many of our fellow islanders had been forceably transported to internment camps at Biberach and Laufen, whilst other Guernseymen had been jailed both in Guernsey and on the continent, whilst farmers had their crops and cattle stolen or requisitioned, whilst for a period, we hovered on the point of starvation, whilst we had been turned out of our homes and lost our furniture, we were still, thankfully, not as badly affected as millions people in occupied Europe.

Ambrose Sherwill, in August 1940, had spoken of a 'Model' occupation and hoped that it would be one which both occupiers and occupied could look back upon without shame. I am not sure about the Germans, but as far as Guernseymen were concerned I feel that 99% of us could look back with pride at the role we played. The vast majority of islanders never collaborated with our occupiers and never forgave them for invading our island.

There were however, a very small minority who collaborated or fraternized with the Germans. Their activities caused a great deal of ill-feeling and resentment amongst the rest of the community. Perhaps the person who in the eyes of islanders was the most blatant collaborator, was a Dutchman who supplied the Germans with large quantities of locally grown food. The Germans allowed him and his company to work large tracts of glass and, in return, he undertook to be both a grower and purchasing agent for them.

In spite of constant representations made throughout the occupation by the States, this man continued to do exactly as he pleased, to the detriment of both the community and the islands food supply. He amassed a considerable fortune during the occupation and we were all pleased to see him later relieved of it by the States through the War Profits Levy. This was a tax on fortunes made by black marketeers as a result of trading during the occupation, to the detriment of fellow islanders. Many islanders, including myself, suffered considerable financial loss as a result of the occupation and it was preposterous that some individuals or firms should, due to their 'doubtful' activities or good luck, reap a financial benefit. The tax was 80% of all profits made during the occupation up to £10,000 and a 100% thereafter.

Perhaps the most contemptible form of collaboration was the activities of informers. Those treacherous, anonymous letter writers were often people driven by hatred, envy and spite, rather than a desire to help the Germans. Their victims were often neighbours and even on occasions relatives, who were sent to French and German prisons, some to die there. It was surprising just how many letters were sent, informing our occupiers of Guernseymen who operated secret wireless sets, or other equally illegal activities.

There was a considerable amount of fraternization, particularly by some young women. Looking back after all these years I find that I now take a slightly more lenient view of their activities than I did at the time. These girls were young, nearly all the eligible men had left the island, and they had a natural desire for male company. There is a time when women of sixteen, seventeen or eighteen bloom and have a natural attraction to the opposite sex. During the occupation the only young men that were around were the German soldiers. Some of them were very charming, very handsome and very gentle, all virtues that will melt a young ladies heart. In retrospect I cannot criticize them too much, it was one of those things that one has to accept inevitably happens. I am sure the same thing happened when the allies were stationed in Germany after the war. There were, however, other girls who fraternized for the benefits that it brought - food, cigarettes and drink.

Of course, at the time we ostracized women who in any way consorted with Jerry soldiers. Naturally they were called 'Jerry Bags' or 'Jerry Bitches'. There were the inevitable children born as a result of these relationships and Guernseywomen made their feeling only too well known to the unfortunate mothers. If a Jerry baby cried in its pram and annoyed the neighbours, someone was sure to pop up and say;

"Hi Mrs So & So, Jarmany calling, Jarmany calling."

During the occupation a practice developed that expectant mothers were allowed to go to the head of a queue. When a 'Hun Chaser' claimed the privilege one day, a woman in the queue called out;

"Make way for a Junkers 88."

There was one local women who fell madly in love with a German soldier. He visited her every day. Whenever 'Fritz' was able to obtain any food he, of course, shared it with her. Later, when the Germans were short of food, she shared what she had with him. One day 'Fritz' said to her :

"You like Kaninchen ?"

"Oh, yes I like rabbit".

"Tomorrow I bring kaninchen, you will cook it, and I stay for supper".

Sure enough, next day 'Fritz' turned up, as promised, with all the meat cut up in portions. She cooked it, then they sat down and enjoyed their meal. Some days later she said to him :

"I don't know what has happened to my 'Pussy', I haven't seen him for three or four days."

"Oh but," he said, "its kaninchen !"

'Fritz' had killed her cat, given it to her to cook, and they had eaten it. The girl was extremely upset and very ill for days.

There were many of our womenfolk who not only treated the Germans with cold disdain, but also exhibited great pluck and courage. A friend of mine had a German officer billeted in her house. She was an attractive lady and the Jerry officer was persistent in his efforts to be friendly. He continually pestered her to go to the cinema with him, but each time she flatly refused. One evening, he threw down two cinema tickets on the table.

"Now," he said confidently, "you come to the pictures with me tonight".

My friend picked up the tickets and threw them on the fire. As they blazed up and were destroyed, she said, pointing to the ashes;

"That is what would happen to my good name, if I were to be seen in public with a German uniform."

My Mother's cousin, Florrie Luff, lived at the top of Hauteville, number seventy eight. She was a widow, her husband had been a Director of Luff's stores. Her home was always immaculate and she was very meticulous about everything being in its right place. I remember her as a lady who did a lot of crochet work. I learned one day that she had three Germans billeted on her, so I went to see 'Aunt' Florrie, to find out if she was all right. She was charmed by these Germans and when I attempted to remonstrate with her in my most tactful way, she said:

"But they are no trouble. They come in and take their boots off on the mat and walk up the stairs in their stockinged feet. They treat me like a lady."

I went home and said to Mabs; "What do you do with Germans like that?"

During the occupation there was not one case, as far as I was aware, of rape or interference of our womenfolk by the German troops. In fact the German Commandant was reputed to have sneeringly said on one occasion that he had to protect his men from our women. Colonel Forty told me the tale of a German soldier who forced his way into a house, which he had mistaken for one of the Jerry brothels and kissed the middle aged lady resident. She telephoned the German police and he ended up being sentenced by their Military Court to a long term of imprisonment. There was no doubt that the German discipline was extremely tough and effective.

When the British troops landed, it was interesting to see some of the young ladies, who had been free with the Germans, welcoming the tommies with open arms. One of these girls was recognised by the crowd, who unceremoniously dumped her in the harbour.

I thought that all the Germans had surrendered and had been shipped out of the island, so I was quite surprised to learn, at the end of June, of a German being arrested after being hidden by a local woman. Apparently this German soldier, named Willie Upson, absented himself from his unit in St Andrews and went to this woman's house where she sheltered and concealed him until he was finally found by the police.

The fact there was a German hiding in the St Andrews area became known locally. The police heard the rumours and searches took place in the locality. Eventually they narrowed down the hiding place to this woman's house, which was searched without success. Further information apparently came to light and the Police again visited the house. They discovered Willie hiding in the roof space, access to which had been achieved through a cupboard in the woman's bedroom. The top of the cupboard had been removed to allow the German to climb up into the hiding place.

The woman's husband was away from the island during the occupation, serving in the forces. She had two children which were born before the war and two more born in 1942 and 1944. This woman met Willie Upson in 1942 and had been friendly with him throughout the rest of the occupation. She was tried and sentenced to four months imprisonment but, before beginning her sentence, she was allowed to take her children to their grandparents in Jersey.

There were repeated calls for action to be taken against those who had collaborated with the Germans, but while a great deal of investigation took place, no action ever resulted. Paddy Doyle, who had informed the Germans of the existence of G.U.N.S, with the tragic result that both Charles Machon and Joe Gillingham died in captivity, was allowed to slip quietly out of the island and back to his native Ireland. Regularly letters appeared in the press demanding action. One letter complained:

'No one seems to have interested themselves in dealing with the situation'. Another asked:

'Are the States going to smoke out these rats and punish them, or are they going to allow them to fatten on their treachery ?'.

The States response came when Deputy Stevenson asked what was the legal position of a particular local Limited Company. Ambrose Sherwill, in reply said:

"A great distress must have been caused to local citizens with the same name as the company in question." He added, "Such matters had been considered by officials of His Majesty Government soon after the liberation and it appeared that, apart from treason and treacherous acts, there was no local legislation instituted. With regard to treason the Royal Court was not competent to punish such offences, a prosecution under the Treachery Act could not be heard without the consent of the Attorney General of England. Any demand made that the States take swift action, apart from the War Profits Levy, is not possible to meet, as the States were bound by the rule of law."

And so the matter rested, no action was ever taken, officially.

Chapter 24

SHOPPING IS FUN AGAIN

An immediate task, as soon as the Germans surrendered, was the clearance of land mines and live ammunition. An enormous number of mines had been laid all over the island. These were largely cleared by prisoners of war using plans which the Germans, to their great credit, had kept of the mine fields as they were laid. By the middle of August virtually all the mines had been recovered, over eighty thousand.

Mabs and I had watched many of the mines being laid all around us and now we took delight is seeing them being cleared. The minefield in the Vauroufs field which had taken a toll of the Germans laying the mines, was successfully cleared without further casualties, so was the garden of Les Faitieres House. The field near the Monument Tavern, which was later to become National Trust property, contained, according to German records, 178 mines. They were all recovered with the exception of one which could not be located. Mabs, as she walked past, heard the British soldiers who were supervising the operation, insisting that the P.O.W.s keep looking for that last mine. Later as she neared home, she heard an explosion, the mine had been found when a German soldier trod on it and was killed.

Almost thirty thousand tons of ammunition and explosives were collected and dumped at sea. The areas selected by the Royal Navy after consultations with the our fisheries experts, was the Hurd Deep, off Alderney, and in deep water some ten miles south west of the Hanois Lighthouse. The depth of water was 40 and 30 fathoms respectively.

Ammunition and explosives were found everywhere. At the White Rock, there were huge shells, parachute mines, depth charges and even one or two torpedo warheads, strapped to the pillars of the piers, which, if they had been detonated, would have caused extensive damage to the harbour and its installations. Bunkers all over the island were full of shells.

Collecting all the ammunition involved British troops searching over three thousand houses that had been occupied by the Germans as accommodation, or for other military purposes. The houses had to be checked over and the ammunition, mostly small arms rounds, removed. Seaplane Bungalow and the Annex both contained considerable quantities.

The task of clearing the mines and the ammunition proved a fairly hazardous operation, four British soldiers and quite a number of German P.O.W.s were killed and many more injured. There were some civilian casualties as well, including youngsters who entered an ammunition dump at Les Caches, St Martin, one of whom was killed.

Other priorities for the P.O.W.s included the clearance of our two harbours, the restoration of roads, tracks and footpaths, the resumption of gas and electricity supplies and the preparation of accommodation for the early return of our evacuees. The German prisoners who were kept in the island to carry out repair and restoration work were housed at Fort Hommet and Fort Le Marchant.

The British Army was of course, also doing a vast amount of rehabilitation work. The Sappers removed the light railway built by the Germans, which connected St Peter Port harbour with the northern and western parts of the island. The captured trains, track and rolling stocks that were so urgently needed on the Continent were returned to France from where they had most likely come.

The Franz Westerman, the German Naval patrol boat, which was sunk on the eastern side of the new jetty by the R.A.F. soon after D Day, was finally raised by the salvage boat Lady Southborough in early July. The wreck of the 700 ton naval patrol boat had been blocking one of the key berths in the Harbour and preventing it's use.

Not only was a great deal of military equipment and supplies recovered by the British Forces after the liberation, there was also a wealth of paraphernalia left behind by our uninvited visitors. Much of this was made available to islanders and local businesses. This included a great variety items from blankets to desks, and cutlery to compressors.

A day or two after our liberation, I noticed a German military car parked in an entrance to Bon Air in Le Varclin. This car was the German version of the 'jeep'. It had been abandoned by the Germans, who no longer dare drive it. I however, didn't give a damn, the Germans had lost the war and the vehicles around were as much ours as anyone else's. So I just climbed into the driving seat and away I went. I drove it around for a couple of days. Everybody else was doing the same thing with any vehicle they could 'borrow'.

It was not long before German vehicles were being rounded up by the British military authorities. An order was issued that all military transport must be delivered to a certain place, by such and such a time. So my little fling was over, but for two or three days it was wonderful. Rather than getting involved in handing the vehicle in, I just returned it to where I had found it. I had no real need of the car, I had my own transport, but just took it out of sheer devilment - that was our mood at that time.

The arena and showground of the pre-war North Show and Battle of Flowers, at Port Soif, was taken over by the British Forces, who used it as a graveyard for captured German tanks, armoured vehicles, guns and other equipment. The area was soon transformed into a massive mound of rusting metal. I don't know if it was all dumped in the Hurd Deep, or taken away as scrap metal. When the first post-occupation North Show and Battle of Flowers was staged in September, it was held in Sausmarez Park. It turned out to be a good choice and the gaiety and splendour, of pre war shows, was recreated despite the ravages of the occupation. The inevitable shortage of cattle, the dearth of poultry and the scarcity of flowers, did not prevent the show from being an outstanding success. It was all part of the process of getting back to normality.

Other equipment, for which no use was found, such as thousands of German helmets, was dumped. Much of it was jettisoned in the sea, but other equipment was thrown into some of the many tunnels and strongpoints the Germans had created, then their entrances were sealed up. Years later many of these storage places were reopened and the equipment salvaged. It wouldn't surprise me if there is not a lot of valuable German war time relics still entombed. Before the British troops left the island they cleared and disposed of vast quantities of German equipment. What they did not do, however, was to clear away the mass of concrete structures that the Organisation Todt had constructed as part of Hitler's Atlantic wall, many of which still exist to this day.

In the various gun emplacements around the island that housed the heavy batteries, there was a wealth of observation equipment. I went and explored the underground passages and bunkers of the Strassburg battery on the Jerbourg peninsula. Some of the telescopic equipment there was so powerful that you could almost see people walking about on Jersey. Unwisely I didn't take anything, I should have helped myself to some of that equipment, it would have been very useful. Over the years I have often regretted missing out on that opportunity. All I managed to 'acquire' at the time of our liberation was the one big jerry can full of petrol.

My thinking then was that I wanted nothing to do with Germans, or their equipment. I hated anything in any way connected with the Jerries and wanted to cleanse our island of everything to do with them and their occupation as quickly and as totally as possible. I was only too happy to see them and their equipment depart. That was I think the general view held by the vast majority of Guernseymen at that time.

There were, however, others who did not hold my view and wanted a limited number of German fortifications retained as show places for tourists. Amongst the sites which it was suggested might be preserved as an attraction for visitors was the battery at Jerbourg. Its 220 mm guns were so placed that they commanded all approaches to the east of the island. A feature of this battery, was the particularly fine range finder which was installed there, together with dug-outs and ammunition stores, which were camouflaged so as to blend in with the landscape of the area.

At the Mirus battery at Frie Baton Saint Saviours, some of the 30.5 centimetre guns were of Russian manufacture. These guns had a chequered and interesting history. They were originally cast for use in the Russian Battleship Volga, which fell into the hands of the Germans during the First World War. After the war it was returned to the Russians, only to go to the breaker's yard in the 1930's. At the start of the Russian-Finnish war the barrels were sent to the Finns, via Norway, only to be again captured by the Germans when they overran that country.

When, in 1941, these massive guns were brought to Guernsey, road improvements had to be carried out before they could be transported to their Le Frie Baton site. They fired 700lb shells with a range of over 30 miles and controlled the waters around the south and west of Guernsey. The immense effort that went into the construction of the Mirus battery, the use of thousands of tons of concrete and steel and the fact that they had little operational use, shows Hitler's folly in diverting men and materials to the Channel islands. It meant that less men, materials and fire-power were available for the fortification of the Atlantic wall.

Although there was a great deal of debate about retaining some of the German heavy batteries, including consideration by the States, no decision was ever arrived at, so the guns and their equipment were cut up and removed.

In Britain after the war there was an acute shortage of steel. Scrap metal became extremely valuable and in Guernsey we had a considerable quantity. George Dawson, the scrap metal king, who was to gain considerable notoriety in Britain during the late forties, came to the island and by skilful wheeler-dealing and the habit of calling everyone 'Sir', cornered the war surplus market. He stayed at the newly reopened Manor Hotel at the top of Petit Bot and quickly clinched a deal with the States to clear all the scrap German equipment that was still in the island for a once and all payment of £25,000. The George Dawson 'success' story started here in Guernsey.

The Germans used a considerable number of pedal cycles, particularly during the last year of the occupation when they were extremely short of petrol. Many of these cycles had been imported from France. The Island authorities collected them and in due course those that were in a reasonable state, some two hundred and fifty, were sold off to the trade. I bought quite a number of the French cycles and, after putting them into proper working order, sold them to the public. The States set a fixed retail selling price of thirty-five shillings. As there was a lack of continental spares to keep them in proper working condition, many of them quickly became unserviceable. Nevertheless, at the restricted price the bicycles were still bargains.

Lined up in row upon row in the car park at North Side St Sampsons were 500 vehicles, motorcycles, and a variety of equipment that had been captured from the Germans. All appeared to be in various stages of corrosion. Every item was to be auctioned off to any islander who might be interested. I naturally, was curious to see what was available and so were about four hundred other islanders.

Some of the cars and lorries up for sale were museum pieces, dating back almost to the start of motoring. There were Red Cross trucks, ambulances, converted vans, power generators, generating units, derelict gas producing lorries, dozens of general transport trucks, troop carriers, trailers, and about 50 cars and 60 motorcycles. My assessment was that in many ways, the tyres were more valuable than the vehicles.

When the motorcycles came under the hammer my fellow dealers, Jack Domaille, Herbie Tostevin and I, held back and let the amateurs do the bidding. The prices were ridiculous, a Norton in very poor condition went for £31, a B.S.A. in need of a lot of work, fetched £29. Continental machines were sold for equally high prices and I knew that we would soon be seeing their new owners in our workshops begging for spares that were not going to be available.

A great deal of furniture and bedding was recovered from German billets. Much of this was made available to returning families, many of whom had lost everything as a result of the occupation. In order to ensure that the vast quantity of furniture and bedding was put to good use, a States Disposal Committee was created. They did a very efficient job - over ten thousand items of furniture, such as tables, chairs, wardrobes, stools and desks passed through their hands. There were beds, mattresses, pillows and over 30,000 military blankets that had been collected from all over the island. One of the most interesting discoveries was a supply of British tinned food, encased in grease. This had been captured by the Germans at the time of the British evacuation from Dunkirk. How that food remained uneaten, when even dogs and cats were fair game for the starving Germans, is difficult to understand.

The Germans had plundered France and stolen millions of pounds worth of commercial and industrial equipment. This had been distributed far and wide throughout every part of Europe, including Guernsey. After the war a great deal of this 'loot' was identified and returned to its owners. French State officials and representatives of the French businesses that the Nazi had pillaged, came to the island and with their help, a considerable quantities of equipment was restored to it's rightful owners in France. Much of it was still in good or repairable condition.

During early August, Frank Stroobant, returned from internment. It was great to see him again, he looked remarkably fit and well. Soon 'Stroo' was back in the swing of his favourite activities. Within a few days he was on the cricket field, displaying all his old guile with the ball. In a representative match he took four wickets for a mere nine runs. His prowess with the bat took a little longer to return, as he made a duck in his first innings.

Soon after 'Stroo' returned to the island, I was passing his shop in Market Hill and there in the window, was the wireless set that he secretly listened to while he was interned at Laufen in Germany. He called it the 'Forbidden Whisper'. It was built in the camp, with parts 'acquired' and smuggled in by a fellow inmate, Billy Williams. Billy, a Jerseyman, was daily escorted out of the camp to work in a local radio shop in the town of Laufen. A stroke of luck which he took full advantage. 'Stroo' and Bill Drinkwater, a trainee Jesuit Priest, helped Billy to construct the set.

The 'Forbidden Whisper' was built at a time when the four hundred men in the camp were desperate for news of how the war was going. 'Stroo' was the radio operator and spent several hours each night, after lights out, in his room, number 722, listening to the B.B.C. news bulletin and then writing out the main items. This

Frank 'Stroo' Stroobant, Billy Williams and the 'forbidden whisper'.

was copied and circulated the next morning to ensure that the camp received a comprehensive news service, which was known as 'Stop Press'. 'Stroo' earned the nickname 'Sparks' for his efforts. He told me that over the last sixteen months of his captivity, he spent over fifteen hundred hours, listening secretly to the radio, Owing to the necessity of maintaining absolute secrecy, the set could only be used after lights out at 10.30 pm. and then only at considerable personal risk.

The 'Forbidden Whisper' was a closely guarded secret and in spite of numerous attempts by the German camp authorities to locate the set, it remained the camp's only accurate source of news until they were liberated. This set, with it's history, was on display in the window of Stroobant and Symes for some time before it was loaned by 'Stroo' to the Guille-Alles Library exhibition. Later it became part of the German Occupation Museum's permanent exhibition.

Whilst the great majority of islanders who had remained in Guernsey during the occupation welcomed back our evacuees with open arms, there were others who were a little apprehensive. Returning islanders were sometimes critical of the 'stay behinds' as they called us. Many came back expecting to find their homes and their possessions just as they left them. They did not easily understand the times and difficulties we had lived through. Returning evacuees found the contents of their houses missing and on occasions suspected, rightly or wrongly, that their neighbours had taken advantage of their absence. For a time, there were quite a lot of difficulties, and feelings sometimes ran high. Fortunately none of the animosity affected Mabs or myself.

There was no doubt that some people had acquired items from other people's houses and this inevitably caused a lot of friction. There was the case of one lady who observed a neighbour of hers using towels on the beach and was convinced that they were hers. The other lady was equally certain they were hers and had always been hers. It was impossible to tell after so many years, but it shows how easy it was to create bad feeling between former friends and neighbours, and how difficult it was to resolve, to everyone's satisfaction.

During the occupation, whenever a house was requisitioned, inventories were taken and these were available to returning evacuees. The Controlling Committee appointed custodians for properties which had been left empty and inventories of their contents were also taken. It was amazing just how many records were kept during such a time of stress. However, there were quantities of surplus furniture collected from properties occupied by the Germans and assembled at central depots, where people went to try to identify their property. Often, three or four people identified a piece of furniture as being theirs. In those circumstances, knowledge of damage or markings helped to settle the question of ownership. Despite every effort being made by the authorities, there were people who many years later were still claiming that 'Mrs So in So' has my dining room sideboard or some other item of furniture.

A considerable amount of furniture disappeared during the occupation, some was shipped to the continent. Antique furniture was sent to the 'Fatherland' and a great deal chopped up and used as firewood.

The demand for furniture in the post-war period, particularly by returning evacuees, resulted in furniture shops being given priority for supplies from Britain. Compensation was available, but only to provide a basic replacement. If you had lost an antique chair, all you could expect by way of recompense was the cost of a utility chair.

The Bungalow Hotel on the Jerbourg peninsula was badly damaged by the Germans during the occupation. Mrs Couch, who ran the hotel before the war, found that half her property had been knocked down and the remainder reduced to a state of chaos. Faced with this heart-breaking situation, she showed great pluck and astonishing energy in the way she set-to restoring the remainder of the building. During the 1946 holiday season, Mrs Couch was able to accommodate a limited number of visitors, as well as serving afternoon teas to holiday makers. Regrettably the Bungalow Hotel, fondly known as the Dog and Lion, was burnt to the ground in the summer of 1962.

As a result of the German occupation, there were 3,000 houses requiring repairs before they could be lived in again. British troops, with the assistance of P.O.W.'s, did a tremendous job of rehabilitation and by the end of July 1945 almost 1,000 homes were once again ready for occupation.

If Guernsey was to get back to its prewar position, the first thing that needed to be done, was to re-establish the island's economic life. As a community we had to regain, as quickly as possible, the means of earning our livelihood.

The German occupation of the island had left the Hotel and Catering industry in a very impoverished and derelict condition. Many hotels had suffered severely, some to such an extent that for all intent and purpose, they were a total loss to their owners. Jersey's tourist industry, in comparison had not suffered the damage and disruption from the German occupation to anything like the extent of ours. Their tourism industry was in a much more favourable position.

The Army's hard work in helping to rehabilitate hotels inevitably caused some controversy. If one owner was helped more than another, then there were complaints. The British officer in charge of the programme of rehabilitation was Major Marshall, who was a member of the family that owned the Manor Hotel, at Petit Bot. One of the first hotels to reopen, with the assistance of the British Army was the Manor Hotel and of course controversy soon followed. Major Marshall, however, was soon demobbed and returned to the island to become President of the Guernsey Hotels and Boarding Houses Association.

Whilst good progress was made with the refurbishment of some of the larger hotels, many of the smaller ones and the boarding houses still needed a lot of attention. Five years of war meant that normal maintenance had not been carried out. The added destruction the Germans created, left many premises in a very sorry state. Hoteliers tackled the work with great determination, despite the acute shortage of building materials.

Hoteliers and boarding house proprietors made every effort to ensure that the greatest possible number of holiday makers were accommodated during the 1946 season. Enquiries and bookings for accommodation for the first post war holiday season started rolling in soon after the occupation had ended. It was realised that a successful tourist season, the first one for six years, would go a long way towards putting the island's economy back on its feet.

Dad and Mum ran the Seaplane Annex as a boarding house before the war, but Mabs and I had no intention of following in their footsteps. I was, however, destined to become involved in the Tourist Industry, but not as an hotelier.

After liberation, growers performed herculean feats in getting their vineries back into shape and production. A great deal of glass was destroyed by the Germans and much of the rest was in a poor state of repair. Virtually no maintenance had been carried out since 1940. All the guts had been taken from the soil by a succession of crops without anything being put back into the ground. Much of their equipment was in urgent need of replacement, but our growers were soon growing crops and exporting their produce. By the 15th July 1945 the first post-occupation tomatoes were despatched to the mainland, our trade with the United Kingdom had been re-established. Also, by that time, over 10 tons of cucumbers had been exported.

Guernseymen, as always, were pretty resilient, they quickly returned to work and before the end of 1945 the island's economy based upon our traditional industries, was once again a going concern.

'Shopping is fun again'. So read a headline in the Guernsey Press in August 1945. Four months previously the majority of Town shops were devoid of stock of any kind and on the whole St Peter Port had presented a very unpleasant picture from a customer's point of view. The dramatic change that had taken place in so short a time, now meant that the Town streets, presented a very different and happier picture. Trading hours were shorter than before the war, but much longer than during the occupation. Most shops had, due to the increase in business, added to their staff. Islanders again found window shopping a joy and a temptation.

In the days after the end of the occupation, virtually all the measures the

Germans had taken to 'Germanize' the island were reversed. Compulsory German in schools was withdrawn, German street and name plates disappeared. Driving on the left was quickly restored, to the relief of not only the islanders but the British Forces. German magazines disappeared from the libraries. German Reichmarks disappeared overnight.

The Gaumont Cinema re-opened in early October, having been thoroughly cleansed of all traces of the occupation including Hitler's portraits. The first film to be shown was 'Pardon my Sarong' with Abbott and Costello. I took Mabs and we both thoroughly enjoyed the film and our visit to the refurbished cinema.

As soon as our freedom had been restored, Mabs wanted to visit her parents and present to them, their grandchild, whom they had not yet seen. Her wish brought home to me, the realization that her freedom would not be complete, until she had visited her parents and the family link had been re-established.

The authorities were prepared to allow Mabs and Margaret to travel on compassionate grounds but I could not go with them. Whilst they could guarantee the outward journey, there was doubt about them being able to come home, as returning evacuees were being given priority.

I was very unhappy at not being allowed to go with them and felt it was wrong that a family could be split up in that way, so at first I would not agree to them going. Margaret was now almost five and I had always wanted to be with her when she saw her first train. I had long dreamed of that moment and I did not want to miss her delight at her first sight of a steam engine. Mabs, understandably, very much resented my not allowing her to go without me, so much so that she complained bitterly about being trapped on the island and of course it was all my fault. After all, it was five and a half years since our wedding day and she had not been home once. Finally I conceded and Mabs and Margaret went by mailboat to visit her parents. They spent about three weeks there before being able to return without too much difficulty.

The period of British Military Government ended on the 25th August 1945, when a new Lt Governor was appointed by the King as his representative. Lt.General Philip Neame V.C., later Sir Philip, came and took command of the island. His arrival as our first post-war Lt Governor was a real milestone in our return to normality.

When, later in 1945, the British forces left the island, they disposed of a considerable quantity of equipment locally. Mr Heggs, the States Engineer, knew of my interest in anything that might be available in the way of surplus motorcycles. He introduced me to a British officer at Fort George who said that they would have a number of motorcycles surplus to their requirements. He invited me to inspect them and make an offer. Being strapped for cash at that time, I approached the bank and, after a lengthy 'inquisition', they agreed to make me a loan so that I could purchase the motorcycles.

Mabs and I met the officer at Fort George, and I particularly remember Mabs being introduced as:

"This is Mr Green's lovely wife", and she was lovely too !

That was typical of the type of compliment Mabs regularly received. There were 25 Army BSA 500 cc, side valve M20 motorcycles available. I offered £25 for each machine, it was accepted. I reconditioned the motorcycles and sold them for £50 each

Some time after the end of the occupation, Charles Hodder, the owner of La Croix, let us know that shortly he would be returning to the island and naturally expected to take up residence again. Mabs and I fully understood that we would have to leave the bungalow that had been our home for over four years. We had been happy there and had grown to like the area.

Although we worked hard rehabilitating Seaplane Bungalow and the Annex, both still required a great deal of work doing to them before either of them would be in a suitable condition for us to move back. Mum, who had spent most of the occupation next door to us in Stanberth, also had to move out. She decided that now she was on her own she would rather move back to Smith Street into one of the flats above the shop. Mum was sure that she would be more at home there and would be more involved with her friends than she would be at Seaplane Bungalow without Dad.

In all the circumstances Mabs and I decided that, rather than move back to Seaplane Bungalow, we would look around for another home. At that time there were plenty to chose from and many were going very cheaply.

The bungalow next door to where we were living, Lyndel, was on the market. That was where Edgar Stacey and his family stayed during part of the occupation and where Mr and Mrs Bourgaize were now the tenants. It belonged to Mr Moullin, whose wife had died there during the early part of the war. He had gone back to live with his mother and he didn't fancy returning to live in Lyndel with his memories. He was keen to sell it, so I bought it, for £650. It seemed a lot of money at that time, particularly as there was only an outside toilet, no bathroom and all the water came from a tap outside the back door. As all my money was tied up in the business, I had to borrow from the bank. I used Seaplane Bungalow as collateral. It was an easy move for us, just next door.

I offered Mr and Mrs Bourgaize the tenancy of part of the Annex, which they accepted. Mum soon became fed up with the flat in Town, the stairs proved too much for her, so she moved into the other part of the Annex. Later Aunt Lil moved in with her, although that was to turn out to be a difficult relationship.

I eventually received £300 from the States to rehabilitate Seaplane Bungalow. It went a long way in those days. We never moved back permanently but let it for many years, sometimes going back for short breaks between tenants. I converted the Annexe into two units and so it remains to this day. Seaplane Bungalow has been my daughter's and my grandchildren's home for some years and recently I transferred the ownership to her. In Court, as the property was transferred into Margaret's name, my thoughts went back to when Dad originally bought the plot for a mere £60. Today it must be one of the most valuable sites in the island.

Chapter 25

IT'S A BUGGEERR

After we had celebrated our liberation, I knew that my first priority in life must be re-establishing my business. Pre war I had enjoyed life, raced motorcycles and run my business, probably in that order of priority. The occupation had left me with no stock and in a very tight financial position. The indebtedness that I had to the bank at the start of the occupation had been cleared, largely due to the sale of my stock. However, in order to keep the business afloat and my staff employed, I again required the bank's support. With liberation I knew that I would soon be able to restock my shop, but that needed money which I did not possess.

My urgent need was capital. I knew the bank would help to a limited extent, but I anticipated that I would need more than they would be prepared to lend me if I was going to take advantage of what I fully expected to be a sellers market. Mr Dekker, a bulb and flower grower, came to my rescue when, out of the blue, he offered me three hundred pounds for Dad's car. As I had personal transport in the form of the Norton motorcycle, I accepted his offer. It was a good price, the car had only cost Dad a hundred and twenty pounds back in 1938.

I also sold some of the surplus furniture, mainly beds, which had come from Seaplane Annex when it had been used as a boarding house. During the occupation the furniture had been stored in the flat above the shop. It fetched inflated prices due to the general shortage and the demand created by returning evacuees. That injection of capital into my business made all the difference to re-establishing myself after the occupation.

I anticipated that for some considerable time there would be a greater demand for motorcycles, cycles and spares, than could be met. That meant that it would be a seller's market, but I realised that in due course, as supplies became more readily available, we would return to the pre-war buyers market. If I wished, once again, to be Guernsey's leading cycle and motorcycle dealer, as indeed I did, I would have to give the public a first class service and the business my undivided attention.

Early in July, a reporter from the Star approached me with a view to publishing my views on the future of the cycle trade in the island. I was only too happy to respond, it was all good publicity for my business.

The reporter wrote:-

> 'Guernsey men and women still rely very much on the bicycle as a means of transport. They will be disappointed to hear that supplies of cycle tyres will still be in very short supply.
>
> Local cycle and motorcycle dealer, Mr Bill Green said:-
>
> Whilst some individuals have managed to have tyres sent to them from friends in different parts of England, the cycle trade has much difficulty in obtaining tyres and tubes from the manufacturers. Stocks of rubber are small. There will probably be an allocation of rubber from the Ministry of Supply to

> manufacturers to meet Channel Island needs. Limited supplies are coming and these will help to relieve the situation. A similar situation exists in the supply of new cycles. Cycles will only come through in small numbers for some time owing to the transport difficulties and the small supply available. Cycle repairs are still the order of the day in the cycle trade. Most tyres now being repaired should have been dumped years ago.'

On reflection I was over pessimistic, supplies did in fact arrive much sooner and in greater quantities than seemed possible when I talked to the Star reporter.

Within a few days of liberation I received my first communication from the Royal Enfield Cycle Company. It was an invoice for a cycle which they had delivered to us five years previously in June 1940, just before the Germans arrived. Artie Selous, who managed the shop while I was away at Armstrong Siddeley, sold the cycle to Mr Wyatt, of The Shop For Men in the Pollet, for his daughter. When I returned from Coventry, Mr Wyatt came to see me, he wanted to pay for the cycle.

"Well" I said, "I haven't received a bill for it, Mr Wyatt, so we have a free bicycle as far as I can tell."

He was a very genuine man and was keen to settle up with me.

I said "Mr Wyatt, I can't charge you if I haven't paid for it myself."

When I received the invoice I went down and showed it to Mr Wyatt and we had quite a laugh about it. He insisted on paying, so I charged him, only the actual invoice price, £3.19.9d. I noticed that their invoice was dated May 1945, so, with tongue in cheek, I deducted 3¾%, seven days discount, and Royal Enfield didn't demure. So I made a small 'turn' on the transaction after all. I wrote to Vic Mountford, the Managing Director of Royal Enfield, and told him the story. He sent me a lovely letter of apology and described their mistake as a 'classic'.

The motor and motorcycling magazines that Ralph Palmer brought back with him, proved to be of great value. I don't think that I have ever written, or rather, typed with two fingers, so many letters in my life. I contacted every possible company that might conceivably be able to supply me with stock. Many of the firms I contacted responded magnificently, due mainly to the island being categorized as an export market. Supplies soon began to come through very well.

I received my first consignment of Enfield and Hercules cycles on the 14th of July. The demand was such that they had all been sold before they arrived in the island. By the end of July I had received and sold 44 new cycles. A little later I received a container-load of bicycles which, as I did not have sufficient room in my Smith Street shop, went straight up to Seaplane Annex, where they were stored. Customers were so desperate to obtain a new bicycle, that they went up to Jerbourg to fetch one, rather than wait for one to be brought down to the Smith Street shop. I would telephone Mabs, she would meet the customer at the Annex and complete the sale.

I was working pretty well day and night trying to re-establish the business. I had a desk in the lounge and often took work home.

Air services were resumed between the mainland and the island in the early autumn of 1945. A service between Guernsey and Southampton was run by Guernsey and Jersey Airways Ltd. The aircraft was the seven seater De Havilland Rapid bi-plane, the fare was £3 single or £5 return and the flight took just over the hour. A service to Croydon soon followed. This was a great boon to me, as it allowed me to visit many of my suppliers in the London area and return home the same day.

I remember on one occasion going across with Edgar Stacey, and he and I had lunch with one of my prewar girlfriends. Although I was married, I liked to keep contact with many of my old flames. Mabs was understandably not so enthusiastic and this inevitably caused a degree of tension between us.

The following summer, Mabs and Margaret accompanied me on a trip I made to the mainland to call on various suppliers and manufacturers. With the old Ford '8' I was driving at the time, we managed to fit in a visit to Mabs family in Carlisle. On the return journey I dropped Mabs and Margaret off at Southampton Airport, so they could fly home - Mabs did not like travelling on the cross Channel ferries. Then I intended to catch the night mailboat to Guernsey but as I was driving past the railway station in Southampton, somebody yelled out, at the top of his voice:

"Bill".

It was my old Motorcycling Club friend of prewar days, Mickey Matthews, who happened to be digging in his garden as I passed his house.

I stopped and explained that I was on my way to catch the mailboat.

"You can't go back today, Alf Bottoms is racing at the dirt track tonight, you must come and see him."

Alf Bottoms was one of the greats of dirt track motorcycling racing and there was no way I was going to miss watching him race.

The next day, Mickey took me over the Dimplex factory where he worked. They made radiators and their production methods and engineering fascinated me. I stayed with Mickey for three days before I caught the boat home. Mabs was understandably frantic, as I had not let her know where I was or what had happened to me.

Mickey, pre-war, had been a regular competitor on the sands at Vazon and we had raced against each other on many occasions. In the twenties he owned a Douglas motorcycle, which he rode on my first encounter with him at Vazon. Despite it being a foggy day, racing continued. I had just completed one race and the starter called us out for the next. As I rode out to the start, Mickey, returning from the other end of course, came out of the fog and hit my motorcycle amidships, just missing my leg. Fortunately neither of us were hurt, but our motorcycles were fairly badly damaged. Despite, or in some ways due to that accident, we became firm friends.

While I was staying with Mickey, I learnt all about his war. He had joined up and had seen service with the 8th Army in the Western Desert as a truck driver. One day, while driving his truck through the desert near Tobruk, he came across three motorcyclists going in the opposite direction. The motorcyclists all wore helmets and goggles. The stance and the way one of them sat on his motorcycle and rode it, impressed Mickey Matthews so much that he was sure it was an old friend of his and mine, Andre Audaber.

Andre Audaber was a Frenchman, who came to work in Guernsey before the war and stayed with the Hubert family. He worked for Hubert's and became a member of the Motorcycle and Light Car Club. Andre was extremely proud of an A.J.S. motorcycle which he purchased from me. He became a familiar figure riding his machine around the island. Andre was a super chap and had a wonderful saying, 'It's a Buggeerr!'

Of course this expression went right through the Motorcycle and Light Car Club. All the boys would say:

"Hello Andre - it's a Buggeerr!"

Andre became very popular and we all missed him when he left the island at the start of the war to join the French army.

Mickey Matthews was so sure that it was Andre that he had seen, that he obtained permission from his Commanding Officer to go into the next town that evening, to see if he could find him. Mickey found Andre - they met only because he recognized the way he sat on his motorcycle. As Andre Audaber said, 'It's a Buggeerr!'

One day, I was walking down Smith Street and there was a Press poster outside the Guernsey Press shop with the headline of the day, which read 'States pass Children's Allowances'. As I walked I felt an arm come around my shoulders, it was Willie Hesse, the former Wehrmacht Sergeant. He pointed to the poster and said:

"Guernsey will soon need living space!"

He had remembered our wartime conversation after all those years. Don't ever say that the Germans do not have a sense of humour, because he laughed and walked on down the Street!

Greens of Smith Street 1946.

Willie was in the island throughout the occupation and after our liberation was shipped to England as a prisoner of war. During the war he became friendly with a girl from our swimming club, Shelia Radford. We had ostracised Shelia because she was going out with this German and in retrospect that is an action I now regret. Shelia was a very good diver, but was stone deaf. After the war when Willie was released from the P.O.W. camp he returned to Guernsey and married Shelia. It was wonderful the way he looked after and cherished her.

Willie, in time, became fully accepted as part of our community. He was a good swimmer and played for one of the island's water polo teams. He managed the 'Restaurant Berthelot' in town, which was owned by the Radford family and later ran the Ellingham Hotel in St Martin. He was a delightful person and one of life's gentlemen.

For a period after the war, Britain's requirement for steel considerably exceeded the supply. The Ministry of Supply sent a representative over to Guernsey, with the job of organising the recovery of the scrap metal from the large quantities of German military equipment which was still in Guernsey. At the end of the occupation, great quantities of equipment had been sealed up in the German tunnels by the British Army.

Jackie Upham, who now ran a company called John Upham Ltd. in Les Amballes, was approached by the representative of the Ministry of Supply and persuaded to take on the job of opening up various tunnels and salvaging the scrap.

Jackie and his team managed to recover over 17,000 tons of scrap metal which was shipped to the mainland to help with the steel shortage.

They opened up a number of tunnels, including the ones at Grand Maison Road, St Sampsons and St Saviours. One tunnel contained thousands of steel helmets, but very little else of scrap value. When they opened the tunnel at Grand Maison Road, they found that a wall had been built just inside the entrance with granite sets, the type used in roads. Apparently, when the tunnel had been filled by the British after the war, they had not been able to get the last tank in as far as they had wanted, so they built it into the wall.

When Jackie and his team cleared away the wall from around the German tank, they then had to remove hundreds if not thousands of empty 303 cartridge cases, that had been literally poured into the crew positions. After the war so many empty cartridges had been found, that they just dumped them any place they could. Each one of these cartridge cases had to be hand picked out by Jackie and his team. They caused a series of shorts to the electrical system. After drying out the magnetos and attending to other necessary maintenance, Jackie eventually managed to get the tank working and used it to pull out a lot of the other equipment in the tunnel. That included such item as eight-inch guns, field kitchens and armaments of almost every description.

'Dreamy' Stranger, who had returned to the island after service in the Royal Air Force, became a Director of John Upham Ltd. One day I met him at one of the tunnels, where he was directing operations. They were cutting up a large gun barrel into smaller furnace size pieces, so that they could easily be transported to St Sampsons harbour for shipment to England. 'Dreamy' and his men were using oxyacetylene cutting equipment outside and inside the tunnel. Some of men were scrambling about in the tunnel on their hands and knees, with the cutting equipment. I would have been scared stiff that there was still some live ammunition in amongst the mass of military equipment.

"What happens if there is some live ammunition in the tunnel ?" I asked 'Dreamy'.

In his nonchalant way 'Dreamy' replied. "God I hope not, we've seen ammunition containers, but no ammunition," adding. "There are a lot of detonators which make a hell of a bang, but they don't cause any real injuries."

During the occupation the Forest Church was extremely popular, the Reverend Finey regularly attracted good congregations. Although, officially we were not allowed to play or sing the National Anthem without permission, and despite often having considerable numbers of Germans in his congregation, he always insisted on finishing the service by singing 'God Save the King'. While the Germans, who always sat on one side of the church, sang their words to the tune, which was a German hymn, the rest of his congregation rendered a lusty 'God Save the King'. Everyone left the church happy. It was a situation which both fascinated and encouraged me, so Mabs and I became regular attenders at the Forest Church.

In consequence I got to know the Reverend Finey fairly well and, after the war, he came to see me.

"Bill" he said "I would like a little motorcycle to get around the parish. I can't afford a car, but a little motorcycle would suit me fine. I am very nervous, so would you please teach me to ride it ?"

"Yes of course I will"

So I chose him what I thought was a suitable machine, a little James Motor bike, with a 125cc, Villiers engine. I arranged to deliver the machine at a time when I could also give him his first lesson. I rode the motor cycle out to his Vicarage, propped it against the wall and rang the bell.

The Reverend Finey came out, looked at the bike and exclaimed;

"Oh dear, oh dear!"

I enquired what was the matter.

"Its the number plate".

"The number plate padre ? What's wrong with the number plate?"

He said, "277, 'Nearer my God to Thee' in the Ancient and Modern Hymn book."

He was extremely nervous, but I managed to teach him to ride the motorbike - eventually. The Reverend Finey passed many happy hours riding around his parish, and he and his motorcycle soon became a familiar sight to his local parishioners.

On August 6th 1945, Police Inspector W.R. Sculpher returned to the island for the first time since he and his wife had been deported into captivity by the Germans in the autumn of 1942. He immediately sought an interview with the President of the Island Police Committee and requested his reinstatement as Chief Officer.

The Police Committee unanimously agreed that he should return to duty. The emphasis was put on his 'return to duty' and not on reinstatement, as he had not been dismissed or charged with any offence. His absence from duty had been entirely as a result of enemy action. As far as the Committee was concerned he had been a blameless victim of German persecution. He took up his duties immediately and I for one was extremely happy to see him back.

Another who returned but who was not reinstated, was former Police Sergeant Jack Harper. He had been sentenced to four and a half years hard labour by the German Military tribunal. Jack, after he returned, showed me marks on his back that were the result of what the Germans did to him in captivity. There were six deep marks, which had obviously been caused by some form of lashing or whipping. He was a big man, but the brutal treatment he suffered at the hands of the German guards had a very serious and lasting affect on him.

Jack told me how he was beaten with a pick and shovel, kicked and trampled upon, and denied food. When the temperature was well below freezing, he was deprived of his clothes. Almost crying at the memory, he related how he was chained to a tree in the snow for long periods. He was made to lift bags of cement and railway sleepers and beaten whilst doing so. When carrying the sleepers, he was tripped and made to fall. While he was on the ground the German guards threw the sleepers onto his chest. He told me of the occasion when he was forced to shower in cold water and then left to dry without a towel. The temperature was below freezing and all the time he was being constantly tormented and jeered at by the guards.

Jack Harper, in fact, should have died from the treatment he received in prison at Augsberg. He related that when he was liberated by the Americans, they said that they had not seen anyone in worse condition than him and still living.

Early in 1946, I was shocked to learn that Inspector Sculpher had been sacked. Apparently, the previous October, the Bailiff set up a Committee of Investigation, comprising Mr C.W. Bickmore, Commander S.B. Mainguy and Major F. Barritt Hills, with the task of:

> 'Enquiring into the circumstances leading up to the offences committed during 1941 and 1942 by certain members of the Island Police Force, with a view to determining whether and if so, to what extent, the state of indiscipline and loss of sense of public duty revealed thereby can fairly and properly be attributed to lack of supervision or other defect in the control of the Force'

If ever there was a predetermined inquiry, this must have been it. The terms of reference undeniably indicated the conclusion required. Inspector Sculpher was seemingly on trial, without having being charged with an offence. The Committee of Investigation, their report clearly showed, relied solely on documentary evidence and called no witnesses, not even the Inspector.

The files of the German Military Authorities, the records of the German Military Tribunal, the evidence presented at the Royal Court hearing and the evidence taken by the Germans, was accepted, apparently without question. The reports which appeared in the press, which were heavily censored by the Nazi's, were also accepted without question. Inspector Sculpher had no knowledge of what evidence was being considered, far less the opportunity to question it. He was only allowed to comment upon their report and findings after it had been completed and presented to the Bailiff. I felt, as did very many Guernseymen, that this was a flagrant case of injustice. I was very bitter and felt outraged at the treatment handed out to a fine upstanding British policeman. Along with many fellow islanders, I hung my head in shame.

How could the Committee of Investigation accept the suspect evidence of a German wartime tribunal, without submitting that evidence to any form of serious questioning ? Where was the justice that I had been brought up to believe in - how could our own authorities condemn and sentence a man without him even being allowed to be heard or being legally represented ? I do not ever remember being so angry, about any decision taken by our States, as I was that day.

Inspector Sculpher, our Chief of Police, a position which he had held since 1930, was instantly dismissed. It was a sad end to a career that had started with the London Metropolitan Police, in which Force he reached the rank of Inspector. He was a stunned and almost a broken man. He immediately packed up and left the island and went to live with his brother in King's Lynn.

I wrote to him, expressing my disgust at the way he had been treated and offering to help in any way I could. He wrote a nice letter in reply, asking me if I would support the petition he was presenting to the Home Secretary. I was only too happy to give him all the support I could and sent a letter as he requested. I understand that many other islanders did likewise.

Inspector Sculpher petitioned the Home Secretary, requesting a new inquiry at which he would be allowed to give evidence and be legally represented. The Home Office carefully considered his request and, through the 'normal channels', informed the States that in their opinion:-

The manner in which the inquiry was conducted by the Committee of Investigation, left much to be desired, in that in particular:-

a. Great reliance was placed upon German documents, to which the Committee had access and these were not checked with witnesses that were available.

b. The Inspector was never given the opportunity at any time before the Committee reached its conclusions, to testify on his own behalf, or to examine or make representations, personally, or through Council as regards the evidence on which the Committee relied.

The Board of Administration, after what they called 'mature' consideration, withdrew the notice of dismissal of Inspector Sculpher. They suggested to his lawyers that they would regard him as officially retiring on the 30th September 1946. This would qualify him for a pension. He accepted what was, in effect, a 'Pardon', subject to the contents of Home Office Report and the decisions of the Board of Administration being given suitable local publicity.

Jurat Johns, President of the Board of Administration, presented a full report to the States. The statement was greeted with applause by members of the House. One member, Douzaine Delegate Ira C. Ozanne, said:

"I was glad to hear something about 'that Blot'." and added, "I think that the whole question has been a scandal, and that Inspector Sculpher has not even been allowed to defend himself."

Now retired, Inspector Sculpher received his back pay and pension and, as far as I know, never set foot in Guernsey again - and I for one did not blame him.

The first post-war meeting of the Guernsey Chamber of Commerce took place on the 25th May 1945. Reg Luxon was still President and the meeting was attended by some fifty members. The Chamber was at last back in the business of representing its members, with the freedom to meet when it wanted and discuss what it wanted. You only appreciate freedom when it is denied you.

At the end of June 1945, the first Annual General Meeting for six years, was held. Our President, Reg Luxon, was keen to stand down, since he had been in office since 1935. Cecil Stonelake, Colin Munro, Ted Laker and I, applied great pressure on Reg in an effort to induce him to change his mind. Finally he reluctantly allowed his name to go forward and he was re- elected by acclamation.

I stood for election to the Chamber Council and was returned for a three year period of office. That period was extended and extended and today, by virtue of my ex-offico position as a past President, I am the longest serving member of the Council.

At the first meeting of the Council that I attended, the subject of commercial radio was discussed. Major Seale representing the Central News Agency was in the island and was invited to address Chamber Council. Major Seale recalled the pre-war success of continental transmitters such as Radio Luxembourg and Radio Normandy. He said that he and his Agency were aware that there were German radio transmitters in Hamburg, Cologne and Stettin that were to be dismantled and sold. If the States was successful in obtaining one of these transmitters, it would be possible to broadcast British trade propaganda throughout Europe and South America.

A company could be formed, that would lease the transmitter from the States with a licence to broadcast. Advertising would produce the revenue necessary to run the station and he was convinced that it would be a profitable enterprise.

I suggested that Guernsey itself could be advertised over the station. Major Seale replied that it would be possible for the States to obtain a concession for free advertising from the company operating the station.

One of our Council members recalled the attempts to set up a 'Radio Alderney' station, a few years before the war. That plan had been thwarted by the British Government. Major Seale said that as the transmitter would be the property of the States of Guernsey, that would prevent it's use being blocked. The States, he said, would have the right to vet and veto programmes and, as he put it, censor them to ensure that they were not vulgarised. After considerable discussion, it was unanimously agreed that the whole question was so involved and that the Council was in possession of so little information, both technical and financial, that it was not advisable to become involved in the project.

Major Seale was a man who had an instant view on every subject or topic and wild ideas by the score. He went on to suggest the possibility of manufacturing penicillin in the island. He emphasised that he was speaking without specialist knowledge of the subject, but he thought that penicillin was best made from the mould of rotting tomatoes. He was not sure whether the spores from which penicillin was developed were better produced in the dark, although he thought this was so. He suggested that the many underground tunnels excavated by the Germans during the occupation could be used for that purpose. By using the redundant tunnels and locally grown tomatoes, Guernsey seemed to him to be an ideal venue for the production of penicillin. For a while he seemed to make sense, but we soon returned to reality !

The main object of Major Seale visit was to discover, for the Central News Agency, the current economic state of the island. He said that he had been able to discover quite a lot. I asked him how he had obtained his information ?

"I went straight to the top" said Major Seale, "I did not get to the saloon by the kitchen stairs !"

"Roughly speaking, you have had a much worse time here than in Jersey, but on the other hand your future looks a lot rosier than their's. Jersey is plagued with Colorado Beetles and their exports are badly threatened. The big question is, where is your future income as an island coming from ?"

For once he did not have an instant answer to his question.

In March 1946, Billy Butlin's personal representative Mr A.J.N Nailer, visited the island with a view to setting up a Holiday Camp. He was met by members of the States of Guernsey's Natural Beauties Committee who accompanied him to the former L'Eree aerodrome site, where it was proposed to build a Butlin's Holiday camp.

Soon it was announced that the 'Holiday King' was definitely going to build at L'Eree. The Natural Beauties Committee approved the holiday site, which would provide accommodation for 2,000 holidaymakers, together with shops, theatre, swimming pool, ballroom and children's play grounds. Billy Butlin soon completed negotiations with the Guernsey Aero Club, owners of the fifty two acre site and bought the land.

Chamber of Commerce members were very concerned at the proposal, as were many members of the States and the public. A petition was presented to the States totally opposing the plan on the grounds that the development would destroy the tranquillity of the area and cause too great a demand on the island's water supply.

In view of the controversy the States decided to appoint a committee under Jurat Pierre De Putron, to investigate the future of Tourism in the island. When the committee presented its report the following November, they supported the establishment of a holiday camp at L'Eree. Then a 'photo montage' of the proposed Camp appeared in the Press and that immediately brought forth a howl of protest.

The 'photo montage' showed just how extensive the plans were. They included a swimming pool with a soda fountain, bowling greens, children's playground, boating lake, miniature golf course, theatre and numerous other buildings. A large sports hall, it was explained, would house 8 table tennis tables, 15 billiard tables, together with lounges, gym, darts and card rooms. Other proposed buildings included a ballroom and dining halls. Space was also left for the construction of numerous tennis courts. Shops on the site would include newsagent, tobacconist, florist, fruiter, shoe valeting service, ladies and gentlemen's hairdressing, chemist, drapery store and Post Office.

It was becoming a serious proposal and Chamber members were extremely concerned at the plan. Mr Nailer was invited to meet members and answer their questions. He sought to play the whole scheme down.

"No it would not be called Butlins Holiday Camp, it would be the L'Eree Chalet Hotel".

"No it would not desecrate the island, far from that, it would only beautify the place".

"How could buildings mar the landscape after the Natural Beauties Committee had approved their construction and shape". "At the moment", he said " L'Eree is in the words of many islanders, nothing more than a neglected barren spot"

He assured the Chamber of Commerce and every islander;

"The artistic landscape garden plans that his Company had in mind would only beautify the area and provide an incentive for campers to go further afield and see more of your beautiful island."

He most certainly was Billy Butlin's silver tongued representative and in my opinion, that evening he earned every penny of his salary ! Despite his eloquence, he totally failed to convince Chamber's members, as he failed to win over the Guernsey Hotel and Boarding House Keepers Association. When the matter was debated in the States they said 'No!' to the holiday camp scheme by an overwhelming vote, only 13 in favour of Butlins, while 35 were against the proposal. Among those who voted for the scheme was Sir John Leale, which surprised me.

Billy Butlin held on to the land for a number of years hoping, no doubt, that the island would change its mind. In 1961 he sold the site to L'Eree Estates Limited, a newly formed local company with English Directors. One Director, Mr Arthur Quadrille, of Arthur Quadrille and Partners of Mayfair, London, said the purchase of the site was the first step towards creating a Garden Village by the sea. Those plans also came to nothing and later the site was purchased as agricultural land by Colin Best.

One of the benefits of having Jurat Pierre De Putron's Committee investigate the future of Tourism, was the setting up of a Tourist Board to replace the States Publicity Committee. I had previously been appointed to succeed C J McCathie as one of the Chamber's delegates on the States Publicity Committee. When the States created the new Tourist Board, I continued to represent the Chamber of Commerce. So, in 1946 I started my long association with that Committee, which continued until recently.

In September 1946, a special General meeting of Chamber members was held to consider the future of Channel Islands Airways, who were being threatened with nationalisation by the British Labour Government under the terms of the Civil Aviation Bill.

One member was of the opinion that if our Airline was nationalised by the Labour Government, then it would be the first step in taking over the Channel Islands. Most members present deprecated the loss of Channel Island Airways and saw it as a clear case of nationalising a Guernsey concern. Many members felt that the Chamber should take a strong stand against the Labour Government's proposals and do everything possible to retain our autonomy and individuality. Allan Grut however, took the other view, saying it was wrong to suspect every move made by the Labour government.

The States sent a delegation to the Home Office to express the island's concern. But it was all of no avail, the Labour Government pushed through their Nationalization proposals and our Airline was swallowed up.

One of the matters that came before the Chamber in 1948 was the pedestrianisation of the High Street, Smith Street and the Pollet. This, of course, raised considerable controversy within Chamber, since members felt their businesses would be affected and a heated debate took place. Some members took the view that their interests were paramount, while others felt that a more public spirited approach should be taken by traders. I personally believed that the banning of cars was in the best interests of the community at large. One member felt it might never have arisen if it had not been for some individuals parking their cars in the streets and causing congestion. It was ultimately agreed that the Chamber would take no action as a body, however there were individual members who lodged personal protests. Pedestrianisation took place, and I think that the centre of St Peter Port became a better shopping centre as a result.

Chapter 26

THE GREATEST REBEL

The subject of reform of the States of Deliberation, the Guernsey Parliament, regularly cropped up in many of the lunch time conversations I had with John Leale as we sat on the wall outside Maison Allaire during the occupation. I quickly formed the impression that Reform was very close to his heart. He was, without doubt a great believer in democracy. The States, which he said derived almost two thirds of its membership from persons who were there only because they held some other office or position, could not, in his view, be considered democratic.

He expounded a vision, where a majority of the States were there because they had been elected directly by the community and were answerable to the people of the island. He greatly impressed me with his sincerity and created an interest in, and a respect for, democracy which I have to this day.

What I was not aware of at the time, was that Deputy Wilfred Corbet, during the later days of the occupation, was laying the foundation for reform. He held discussions with other members of the States, who he knew to be interested in the principle of reform. The subject was quietly raised with the Bailiff, Victor Carey, who thought that it was premature to openly discuss the matter then, but agreed that as soon as the island had been liberated, a Requete, or petition could be presented to the States of Deliberation.

Soon after liberation, Deputy Corbet took the Requete that he had drafted out of his desk, where it had lain for eighteen months, and proceeded to collect the signatures of fourteen States members. It was presented to the Bailiff on the 28th June 1945. This was to lead to the enactment of the Reform Law of 1948.

The Requete was signed by:-

> Deputy W. Corbet, Deputy E.T. Wheadon, Jurat John Leale, Jurat Sir Abraham Laine, Jurat Pierre De Putron, Deputy C.H. Cross, Douzaine Delegate E.A. Dorey, Deputy C.W. Arnold, Deputy R.H. Johns, Douzaine Delegate R.G. Luxon, Reverend E.L. Frossard, Douzaine Delegate T.E.G. McCathie, Deputy the Rev W. Kilshaw and Douzaine Delegate H.M. Mahy.

The Requete read:-

> 'That on the first day of January 1900 membership of the States of Deliberation was increased by the inclusion therein of nine Deputies of the People. After a due period of successful trial the number of Deputies was increased to eighteen on the first day of January 1921. That experience during the last 25 years has vindicated the democratic system of government and that the time has therefore arrived both from an Island standpoint and from the

view of world experience to study once more the question of direct representation in the States of Deliberation as well as other means whereby the Government of the Island may be brought more into line with the present day requirements'.

The Petitioners requested that a Committee be appointed to study carefully and report as soon as possible to the States of Deliberation regarding:-

A The desirability of increasing the number of direct representatives in the States of Deliberation

B Any other alterations in the Constitution of the States or the rules and customs regulating procedure therein whereby this house may be brought more into conformity with the requirements of present day government.

The Requete was presented to and discussed by the States on 18th July 1945. John Leale pointed out that the obvious criticism that could be brought against the States was that the Deputies, the only elected representatives of the people, were in a hopeless minority.

"That means," he said, "that the electorate have no powers through the ballot box, of insisting that its will be carried into effect." He felt "It was wrong, in an assembly, such as ours, that some members of the States should be responsible to no one but themselves, once they had taken their seats."

As a result of the interest that my talks with John Leale had generated, I went along to the meeting of the States when the Requete was debated and sat in the public gallery. Despite the importance of the matter under consideration, very few other islanders took the opportunity of attending.

The Reverend Macartney, the Rector of St Andrews - who like all the Parish Rectors were by virtue of their office, members of the States - questioned whether the signatories were anticipating the formation of political parties. He expressed the view that;

"It is one of 'the glories' of this House that it has stood for centuries without falling into political parties." He observed that; "Whatever else might be put in its place, it will take centuries for it to work as well as our present constitution. Because a thing was old it was not always bad. The people of Guernsey as a whole," he said, "seemed to be prepared to leave the conduct of their affairs to those in charge."

Jurat De Putron reflected that democracy was an excellent, but a very dangerous word.

His Majesty's Procureur, Ambrose Sherwill, observed;

"Considerable skill will be required if this little ship of state is to be steered into calmer waters."

He went on to propose an amendment to the Requete, that a Committee, which became known as the Constitutional Reform Committee, be appointed consisting of seven members, four from the States and three non-States members, to consider the matters raised in the Requete and report back to the States.

John Leale, who became President of the Committee, Deputy W. Corbet, Rev F.Garfield Waterbury and the Rev K. Macartney were elected as the States members. The three non-States members had to be nominated by the public by the 31st July 1945.

During the week following the States debate, a meeting was held at the Victoria Road Schoolroom to form the Society for States Reform. Some eighty potential reformers were present. I attended and found myself in hot water as far as Deputy Corbet was concerned.

I asserted that;

"The States treated the public like schoolboys, and did not show any confidence in them." I added, "That whilst I was keen on States reform it should be done by evolution and not revolution." These remarks were greeted with great applause!

I argued "No matter how good the men on the Constitutional Reform Committee were, the States still have the power to veto any proposals they put forward." I continued, "I think it unfair that the States have the power to elect the three non States members to serve on the Committee. They would only elect those who represented their view. I feel that they should be elected by the general public."

Deputy Corbet replied saying;

"This is not a public election. In my view the States have probably gone farther than they have ever gone before. I say this to Mr Green - the States have given you a foot and now you say you want eighteen inches."

My comments were well reported and when I next met John Leale in the street he said to me:

"Bill, you ought to be interested in the Constitutional Reform Committee, we would appreciate having someone like you with us. You should think about it."

I was highly flattered by his comments and encouragement. I did not need any further persuasion. Two members of my staff proposed and seconded my nomination, Artie Selous and George Cave. Mine was one of the last nominations submitted.

Soon a list of those put forward for the three non States places on the Constitutional Reform Committee was published in the Press.

Henry Martin Mahy, Vale.
Harry Dean, Plough Inn, Vauvert.
Allan Grut, Green Lanes, St Peter Port.
Thomas James Ogier, Myrtle Lodge, Vale.
G.H. Gale, Bordeaux View, Vale.
Robert Hale, Havilland Vale, St Martin.
Miss Nina Worley, St Johns Terrace, St Peter Port.
C.H. Cross, New Road, St Sampson's.
Francis John Le Vallee, Les Amballes, St Peter Port.
Albert O. Blatchford, Les Amballes, St Peter Port.
William Green, Smith Street, St Peter Port.

A newspaper report commenting on the nominations stated:-

> 'There are two young men both in their thirties, who are having an increasing voice in island affairs. They are Mr Allan Grut and Mr William Green who's names are well known to the public through their business enterprise, and through their association with the Chamber of Commerce. Both are progressive thinkers and are likely to represent very strongly the point of view of the present generation.'

When the States met on the 17th August, despite my reported comments, I was elected to the Committee, along with Allan Grut and Thomas Ogier. It is only in recent years that I have fully realised just how privileged I was to be a member of that historic Constitutional Reform Committee. That I think, was the start of my public service to my island which, I am proud to say, still continues to this day.

The next time I saw John Leale was when he bumped into me, I am sure on purpose. He said;

"Oh I am pleased you are going to come and join us."

The Committee quickly got down to work. We met at about 5 p.m. in Dr. Bostock's house, next to Maison Allaire at the top of Smith Street. One of our members, the Reverend Macartney, was blind though this did not in any way prevent him from taking a full part in our deliberations. He took notes in braille, and carried a little machine for that purpose. He was highly intelligent, with a brilliant political mind. Although he did not agree with all our recommendations, he must be given the credit for initiating much of our thinking. In many ways he was the driving force within the Committee.

In order that I could give the Reverend Macartney a lift home to the Rectory in St Andrews, I would park my Norton motorcycle outside Dr Bostock's house. As the Rector was blind, he did not know quite what to make of the sidecar - he was never quite sure what he was in. On one or two occasions it poured with rain and he was thoroughly soaked He was a grand character and although I don't think he knew what to make of me, I totally respected him.

Wilfred Corbet was a very shrewd and capable politician, who was a great asset to the Committee. I admired and envied his political ability. I don't think, however, that the Reverend Waterbury, the Rector of Castel, contributed a great deal to our deliberations, although he was an interesting character. Allan Grut, who was about my age, had a great command of the English language and was another member of the Committee with a splendid political mind. I certainly admired him then and did so throughout his subsequent successful political career in the States. Little Tom Ogier, a grower, and a very stable sort of person was like me, politically a little green. Although he was quite a bit older, we got on well together, but we were both very much the 'Political Juniors' on the Committee.

To be honest I was very much out of my depth and I have always been grateful to Wilfred Corbet for being so helpful to me. He, I think took a liking to me, realised that I was paddling in deep water, and often came to my rescue. John Leale, who was always a very courteous and charming man, also sought to encourage me.

He had the great ability of getting to the heart of the matter under consideration and of guiding others in the same direction. If a Committee member went off the point he would steer us back, albeit with a touch of charm.

He would say:

"That is not what we were really thinking about Mr Green, it was such and such....."

He always retained total control of the Committee, although at the time members probably did not fully appreciate the fact. John Leale had a masterful control and was, without doubt, very experienced in the art of handling committees.

I remember an occasion when I made a fool of myself by mixing up the Royal Court with the States of Deliberation. There was a hush in the Committee and I was allowed to realise my mistake in total silence. I can still see the members of the Committee looking at each other as if to say 'We have got a right one here!' John Leale very quietly and courteously straightened me out, pointing out the difference between the Royal Court and the States. That showed how totally inexperienced I was at that time.

On another occasion when I had made one of my outrageous suggestions, John Leale pulled his glasses down over his nose, looked at me and said:

"You know Mr Green, you can take the greatest rebel, which you are, and put him in a position of responsibility and trust for long enough and do you know what happens to him?"

"No Sir".

"He becomes a conservative." And boy - was he right!

I freely admit that I was a rebel and, to be candid, a bloody nuisance. I formulated ideas that were absolutely impracticable, only to have them savaged by the more experienced members of the Committee.

When the States set up the Constitutional Reform Committee, it had needed a blend of experience and youth. In many ways my presence most certainly helped to make it a representative Committee, although I think in some ways I was being used, more than being useful.

Whilst I was without doubt a 'lightweight' as far as the other members were concerned, I was fascinated by it all and learned a great deal about 'Committees', 'procedure' and the States in a very short time. I was thrown in at the deep end and learnt to swim the hard way. Most certainly I learned a great deal more than I contributed. That experience, I believe, stood me in good stead throughout the rest of my public life.

From the first, I was impressed at the way John Leale controlled and guided the committee. He encourage us to determine, at the very beginning of our deliberations, what was our basic objective.

We perceived that it was our duty to lay before the House proposals that would have the effect of making the States more truly representative of the people of the island, whilst and at the same time creating the best possible instrument for the government of Guernsey. I found that declaration extremely helpful in concentrating my mind.

The States of Deliberation at that time was composed of

The Bailiff.
The Procureur.
The Comptroller.
12 Jurats.
10 Parish Rectors.
15 Delegates from the Parish Douzaines.
18 Peoples Deputies.

The Bailiff and the two law Officers were appointed by the Sovereign. The Jurats were elected by the States of Election, a body consisting of the Bailiff, the Law Officers, Jurats, ten Rectors, eighteen Peoples Deputies, the twenty Parish Constables and one hundred and eighty Douzeniers. Once elected Jurats held their Office for life. Candidates had to be British subjects, although Roman Catholics, Brewers and Publicans were disqualified.

Each of the country Parishes appointed a Delegate, who could be either one of the Constables, or a Douzenier to attend a particular sitting of the States of Deliberation. St Peter Port appointed two from their central Douzaine and one each from each of the four Cantonial Douzaines. The Delegate was under an obligation, if so requested by his Douzaine, to put forward it's views and vote as instructed. They were, however, free to state their own views. In practice, a different Douzenier attended each States meeting. Delegates were often selected on the basis of the knowledge of a particular subject that was coming before the States.

The eighteen People's Deputies were the only members of the States who were directly elected by the electorate. Only eighteen out of fifty eight members were accountable to the people, less than one third. That meant that more than two thirds owed their seats to the fact that they had been chosen to fill some other office or position.

We looked upon our task as going right back to fundamentals and questioning the basic philosophy of governing our island. The desirability of having a two chamber Parliament, an upper and lower House, was considered. Whilst almost every other democratic country in the world had a two-tier Parliament, we concluded that we were not a large enough community to support such a democratic luxury.

The future position of the Bailiff was very carefully considered. We questioned the desirability of the Bailiff being both President of the Royal Court and President on the States, on the grounds that those that make laws should not administer them. Again, we felt that only being a small community, it seemed unlikely that either position could become full time. If the office was divided it would almost certainly lose some of its prestige. We concluded on balance that the dual role of the Bailiff should continue. We did however recommend that, as President of the States, the Bailiff should only have a casting vote.

We felt it essential that the advice of the two Law Officers should continue to be available to the States, though some members believed in a consultative capacity only. However the majority view, which I strongly supported, was that the Law Officers should continue to be full members of the States.

The area where there was considerable debate and division within the Committee concerned the future of Jurats, Rectors and to a lesser extent Douzaine Delegates. The Reverend Waterbury was totally against any move to exclude Rectors and Jurats from the States. He took the view that any reform would be artificial and, as he put it, be:

"The inevitable outcome of post war agitation."

He felt that if reform was to be considered, then it should not be until all our evacuees had returned to the island.

The Reverend Macartney also desired to keep a link with both the ecclesiastical authorities and the Royal Court by retaining representatives of the Parish Rectors and the Jurats. Initially I had supported that view, as I felt that the States had derived considerable benefit from their contributions. However, John Leale succeeded in persuading me that our objective was to make the States more representative and by the retention of Jurats and Rectors we could not achieve that aim.

The majority view was that Jurats and Rectors should no longer hold seats in the States by virtue of their office. A Jurat was chosen because of his ability to appraise and evaluate and the committee did not see that as a qualification for a seat in the States. A Rector, who might be a newcomer to Guernsey and have no knowledge of the island, should not have a seat in the States simply because he had been appointed by the ecclesiastical authorities to a 'living' in the island.

The position of Douzaine Delegates was a matter that was difficult as far as I was concerned. Up to that time they had been members of the States on a meeting-to-meeting basis and as a result had not played a full part in the proceedings of the House. Whenever I sat in the public gallery, I rarely heard them speak. In fact they were renowned for their silence. Some members felt that whilst they were Delegates, with a duty to speak and vote as instructed, they could not be full participating members of the States. Others felt their continued presence, with the exclusion of the Rectors and Jurats, would help in the representation of the island's agriculture and horticulture industries.

Some believed that the Parishes would be better served if their place in the States was taken by directly-elected members who would contribute to the debates. The States should not carry more silent members than need be. Personally, I very much wanted to ensure that the Douzaines continued to have a direct voice in the States. I wanted to support the existing system, provided a way could be found of better involving the Delegates in the work of the House. My inexperience prevented me from making any practical suggestion so, reluctantly, I went along with the majority in proposing that they be excluded from the House along with the Rectors and the Jurats.

The Reverend Macartney believed that we should never have an election in which the whole of the States was changed at the same time and in that he had my full support. I felt strongly that there should be continuity of the States and, in consequence, I supported his suggestion that a new office be created to provide that continuity.

He proposed that the office of Senator should be created, that they should be chosen by the States of Election and serve for a longer period than Peoples Deputies. The Senators would represent within our single house Parliament what might otherwise be a second chamber. They would provide the stability and continuity, that he and I were seeking.

We were all aware that there are occasions when waves of feeling sweep over the people and hasty judgements can be taken, which on mature reflection are regretted. It was felt that the inclusion of a bench of Senators would to some extent mitigate that danger. We believed that the calibre of men appointed to the Senatorial bench would not be easily swayed by any foolish outcry.

We were also concerned that the States should not be overloaded with inexperienced members. The presence of persons of tried ability and experience, sitting for a longer term than other elected members, would exercise a stabilising influence. It was also felt that many of the people who would be well suited to hold the position of Senator would be unwilling to submit themselves to the hustings.

The office of Senator would, the Committee believed, be regarded as a high honour and would also allow for the possible retention of Jurats and Rectors whose services might otherwise be lost to the community.

Under the Presidency of John Leale, the Committee made rapid progress in preparing our recommendations for consideration by the States. We had only been appointed in the middle of August and our report was published in the Billet d'Etat on the 29th September 1945. That says a great deal for the leadership and drive of John Leale.

Our proposals recommended that the States be composed of The Bailiff, the two Law Officers, twenty-one Senators, who should serve for nine years and forty Peoples Deputies, who should serve for three years.

The Bailiff and the Law Officers should be in the States by virtue of their Office. The Senators would be elected by the States of Election, seven being chosen every three years, to provide continuity. The Deputies would be representatives of the people.

I felt that we had achieved the objective that we had set ourselves at our first meeting, to create both a representative States and the best form of government for the island.

We made a number of other proposals, including the dropping of the French language in matters of legislation and procedures, although we accepted that it be retained for traditional and ceremonial purposes. The possibility of evening meetings of the States was suggested in order to encourage younger members of the community.

In formulating our recommendations we had the benefit of the opinions of the unsuccessful non-States candidates who had been proposed for the Constitutional Reform Committee. I think that it was unique that they were asked for their views on the reform of the Constitution.

Our report was signed by all members of the Constitutional Reform Committee with the exception of the Reverend Waterbury, who submitted a letter of dissent. He argued that the existing Constitution had worked well and believed that both the Jurats and the Rectors should continue as members of the States. The Rectors, he believed, were valuable as they were politically independent representatives of their Parishes.

The Reverend Macartney signed the report, but added an addendum to the effect that he wished to see four of the Senators seats reserved for Jurats and three for Rectors.

The States Advisory Council considered our report before it went to the States and declared that, whilst they approved of the general approach, they believed that the changes proposed to be of too violent a nature. They were of the opinion that there should be some form of representation of the Douzaines in the States. They suggested that one Douzenier from each Parish should be chosen to serve for one year and be eligible for re-election. It would be their duty as a representative of their Parish, to express the view of the Douzaine, but they should be entirely free to vote as they wished.

When our Report was debated by the States on 17th October 1945, I went and listened in the public gallery. On this occasion there were many more members of the public present than there had been when the Requete was first considered.

The Reverend Macartney made the outstanding speech of the debate when he made a strong plea for spiritual representation in the States. He pleaded for four of the seats on the Senators bench to be reserved for Jurats representing the Royal Court and three for the Rectors representing the ecclesiastical authority of the Crown.

When the member of our Committee who had refused to sign the report, the Reverend Waterbury, spoke in the debate, he suggested that the proposals had been inspired by socialists from the other side of the Channel. He quoted from a pre war-issue of the National Geographical magazine, that described Guernsey as 'a contented island'. He was against change for change's sake.

Our proposals for the removal of the Rectors and Jurats, as well as the creation of the office of Senator and the increased number of Deputies, were easily passed. The suggestion by the Advisory Council that Douzaine Representatives continue to sit in the House was accepted. The States, however, decided to delay a final decision on the Constitutional Reform until after the General Election, which was to take place on December 27th 1945. This was to be the first General Election since before the occupation.

I was sure there was going to be a considerable change, with a number of sitting Deputies losing their seats to left-wingers. This, I think, was the general view of many States members. Britain had held a General Election earlier in the year and returned a Labour Government. Virtually all our evacuees were back in the island and I expected them, with their mainland experience, to influence the result.

The 'lurch to the left' did not happen, in fact all sitting Deputies who stood for re-election were returned. The Progressive Democratic Association and other left-wing candidates all failed to be elected. The general election of the Deputies, in many people's opinion, really only confirmed the status quo and showed that the strength of feeling for reform had been greatly over-estimated.

The result of the election encouraged a number of States members who were against major change to put forward their own plan for more limited reform. The Reverend Waterbury, Jurat de Putron and Douzaine Delegate J.E.L. Martel, presented what they called an alternative, but in fact was the reversal of what the Constitutional Reform Committee had put forward.

They proposed the retention of the Jurats and four of the Rectors, together with fourteen Douzaine representatives. The number of Deputies under their plan would be increased to thirty two.

We put forward two further reports, the first proposing the inclusion in the States of ten Douzaine Representatives, along the lines suggested by the Advisory Council and the reduction in the numbers of Senators to fifteen and Deputies to thirty two. Our other report dealt with the possible payment of members for the loss of wages, so that it would be easier for working men to become members of the States. We also proposed that in future the States should meet in the former Church of St Pauls, as we felt that the layout of the Royal Court was unsuitable for States meetings.

In January 1946, the States of Deliberation, after three days of what I can only call confused debate, decided that the Reformed House should consist of:-

The Bailiff, with only a casting vote.
The Two Law Officers with the right to speak, but no vote.
10 Douzaine Representatives with a duty to represent, but freedom to vote as they thought fit.
15 Senators, serving for a period of six years.
39 Deputies, elected for a period of three years.

Rectors and Jurats were be excluded from the Reformed States.

These proposals were considered by a Privy Council Commission that came to the island in September 1946. The Right Hon. Chuter Ede, the Labour Home Secretary, was Chairman and the members were Viscount Samuel, Lord Ammon, the Right Hon. R.A. Butler MP. and Sir John Beaumont K.C..

'Rab' Butler, as he was universally known, was a senior Conservative Member of Parliament and a former Minister of Education. He was responsible for the 1944 Education Act, which did so much to change the whole concept of education in Britain.

The Constitutional Reform Committee's proposals, as amended by the States, were put to the Commission by Sir John Leale, as he now was. He was cross examined by the members of the Commission and very skilfully explained ours and the States thinking in arriving at our conclusions.

The Commission was prepared to hear from any witness, whether they were a States Member or a private individual. They arranged to hold one of their meetings in the evening so that workers could attend and put their views forward. It was called 'a workers session' and the Royal Court was packed, with additional seats being provided in the gangways.

Inevitably some of the left-wing activists presented their case. Mr Siddle, the Chairman of the Guernsey Communist Party, gave evidence and, in the course of examination by the Commission, revealed that the Party's membership in the island was twenty nine! Miss E. Blatchford was a witness on behalf of the Guernsey Progressive and Democratic Association, which had done so badly at the General Election. Her evidence won prolonged applause from the public gallery and gained a commendation from the Home Secretary, Mr J. Chuter Ede.

A substantial number of witnesses disagreed with the proposal that the Senators should be elected by an Electoral College and favoured election by universal franchise. Many people were greatly concerned with the need to ensure the retention of experienced persons in the service of the community. Without those people our good government would not be able to function effectively.

Mabs came with me one day and listened to the proceedings. She was intrigued when a lady who lived just down the Jerbourg Road from us, a Mrs Thoume, gave evidence. She really let fly with her views, which were all about the lack of facilities in the island. Rab Butler recognised her contribution for what it was, a good moan and countered by asking her: "Don't you have a Women's Institute in Guernsey ?"

A suggestion by one witness that the Bailiff should be excluded from the States, found little support. Another put forward the view that the Civic head of affairs should not necessarily be a person with legal qualifications. The States, it was suggested, should elect from amongst it's number, a person who would represent the States and have executive powers. The support for that view was, however, very limited.

I attended every session of the Privy Council Commission and at one time contemplated giving evidence. Bill Arnold, who had been appointed as H.M. Comptroller, our Solicitor General, gave evidence. Chuter Ede cross examined him and took Bill apart. Any ideas that I had of giving evidence quickly evaporated, I was not up to that kind of cross examination, the witness box was no place for me!

I did, however, get to know the members of the Commission and talked to a number of them informally. I was walking down the road with 'Rab' Butler, discussing things generally, when he said;

"I am a conservative with a small 'c'."

That comment summed up and explained to me his general approach to politics and made me better understand why, many years later, he twice lost the opportunity to become leader of the Conservative Party and Prime Minister.

The Commission's report was published in March 1947. In general, it concluded that the proposals for the reform of the States and the Royal Court were acceptable, although it did propose some amendments.

The report of the Committee of the Privy Council was considered by the Constitutional Reform Committee. We felt that we could not agree with their recommendation that the size of the States be increased to 68 members. That, in our view, was going to be too large a House. We therefore proposed that there should only be twelve Senators and this was accepted by the States. There was, however, still controversy over the title of the Office of Senator.

Whilst some members liked the term, as they said it had dignity and a sense of history, others just hated the word, which they felt was pure American. Members floundered about for a better title. At one meeting the title 'Jurat' was proposed but rejected. The matter was settled when the Bailiff asked John Le Patourel, the historian, for his views and suggestions. He came up with the title, Conseiller, which was gratefully accepted

The States of Deliberation finally accepted the Project de Loi on the 16th of January 1948, and Royal approval was received in the following August.

Our new States would consist of:-

The Bailiff, with only a casting vote.
The Two Law Officers with the right to speak, but no vote.
10 Douzaine Representatives elected by their Douzaine for a period of one year, with a duty to represent, but freedom to vote as they thought fit.
12 Conseillers, serving for a period of six years, half being elected every three years.
33 Deputies, elected for a period of three years.

The States had established the principal that the House should be composed of directly elected and non directly elected members in the proportion of three to two. That achieved the objective, we as the Constitutional Reform Committee had set ourselves when we commenced our task, to make the States more truly representative of the people of the island. The creation of the Conseillers bench provided continuity and the reformed States was, in my view, the best possible instrument for the future government of Guernsey.

On the 12th November 1948, the election took place of the first twelve Conseillers to sit in the States of Deliberation. Eight of their number previously sat in the House as Jurats. At the end of the year thirty three Deputies were elected and on January 1st 1949 the new States, without Rectors or Jurats, came into office.

The new Constitution of the States, in which I had the privilege of playing a small part, provided Guernsey with a stable and representative government that has served the island well during the second half of the twentieth century. Our system of government has been respected and envied throughout the world. I am proud to have been involved in its conception, and, in later years, as a Member of the reformed States of Deliberation.

Chapter 27

DAMN THE GERMANS

Before the war, swimming, water polo and motorcycling had been my main sporting interests. I had been an active member of the Guernsey Swimming Club, the Water Polo Association and the Motorcycle and Light Car Club. As soon as we were liberated I was impatient to restart these activities.

I was now thirty five, soon to be thirty six and I realised that it would not be long, in sporting terms, before I would be in the veteran class. There would be a lot of youngsters returning to the island after being evacuated and from service in the forces, who would be keen to challenge pre-war sporting champions, including myself. However, I was in no way ready to stand down, the youngsters would have to challenge me and beat me. I was certainly not going to make it easy for them.

When I first started motorcycle racing there were a number of 'old stagers' around and they went on for years, defending their reputations. I well remember in 1927 racing against old Tom Le Cheminant, when he was over sixty. 'Pop' as we called him, rode a long stroke Sunbeam, with sit up and beg handlebars. In those days the races were long distance handicap events, sometimes over as many as eighty laps. 'Pop' often received a six or eight lap start and would just go around and around, with all the other competitors passing him every five or six laps or so. He was a grand old character. At one time it was my ambition to race until I was sixty and beat his record.

In the middle of June 1945, barely a month after our liberation, a meeting was held in the large room above the St Peter Port Constables Office, to re-form the Guernsey Water Polo Association. It was a well attended meeting with a great deal of enthusiasm about the future. Ted Williams was elected President and I was appointed Honorary Secretary. Sergeant 'Nobby' Hamon, who returned with the British Liberating Force and had been a member of the Association before the war, volunteered to raise a Forces' team to play us.

On July 6th, at 6.45 pm after work, the first Water Polo match since the occupation was held in the old Harbour. There was a large crowd to watch the match between Guernsey and a British Forces team. Who won really did not matter, what was important, was that the sport was getting going again in the island. The Guernsey team consisted of Frank Le Page, Reg Marsh, Roger Bichard, A.C. Tanner, Bill Green, Basil Rabey, and Frank Hubert.

Later that month we again took on a much strengthened Forces Team and beat them by two goals to nil. I was back in form as I scored both goals. I remember that we were fortunate, as the Forces side also scored two goals, but both were disallowed for being offside.

Towards the end of August that year the Water Polo Association staged the first post war Swimming Carnival. Over two thousand people flocked to the mixed bathing pool at Valette to enjoy the afternoon's competitions and fun. Ralph Palmer and Gerald Sparkes put on an excellent display of double diving and generally fooled about, as only they could, much to the crowd's delight. I came

A large crowd watch Water Polo in the Careening Hard.

second to Ernie Mahy in the men's five lengths event. There were a lot of prizes to be won and what did I win - a cycle repair outfit, which I had donated !

It was not long before water polo was regularly being played in the Careening Hard. There was a water polo league with five teams, I was a member of the Old Amherstian's. We were a pretty good team and frequently won the the plaque which was awarded to the winning team in the league.

In those days we always had a good crowd to watch any of our matches, even our friendly matches. On one August evening, when the weather was at it worst with rain and almost gale force winds, we still had a crowd of hardy supporters. The goals and the netting had been placed in position some hours previously, but an amateurish yachtsman had cast them aside so that he could move his boat into the outer harbour. When the match was due to start Frank Hubert and I were still desperately trying to re-position the goals, which were being blown all over the dock by the strong wind. By the time we had re-located them, we were in no condition to play polo, but we did.

All our matches were fully reported by the press. One write up stated:-

> 'The game seemed lost, when Green chased a long pass. He robbed Oliver, then swam to the left of the pitch and with a fine back shot put the teams on level terms just before the final whistle sounded, a typical Green move!'

The Guernsey Swimming Club was not re-formed until February 1946, when a General Meeting was held under the Chairmanship of our pre-war President, Mr F.E. Fulford, my old headmaster at the Intermediate School. I was elected President with Ralph Palmer as my Vice President and Mrs W.V. Frampton as Honorary Secretary. My election was greeted by loud and long applause, which gave me great confidence for the future. I said in my presidential address, that I wanted to recreate the club so that it would again attract the younger swimmers, as they were, in my view, the future. I pledged to do my best in my new office and asked for member's support to ensure the success of the Club.

The mixed swimming pool at Valette was in very poor condition, as a direct result of the rough treatment it received during the occupation. A great deal of repair work, including the removal of a gun emplacement that had been erected above the pool was necessary before it could be brought back into full use. The Horse Shoe bathing place was, however, in a reasonable condition, but the changing accommodation had been completely destroyed. I was very keen for the States to give priority to the repairs that were necessary and made personnel representations to Cecil Stonelake, who was the President of the States Bathing Pools Committee.

Despite all the difficulties, we restarted club nights early in the summer. On the first one held for six years over one hundred swimmers turned up and our Secretary, Mrs Frampton, was kept busy issuing membership cards to the throng of old and new members. I was very happy to see Monty Manning again giving expert advice, in his usual masterly fashion, to youngsters learning the art of diving. 6.30 pm on a Tuesday night once again became a 'must' for all members of the Swimming Club. I was pleased that Baron Pontin and Hubert Nicolle, two of the island's best swimmers, were turning out on Club nights. The Club was most certainly getting back on its feet.

The Swimming Club's first post-war Gala was held on Thursday 29 August 1946, under my presidency. We drew a very large crowd of spectators and, although there were no records broken, a very high standard of swimming and diving was achieved. I invited Jurat Sir Abraham Laine to watch the Gala and present the prizes. Whilst I was introducing him to the large crowd, I took the opportunity of paying tribute to his work for the island during the occupation. He was Vice President of the Controlling Committee.

"I do not think, Sir," I said, "you have been publicly thanked before and I would like to take the opportunity of doing so now." Sir Abraham received a standing ovation.

After the success of that first Gala we quickly organised a series of floodlit Galas at La Valette. I managed to 'locate' a German Mercedes generator, that was

A large crowd at La Vallette Pool July 1939 watching the Guernsey Swimming Club -v- Royal Naval College, Dartmouth Hubert Nicolle in lead, far left.

of a large enough capacity to floodlight the whole of the pool and the surrounding area. I came across this wonderful piece of equipment at the German Underground Hospital in St Andrews. The generator was on wheels, so we would tow it down to the pool for each gala and afterwards tow it back again.

There was very little entertainment just after the war, so we used to attract large crowds at our floodlit events and, in consequence, made the Swimming Club a great deal of money.

Everyone had great fun at the Gala's in those days. All the deck chairs were set out along the wall on the east side of the bathing pool, for spectators to sit and watch the Gala. The tides very much determined when we could hold Gala's. Ideally the tide would be just about coming towards the top of the wall as the Gala was nearing its conclusion. This was usually about the time the Mail boat arrived from Jersey. The swell from the mail boat would wash over the wall and we used to enjoy seeing everyone sitting in their chairs with their feet in the air. We would pray for the mail boat to come before the Gala finished, in fact once or twice we actually put on extra events, to make sure we did not miss that spectacle.

At the Swimming Gala's we used to get up to all sorts of antics, mainly because of Ralph Palmer's ability to play the fool. He was game for anything. One of the stunts we performed, on the five metre diving stage, was the enactment of a Pirate being captured. This was very reminiscent of the 'Bluebeard' stunt Gerald Sparkes and I performed at the first occupation Gala in 1940.

Ralph Palmer was the pirate. We made a great performance of capturing him and taking him up to the top of the diving stage. There we tied a rope around his neck and apparently tied the other end to the diving stage, then pushed him off into the pool. Actually it was two different ropes, but the audience did not realise this until Ralph had been pushed off the diving board.

At one of the evening Gala's, Eddie Luff was standing down on the pool side, obviously he had not seen our stunt before and was calling out:

"Bill, don't, don't do it, don't do it, stop it, stop it you will bloody kill him!"

Of course he couldn't see the other end of the rope. As we shoved Ralph off the diving platform, Eddie fainted and had to receive medical attention !

We were performing this stunt on one occasion and Eric Martin was assisting me on the top of the stage. Ralph was yelling to him and Eric, who was very deaf, was saying:

"Eh?, Eh?".

As I pushed Ralph off, I saw what he was shouting about, Eric was standing on the rope. I only just pushed him off the rope in the nick of time. We made Ralph do all sorts of foolhardy stunts. We would ignite the surface of the water by throwing bags full of petrol into the pool and setting it alight. The surface of the pool would be a sea of flame and Ralph would dive through the flames, a feat which always looked spectacular and earned him a lot of applause.

Another of our favourite stunts, the 'Sack Dive' was performed by Monty Manning. Ralph and I trussed Monty up in a sack, tied the top up with a double knot and pushed him off the high diving board. Monty would sink to the bottom of the pool, while the audience held its breath. After a few moments Monty would free himself and surface to the cheers of the crowd. The trick was when we tied the top of the sack, Monty would have pulled a considerable length of rope down inside the sack. As soon as he hit the water he would let go of the surplus rope and the top of the sack would open up and he would escape to the surface. It was a very impressive stunt which always had the audience on the edge of their seats even when they had seen it a number of times previously.

On other occasions we obtained a quantity of torches, the type which are used in torchlight processions, and we would bring the Gala to a spectacular conclusion

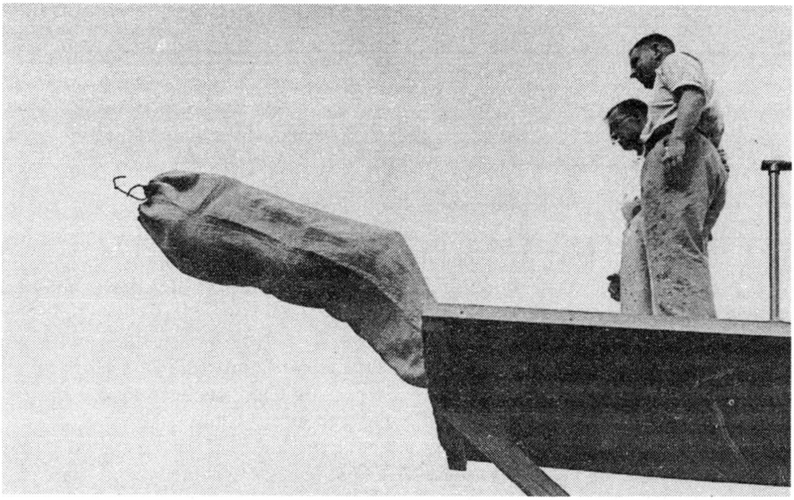

The Sack dive. Bill Green,(right), Ralph Palmer and Monty Manning in the sack.

by spelling out the initials of Guernsey Swimming Club. The floodlights would be turned off and the flames from these torches would light up the area whilst the National Anthem was played. As the last strains of God Save the King faded away, these torches were dowsed in the water.

During my two years as President, the Guernsey Swimming Club regained its pre-war position as the island's largest and most active sporting club. Pre-war there had been a membership of some four hundred. This number had fallen during the occupation to less than two hundred in 1942 and nil in 1945. When I retired as President in 1948 there were six hundred and fifty two members. This success had been brought about by the great team work of colleagues like Danny Williams, Eric Martin, Ralph Palmer and Con Lacey. Together we managed to rebuild the club and to this day it is still very successful.

Regrettably, my period of Presidency not only brought success, but was also marked by controversy.

We appointed Roy Langlois as the swimming club coach, an honorary position. Later, however it was decided to advertise for a paid professional coach. Somehow the advertisement in the mainland swimming journals appeared before I had informed Roy of our intention to appoint a professional coach. This led to him complaining to a Star Reporter, and inevitably an article critical of the actions of the Swimming club appeared.

As President I wrote a letter explaining our position, pointing out that pre-war we had both a Honorary Club coach and a professional, in Pop Osborne and Mrs Hughes. I unwisely criticized the Star and its reporter, and inevitably they responded with all guns blazing. As a result I learnt the lesson of doing one's homework thoroughly before attempting to criticize the press.

When I retired as President of the Club, Jimmy Ross succeeded me. Jimmy was a great character, who returned to the island as a Colonel with a fine war record. Later he became headmaster of the Grammar School and on one occasion asked me to go and present the Prizes at the school Prizegiving. In his introduction, he gave me a big build up as being one of the finest sportsmen Guernsey had ever produced.

Twelve months later, at the Annual General Meeting of the Club, Jimmy proposed that I should be made Honorary President, a new position in recognition of the work that I had done for the Club over many years.

In making his proposition he said:

"It is generally felt that Bill Green has carried the club through the most difficult time of it's existence and, although he only served for two years, it was the climax of the great role he has performed as a Swimming Club member. Bill Green knew exactly when to throw the wet blanket on something that was not too hot and when to set the spark to something that was too cold. It was only this season that the club had fully reaped the benefit of Bill's hard work."

I remember being very proud of Jimmy's remarks, whilst also been somewhat embarrassed.

From the time when I learnt to swim as a very young boy, with the encouragement I received from the Bassett-Lowke family and Mrs Hughes, my interest in swimming and the Guernsey Swimming Club has been total. I must be one of the oldest and the longest serving members of the Club.

Whilst I have enjoyed swimming, and still do, I was never very good from a competitive point of view. My build, or to put it more succinctly, my shape was never conducive to speed. I enjoyed competing, but wasn't very fast. The Club selected me for long distance races, such as ten lengths, against Jersey, because I was fit and could last the distance. George Symons who was ten years older than me and also swam for the Club, always beat me in a one length race, but he could never defeat me over five or ten lengths.

I always tried to get fit for the swimming season, but this usually meant little more than giving up smoking. I used to smoke in winter, starting around October after the swimming season ended and smoked until Lent. Then I would give up, not for God but for me. I carried out that routine for many years, although I never smoked during the occupation. Fortunately the cigarette never became my master, as it did with many of my friends and colleagues. I would enjoy a smoke but never found it difficult to give up. In fact when it was first established that there was a link between smoking and cancer, I gave up and have never smoked since.

From time to time over the years I attempted to smoke a pipe, but never mastered the art. Dad loved his pipe and when I was younger I tried to emulate him by carrying a pipe around in my top pocket. Whenever I tried to smoke a pipe I dribbled so much that I put it out.

Whilst I always tried to keep as fit as possible, by not smoking during the swimming season, I also did some road running and exercises for flexibility. Swimming was a great way of keeping fit, but age was now beginning to catch up with me. I was approaching forty and as far as Water Polo was concerned, about to join the ranks of the veterans. Even the Press started to refer to me as a veteran. It was only then I realised that the occupation of the island by the Germans had deprived me of five of the best years of my sporting life. I was thirty when they arrived and approaching thirty six when they departed. Those were just the years when I would have been at my peak as a water polo player. Now, as the Star put it in July 1947, 'Bill Green has slowed down a lot and his back flips are almost a strain'.

Damn the Germans!

The lure of the long distance swims between Sark and Guernsey, and Guernsey and Jersey, attracted swimmers not only from Guernsey and Jersey, but also from the mainland. In 1927 Jack Heyward was one the first persons to swim the gruelling nine miles from Sark to Guernsey and the only swimmer to have swum both ways. Jack was a very slow swimmer, but by jove he could stay in the water a long time - just what was required for long distance swims. He lived along The Banques, on the Delancey Lane corner and often when the tide was suitable he would swim from the Halfway to Salerie Corner. He looked upon it as a training swim and a convenient way of getting to his office at White Rock.

After completing the Sark to Guernsey swim, Jack was keen to have a crack at the Guernsey to Jersey swim. In 1937 he organised an attempt and I agreed to accompany him, at least part of the way. In order to get the most favourable tide conditions, we set off from St Martin's point very early in the morning while it was still dark. Jack disliked swimming in the dark so a number of us accompanied him when he entered the water. After about five or six hours of swimming he was six miles south of Sark, when the mail boat passed very close to us. The wake made Jack sea sick and he had to be taken from the water. I clearly recall the difficulty we had in getting him into the boat. He was sixteen stone, wore no bathing costume and was smothered in grease. Eventually the only way we managed to get him into the boat was by a number of us jumping into the water and pushing him up over the side. Jack just lay on the bottom of the boat, crying at having been beaten by seasickness.

On another occasion Colin Duquemin and I attempted to swim from Guernsey to Sark. We swam as far as Brecqou and failed to get any further. Our friends and supporters in the accompanying boats tried in vain to persuade us to complete the swim. The tide had turned against us and we knew we were beaten.

After the war Jack Heyward offered to present a cup to the next person to make the swim from Sark to Guernsey successfully. This was a challenge that some of our Swimming Club members could not resist. In the middle of August 1948, Harry Bisson, a schoolmaster, and Frank Hubert set off in an attempt to secure the Cup. The weather conditions were far from ideal. They were to have been joined by Terry Sowden, one of Jersey's best swimmers, but he failed to turn up at the rendezvous, which was the most northerly tip of Sark. Waiting for the Jersey swimmer delayed Harry and Frank's entry into the water and lost them valuable time against the tide.

Both the swimmers were well greased against the cold and wore goggles. Kenny Bell was their pilot. Jimmy Ross, Colin Duquemin and I acted as official observers. Jack Heyward was also in the boat.

Harry set off swimming at a steady pace of 28 strokes to the minute and Frank 32 to the minute, later both slowed down to 22 strokes a minute. They were swimming in the face of a strong tide and in the initial 45 minutes little or no progress was made. Jack Heyward, who at sixty-two was still a powerful swimmer, joined the two in the water to give them encouragement, but could not keep up with them.

Colin joined Frank in the water, who by now was trailing Harry. Frank was being badly buffeted by the sea and leaking goggles added to his problems. After just under two hours Frank's shoulder muscles began tightening and he decided to give up the attempt. I joined Harry in the water just as he caught the strong tide which propelled us past Herm's Shell Beach and Belvoir Bay.

After I had been in the water with him for about an hour and a half, we were nearing Jethou and only three miles from Guernsey. Harry was given some brandy to warm him up, but I could see that he was very nearly exhausted. My place in the water was taken by Jimmy Ross, who after a few minutes suggested to Harry that the time had come to accept that he could not complete the swim. After touching the rocks of Jethou, he was helped into the Pilot boat. Harry had swum himself to a standstill, but by sheer will power had succeeded in getting as far as Jethou. Looking back after all these years, I think that Harry would have completed the swim if he had not been delayed at the start waiting for the Jersey swimmer.

A few days later Terry Sowden telephoned me to say that he wanted to come to Guernsey and attempt the Sark to Guernsey swim. I invited him to come and stay with us, and offered to help organise his swim. That was on the Thursday evening - he only wanted to attempt the swim on the following Sunday morning !

I hurriedly contacted Kenny Bell, who agreed to act as his pilot. Ralph Palmer and Eric Martin were talked into being the Official Observers. Jack Heyward, when told of the attempt, naturally insisted on being in the pilot boat. There were so many who wanted to accompany Terry on his swim that we organised two boats. Kenny was in the pilot boat, 'Newton's Faith' and Gerald Sparkes in his own boat 'Fisher Lass'. Unlike the previous week when Harry and Frank had made the attempt, the weather was perfect, so Mabs and Frank Hubert's wife wanted to come as well. Colin Duquemin, Roger Bichard, Colin Gurney, Peter Bonnefin, Brian Croucher and of course Harry and Frank all joined the party in the boats.

Terry was only nineteen, but was already one of the stars of the Jersey swimming club. He travelled over on the Saturday evening Mailboat and stayed the night with us at Lyndel.

It was perfect weather when Terry entered the water at Les Autelets rocks on the western coast of Sark at 2.50 pm. The Jersey swimmer had huge hands, with which he literally picked up a chunk of the ocean with each arm movement and deposited it behind him as he went along. I accompanied him, in the water at the start. He set off at a fast pace of 32 strokes to the minute, so fast that I could not keep up with him. Other Guernsey Club swimmers took over, but he exhausted us all with his astounding speed.

I was frankly astonished at the pace Terry set and thought he would burn himself out in no time, But as we watched his confident swimming, I began to think again - it was an amazing swim.

Arriving at the White Rock in 4 hours 10 minutes to the cheers of the large crowd, Terry Sowden said he felt 'fighting fit' and, to prove it, he started jumping up and down on the spot !

Terry was the first person to have completed the swim from Sark since Jack Heyward accomplished it in 1927. Jack was amongst the first to congratulate Terry and present him with the magnificent Trophy.

After completing the swim Terry came back to Lyndel and stayed the night, before setting off on holiday early the next day. Mabs had expected that everyone who accompanied Terry would be cold and hungry afterwards and had prepared a great urn of broth. When we all arrived home the telephone rang. It was Mabs sister with the sad news that her father had died. Without telling anyone the bad news, I quietly encouraged everyone to leave. Mabs was left with the whole urn of broth as no one had touched a drop.

I told Mabs that her Dad was very ill and that we had better go over on the mailboat the next morning. On the train going up to Carlisle, I broke the news to Mabs that her father was dead.

Chapter 28

SOUND ADVICE

As peacetime conditions returned to Guernsey, my business prospered and expanded. Motorcycles quickly become a major part of my turnover and in the Smith Street shop I didn't have enough room to cope with the expansion. For a time I continued to have the use of Dr Bostock's garage and paid him a rent. When he eventually returned to the island I moved out.

If I was to take full advantage of the fast expanding motorcycle market, I required either new or additional premises. So I started looking round for a suitable site, or property. There was a vacant site on the South Esplanade, opposite the slaughter house and the Castle Emplacement. The site was owned by a lady in Jersey who I understood was prepared to sell. I looked very carefully at the site and decided that in many ways it would be an ideal position for a motorcycle business. The one drawback was that it did not have a rear entrance. I felt that if the site could be purchased for around £1,000, then I could afford to spent another £2,000 erecting a suitable building. I was confident that the bank would be prepared to back me to that extent. Trade was booming and I was satisfied that the business was capable of servicing a loan of that size.

Mabs and I went over to Jersey to discuss the matter with the owner, but she shocked us by asking £2,500 for the site. Mabs felt strongly that £2,500 together with the building costs, was too much of a commitment to undertake at that time. Despite returning to Jersey for further negotiations, it became clear that the owner was not going to budge on the price. While I felt it was a good site, I had to agree that it was more than the business could finance.

Dreamy Stranger and his father owned a former stonemasons yard and shed in George Street, that had been used by Lucas as a battery depot before they moved to other premises. I knew it in my schooldays as Le Tissier's tombstone yard. In the summer of 1947, I heard that it was empty and on the market, so I went to see Mr Stranger senior, who agreed to sell it to me for £700.

As soon as the purchase was completed, I also bought, very cheaply, two adjacent houses. Both were in very poor condition so I pulled them down. One of the houses was built of lath and plaster and was easily demolished. The only items that were of any value were the tiles on the roof, so I decided to save them. I remember picking them off the roof, one at a time, and handing them to Mabs through a window. She then had to climb down the ladder and stack the tile, before returning for the next one. Mabs was game for anything ! Later I managed to sell the tiles, a rare type that was no longer available. The garden of that house was higher than the rest of the site, so I physically dug the soil out to make the entire yard the same level.

The second house was on the other side of the yard and required a crane, with a swinging ball and chain, to effect the demolition. The tenant had been an elderly Scots lady who had readily moved out, so the house was empty, or so we thought. However, as soon as the crane went into action, we heard a scream and this old

George Street redevelopment. Mabs, Margaret, Richard Hardwick, Cecil Hardwick, Bill.

dear came rushing out of the outside toilet in no fit condition for a lady to be abroad. She had, we later learned, only moved next door and continued, unbeknown to me, to use the outside toilet. The toilet was a small lean to hut with a tin roof. When the first wall of the house was demolished some of the bricks fell onto the tin roof and terrified this dear old lady. I apologised to her profusely, fortunately she was unhurt, except for her injured dignity!

On the area of the former raised garden I built the showroom, which I later extended. In 1949 I personally dug the pits for two large underground petrol storage tanks. With the installation of a blender petrol pump, the site became a modern Motorcycle Service Station. I was now the owner of the biggest and most successful motorcycle business in the island. I reckoned that Dad would have been proud of my achievement.

Pre-war, one of the flats above the Smith Street shop had been let to Mr and Mrs Butt, but they moved to St Martin about six weeks before the occupation. While Ted Butt remained in the island, Edna evacuated with their children. After returning to the island, she came to see me, to enquire how I was getting on. I remember sitting talking to her in my little office and asking her what she was going to do with herself:

"Work I suppose!" she replied.

"Would you like to work for me ?"

"I will have to think it over and talk to Ted about it. I've been away five years and it would be mean for me to go straight to work and leave him on his own."

Her husband agreed, so Mrs Butt came to work for me at Smith Street, initially as a general 'Cleaner Upper', but ending up as Manageress.

Edna managed the Smith Street shop for me. She was a very efficient lady and most certainly did a 'mans job'. After she had been with me some time, I would go into the shop, put in an appearance, satisfy myself that everything was under control and let her run the show ! So much so that on occasions she would not have the faintest idea where I was, or when I would reappear. That annoyed her, as customers would come in and ask to see me and all she could say was that I was out and that she had no idea when I would be back. However she did a marvellous job covering for me.

I tried not to interfere with what she was doing, especially when she was window-dressing. If I did, she'd ask:

"Who's doing this job, you or me.?"

Edna did an extremely efficient job of running the Smith Street shop and it was to her credit that cycle sales reached a peak of over 350 in the early post war years.

Edna was an excellent sales lady, she always knew what the customer wanted, even if they had not yet made up their own mind. Herbert Winterflood, who was one of my cycle salesmen, often got mad with Mrs Butt because she would interrupt him in the middle of a sale and tell the customer they would be much happier with a different model. Herbert was convinced that whatever model he was attempting to sell to a customer, Mrs Butt would always suggest something different in order to get the credit for the sale. I suspect that he may well have been correct in his thinking.

Bert Coutanche returned to the island and my employ after the war, having served in the Royal Air Force. Pre-war he regularly competed on the Vazon sands but never up the Val des Terres. Although he obtained a new racing motorcycle soon after the war, he never raced it seriously. He was happy to be my mechanic in the pits. Bert, in my experience, was sometimes a difficult person to get on with. but I have always been very fond of him, awkward as he could be - a grand character and a wonderful man.

Bert was absolutely straight, totally reliable and very loyal. He rejoined the business as a mechanic. Later when I opened George Street, he went there, first as foreman and later as manager. For many years he was the mainstay of the George Street business.

After I opened George Street, Artie Selous remained at the Smith Street shop, dealing with all the cycle repairs. However, after a time, due to the expansion of the repair side of the motorcycle business and because Artie was a very good engineer, I transferred him to George Street. Sidney Smith took over the responsibility of cycle repairs at the Smith Street shop.

Artie was particularly good at accident repairs, he had a great ability to straighten out frames of motorcycles that had been involved in accidents. He made himself a set of jigs and used them to straighten out and realign the frames. Give Artie a smashed up, twisted motorcycle and he was in his element. He'd straighten it out and re-furbish it, as new. He was very proficient at brazing and did all our paint spraying. Artie with his ability as an artist, was naturally given the job of hand-painting the numbers on all the motorcycle registration plates. One day the Motor Taxation Department contacted me to let me know that there were three motorcycles on the roads with the same registration number.

Fortunately, we were able to sort that problem out without too much fuss. What caused Artie to duplicate, or rather triplicate the number, I do not know, but he did have a reputation for liking a little drop to drink. He never drank at work, so he assured me, but I had a suspicion that the tonic water he often brought to drink with his lunch was more than it seemed!

Artie's painting was not confined to his working hours. He was a good artist, with many of his pictures being highly regarded by art experts. One of his pictures, a painting in oils of the Dog and Lion rocks, was put on display in the window of the Singer Sewing shop and drew much favourable comment. Another hilarious example of his use of paint came when he was invited to a wedding and was expected to wear his best suit and shoes. His shoes were patent leather and the surface of one of them was in a very poor condition. Artie thought that if he sprayed them with shiny black lacquer it would make them more presentable.

After spraying them, he was drying the shoes over the gas ring when one of them caught fire. He threw it into the bath tub and quickly turned the water on it. Despite everything Artie still wore the shoes to the wedding and reception.

Artie, a man of considerable ability and invaluable to the business, joined me in 1936 from Jack West's cycle shop in St Sampson's and remained for over thirty years before retiring in 1968. For many years his great passion was a Matchless motorcycle, which he religiously polished every day so that the chrome was always in immaculate condition, .

Later he developed a passion for his stereo, which had a Leak amplifier, reputed to be the best available at that time. Artie would turn the volume right up and blast and vibrate the neighbourhood. One of his favourite records was of the 1812 Overture, with the gun fire. Artie insisted that I went to his house in Victoria Road to listen to this record being played on his stereo. I think that most of the staff were also cajoled to visit his music room at the top of the house.

Whilst motorcycles were initially the growth business after the war, it was the advent of the scooter boom that really escalated my turnover. Soon after the war I was walking around the Motor Show at Olympia, when I ran into Claude Rye, an old business acquaintance. I told him that I was looking for a British scooter which I could sell.

Claude, who was a very large dealer on the mainland said:

"You'll not find a good British scooter, why don't you get the Lambretta?"

"My father wouldn't sell anything foreign in the shop when there was a British product available and nor will I."

"What agencies do you have?" enquired Claude.

"Royal Enfield, James, Excelsior and A.J.S., all British machines, through and through." I replied.

"Ah, you sell James and Excelsior."

"Yes."

"Both Villiers engines - Bill, you had better go along to their stand and take a close look at their engines."

Villiers used to boast that every part of their engines was made in their own factories. So I went to their stand and was disappointed to see German manufactured Dynastart units fitted on to the Villiers engines. I looked askance at these foreign parts - I just couldn't believe what I was seeing.

I approached one of the salesmen on the stand and enquired:

"Is the man who is responsible for fitting these German Dynastart parts to the engines at the Motor Show ? If so, would you ask him to come and explain your Company's change of policy to me."

He went to a telephone and soon a gentleman appeared and asked how he could help. I tore him off a strip for fitting these dynastart units on the engines.

"Well", he said "I'm sorry Mr Green, but we in Britain cannot manufacture that equipment at anything like the price we can buy it from Germany and we have to keep up with the times and remain competitive. That is what it is all about."

Clearly I could not give up the James or Excelsior agencies and there was no British company manufacturing a suitable scooter. I had tried the Swallow 'Gadabout', but that was far too heavy and quickly became a commercial flop. Later that day I had a meal with Claude Rye and talked the matter over with him. I followed his advice and took on the Lambretta scooter agency for Guernsey. It turned out to be very sound advice and we were extremely successful with the agency. We sold hundreds of Lambretta scooters, in fact they sold like hot cakes, quickly becoming our main agency. In many ways I was sad that it was a foreign product that was so successful, it watered down ones patriotism.

One of the reasons why they sold so well was that they were equally suitable for women, as men. A lady in a skirt could not ride a motorcycle, but a Lambretta scooter presented no problems. Well no problems for the ladies, but the ladies presented us with problems ! They soon realised that the two side panels could be resprayed any colour they wanted. So Artie was soon spending hours spraying panels to colours of the ladies particular choice. They wanted pink panels to match their skirts, red ones to match their handbags and one young lady had to have hers resprayed to match her lipstick. For a time we made a good living respraying Lambretta's to the ladies' requirements. On reflection that was the nearest I ever came to running a boutique.

In the post-war years there were really only two commercially successful scooters, the Lambretta and the Vespa, both Italian. Lambretta, in my experience, was the better of the two. There were several attempts by other manufacturers, to manufacture a scooter, but, with the possible exception of the German Adler, none were real competitors for the two Italian machines.

Lambretta's were manufactured in Milan by a private family concern named Innocenti. On a visit I made to the factory to see the scooters being built, Seignior Innocenti said to me:

"I am sorry, Mr Green, I have nothing to show you, my workforce are on strike. They want so much money these days to work, that I can't afford to make scooters."

A few months after I visited Milan, Seigneur Innocenti told his workers that he could not afford to continue to manufacture scooters unless they tempered their demands. The workforce retaliated by going in and smashing up the factory. Seignior Innocenti responded by announcing that he would not repair the damage or restore the factory and went off and manufactured Lambretta's in Spain.

In the post-war period, the Unions in the free world found that they were able to force through their demands by various means, particularly strike action. The demise of the Lambretta factory in Milan was a direct consequence of militant Trade Union action. Britain was suffering with the same problem and many industries were becoming totally un-competitive as a result. Japan was the real beneficiary of much of the dogmatic union action. Gradually, but inevitably, the British motorcycle manufacturing industry disappeared and was replaced by the Japanese.

The magazine 'The Motorcycle', at one time produced an annual 'British Supremacy' number. It contained a list of all the British motorcycle achievements during the previous year. There came a year when they couldn't produce that list, because British motorcycles achievements were no longer supreme.

On a visit to the Motor Show I closely inspected some Japanese machines and realised that their engineering was very advanced. Vic Mountford, of Royal Enfield, told me that they had stripped down a Japanese machine in their workshops and were extremely impressed with its clever design and advanced engineering. Vic said that they couldn't possibly build a similar motorcycle in Britain for anything like the Japanese price. It quickly dawned on me that if we were not careful the Japanese were going to take over our market.

A few years before the Japanese supremacy had finally taken hold of the British market, I was invited to be the guest of honour and speaker at the National Motorcycle and Cycle Trades dinner. I told the story of a young lad going fishing, with his Japanese rod and line. He thought that it might rain, so he took his Japanese made anorak and as he liked to be entertained, he took his Japanese radio. I continued in that vein and described how with all his Japanese equipment he travelled on his Japanese motorcycle.

I said, "You see Gentlemen, one of the most important things that happens to any young lad when he reaches the age of fifteen or sixteen, is that he becomes the proud owner of a motorcycle. Today his motorbike will be Japanese and, if we are not very careful, his pride for his Japanese bike will mean that from that moment in time his patriotism will be watered down."

They all laughed and thought I was talking through my hat, so much so that I thought I was going to be thrown out. At that time the British motorcycle industry was still pretty virile, but I could see what was going to happen, and regrettably it happened.

In 1951, I took on the agency for Cymota, reputed to be the world's best cycle motor. It consisted of a motor unit attached to the front of a bicycle, which drove the wheel. The manufacturer claimed that the Cymota was the cheapest form of transport in the world, 250 miles per gallon, 7 miles for a penny. It could be fitted to almost any make of cycle, and speeds up to 20 mph could be achieved. There was no clutch or gears and only one control, the accelerator, which fitted on to the handlebars. The Cymota was available in five colours and retailed at £18.18s.0d. Initially we sold quite a number of these machines, but very quickly it was found that the motor drive wore out the front tyres in next to no time. The Cymota turned out to be another seven day wonder.

Throughout the whole period that I was in business I always employed two or three boys. Some of these boys ended up staying with me for thirty years or more. Looking back, I'm amazed just how many staff I actually employed over the years. Never throughout the whole of my business career did I sack an employee, with just one exception. This particular boy had been sent to me by Vauvert School. It quickly became obvious that he was not going to make the grade as a mechanic, however much time I gave to him. So I took him on one side and said:

"Look lad, you are not suited for this job and you are not going to be happy in it, you had better go and find yourself another job."

Unbeknown to me, this lad was a union boy. Dave Shenton, the Trade Union Officer came to see me about sacking this lad. Dave started off on the wrong foot when he made a derogatory comment as he was coming up the stairs to my office.

I was standing at the top, and responded by saying

"Nobody tells me what to do in my own premises."

"I am going to tell you what to do." replied the Union man.

"Well you do that and you'll go down those stairs, faster than you came up."

He was in an unfortunate position, almost at the top of the stairs - Dave didn't press his luck.

I am thankful to say that I didn't get involved with Unions, that incident was my only business encounter with any Union official. Basically my attitude has always been anti-union. I have a belief that if there had never been any unions at all, England would have been a much better and a more prosperous country. I believe that in the immediate post war years the unions virtually ruined Britain. If there had been no unions, evolution would have taken care of the worker far better than unions have and without doing the immense damage to the British economy that occurred.

British industry would have been so busy working flat-out to supply the rest of the world that the workforce could have commanded its price. There would have been a shortage of staff and, as a consequence, far better working conditions would have been achieved. That has been the situation in Guernsey in recent years, whether employers have liked it or not, labour could, and has commanded high wages and better conditions. I am thankful that Trade Unions were never part of my working life.

Over the years, working people and workforces have been criticized by management, in my experience often unjustly. I have always believed that how employees react depends on how the boss or the management treats them. In business, I always looked upon my staff as my friends and treated them accordingly. We worked together as a team and I was the captain. If we had had a good day, then it was the result of team effort and I would try to reward them with a little extra in their pay packet. In those days it was welcomed and appreciated. I tried to pay them well, or at least I thought I did. On hours, we had a very flexible arrangement, if they wanted to go off for any purpose I would, whenever possible, say:

"That's all right, put the time in when it is convenient to you," which, in fairness, they always did.

In the fifties and sixties, I had a fairly large staff and it was not difficult to make arrangements for someone's work to be covered. There wasn't any jealousy, if somebody wanted a few hours off and it could be arranged, nobody complained. It was all part of the give and take that existed when you were working with friends

'Greens' of Smith Street recreated in the Occupation Museum. Note the original little bike.

and mates. I am happy and proud that many of my former employees now rank amongst my wide circle of friends.

However, I did not get on well with everyone - 'Officialdom' was often the exception. The little bike that Dad made for me when I was a very small boy had for many years hung outside the Smith Street shop. When the Germans arrived I received numerous 'requests' to sell it. I realised that it would only take one persistent and forceful German to insist that I sell the bike, so I removed it for the duration of the occupation.

When, after our liberation I proposed to put back my little bike on the hangers above the shop front, the States Natural Beauties Committee informed me that they would not allow it to be replaced. Argue as I might, they won the day and it was never reinstated. I kept it for many years and when Richard Heaume wanted to recreate my cycle shop as it was during the war, as a feature of his occupation Museum, I handed it over to him. It now hangs over my recreated shop, a credit to Dad's workmanship after over threequarters of a century.

When I opened my premises in George Street, I was looking for any new agency, any new product or vehicle which would help me expand my business. I heard that the Dot Cycle and Motor Manufacturing Company of Manchester, was producing a three wheeler truck suitable for carrying loads of up to 300lb. It was based on a type of truck used during the war by Government departments. Powered by a 122cc Dot Villiers two stroke engine, with three speed gears and it did over 85 miles to the gallon.

I was very impressed with all the reports that I heard of the vehicle and was sure that it would be ideal in the island, either as a milk float, ice cream wagon or for other delivery work. In practice, however, it was very under-powered and only suitable for use on the flat. When it came to a hill, its lack of power became only too obvious, particularly with a load aboard.

Not knowing its limitations I ordered one, and in due course it was delivered. The press came and took photographs of it and published a story, suggesting that it was the first of what might become a large fleet of these delivery trucks. The write-up claimed that it was easily handled by women drivers and that the steering was simple and effective. What the press did not report was that I had taken the vehicle out for a trial run and, while taking the bend in Brock Road by the school, had turned it over.

The handlebars were attached to the back of the truck and as a result, it was extremely easy to oversteer. Added to that, the motor drove the rear wheel, so the slightest oversteer and a touch on the throttle, turned the vehicle over. I came a real cropper with this truck in Brock Road and as a result lost all confidence in it. That was the only one that I imported into the island. I finally sold it to Steve Jones who ran a small shop and factory, near the Little Chapel, at Les Vauxbelets. He manufactured plaster of paris models of the Little Chapel for the tourist trade and used the Dot truck as a delivery vehicle.

I warned Steve about the difficulties of oversteering and despite that he willingly purchased it and drove it successfully for a long time. For many years after, whenever I ran into him I would ask:

"How's the Dot Truck ?" and Steve always reacted by bursting out laughing - I never really knew why.

By the early 1950's my motorcycle business, along with the businesses of my main competitors, Theo Millard and Herbie Tostevin, were sufficiently established and successful to claim that we had developed the motorcycle trade in Guernsey to a level which was both healthy and profitable to us all. Motorcycles were much cheaper than cars, supplies were readily available and there was a growing demand. The island roads were very suitable for the increasing number of motorcyclists. Of course, motorcycles were mainly favoured as a means of transport by the younger generation. Some older people still rode motorbikes but many, as and when they could afford it, transferred their allegiance to the motor car.

The motorcycle in the hands of the young tended to be a fairly noisy form of transport. Single cylinder machines, by and large, were the noisiest. Youngsters, and indeed some of us older motorcyclists, enjoyed the full blooded sound of a well tuned engine and indeed a little expert 'interference' with the silencer made them even noisier. As a result there was an island wide anti-motorcycle campaign, which did not help the cause of motorcycling, or indeed the business of the traders.

During the height of the controversy on motorcycles, Sir John Barbirolli, the well known orchestral conductor, came to the island on holiday and stayed at the Manor Hotel. The Guernsey Press interviewed the great man, and asked him such questions as what he thought of his hotel:

"It was very nice indeed."

Did he like the island ?

"Oh yes, it was a lovely place."

One or two other questions were asked and then they put the loaded question to Sir John, "What do you think of our motorcyclists ?"

He took his cue, "Well you know, they make a terrible noise, a really terrible noise."

The Press headline read, 'Sir John Barbirolli thinks that our motorcyclists make a terrible noise'. This criticism of my livelihood incensed me so, that I telephoned him one evening at the Manor Hotel. Much to my surprise, I was put through to him, just before he was going to sit down to dinner.

I said, "Sir John Barbirolli, my name is Green, which won't mean anything to you at all, but I have taken particular exception to your remarks about our motorcyclists."

"Well you know, Mr Green" he said, "they do make a terrible noise."

"You know Sir John, what you don't appreciate, is that when you are conducting one of your symphony concerts, to me it is one of the most God darn ruddy noises I have ever heard in all my life. But to me, the sound of a well tuned motorcycle engine is sweet music."

He laughed and said, "Come out and have a drink."

I didn't have the nerve to go !

As soon as my George Street premises were open for business, I transferred George Cave there. Later I asked Herbert Winterflood to move up there as well. Unfortunately he couldn't get on with George. At the time, Herbert had something the matter with his hands and needed to wear gloves to work on motorcycles. George took this to be that young Herbert didn't like getting his hands dirty, and in consequence ribbed him unmercifully. Artie Selous would also tease the life out of Herbert, saying to him:

"Why the hell do you work here?" and before Herbert could respond. "No you don't work here, you just come to supervise."

Herbert, at one time had thoughts of becoming a Minister of the Church. He preached locally and I believe was offered the opportunity of undertaking an ecclesiastical training course in Bristol, but for some reason did not follow that vocation. One evening I went to hear him at a church in St Andrews, he preached an excellent sermon. Herbert left us in 1957 when he was offered a job as a reporter with the Evening Press.

One of the stalwarts of the George Street business was Charles Pratt. He joined me soon after we opened there and remained with me until I sold the business in 1973. Charles was a first class mechanic, having been trained in the Navy during the war. He was a very quiet lad who would get on with his job without causing any problems. I found that I had an easy rapport with him, particularly with regards to repairing and tuning motorcycles. I had the good fortune, or ability, to be able to listen to a motorcycle engine and know precisely what was wrong and how to put it right. Charles would start the bikes up, I would listen and tell him what I thought was wrong:

"She's a bit over rich" or "She needs pulling back a bit on the timing" and he would put them right. I think that he was just as good at diagnosing faults as I was, but we enjoyed working together. We were a good team.

At the time that I had been keen to acquire the South Esplanade site, Mabs had said that I would do better by buying the shop and premises in Smith Street. Mabs thought that as we had been there for over forty years and were the sitting tenants, we should be able to buy it for a very reasonable price.

In 1948, the business was doing well, so I decided to approach our landlord, Miss Anderson, with a view to buying the whole of the Smith Street premises. Marjorie Anderson, who I always found to be a very kind and caring landlord, inherited the property from her uncle, Mr Ashplant who had given Dad our original lease.

"Well Mr Green", she said, "if you would like to make me an offer I will think about it."

I went to see my bank manager, Alec Hooley of the Midland Bank, and with his assistance worked out that with, the income from Rabey's Book shop and the flats, it would be possible for me, with the bank's support, to pay up to £10,000 for the Smith Street premises. On the manager's advice I made Miss Anderson an offer of £7,000, which I was convinced that she would never accept.

"O.K. Mr Green," she said, "that's all right with me."

So in 1948 I became the owner of the Smith Street premises for what, even at that time, was a very low price. There were two shops, five flats and a cottage at the rear. Some years later I had to spend over £20,000 on a rebuilding programme that was necessary due to the condition of the premises. In fairness, both Miss Anderson and I knew that a lot of money was needed to be spent on the property at the time I purchased it. However, the acquisition of the Smith Street premises was one of the best business investments I ever made.

I was very conscientious about training youngsters who bought their motorbikes from me. I trained a great many young people in the correct, safe and responsible way to ride a motorcycle. Often fathers would come and ask me to train their lads and I used to like to do it. I took the learners down to La Valette, the stretch of road between the Brewery and the Aquarium. That road was very quiet in those days, rarely was there a car parked in the area of the bathing pools. Paul Le Marquand, one of my mechanics, usually came down with me to assist with the training. Paul went up to the far end near the site of the Aquarium and I stayed by the Brewery and we would get the trainee to ride up and down between us.

On one occasion, I sent a young trainee with his brand new motorcycle on his way to Paul and settled down with a newspaper to await his return. When, after some considerable time there was no sign of our pupil, I started strolling towards Paul, only to to meet him walking up towards me, "Where's our trainee?" I asked.

"I haven't seen him" Paul replied.

"Well I sent him to you."

We could not see him anywhere on the road, so we looked over the sea wall. There he was, motorbike and all, down on the rocks. Apparently, he tried to turn around in the road, had gone down the steps at the Horseshoe Pool, over the side and finished up on the rocks. Fortunately he didn't injure himself and did little damage to his brand new 175cc Excelsior.

The number of youngsters that I trained to ride a motorcycle must run into many hundreds. After all these years I still run into some of these lads, now mature men, who remind me that I trained them. I like to look back upon all that time I spent as an investment, my contribution to road safety.

I was always very keen to promote 'Road Safety' particularly for new or prospective motorcycle owners. I published a small booklet of 'Hints for Happy Motorcycling'. In it I emphasised that motorcycles in themselves, were not dangerous, 'It is the misuse of a motorcycle, or for that matter a motor car, a tractor, a gun, or even a machine tool, that makes these things dangerous.'

Another aspect of riding a motorcycle, which I have always believed to be important is 'Road Manners'. I wrote;

> 'Road manners mean so much. Do you realise what a wonderful privilege you enjoy when you attain a licence to use the road. Value that licence, keep it clean, give no man the chance of taking it away from you. A clean licence will stand you in good stead all your life, it is a valuable thing to possess. Do not therefore ride in a manner that annoys others. Your machine can be ridden harshly, noisily, or quietly and smoothly. Remember that what to you, may be a joy, to others may be very aggravating indeed: and so, don't rev the engine late at night or very early in the morning in any unnecessary way, either stopped or travelling. Don't overtake another vehicle with a roar and a swerve, but modestly and reasonably. Don't ever be tempted to take a chance.'

On reflection, that advice holds good for today's motorcyclists, particularly with regard to road manners and excessive noise .

Over the years, my marriage had suffered as a result of my friendship with a number of young ladies. Little by little one girlfriend, in particular became part of my life. Mabs understandably, took exception to our continuing friendship.

Despite trying to maintain her composure in public, the situation regrettably, became very detrimental to Mabs' health, so much so that it led to her having a nervous collapse in early 1947. Mabs told Dr Rose the whole story of my misdeeds - he took me aside and spoke to me like a 'dutch uncle'. He told me that I had a very good girl as a wife and to pull my self together. It wasn't, he said, worth breaking up my marriage for a 'Chit of a Girl'.

Despite his advice I continued to see the young lady. I have always found it difficult to say "No" to ladies, even up to the present day !

Mabs, on Dr Rose's advice, went for an extended stay with her parents in Carlisle to help speed her recovery. Margaret went as well and attended school there for over a term. I regularly telephoned Mabs, pleading with her to come home. Eventually I went over and brought her and Margaret back to Guernsey.

Inevitability the situation came to a head and there was a showdown meeting between Mabs, the young lady and myself. As a result of the confrontation, I walked out, saying to the young lady;

"Cheerio, sadly that's the end of our friendship, obviously it can't go on."

I telephoned her the next day to say how sorry I was and that it was quite obvious the situation could not continue and had to end. She was in tears, so I said to her;

"If ever you have real need of me, call me, I will be there."

A fatal thing to have said, as it wasn't too long before she called, I responded and our friendship was rekindled.

When the young lady married, Mabs hoped and believed that the problem had been solved. For a time the situation between Mabs and me did improve.

Mabs and I received an invitation to attend the Lt.Governor, Sir Philip Neame's, Garden Party, at Government House. Mabs first question was:

"How are we going to get there ?"

"In the Riley!"

"We can't go in that." she exclaimed.

"Yes we can, it's my car and they invited me".

I'd acquired an old Riley from a friend of Len Rouget, who had kept it hidden throughout the occupation. It was a car that had certainly seen better days. It was an open-top model with a fold down canvas hood. It was powered by a six cylinder engine, but there were two pistons short, so I took the two con rods out and ran it on four cylinders. So, of course, it made the most extraordinary noise.

Mabs was very strongly against going to the Governor's Garden Party in the Riley.

"It's a tatty old thing, it's disgusting, I can't possibly go in that, I am ashamed of it".

Well we did.

We drove along Queen's Road and turned into Government House, where we were met by a 'flunkey' who motioned us on. Then another 'flunkey' beckons us further on and by and by we found ourselves driving out of Government House and into Mount Durand !

Mabs turned to me and said "You damn fool, leave it here, we'll walk in, you've embarrassed me enough."

Despite owning the Riley, I much preferred to use my Royal Enfield motorcycle. When I eventually replaced the two missing pistons and restored the engine to its original design, I sold it and bought a post-war Ford Popular. Mabs enjoyed driving the Ford, so I happily continued to ride my motorcycle.

After Margaret transferred from Blanchelande College to Ladies College, I regularly took her to school on the back of my motorcycle. She called it her daily 'trip of terror', because I went so fast. Getting her out of bed in the morning was always a problem, so inevitably we were late. By the time she was up I had usually been down to Town for a swim at the bathing pools, returned home and breakfasted. On the way to school we were always in a hurry and consequently sped down Ville au Roi at sixty miles per hour, passing everything in sight. Fortunately there was less traffic on the roads in those days. I remember that as we drove down King's Road, I had to slow down, as Margaret liked to wave to a Dalmatian dog that was always looking out of an upstairs window.

Towards the end of 1950 Frank Tuck, one of the policemen 'convicted' and imprisoned by the Germans in 1942, returned to Guernsey from Liverpool, where he had settled after the war. His visit was to enable him to examine documents, files and other material in support of the efforts that he and his fellow ex-policemen were making to obtain a review of the judgement and sentences passed by the German Military Court and the Royal Court in 1942.

The former policemen, with the exception of Bert Smith who died in Augsberg Prison as a result of the treatment he received from the Germans, pooled their life savings in an effort to obtain special leave to appeal against their convictions. They engaged a distinguished British lawyer, Mr E.C.Goldrein, of the firm Silverman and Livermore in an attempt to prove that, far from being thieves, they were saboteurs fighting the occupying Germans.

Frank, who was staying in the Pollet, dropped into my shop one day and spent over an hour telling me the gruesome details of their arrest and interrogation. He also explained to me the difficulties they had in defending themselves at their trials.

Like many of the other ex-policemen, Frank wanted to enlist in the Armed Forces when war broke out. After the island was demilitarized, the whole Force was assembled in the room above the Police Station and Ambrose Sherwill lectured them on their duty to remain in Guernsey. He said that the British did not consider the islands to be of any strategic value and he believed that would also be the German view.

Ambrose said that any policeman leaving would be deserting his post and there could be no guarantee of a job for them to come back to after the war. If the island was to be totally evacuated the Police Force would be the last to go, and the plan was, he said, for them to leave in the lifeboat. Ambrose's plea must have been successful, as virtually the whole of the Police Force remained in the island.

Frank recalled that as the occupation had gone on he and others became progressively more frustrated and incensed by the near collaboration of some people in authority, who willingly attended garden parties and other functions held for the Germans. Frank told me that he and other members of the Force listened to the broadcasts by Colonel Britton, directed towards occupied Europe, encouraging the Underground fighters to commit acts of sabotage against the Germans.

They knew that the French resistance workers were operating with great skill and ingenuity and doing their bit to win the war. The policemen also wanted to do their patriotic duty, by harassing and harrying the Germans. "We knew" said Frank "that any major act of sabotage was entirely impossible due to the smallness of the island and the presence of so many Germans. We regarded the taking of food as being an act of sabotage against our occupiers".

"After being caught, we dare not admit that we had intended to carry out sabotage. We knew that we would have been shot, the penalty for sabotage was death. When we went for trial we pleaded guilty to theft, denied all intention to commit sabotage, pleaded hunger and pretended to be sorry. We did all we could to make our penance seem real."

"We all hoped that the Committee set up by the Bailiff after the end of the occupation would give us the opportunity to have our cases reopened. We were disappointed that we were not allowed to give evidence or to be legally represented". "Now", Frank said "we want the British Government to review the case so we can all be completely vindicated".

Frank told me what he and his colleagues had been through when they were arrested. They were subjected to hour upon hour of questioning by a team of German inquisitors, who fired question after question in rapid succession, scarcely giving them time to answer.

"They not only asked particular questions, they also made allegations and kept repeating them, no doubt in the hope that in time we would agree and sign statements accordingly. After days of questioning, which brought the Germans little success, they resorted to beatings and brutality."

The Statements and 'Confessions' which the ex-police officers eventually made were wrung from them in the best traditions of Gestapo savagery. Frank recalled that every so often a German would tell him that another policeman had confessed and implicated him. Then they would try to get him to confess. "If I didn't then they would beat me, not just a few kicks, but a long sustained beating. After a few days of that treatment I scarcely cared what happened to me and was willing to sign anything."

"I was given a long sheet of paper and told to sign. It was all in German, none of which I understood. Anyone who refused was beaten again and again until he signed."

Frank, who was very emotional about the whole episode, concluded:

"When the evidence is assembled, I think that no one will doubt that those so called confessions were wrung out of us by sheer torture, which few people could have ever withstood. The general public do not know how we were tortured in order to make us confess."

The Liverpool Lawyer, Mr E.G.Goldrein, who the former Guernsey policemen engaged to prepare their case, came to the island and took dozens of statements from the men concerned and from many other independent witnesses. Before returning to Liverpool, he commented:

> "I am satisfied that the German and civilian trials, which led to the conviction of these men, were a mockery of justice and I am placing the whole of the facts before the Home Secretary."
>
> "I am satisfied beyond any reasonable doubt that the taking of food in these circumstances by Police Officers, who up till then had borne exemplary characters and have since, was regarded by them as an act of sabotage against the occupying power. The most important factor in the matter is that they were unable to plead sabotage in their own defence at the German trial because sabotage was punishable by death, and it was wholly for that reason that they made such a poor showing in cross examination in the German court."
>
> "The most terrible feature of the case is the way in which evidence against them was obtained by the Germans in the first instance. The brutality by the Germans against them was not disclosed at the trial, but it was quite clear that threats of every kind were used against them. There was duress and physical assault of all kinds, that included threats of instant death and a very violent assault which in fact incapacitated some of the men completely. It included such assaults as brutal kicking in the course of which one of them was permanently injured. It was indisputable that the statements were written in German and that the accused men had no means or opportunity of checking them. They were presented with statements made by their fellow police officers in order to extort statements from them."
>
> "The whole circumstances in which the so called evidence was obtained would be completely unacceptable to normal British justice. When the trial was held, a Swastika flag was hung in the background and even at the civilian trial there were many Germans present and the same limitations were therefore placed on any defence they might otherwise have had".

In due course, the eight ex-police officers, who appeared in the civilian case, were granted special leave by the Privy Council to appeal against their conviction before the Royal Court on June 1st 1942. The other eight men, who only appeared in the military case, could not be included in the appeal as the Privy Council had no jurisdiction in regard to the German Court and its findings.

Ex-sergeant Alf Howlett, Ex-constables Ken Bailey, Frank Tuck, Charlie Friend, Bill Quin, Fred Short, and Frank Whare were all given leave to appeal against their convictions of stealing civilian stores, and Ex- sergeant Jack Harper of receiving.

Ex-sergeant Fred Duquemin Ex-constables Bill Burton, Archie Tardif, Eugene Le Lievre, Tom Gaudion, Alf Le Gallez, Harold 'Snip' Piesing and Peter Bretel, were, however, unable to appeal against their conviction by the German Court. Despite the fact that the 'Confessions' were literally beaten out of them, they lost their good names, their positions as members of the Guernsey Constabulary and their pension rights. In my view, a thoroughly unsatisfactory situation and a total miscarriage of natural justice, that has never been corrected.

For no doubt good legal reasons, which I have never been able to understand, the appeal of the eight ex-police officers was not heard by the Judicial Committee of the Privy Council until October 1955.

The ex-police officers' case was put by Mr Geoffrey Bing QC, the former Labour Member of Parliament. He pointed out that in the first place they were arrested by the German authorities, questioned and then tried by them for offences against German property. Afterwards at the request of the Germans and on the basis of the information collected by them, the former policemen were tried in the Royal Court and sentenced to further terms of imprisonment.

The police officers, their barrister said, were engaged in patriotic and proper activities and it was wrong that they should be penalized by having a conviction recorded against them which was a result of them merely doing their duty by their Country in the very difficult circumstances of the German occupation. The eight ex-policemen claimed that their trial before the Royal Court was held under pressure from the German authorities, and that in the circumstances no fair trial took place, particularly as they could not put forward any real defence.

Mr Bing said that records of the German trial had largely disappeared, but from the few that were available it seemed that the form of interrogation was to obtain a statement from one person and then go to another, confront him with it and on that basis obtain a confession from him. The German trial was reported in the Guernsey newspapers, but, for some reason or other, the Germans afterwards became extremely reticent about the proceedings.

After the Military and before the Civilian trial in May 1942, Doctor Biel, the German's Judge Advocate, wrote to His Majesty's Comptroller in Guernsey saying;

> "In the event of the accused denying the admissions made by them to the Feldgendarmerie, please advise me immediately as in this case the Germans will take up the proceedings regards the thefts committed at the expense of the English traders".

Mr Bing pointed out that some of the defendants were shown a copy of Doctor Biel's letter and, as a result, changed their pleas from 'Not guilty', to 'Guilty' to avoid the risk of being tried again by a German Military court.

There was no doubt that the men had been successfully taking great quantities of German property, and their defence was that the non-German property was taken in mistake. They would never knowingly have taken anything from the civilian population. Mr Bing suggested that the Germans were very anxious to prove that the Guernsey police were taking property not from the Germans, but indiscriminately, therefore they put pressure on the Royal Court and this letter was the method they used.

Despite the very strong case Mr Bing put forward on their behalf the Privy Council Judicial Committee turned down the appeals, with the exception of one charge against ex-police officers Quin, Short and Friend for breaking and entering one store and stealing spirits and wines. They dismissed all the other appeals. The committee said that having regard to the fact that they were convicted in other cases their sentences would not be reduced.

The ex-police officers went on to petition the Queen in a further attempt to clear their names, but regrettably without success.

The British Judicial system was just not equipped to deal with the situation which arose in Guernsey during the German occupation and, as a result, seventeen members of the Island Police Force were, in my view and the view of many islanders, denied natural justice. They all paid a heavy price, Bert Smith with his life and the others with their health, reputations and livelihoods. As a community we should, even after all these years, hang our heads in shame at the injustice.

Chapter 29

OLD FAITHFUL

Throughout my life I have had many interests. Sport has, however, always taken a high priority, and of all the sports in which I participated, motorcycle racing was the one which I took most seriously. Once I had become proficient and successful in the sport, it took an undeniable precedence in my life. Over the years, I developed a fighting spirit, so that loosing a race was never part of my thinking. Motorcycling very much became my life and, whilst being dedicated to success in that sport, I promised myself that I would never take any of my other sporting activities as seriously.

I swam for enjoyment, I didn't stretch myself too far and if in competitive swimming I didn't win, it didn't really matter. That was my philosophy and, as a result, I have enjoyed swimming all my life and still do. I have always been prepared to become involved in the administration of any sport, or club, in which I was involved, with the possible exception of motorcycling. Fortunately I enjoy that side of sport, in many ways as much as I enjoyed competing. As I became older I found that I could still maintain an interest, as an administrator, despite not being able to take such an active part.

Motorcycling and motorcycle racing has always held pride of place with me. If there was a clash of sports and there often was, such as when a swimming gala and sand racing took place on the same afternoon, then motorcycling always took precedence. My sporting religion often forced my business into second place. Although I don't think Mabs liked the thought of me racing, she was, however, very supportive and loyally involved herself in the activities of the Motorcycle and Light Car Club. She attended meetings and took an interest in Club affairs. On a number of occasions after our race meetings, she was asked to present the prizes.

The only period of my life when motorcycling was displaced as my number one activity was during the occupation. Had it not been for the war and the Germans, I think it very probable that my desire, and indeed my ambition, to compete on the national and international circuit would have been realised. Dad successfully deflected my thoughts of turning professional with A.J.S. by handing over the running of business to me. But by the end of the nineteen thirties the temptation and pull of the British and International racing tracks was once again very much in my mind.

The opportunity which occurred when I was still in my teens, of racing with the A.J.S. team, had certainly passed. At thirty, I was too old as far as A.J.S. were concerned. But many mainland motorcycle dealers were promoting their businesses by riding on the International Circuit. Fred Lawson and Alec Bennett were both successful on the track and this had benefited their businesses. I was very tempted to follow their example.

My Smith Street business was well established, I had a good staff, who would have been able to carry on in my absence. Artie Selous could easily have taken over the management. I was by then a very experienced and successful racing motorcyclist. I was Channel Islands champion and, at the age of thirty, I knew my limitations and I knew just how far I could push myself and my racing machine. I always left a small margin so that, if ever I needed that little bit extra, it was there. But for the war and the German occupation, I am sure that I would have succumbed to the temptation of turning professional, perhaps even to the detriment of my business, my marriage and my Guernsey way of life. However all thoughts in that direction were swept aside by the advent of the war and the occupation.

By the time that motorcycle racing was re-established after the war, I was getting too old for the professional circuit. Perhaps it was for the best that the war intervened, as Dad always said I would have either been very successful, or very dead. Professional motorcycling has always been a very risky sport.

During the occupation, my 349 cc A.J.S. racing motorcycle had been down at John Crouch's premises in the Pitronnerie Road. I had left it with him during the early part of the war, when I went to work at Armstrong Sidley's. Fortunately it was not discovered by the Germans. Shortly after liberation I reclaimed it and set about reconditioning it ready for my return to the racing scene.

In Guernsey, we were very slow in re-introducing the hill climbs and the sand racing events. The Motorcycle and Light Car Club was virtually inoperative until the spring of 1946. Fred Cohu organised one hill climb before the Club found its post war feet. Jersey, meanwhile was much quicker off the mark and I went over to compete in many of the events they organised. I recall on one occasion I was accompanied by Mrs D. Van Draege and Geoff Cohen, who both competed in the car event. The press described us as the Guernsey Kings and Queen of speed.

Early in 1946, the Motorcycle and Light Car Club decided that future Hill Climbs would be staged at Le Val des Terres. On August Bank Holiday, a Hill Climb was held, that put Guernsey back on the road racing map. Well over ten thousand people turned out to witness the event. Whilst it was extremely successful as far as the Club was concerned, it did not turn out that way for me. First I was allocated the number 22, instead of my previously well known and, in many ways, lucky number 2. Although I had a very successful first practice run, the timing on the A.J.S. was not quite right. Bert Coutanche and I worked hard to correct the fault, and it was with a certain amount of apprehension that I went to the starting line for the first race. With a great roar from the exhaust, I left the starting line, only for my engine to pack up with valve trouble before I reached the end of the flat. Regrettably I was unable to compete in any of that afternoon's races.

The first sand racing meeting at Vazon after the occupation, was not held until 29th July 1948. There were over four thousand spectators, and it was obvious that sand racing was going to be as popular as ever. I still possessed my, by now famous, yellow and black A.J.S. sweater, which I always wore when I rode my vintage 349 cc A.J.S.

I was, however, soon in trouble. Before the first race, all competitors were allowed two practice circuits of the course and on my second lap my motorcycle packed up. However I was able make a temporary repair to the drive chain, although it was to let me down again in a later race.

In the first race, a ten lap scratch event, there were nine riders:-

Eddie Gavey	1946 B.S.A. 350cc.
Frank Seabrook	1947 A.J.S. 498cc.
W.L. Gavey	1947 B.S.A. 500cc.
J.A. Giles	1946 Triumph 500cc.
Jimmy Lanyon	1945 Triumph 350cc.
Jigger Giles	1948 B.S.A. 498cc.
Jack Cochrane	1947 Triumph 498cc.
Eric Rabey	Velocette.
Bill Green	1925 349cc A.J.S.

Bill Green and 'Old Faithful' waiting for the 'off' on the South Esplanade, to speed up Le Val des Terres.

I went straight into the lead and at the end of the first lap had put over 100 yards between myself and the second rider Frank Seabrook. Frank's motorcycle, a 1947 A.J.S. 498cc, was faster than my old machine, but I beat him on the corners and the 'S' bends. I continued to lengthen my lead over him and won in 8 minutes 5.6 seconds.

I started from scratch position in the 15 lap motorcycle handicap race, but after 2 laps I was up amongst the leaders. Jigger Giles, on his 1948 B.S.A. 498cc, was forced to retire early in the 3rd lap when he came off his machine. Jigger was the hardest man to beat if he stayed on his bike but, fortunately for his fellow competitors, he fell off more often than he stayed on ! Frank Seabrook and Eddie Gavey, on a 1946 B.S.A. 350cc, were fighting out the lead, when newcomer Jimmy Lanyon came up and challenged them. Getting every ounce of speed from my machine, I was rapidly fighting my way up through the field. Frank came a cropper when he skidded and was thrown off at the 'S' bend on the eighth lap and retired. I caught Jimmy up on the twelfth lap, and the crowd roared when I overtook him on the 13th. We both passed Eddie Gavey and I entered the fourteenth with a slight lead.

At that point my drive chain parted company and I was left to push the machine back to the pits from the Fort Hommet end of the circuit. Jimmy Lanyon on his 1945 Triumph 350cc, went on deservedly to win the first race he entered on the Vazon sands.

An extra five lap race was held, in which all riders had to run to their machines. Jimmy, being more agile, managed to jump into the lead and although I chased hard on my 'again' repaired motorcycle he held on to the lead. In the final lap I was still chasing him when I was compelled to retire with strange noises coming from my engine. Jimmy Lanyon certainly had a successful and memorable first Vazon sand race meeting. Over the next few years he was to prove a very able and courageous competitor.

Bill Green - Sand Racer.

That first sand meeting after the war was significant for the fact that every rider who competed did so on a British manufactured motorcycle. Regrettably that domination did not last long, and foreign machines soon became much more predominant. I am proud that I never rode a foreign motorcycle in any race in which I competed, British bikes were good enough for me. The Germans, the Italians and particularly the Japanese were later to make great inroads into the British market.

By this time, not only were the Motorcycle and Light Car Club organising Hill Climbs and sand racing meetings at Vazon, they also participated in other events. One such was the Saumarez Park Gymkhana. It was described as a 'Joy Day' with everyone enjoying themselves. There was a 'Bending' race where competitors had to wind their way through various obstructions. I won both my heat and the final on a scarlet Swallow 'Gadabout' which I was marketing at the time. The fact that I entered the race with the spectacularly coloured machine created a great deal of interest and we received a lot of enquiries about the 'Gadabout' in the shop, although it never became a commercial success.

After a considerable number of breakdowns, many people, including the Press, were writing off my 1925 A.J.S. as an 'old faithful', in danger of becoming worn out. The great Guernsey public who supported motorcycle racing, had a soft spot for 'old faithful'. They had taken it to their hearts and enjoyed watching me ride my venerable old racing bike nearly as much as I enjoyed riding it. One newspaper comment was:-

> 'It will be a sorrowful day for Bill and a sad blow to the local motorcycling fraternity, when the old A.J.S. has finally to be cast aside. His daring and beautiful handling of the machine has always been a delight to us all.'

I was certainly not yet ready to cast aside my 'old faithful' A.J.S., it was still going to win me a lot of races and provide me with a great deal of enjoyment. Needless to say, it required constant attention to keep it in anything like racing condition. Bert Coutanche and I spent many hours stripping down and rebuilding the engine. With 'old faithful', I continued to compete in many races, both in the island and in Jersey, against machines which were much newer and more technically advanced. 'Old faithful' was never the master on the straight, but on corners and 'S' bends it was still in a class of it own. It was, without doubt, a magnificent machine.

Nevertheless, it was getting a bit un-reliable and I began to feel the need for more power. So in 1949 I came to the conclusion that 'old faithful' would have to be retired. By that time I had developed the business to such an extent that it was sufficiently profitable to support my racing passion. I was then approaching my fortieth birthday. I discussed the choice of a new racing machine with Bert, as I

Bill Green's hand on Old Faithful while admiring his new racing A.J.S.

greatly valued his opinion. In the end I acquired a new 500cc A.J.S., Model 18. which was assembled, in the factory, according to Clubman Tourist Trophy specifications. It had a close ratio gear box and high lift cams.

My new racing machine caused a lot of interest. The Press came and photographed me with both the old and new bikes. The photograph was published under the heading of 'Old Faithful in retirement' and the story was almost an 'obituary'.

> 'Bill Green looks at his new bike in admiration, but has an affectionate hand on his 'old faithful'. Bill Green's famous old A.J.S. may no longer be seen in local motorcycle races. This news will probably be read with regrets by hundreds of Guernsey motorcycle racing enthusiasts, who have come to regard Bill's 'old faithful' as an essential part of every motorcycle meeting in the island. Many think without it, the meetings will lose half their attraction.
>
> The old machine may still thrill crowds, but it seems unlikely as it's owner has bought a new modern bike. The old A.J.S. has quite a history. It was bought in the Isle of Man in 1925, by Bill Green's father after Jimmy Simpson finished second on it in the Tourist Trophy. Reconditioned by the manufactures, the bike was brought across to Guernsey for the well known racer Terry Bougourd who won several events on it. After ten years it was reckoned the bike had already covered a thousand miles of races, and in its time the machine had raced in both Guernsey and Jersey with Bill Green in the saddle. It will be with very great deal of reluctance that Bill finally discards 'old faithful', but he admits it is getting a bit unreliable now'.

'Old faithful' was one of three specially built by A.J.S.for the 1925 Isle of Man 'T.T.'. Its weight was a mere 190 lb. This was achieved by drilling holes in everything possible, such as the engine and gear box plates. Originally the sprockets were made of a lightweight alloy and needed replacing after every race. For the sake of economy and time, I replaced them with steel sprockets. Originally she was also fitted with alloy mudguards and stays. Duralumin was used in the manufacture of the rocker gear and push rods. It had an 8:1 compression ratio, with a close ratio gearbox, hand changed, with a 5:1 top gear. It was a very advanced racing machine when it was ridden by Jimmy Simpson into second place in the 1925 'T.T.'.

After I retired 'old faithful', I parked it in our garage at Lyndel, which Mabs was always complaining was full of my old junk, and forgot about it.

A.J.S. advised that I should run-in my new racing machine by putting in about 500 miles of quiet running. Whilst the engine had been run up on a dynamometer at the works to measure the potential power, I wanted to make sure that it was properly run-in at comparative low speeds. I spent a great deal of time, mainly in the evenings, gradually clocking up those first 500 miles. I fixed up some temporary lighting on it because, being a racing machine, it wasn't fitted with any lights. One evening I was riding along at about 35-40 mph by Saumarez Park, at a point were the trees hung right over the road, making it one of the darkest stretches of road you could possibly find, when my temporary lighting failed. That was a frightening experience, however, fortunately I managed to stop. That episode taught me a valuable lesson. The thing to do is look up, straight away, so that you can see the sky, between the trees, whereas if you are looking ahead it is total darkness and in those circumstances, the inclination is to pull over to the right and possibly into danger. I have since had similar experiences when riding motorcycles.

One day I was testing a motorcycle for a customer who complained that it had a very bad miss-fire at about 60 mph. Coming from St Martin towards town, along the Fort Road, I was approaching the Morley Chapel corner at the critical speed, when my mackintosh, which I had laid on the top of the petrol tank, flew straight up over my head and covered me so that I couldn't see a thing. I was extremely lucky because I didn't take the bend, I went straight on and ended up on the pavement on the other side of the road, just missing the wall. If there had been anything coming the other way, it could well have been a total disaster.

It was some time before I raced my new 500cc A.J.S. as I took time to fully run it in before racing it flat out. In order to compete in the 1949 Liberation Day Motorcycle and Light Car Club sand racing at Vazon, I borrowed Frank Seabrook's Royal Enfield for the afternoon.

The first race of the meeting was a five lap scratch event. Astride his Ariel, Dick Henry quickly raced into the lead and at the end of the first lap was well ahead of the rest of the field. Jimmy Lanyon and I were battling it out for second place. Towards the end of the second lap Dick had to retire with engine trouble, so from then on it was a race between the two of us. We had a grand scrap, I managed to use my experience on the corners to establish a small lead, but Jimmy would make up ground on the straights. There was still very little separating the two of us on the fourth lap. I managed to increase my lead with some clever manoeuvring around the 'S' bend, then Jimmy really opened out his machine in the final lap, but couldn't catch me, so I won by a matter of a few feet. A really good scrap, which I managed to win on the borrowed Royal Enfield.

At that meeting, some prankster stuck an 'L' plate on the rear of the Royal Enfield because I was celebrating my twenty-fifth year of competitive racing on the sands at Vazon. That meeting, however, was marred by the fatal accident to David Bougourd who just failed to negotiate a tricky bend. He was driving his M.G. racing car and turned it over. No one at the time realised the severity of the accident. We all were aware that he had been taken to hospital, but the racing went on and all the events were completed. On my way back to Town afterwards, I came up behind the car of David's father, Eddie Bougourd, as he was entering the Grange from Queen's Road. I pulled alongside on my motorcycle:

"How is Dave, Eddie ?" I enquired.

"Dead." came the curt reply.

I was stunned. I dropped behind, not knowing what to say.

I raced my A.J.S. for the first time on the sands at Vazon in June 1949. It was fully run in and I was keen to put it through its paces. Initially that afternoon though, I was a little careful as I wanted to build up my confidence, before turning on full power. By the time the main event of the afternoon, the Challenge Tankard, was run, I was full of confidence and raring to go. It was a 'Select' race, with only four motorcycles in each class, from Jersey and Guernsey. Representing Guernsey were Jimmy Lanyon, Les Lane, John Machon and myself, while the Jersey colours were carried by Fred Renouf, Dennis Le Sueur, Ralph Vibert and Sid Logan.

Sid and I set off at a terrific pace from the start and after we had completed three laps the rest of the field was straggling a long way behind. As in nearly all my clashes with Sid, he had the pull on the straight, whilst my cornering at speed still gave me the edge. It was a wonderful race, not only for Sid and myself, but also for the spectators, because the lead was constantly changing. I would come out of a corner just in front, then Sid would pass me on the straight. Unfortunately, at the end of the fourth lap Sid's bike let him down and had to retire. I went on to have a clear-cut victory on my new A.J.S. over John Machon and Ralph Vibert.

The press report was highly complementary, it read.

'Local ace Bill Green was slow at getting going, but with the arrival of the rain so his confidence and daring mounted to leave him always in the running. A grand performance of nerve, and uncanny judgement earned him a first place in the most prized event of the afternoon, fought out in the best company in the Channel Islands'.

Later that summer I was to have success in Le Val des Terres Hill Climb. Jersey's Sid Logan came across for the race, so I looked forward to a good scrap between us. While from a motorcycling point of view, we were both in the veteran class, we were still Hill Climb champions of our respective islands. When it came to the final run up the hill, I was the first to make my run. I set off at a tremendous speed, but unfortunately the timing apparatus failed to function. The marshal, tried to flag me down, but I was well on my way to the top, making a good time but what it was no one knew. I had to go back to the start and make the run again after all the other riders had made their final runs. In those days we were using the 'Long Course', which started half way back along the South Esplanade.

Sid held the lead with a run of 48.4 sec. Every member of the large crowd that lined Le Val des Terres, and there were thousands, knew that Guernsey's honour

Jersey's Sid Logan in action up Le Val des Terres.

Bill Green in action on 500cc. A.J.S. up Le Val des Terres.

depended on me and my last run. Being certain that the A.J.S. was capable of a fast time, I realised that it was now up to me to use all my skill in negotiating the corners. Setting off from the starting line at a very fast speed, I negotiated the bends virtually without throttling back. The crowd cheered me on and the bike responded magnificently. Roaring into the final straight, I crossed the finishing line at over 50 mph. and clipped 0.1 of a second off Sid's best time, with 48.3 seconds at an average speed of 38.6 mph. and stole the honours for Guernsey. That ride also won the Munro trophy, awarded to the fastest time of the day on a motorcycle.

Looking back on that race, it was one of my most memorable and enjoyable. I was delighted when the press nicknamed me 'Corner King, Bill Green'.

Often I would go out on my motorbike, sometimes, in the summertime, as early as half past three in the morning to be able to get clear roads and 'track' around the island. In those days you could do that and get away with it without being caught for speeding. Whilst I admit that I often broke the speed limit, I never did so in a way which I considered dangerous. When, kindly police constable Kimber caught 'Dreamy' Stranger and me speeding along the Jerbourg Road, that was the only time I was actually apprehended. P. C. Kimber never reported us, so I still have a clean record as far as speeding is concerned.

On one of my early morning rides around the island, Mabs was on the pillion. As we approached Vazon, I said to her:

"This machine will do the ton down here, do you fancy it ?"

"Yes all right."

So we were accelerating up towards the hundred, when the engine seized. We were doing about ninety miles per hour when it happened. I managed to get the clutch out and we drifted to a standstill. The seizing of the engine produced a very long skid mark along the road at Vazon. Fortunately we slid in a straight line, largely because of the speed we were doing. If we had been going slower the back wheel would have drifted out and who knows what would have happened.

'Dreamy' Stranger and I practised cornering early in the morning, both before and after the occupation. There was one particular corner we used to call the '70 mph bend'. Coming from L'Eree, on the coast road, after the sharp corner, there is a long sweeping bend as you go towards Perelle. We would enter the bend doing

70 mph, and hold our bikes at that speed right the way around. It was the ideal bend as there was total visibility and no blind spots. 'Dreamy' and I practised our cornering a great deal there and could both go around it at 70-73 mph. That was not bad for the racing bikes of those days, today, no doubt modern machines would be able to take the bend at around 80 mph. I never went around a blind corner at excessive speed, I always ensured that I had six inches of margin in case of emergency. I never went right to the edge. If you went into a corner, two or three miles too fast you were in trouble, the art was to approach the corner a mile or two down, and then accelerated through it. That way you retained full control all the way around the bend. Cornering was an art and I like to think that I mastered it.

I took pride in the fact that I could overtake other competitors on corners, as cornering was the secret of motorcycle racing in Guernsey. Unlike mainland circuits, Guernsey tracks were short laps with many corners and very little straight. In my day many of the events on the mainland were road races. Today that type of racing has become too dangerous, the machinery is too fast, so now it is mainly track racing.

Later in 1949, I went across with other members of the Guernsey Motorcycle and Light Car Club to Jersey for their last meeting of the season at St Ouens Bay. In the thirty lap handicap event there were 36 riders in a very strong field, which included Sid Logan. He and I were the only two scratch riders, all the others benefiting from the handicapper's 'generosity'. In the first lap I came off my machine on a corner but quickly remounted and rejoined the race. A few laps later, at the chicane bend, I came off again, a cropper this time. I remounted, and being very annoyed with myself, proceeded to burn up the course at an even faster speed. Despite my two falls I finished fourth, Sid of course won the race. Throughout the whole of my motorcycling career I rarely came off my machine, but that afternoon was the exception. One of the reasons, I believe, was that the sand on the Jersey circuit was much softer than on Vazon beach.

Looking back, 1949 must have been one of the most successful, if not my most successful season. My new A.J.S. racing machine performed superbly, I consistently beat off challenges from all-comers and became a firm favourite with the crowds. In those day's, before the cult of television, when entertainment was much more homemade, the crowds at Le Val des Terres hill climbs would regularly number over 10,000. At Vazon there were usually as many as four thousand spectators. As the leading racing motorcyclist in the Channel Islands, I was in many ways looked upon as one of their sporting hero's. Young lads put the number '2', my racing number, on their bikes and pretended to emulate my cornering skills.

The press gave me great support during those years and in a review of the Sporting Year, I was listed as one of those who became Guernsey sporting stars in 1949.

'Bill Green'

'The brilliant and daring riding of the Corner King'.

> 'Bill Green has been a feature of this years motorcycle racing in Guernsey. He has provided speed enthusiasts with countless thrills both on the Vazon sands and at Le Val des Terres, he has kept the Guernsey flag flying on the inter-insular events, following the strong challenges of the Jersey aces, astride their high powered machines. We think Bills most meritorious showing, was when he climbed Le Val des Terres in the fast time of 48.3 seconds. It will

> be recalled that this was thc last run of the day and Sid Logan of Jersey was holding the lead with a time of 48.4seconds. Seldom has the crowd seen Green ride so superbly, his average speed was 38.6 mph.'

The local Press would conjecture from time to time as to the up and coming local boy, most likely to take over from me as the islands most successful motorcyclist. At one meeting in the summer of 1950, Les Lane rode his 346cc Royal Enfield so beautifully and easily that he won five races. Les had for sometime been attracting more and more attention and that successful afternoon was certainly Les's way of staking his claim. Les was, without doubt, a very good sand racer. He was a flamboyant character and a bit of an extrovert.

Les, was seven years my junior and he and I had many battles on the track - he won some and I won others. Off the track we became firm friends, a friendship which has strengthened over the years. Les was one of those people who enjoyed life and lived it to the full. He was brimming over with devilment and always playing the fool.

The first time I met Les was in 1947, at a motorcycle trial in the island. It proved to be a very difficult course and there was one tricky section that no one had completed without putting their feet down on the ground. Les, who at the time had a Velocette, was one of the last to go and completed the section without his feet touching the ground.

"How did you manage that Les ?" I asked.

"I will let you into a secret" he said, "I let the back tyre down almost flat."

It was a little trick he had learnt on the mainland, it was obvious when you thought about it, but I hadn't.

Les added "I had to stop just around the corner and pump the tyre up again."

Les earned himself a reputation as a sensible rider. One of my mechanics, Charles Pratt, used to get Les's Royal Enfield ready for him. Charles was a the past master at creating a reliable engine and Les was a wise and astute rider. He would never over rev the engine, something which some riders would regularly do in

Les Lane in action up Le Val des Terres.

order to get the last ounce out of their machines. Inevitably in time, that blew up the engines.

In the evenings, after the racing on Vazon Sands was over, many of us would congregate in the Peary Nook Tearooms across the road. Edie and Billy Wilcox, who ran the tearooms were a lovely couple. It almost became an unofficial headquarters for the Motorcycle Club. They kept open all hours and often we would still be there, drinking coffee, at three in the morning. The tearooms were unlicenced, so there were no problems with licensing hours. It became the post-war Stainers as far as us boys were concerned.

My nephew Noel Trotter, a constable in the Island Police Force, was involved as a witness in a case in the Royal Court which was well reported. During cross examination by the defending advocate, he was asked:

"Police Constable Trotter, you were off duty at the time ?"

P.C.Trotter replied "Sir, a policeman is never off duty".

Les read the report and one night after a group of us had enjoyed a convivial time down at the Peary Nook tearooms, he telephoned P.C. Trotter at his home. It was three in the morning and he spoke to Zoe, Noel's wife.

"Can I speak to Constable Trotter please."

"What's the matter, he's asleep."

"Oh it's important." says Les.

So Zoe gets her husband out of bed and he comes to the telephone.

"Police Constable Trotter here, what is the problem ?"

Les Lane says; "Can you tell me the time please ?"

Trotter explodes: "What the hell are you ringing me for ?"

"You're 'The' policeman who is always on duty, so you said, and my mother told me that if I want to know the time, ask a policeman, can you tell me the time please ?"

Les did not wait for the eruption, but put the telephone down.

I don't know if he ever discovered who made the call. Noel did, however, have a sense of humour and was not past playing the part on occasions. I remember once, down at the White Rock Cafe, someone got him to play the 'heavy hand' with one of their friends. He really put the fear of God into this chap, who really thought he was in dire trouble until Noel came clean.

My sister Daisy had two sons, Noel and Ian Trotter. Noel who was fifteen years younger than me, was not my favourite nephew. In my view he was very arrogant and when he became a policeman I felt that it was his natural vocation as he liked dominating other people.

Noel eventually became a motorcycle patrol policeman. Many people have said that he did a very fine job in that particular capacity. I would disagree because he set out to trap motorcyclists and created a great deal of unnecessary aggro between the public and the police. The young motorcyclists that I was dealing with at that time through my business had a wonderful time challenging his authority. Police constable Trotter had a habit of hiding in gateways and other places in order to catch the boys speeding. On Thursday and Saturday afternoons the game was to find out where Police constable Trotter was hiding. One of his regular places was along the Vazon Road where the youngsters liked to open up their motorcycles and have a race.

Once they had located P.C.Trotter, they would send out a decoy in one direction going like the clappers. Police constable Trotter would pull out in pursuit and then this chap would slow down to a crawl. The local T.T. race, then took place in the opposite direction, because they knew where the law was otherwise occupied.

I saw Noel quite often because, as a motorcycle patrolman, he would bring the police motorcycles into George Street for repair. We supplied their bikes and repaired them. As a consequence he was around the George Street garage much more than I would have liked and I suspected that he was doing my business a great deal of harm. Many of the young motorcyclists who were good customers of mine didn't like to be in the garage when he was there. Eventually I approached Deputy Jack Hart, President of the Police Committee and asked him to take his business elsewhere.

During this period, the 1950's, my friendship with the opposite sex continued despite all the pressure applied by Mabs and my many friends for me to come to my senses. As a consequence, my relationship with Mabs, to say the least, was strained. In public, Mabs continued to be very supportive, but in private it was a very different matter.

Mabs joined in the social side of the Motorcycle and Light Car club, taking a leading part in some of the events. With the then President's wife, Mrs Ruth Randell, one of my former girl friends, and Mrs Les Lane, she organised social events at the St John Ambulance Brigade hall. At one of the events Mabs and I won first prize in a competition in which the ladies had to 'make up' their partners. Mabs, with lipstick flowing freely, made me look a real idiot, perhaps that is why we were the winners!

On occasions Mabs wrote sketches, which were performed at the Club's socials. One sketch featured a veteran racing motorcyclist who suffered terrible tensions and stresses before each race. The principle props were a very large bottle of aspirin and a tow rope. The final scene depicted the veteran's young son announcing that, despite the effects racing had on his father, he also wanted to race motorcycles.

Another sketch Mabs wrote, was the result of seeing the sand racing at Vazon continue after the incoming tide had almost covered the course. Mabs acted the part of Mother Neptune, wigging the motorcyclists for daring to ignore the tide.

Despite trying to maintain her composure in public, the situation again became very detrimental to her health and, fearing another collapse, Dr Rose was called in. He told me in no uncertain terms to pull myself together.

While domestic battles continued, my motorcycling battles with Les Lane became more memorable. One such encounter with Les was in a five lap handicap race. He was on his 346cc Royal Enfield and me on my 500cc A.J.S. As he had the lower powered machine he was given a half lap start. Les went away at a tremendous pace. He quickly caught Jimmy Lanyon and the other competitors in front of him and took the lead. I was lying in seventh position at the end of the first lap but soon fought my way through the field, so that I was in the third spot by the end of the third lap.

By the end of the fourth lap I had overtaken John Machon, who had been lying second, and only had Les to pass. Les Lane was tearing along using every ounce of power he could coax from his machine. He was riding beautifully. The crowd were cheering us on, they loved a good scrap, and Les and I were giving them great value for money. Inch by inch I was gaining on Les and, as we entered the last 'S' bend, only about ten yards separated us. As we came out of the bend I had closed the gap and we both roared towards the finishing line, which Les reached first, just a foot or two in front of me. A very exciting race which we both enjoyed and which kept the crowd at boiling point with excitement.

During 1950 the Star newspaper published a series of cartoon's of leading islanders, called 'Le Ray's Picture Gallery'. I figured in one of these cartoon's, drawn to depict me on my racing motorcycle, wearing my helmet, emblazoned with the letters A.J.S. in their instantly recognisably style. Accompanying the cartoon was a flattering write-up.

> 'Finest motorcyclist in the Channel Islands. That is what the experts say about Bill Green, seen here in another Le Ray cartoon. One of the pioneers of motorcycle racing in Guernsey and he's been cycling since he was a nipper. He sells motorcycles, but he's more than that. He is a first class mechanic on them too. He is a fine swimmer, was first post war President of the Guernsey Swimming Club and is on the committee of the Water Polo Association. Bill Green was born in Guernsey and went to the Intermediate school'.

The original of the cartoon was framed and presented to me and hangs in pride of place in my home. I was, and still am, very proud of the honour the Star paid me in publishing that cartoon.

During the early and middle nineteen fifties I continued racing, but I was now very much regarded as the 'Grand Old Man of the circuit', and the crowds 'Favourite Veteran'. Over forty and a veteran I might be, but I was still as keen on winning as ever. During the fifties one of my favourite opponents was Jersey's Steve Perchard. A great many races developed into thrilling personal duels between us. Perchard usually managed to find that little bit of extra power on the straights, but my superior cornering always made up ground for me on the bends, which meant that I generally managed to steal the honours.

Way back in 1929 I won the Pealling-Carey Trophy, in a thirty lap handicap race on the sands at Vazon. The Guernsey Motorcycle and Light Car Club's activities were drastically curtailed by the depression, and for a few years the Club virtually ceased to function. Dad was involved in the administration of the Club at that time and arranged for the trophies and cups to be looked after by other organisations. The Pealling-Carey trophy was entrusted to the British Legion. They made use of it as a Darts Trophy, until it was returned to the Club in 1952. So after a period of twenty three years, the trophy was to be competed for again.

There was a great deal of publicity given to the race for the returned trophy. I was generally regarded as the hot favourite to retain the award. On the day of the race, huge crowds lined the grey sea walls at Vazon - everyone had come to witness the thirty lap race for the trophy. I was determined that I would use all the skill and experience gained in twenty nine years of sand racing to beat off all challengers and retain the Pealling-Carey trophy.

The meeting started with a five lap handicap race for 350 and 500cc machines that I won easily. Then I went on to win another five lap race for motorcycles of unlimited power. Being in fine form, I was keenly looking forward to the thirty lap Pealling-Carey Trophy event.

I had a great race and retained the cup for a second time, twenty three years after I had last won it. Dick Henry pushed me most of the way, but had a nasty spill at a bend on the twenty-ninth lap. Jack Cockayne and J. Fox followed me home in an excellent time of 19 minutes 8 seconds. Young Fox rode a fine race. It was his first attempt at sand racing but he rode very sensibly, taking no chances. Gradually many of the riders in front of him dropped out, mainly due to the risks they were taking. He came in third.

After the race I told the huge crowd over the public address system, that I would carry on motorcycle racing for one more year, complete thirty years of competitive racing, and then retire. I may have believed it at the time, I may have made that statement as a result of the persuasive pressure that Mabs and others were applying, but it did not happen. I was to race on for a number more years before finally deciding to 'hang up my helmet'.

When in 1955 I gave up competitive motorcycling racing for the first time and resigned myself to being a spectator, the Club invited me to join their Commentary team on the Val des Terres hill climbs. Reg Randell was at the start, I covered the middle of the course and Richard Ozanne the finish. I think wc did a good job keeping the spectators in the picture and also providing a valuable communication system for the race organisers. However, it was never the same, I longed to be back in the saddle and back in the race. The day after my fiftieth birthday, 20th August 1959, I could no longer resist the pull of the sport I loved, and despite vigorous pleading by both Mabs and my daughter Margaret, I came out of retirement to compete in the sand racing on Vazon beach.

In my first race, a ten lap event, I had a good ride and was satisfied when I came in third. The main race, the thirty lap Pealing-Carey Trophy, was what had really tempted me out of retirement. Having won the trophy twice before I thought it would be a fitting conclusion to my racing career if I could win it for a third time. I had completed twenty laps, was lying second and well placed, when negotiating the Hommet corner I was thrown from my machine.

The race was stopped and I was taken by stretcher to a waiting ambulance. Apparently I steadfastly refused to be put into the ambulance. Dr Rose who was in attendance, asked Mabs to persuade me to get into the ambulance, as no one else could. Once inside, I was heard to say;

"I cant win in this thing, it doesn't go fast enough!."

Fortunately I was only slightly concussed and after the three days in bed, that the doctor prescribed, I was as good as new.

The Pealing Carey Trophy was re-run at the next meeting of the Motorcycle and Car Club in September and I again took up the challenge. Earlier during the meeting I achieved a third place behind two of my employees, John Guilliard and Roger Sparkes, in a twenty lap race. In the Pealing-Carey trophy I once again had bad luck after making a good start to the race. I was following Derek 'Moke' Le Marquand into the Hommet corner when his motor cut out. I was so close behind him that I couldn't avoid him and we both found ourselves sitting on the sands. Neither of us was hurt. As I sat there I decided that I had raced my last race, I had finally retired.

A few weeks later, at the Club's Annual Dinner, the Club's Honorary Doctor, Dr Strickland, who was the main speaker, paid a tribute to me on my retirement. He described me as:

"The 'Doyen' of Guernsey motorcycling racing and a truly wonderful sportsman".

I raced for over thirty-six years and thoroughly enjoyed ever moment. I was remarkably fortunate that I was never seriously injured. I always had total support from all my family and colleagues. I had the undoubted advantage that I was born into the motorcycle trade and was privileged to have had a very indulgent father who ensured that I was always well trained and equipped. Dad encouraged me to use the ability that I was undoubtedly blessed with, rather than taking the unnecessary risks that many of my fellow competitors took.

On reflection, Mabs and Margaret must have been greatly relieved when I finally retired from competitive motorcycle racing. Margaret particularly was scared stiff every time I raced, as she was sure that I was going to come to grief. For days before a race it would affect her so much so that she was almost ill with worry and went right off her food. She was furious with me for attempting a come-back. Now, it is obvious to me that I should have retired a great deal sooner, but I loved the sport so much that in some ways it was surprising that I gave up when I did !

My one regret, looking back on my racing career, is that I did not turn professional and compete on the international circuit. Had I been born and brought up on the mainland, not only would I have ridden in the Isle of Man and at Brooklands - but, almost certainly competed at Silverstone and Brands Hatch. I can only dream of what might have been.

Chapter 30

I AM INTERESTED IN SWIMMING, NOT BALLYHOO!

One of the most outstanding long distance swimmers, in the post war period, was a young London University student, Ruth Oldham. Before coming to Guernsey in 1961, to attempt the Sark to Guernsey swim, Ruth swam Lake Windermere in record time. She was a very determined and courageous little swimmer

For her attempt on the Sark to Guernsey swim, Ruth asked me to act as her swim manager and recruit Kenny Bell as her pilot. Before she slipped into the sea off the northwest coast of Sark in her attempt to swim to Guernsey, I ensured that she was covered with a protective coating of grease and chilli paste against the cold.

She set off strongly and within threequarters of an hour had passed Brecqou and was well on her way towards Jethou. A problem with leaking goggles slowed her down and Ruth missed the tide by a few minutes. Although she gallantly fought against the tide, she was swept steadily southwards, away from her planned destination, St Peter Port. So Kenny and I directed her towards Fermain Bay, but she continued to be swept southwards by the fast flowing tide.

Shortly before 7 pm. she clambered ashore on the rocks below the Pine Forest on the Jerbourg peninsular, only the third person and the first woman to have swum from Sark to Guernsey. We put her aboard Ted Laker's boat and Ruth was brought into St Peter Port Harbour, where she was heartily cheered ashore by a small crowd.

Once she successfully accomplished that challenge, Ruth was determined to conquer the Guernsey to Jersey swim, which had never previously been accomplished. I had swum with Jack Heyward on his attempt before the war when he was forced to give up through sea sickness, caused by the wake of the mailboat.

The success that Ruth achieved with her Sark to Guernsey swim brought a flood of publicity for both Ruth and Guernsey. Many local people felt that the challenge of a possible Guernsey to Jersey swim could be used to promote the island from a tourist point of view. Eric Martin, who was a keen swimmer and an astute businessman, suggested that a properly staged and publicised swim, with a substantial prize, would generate a great deal of world wide publicity.

Support for Eric Martin's suggestion came from local impresario, Sydney James, who the following year put up a prize of five hundred pounds for the first professional swimmer to complete the Guernsey to Jersey swim. His organisation, Sydney James Production Limited, placed very stringent conditions on the £500 challenge. The requirements were clearly designed to ensure that the publicity arising from the swim would all be to Guernsey's benefit.

Every swimmer was required to sign a form, agreeing that they would forfeit the prize if any of the conditions were broken. Swimmers had to agree to being based in Guernsey and return to the island as soon as the swim had been completed. Sydney James or his representative was to accompany the swimmer in their escort boat and if successful, he would become their personal manager. No competitor could attend any reception or other function without the prior approval of Sydney James, nor could they appear on television without his permission. He was determined to ensure that all the publicity came Guernsey's way, with Jersey being denied a look-in.

One further condition was that professionals could only attempt the swim in September 1962 and if an amateur had been successful before that date, the £500 challenge would be withdrawn. Inevitability Sydney James obtained a great deal of publicity for his challenge. National newspapers carried many stories in which Guernsey was featured.

Ruth Oldham contacted me and asked if I would organise her attempt to swim from Guernsey to Jersey and again act as her swim manager. She announced to the British press that she was going to attempt the swim towards the end of July and naturally received a considerable amount of publicity. Some of the National newspaper articles suggested that the swim could be dangerous. One experienced Channel swimmer was reported as warning Ruth to forget the idea, because of the danger from the un-predictable tides.

I was incensed by this 'scaremonger' publicity, and I suspected that Ruth might be behind it. In my limited dealings with Ruth I soon became aware of her ability to 'generate' publicity. I suspected that some of the published criticism of the swim had in fact originated from Ruth herself.

On the day before she was due to arrive in the island for the attempted swim, a letter from me was published in the local press. I said that it had come to my notice that 'certain wild statements' had been made in the national press on the dangers Ruth Oldham was taking in attempting to swim from Guernsey to Jersey. I went on 'well knowing this ladies flair for publicity I suspect some of these statements to be inspired by herself'.

I emphasised, in my letter, that the swim would only take place if I and my fellow organisers were totally satisfied that conditions were safe for Ruth to make the attempt. I was asked by the press about my position as her swim manager and I was reported as saying;

"When she arrives in Guernsey, young Ruth and I will have a heart to heart talk, I feel she and I should understand each other before we go any further".

Ruth had been staying at the Water's Edge Hotel, at Bouley Bay, in Jersey, where her fiance was appearing in cabaret. Leonard Matchan, the millionaire proprietor of the hotel put his private plane at her disposal for her flight to Guernsey. When I heard this I realised that Leonard Matchan was intending to muscle in on the swim publicity, no doubt at Guernsey's expense.

I, and the rest of the swim organising team, met Ruth at the Albion Hotel, and it soon became clear that she was very upset about my letter to the press, particularly my use of the phrase 'certain wild statements'. I was sacked as her swim manager, although she required my presence on the swim as I was the Guernsey representative of the British Long Distance Swimming Association. Without a representative of the Association the swim, if successful, could not be officially recognised.

At the end of our meeting Ruth read a prepared 350 word statement to the press, in which she said that she was surprised that Mr Green had taken offence at some remarks which appeared in the national press. And she added that her amazement changed to incredulity when she read my published letter.

Ruth Oldham went on "In reply to this letter I wish to confirm that the newspapers certainly received the comments on the hazards of the swim from me. However I do not feel that the statements can be described as 'wild' since they originated from people who's views on the matter are much respected. These include boatmen, who have intimate knowledge of the waters and a senior official of the British Rail Channel Island Ships."

She also agreed that she had a flair for publicity but did not like the impression the remark must have given to those who read it. Ruth concluded "I cannot help feeling that Mr Green's attitude arises from my decision to stay in Jersey while waiting for the swim to start".

After Ruth had read her prepared statement, she answered questions. Where was she going to be based for the swim, in view of her row with Mr Green ?.

"The Water's Edge Hotel has kindly offered to accommodate me and put their speed-boat, plane and car at my disposal. These arrangements offer numerous advantages to me, including an air preview of the course. I feel that I must now also take up their further offer to supply a boat from the Hotel's underwater centre, for my attempt on the swim."

I realised that it was Leonard Matchan and the Water's Edge Hotel that were now calling the tune, and winning the publicity battle. Ruth and I were just pawns in the game. The press asked me for a comment. I thought of all that I could have said, but finally bit my tongue and commented:-

"It only remains for me to wish her jolly good luck," and added, "I am interested in swimming, not ballyhoo!"

So Jimmy Webster, from the Water's Edge Hotel, became her Swim Manager and organiser. He was an expert skin diver and boatman, but whether he knew the tides and the waters between Guernsey and Jersey remained to be seen.

Before I was sacked as her Swim Manager, she had talked to me of the possibility of turning professional and delaying her attempt until September, so that she could qualify for impresario Sydney James's challenge prize of £500. However, she wanted to be the first person to complete the swim, amateur or professional.

Two days later I was down at St Martin's point to welcome Ruth as she stepped ashore from her boat to start her attempt to swim from Guernsey to Jersey. I handed her a telegram I had received from a Lancashire friend of her's, wishing her luck. As she entered the water, I called out:

"Good luck, you can do it Ruth".

For some hours Ruth, despite swimming strongly, was swept by the tide in a southwesterly direction. When the tide turned she made good speed towards Jersey. However the north easterly drift of the tide was such that she was being carried past Jersey in the direction of France. Although getting to within three miles of Jersey's Grosnez Point, the tide and weather were against her and she had to be pulled into the escort boat after being in the water for almost twenty four hours. My own view was that she started the swim too early and, as a result, had to swim into the tide instead of across it.

A few days later Ruth made a second unsuccessful attempt, again being thwarted by the flood tide. To conquer the tidal conditions successfully a swimmer needs to make good headway south before being carried east and then north easterly by the flood tides towards Jersey. I believe that it is necessary to swim to a point more than ten miles south of Guernsey, before the tide turns and carries the swimmer towards Jersey and the French coast. When the tide is in full flow it carries swimmers towards France faster than they can swim. It is very easy to be swept past the coast of Jersey altogether and that is why it is essential to swim so far south. Ruth failed on her first two attempts because her swim plan did not make sufficient allowance for the flood tide.

After her second failure to swim from Guernsey to Jersey, Ruth declared:-

"I will do it if it kills me!"

There was no doubt that she possessed the dogged determination to succeed.

On the 13th of August, Ruth set out from St Martin's point on her third attempt to conquer the tides and elements. For this attempt Master Pilot Henry Bisson, was in charge of the swim and the escort boat was crewed by Graham Cowley and Peter Helmot, all from Guernsey. I did not receive an invitation to travel in the escort boat and therefore the British Long Distance Swimming Association was not represented.

On this occasion, Ruth made better use of the tides and reached a point eleven miles south east of St Martin's point before the flood tide started taking her in a north easterly direction. Apparently she got within a mile of Grosnez Point before the tide again turned against her. Although desperately cold and tired she summoned up enough strength to fight her way towards shore. The last three hundred yards took almost an hour to complete. The sea was quite rough at the foot of Grosnez Point where she landed and she had to make several attempts before being able to haul herself out of the water to become the first person ever to swim the eighteen mile stretch of water between Guernsey and Jersey. It had taken her fifteen and a quarter hours. Incidentally, Ruth completed the swim in my daughter's swimming costume. Earlier when she had needed a costume, Margaret had lent Ruth her maroon nylon racing costume, which, incidentally, was never returned.

Once she completed the swim, Ruth was taken by launch to Bonne Nuit Bay, where she went ashore. On landing, she was reported as saying:-

"I can hardly believe that I have done it".

From there, Ruth went straight to the Water's Edge Hotel, where she had a hot bath before being introduced to the diners in the Restaurant by Leonard Matchan. The publicity bandwagon had begun to roll and Guernsey was nowhere to be seen.

Later, she was presented with a magnificent solid silver trophy by State Express, the cigarette company. While not as valuable as the £500 prize offered by Sydney James, it was still a very acceptable reward. The success of Ruth's swim meant the end of all Sydney James plans to publicise Guernsey.

Monty Manning was a diving enthusiast and had been a Guernsey Swimming Club coach for over twenty two years. He was extremely good with youngsters and spent hours encouraging and teaching them the finer points of diving. Monty, however, suffered from a stammer, which produced one or two embarrassing moments. On one occasion we were in a lady's house for a Swimming Club meeting and before everyone had arrived Monty, having noticed the cat was licking the back of it's neck, had, for the sake of making conversation, said to me:

"I b-b-bet y-y-you c-c-can't d-d-do what the c-c-c-cat is d-d-d-doing n-n- n-now?"

By the time he had stuttered the words out, the cat had finished washing the back of its neck and was attending to another part of it's anatomy, which caused Monty to turn a bright shade of pink!

Although over sixty, he still performed spectacular dives as part of the entertainment at our Galas. His 'piece-de-resistance' was a 24 foot double back somersault dive from a ladder on the diving stage. His favourite dive, however, was the 'running Moulburg', for which he ran along the diving board, sprang up into the air and performed a reverse somersault before entering the water head first. He used to miss the end of the diving board by a matter of inches. I often said to him:

"Monty one of these days if you're not careful, you are going to crack your head on the board!"

Monty was very supportive of the younger members of the Club and often accompanied swimming and diving teams to the mainland. When he resigned as the Club's diving coach, Ralph Palmer took over. However he was still very active, and on one occasion, in August 1963, he went with one of the Swimming Club's most promising young divers to the Southern Counties Diving School at Chigwell in Essex. Although he was sixty eight, he was still keen to swim and dive each day for sheer personal enjoyment. While at Chigwell, he got up early one morning and went on his own to the baths for some diving practice. Later, he was found dead in the pool, with a big bruise on his head. Apparently he had being practising one of the running Moulburg dives and must have struck the diving board sufficiently hard to have knocked himself unconscious, and drowned.

Frank Le Poidevin, who was then the President of the Swimming Club and I, went across for Monty Manning's funeral. We stayed in central London over night and next morning went to the funeral by tube. Unfortunately we missed the stop and overran the station. So Frank and I had to catch another tube train back, which meant that we were almost late for the funeral service. As we were hurrying through the gate of the Crematorium, the Commissioner stopped us and asked;

"What name please."

"Green." I replied.

He looked down his list and said. "No Green, this morning."

"I am very relieved to hear that" !

After the war commercial flying came into its own. Everyone was flying and Mum did not wish to be left out. She had never flown and it became her ambition to do so while she was still able. I organised a flight to Alderney for Mum and Mrs Edna Bourgaize, a lady friend of hers. Mum really looked forward to this flight, I hardly ever remember Mum being so excited as she was at the prospect of flying for the first time.

The great day arrived and we duly took off from our airport. The weather was perfect and the visibility was excellent. Mum was thrilled to see her home island, for the first time, from the air. As we came in to land at Alderney Airport there was a lady pushing a pram across the grass runway, which was not an unusual occurrence in those days. The pilot lifted off again, circled with one wing dipped down over the sea, flattened out and landed. When we got out of the aircraft Edna asked Mum :-

"Did you enjoy that Gran ?".

"Oh yes!"

"You weren't frightened ?"

"No, no," said Mum, "I thought were were going to land in the sea."

"And you weren't frightened ?" asked Edna.

"Oh no, I've seen them land in the sea sometimes."

She was quite happy, she was no doubt thinking of the French seaplanes during the first war. I was petrified because I thought we were going to land in the sea as well and I knew what the consequences would have been.

Mum was living in the annex at Seaplane Bungalow, she was occupying one end and Mrs Bourgaize the other. Edna was a trained nurse and was a godsend to Mabs and I, because she gave Mum all the attention she needed. Later, Aunt Lil went to live in the Annex with Mum, but they did not get on at all well together. By this time they both used walking sticks to assist them in walking. If they sat too near each other, these two elderly ladies would poke each other with their sticks. I can well remember seeing a number of round bruises on my Aunt's thigh as a result of Mum prodding her with her walking stick. We always had to ensure that they were far enough apart, so that they could not 'duel' with each other.

When Mum was unable to look after herself she went into the Le Platon Home, in Clifton. She was there for about eighteen months before she had a fall and broke her thigh. Mum was transferred to the Princess Elizabeth Hospital, where she died in 1961, aged 94.

Aunt Lil had previously gone into the Old Town Hospital, where she became one of their 'pin-up's'. My Aunt had a great sense of humour and, like the rest of that side of the family, was full of fun. In the Old Town Hospital, she used to sit in her cot and sing little ditties.

I was very fond of Aunt Lil. She never married, but when her mother died at the age of thirty-nine, she brought up the family. Aunt Lil had a boyfriend at the time, but turned down marriage and devoted her life to the rest of her brothers and sisters. When she died, I was her executor and made a mistake with her age. Barry Lovell was the undertaker and between us we recorded her age as eighty-four on the coffin plate instead of ninety-four. As her coffin was being lowered into the grave, her brother Harold, looked down and noticed the mistake.

"Well it is too late to change it now,"I said, "anyway she would have chuckled at the thought that she could, even now, be boastful about her age."

My daughter Margaret left the Ladies College at sixteen, after having first been expelled and then being reinstated. Four of the girls, including Margaret, led the whole of her class out of school, without permission, to watch the boys of the neighbouring school play cricket. The four ring-leaders were expelled. It was going to be Margaret's last term, and she was due to take her 'O' levels in a matter of weeks. Together with another parent, I went to see the Headmistress, and we pleaded for our daughters to be allowed to stay on to complete their examinations. We were successful, but Margaret was made to apologise in front of the whole school.

After leaving school, Margaret trained and qualified as a British Horse Society Instructor. For a year she taught riding to the boys at Wellington College in Wokingham, but left when she fell in love with a Royal Horse Guardsman. After a spell in London, Margaret went to France as an au-pair. Mabs and I took a holiday in Paris, so that we could assure ourselves that she was alright. Margaret persuaded me to pay for her to study French at the Sorbonne, the Paris University.

I suspect that she perfected her French more from boy friends in the Paris cafes than from her rare appearances at the Sorbonne. However, she achieved what she set out to do, a mastery of the French language.

While Mabs and I were in Paris, I was impressed with a small car that I noticed running about the city streets. It was the Vespa, produced by the scooter people. I thought that, in view of its small size, it would be ideal for Guernsey. I made inquiries and found the company showrooms, just off the Champs Elysees. As a result of our visit to Paris, I obtained the agency for the Vespa Car in Guernsey. I imported over thirty of them before the company ceased production, as a direct consequence of the success of the British Mini.

The Vespa was smaller than the Mini and had a twin cylinder air-cooled engine. It was a marvellous little car to drive, and achieved almost 50 miles to the gallon. Although only thirty thousand were produced, they proved to be very popular, particularly with my staff and family. Edna Butt, Roger Sparkes, and Len Holmes all drove Vespa cars at one time. For many years Mabs loved her little Vespa and Margaret was also a devotee. It was a tragedy when they went out of production.

After experiencing Paris, Margaret returned home to Guernsey. I persuaded her to work with me in the business. I had hopes that she would enjoy the motorcycle trade, as I had always done and join me on a permanent basis. I looked upon Margaret as my only hope of being able to keep the business in the family. But it was not to be. Although she worked with me for two years, running the administration side of the business very efficiently, the motor trade was not for her.

Margaret had always known the difficulties Mabs and I were having with our marriage and tried to do everything in her power to keep us together. On our twentieth wedding anniversary Margaret presented us with a small sailing boat which she bought from one of my employees, Dave Allett. It was lying on the Careening Hard, so she wrapped it in cellophane and tied it up with a great big bow. Mabs and I, and indeed Margaret, obtained considerable pleasure from sailing that boat in the waters around Guernsey.

Whilst we enjoyed boating, I was the most hopeless boatman ever - rarely could I do anything right. On one occasion I remember throwing out the anchor at Bec du Nez, only to realise that it was not attached to the rope. I had to dive down to retrieve the anchor.

On another occasion, Mabs, Margaret, her boyfriend and I went to Herm for the day. I had fitted a small Seagull out-board motor to the boat, as I was not very proficient in handling the sails. The motor was the type that tilted up out of the water and there was a little spring clip which held it in place. Margaret fitted the out-board motor onto the boat earlier in the day, and unfortunately I did not check that the little clip was in place. We motored our way to Herm and when we arrived, there was a queue of boats waiting their turn to enter the harbour. We waited, and when it was our turn, I pulled the starting cord to restart the motor. Instead of springing into life, the motor jumped out of its mounting and plunged into the sea.

Although I could see the motor lying on the seabed, it was in quite deep water. So I rowed the boat into the harbour, put on my bathing costume and swam out to try to re-locate the motor. Eventually I found it and dived down, picked up the engine, trundle it a few yards towards the shore before dropping it, to come up for air. I then took another deep breath and repeated the procedure. Gradually I managed to bring the motor to a position from where I landed it on the quay. While Mabs, Margaret and her boyfriend enjoyed the wonderful summers day in Herm, I was on the quay, stripping down and re-assembling the Seagull outboard motor. Being a very hot day, the heat helped to dry out the ignition. When I finally re-assembled the motor, it was time to return to St Peter Port. So I fitted the motor to our boat, and with the pin in place, we motored home.

Chapter 31

A STRANGE COINCIDENCE

After buying the Smith Street property from Miss Anderson in 1958, I knew it was only a matter of time before I would have to spend a considerable sum of money on repairs and modernization. So early in 1963 I transferred the cycle business to George Street and the builders moved into the Smith Street premises. The property required an almost complete rebuild. Originally the estimated cost was going to be in the region of £14,000, but because of difficulties with the foundations the final figure was well over £20,000, nearly three times the purchase price I paid Miss Anderson for the property only five years previously.

Smith Street rebuilding Sale. Daughter Margaret, Bill, John Couch, Edna Butt, Bert Coutanche.

When the builders took up the wooden floor in the shop, they found a large drain that served the area of the prison and the Royal Court, running from one side of my property to the other. The States Building Inspectors required the drain to be protected by a framework of steel girders and covered with concrete. I, of course, paid for all that extra work.

Clearly, I could only embark on such a large expenditure, if I had the backing of the bank. Alec Hooley, the Manager of Midland Bank was very supportive and I soon found myself servicing a substantial overdraft. As I was operating with the bank's money, Alec came up one day to look at the premises to see where the money was going. He looked around and said to me.

"By jove Bill, you have got some very fine premises here. Do you want to sell them ?"

"No way !" I said, "My Father started business in Smith Street, not in these premises, but almost next door. I won't pull out of Smith Street. My daughter may, in years to come, but I will not."

As far as I was concerned that was the end of the matter and put Alec's inquiry to the back of my mind. My thinking was that, as I became older, it might not be

Bill Green, President of Chamber of Commerce.

possible for me to run a motorcycle business but I was sure that I would be capable of running a cycle shop. Events however, were to dictate a different course. When the builders eventually completed their work, I moved the cycle side of my business back to Smith Street.

I considered it a very great honour, when on the 19th April 1963 I was elected President of the Guernsey Chamber of Commerce. I was proposed as President by Frank Stroobant and seconded by Rex Bragg. After my election, I paid a tribute to Ted Laker, whom I succeeded as President and thanked him for the great work he had done on behalf of Chamber during his period of office. He was, consequently, a difficult man to follow.

I had long been associated with the Chamber, first as a subscribing member, then as a member of Council and since 1954 as a Vice President. I must have been one of the longest serving Vice Presidents in Chamber of Commerce history. I was first elected as Junior Vice President under the Presidency of Mr C.J McCathie. When Ted Laker was elected President I became Senior Vice President.

One of my first actions, after taking office, was to make a thorough study of the origins and history of the Guernsey Chamber of Commerce. I was helped in this task by the fact that there are still, in Chamber's possession, a great many minute books and records stretching way back into the last century.

The Guernsey Chamber of Commerce was constituted in its present form on the 16th December 1808. However the Channel Islands led the way in the formation of Chambers of Commerce. The Original Jersey Chamber was formed in 1768, and the Guernsey Chamber soon afterwards in 1769. In the United Kingdom the first Chamber was not formed until 1783, when the Glasgow Chamber of Commerce came into being.

The Chamber was formed primarily to suppress smuggling. For many years prior to 1808 Guernsey merchants played a big part in the 'free and illicit trade' of the island, to the dismay of the Customs Authorities. The island achieved great prosperity from that 'industry'. For a long time local traders turned a deaf ear to the British Government's plea that a stop should be made to these practices and that a Customs-House should be erected in the island.

Finally, in 1808, there was a change of heart in Guernsey, I suspect largely brought about by self-interest, and it was resolved to co-operate wholeheartedly with the authorities in the eradication of smuggling. The fact that this 'free trade' died out locally, was chiefly due to the Guernsey Chamber of Commerce. On December 16th, 1808 a General Meeting of traders and merchants took place in rooms at the Market Place, which Daniel de Lisle Brock chaired. So the Guernsey Chamber of Commerce, was constituted in its present form, with Daniel de Lisle Brock as its President.

One of the first events I was involved in as President was the visit to Guernsey by the President of St Briac Chamber of Commerce. He and his party were entertained by my two Vice Presidents and myself. I was interested to learn that French Chambers of Commerce possessed considerably greater powers than we had, those being vested in them by French Law. There is a compulsory requirement for French Companies to become members of their local Chambers of Commerce.

Amongst my early duties I visited Basle, at the invitation of the British European Airways. Afterwards, I took the opportunity to extend my visit by having a short holiday in Switzerland. As part of the trip had been for pleasure, I felt that I should make a contribution towards the cost and accordingly sent a cheque to the Treasurer of the Guernsey Chamber. It was my way of saying thank you for the invitation I had received from British European Airways. I got into trouble with the Chamber Council over my donation, as they felt that I was representing the Chamber and should not therefore make a contribution.

British European Airways, who operated into the island in those days, were very keen to capture a share of our freight business. I invited a delegation led by Mr R B Crabtree, their London based Cargo Sales Officer, to a Special General Meeting of the Chamber so that our members could judge for themselves the practicality of transporting freight by air. We were shown a film called 'Gateway to Europe', which depicted how modern jet aircraft, could carry freight to all parts of Europe.

As President, I expressed the view that we were living in an age of progress and change and that many of the old traditional methods of trading were changing. Guernsey traders would have to adapt and change with the times. As always, members were more concerned with what it would cost them. The response of Frank Stroobant, my Senior Vice President, was typical - he insisted that traders wanted goods Carriage-Paid to Guernsey, which meant that the transport arrangements would have to be made by the manufacturers at the airport or port of departure. I had tried to get members to be more forward looking but, as usual, they were more concerned with the contents of their wallet today, rather than the opportunities of tomorrow.

Around the time I became President, Green Shield Stamps were in their heyday in the United Kingdom. Many of our members, particularly those in the Motor Agents Association, the petrol retailers, were concerned that Stamp Trading would spread to Guernsey and be detrimental to their businesses. In the United Kingdom, trading stamps had become an extremely popular way of promoting sales, particularly in the petrol and grocery trades. The matter was debated at one of our quarterly meetings and it was clear that members felt that the introduction of trading stamps would have an adverse effect, both on the profitability of local businesses and the price of goods to consumers.

I approached the President of the Advisory and Finance Committee, explained our concern, and requested that consideration should be given to making trading stamps illegal in Guernsey. As a result a special investigation Committee, headed by Deputy C.K.Frossard, was set up to look into the whole issue.

When the Committee presented its conclusions, they could not see the need to ban trading stamps. They were un-convinced that they would have an adverse effect on the island's economy but did however propose that legislation be introduced to regulate their issue, use and redemption. An important clause in the resulting Law was that any promoter of trading stamps must deposit, or secure a sum of money with the States, to be used in the event of the promoter going into liquidation. In the event there were no attempts made to introduce trading stamps into Guernsey.

On the 22nd November 1963, President Kennedy was tragically assassinated in Dallas. On behalf of the Chamber, I sent a message of condolence to the American Ambassador in London. Ambassador David Bruce sent me an official acknowledgement. Unbeknown to me, in sending that message, I had repeated history.

Cecil Gicquel, who was the Secretary of the Chamber of Commerce for over thirty years, and I were clearing out our office and meeting room at Austin House in the old Star newspaper premises in the Bordage, when we came across a very old book. It was dirty with age and contained the dust of years. Thumbing through the book, I became interested in its contents, so I took it home for closer inspection. Mabs was fascinated with the book and found that it contained all the messages of condolences sent by people and organisations from all over world at the time of the assassination of President Abraham Lincoln.

Included were details of the Guernsey Chamber of Commerce's Resolution passed at a General meeting, held on the 2nd of May 1865.

'Resolved, That this Chamber, deeply impressed with horror at the intelligence recently received from America of the assassination of President Lincoln, and others, thinks it a duty to publicly express its abhorrence of such dastardly crimes, the authors of which deserve the execration of mankind.

The inhabitants of these Norman islands of the Channel, the apex of the great Norman Anglo-Saxon social edifice, venture to hope that the fratricidal struggle that has endured in America during a period of four years, and affording on both sides so many proofs of heroism and endurance, may be closed, and, uniting again, peace and prosperity may be restored throughout America ; and that the great Norman Anglo-Saxon family in all its branches throughout both hemispheres, all sprung from the same race, may hereafter live in brotherly union and love, contributing to the happiness and welfare of each and all, and giving the world a bright example of concord, progress, and civilization.

Thos. Helary Agnew, Secretary.'

It was a strange coincidence that we should find that book so soon after I sent the message of condolence to the American Ambassador. I wrote again to David Bruce and told him of our find. After the book was rebound, I sent it to him for his inspection. The Ambassador responded;-

"It was not a coincidence, but rather an indication that your members continue to entertain strong feelings of friendship for my country."

He went on to say that a copy of the Resolution passed by the Guernsey Chamber of Commerce in 1865 had been forwarded to the Kennedy Memorial Library, in Cambridge, Massachusetts, together with a copy of my letter.

We also found other historical documents on the formation of the Chamber of Commerce, dating back to the early eighteen hundreds. I felt that the book and documents should be placed in safe custody and they were accordingly offered to the Priaulx Library on permanent loan. The value of these documents and book is recognised by the fact that a note of their existence is included, each year, in the Chamber's annual accounts.

Over the years I had been a strong critic of British Railways, but during my period of office as President of the Chamber of Commerce, I found myself defending that nationalised industry.

As a result of the Labour Government's nationalisation of the United Kingdom railway system, the ferry services between Guernsey and the mainland became part of British Railways. Rumours started circulating in the island that British Railways were contemplating pulling out of the Guernsey service. The nationalised Board issued a statement from their London Headquarters categorically denying the rumour. The moment the denial appeared in our press, I realised the damage that such stories, true or false, could have to the island and our tourist trade.

I set about trying to trace the source of the rumour. I quickly discovered that there were several business interests involved in plans to run shipping services into the island. Some of these had little or no financial backing whatsoever, being merely promoters who thought up schemes in the hope of subsequently raising the money.

It transpired that two of these promoters had written to British Railways suggesting that they might be glad to close the unprofitable Channel Islands routes. These 'Gentlemen' would then offer to set up a Company to run new services. They claimed that they had 'official' support for their proposal. As President of Chamber I contacted British Railways and they assured me that they had no intention of withdrawing from the service. I was therefore able to reassure traders and the public alike that, contrary to pulling out, British Railways were planning to improve the service.

I suggested that too much criticism had been levied at British Railways from the island of late and, if continued, it could only undermine the service. I said that, in my view, it was in every islander's interest to see that British Railways operated at a profit and so ensure the continuance of the fine service that we had enjoyed for so long. Jumping on the band wagon of cheap rates might be to our short term advantage, but could result in long term tragedy. British Railways had placed orders for two new passenger ships for the Channel Islands run which, I felt, showed the confidence that they placed in the future of the service.

I emphasised that the economy of the island was bound up in sea transport for as far into the future as it was possible to see. It was therefore extremely important that we did not place ourselves in the hands of any organisation that could, because of changed circumstances, pull out and leave us high and dry.

As a strong critic of nationalised industries and a firm believer in private enterprise and competition, I found it difficult to justify my temporary conversion. When a press reporter challenged me on my apparent transformation, I responded by saying :

"No doubt I shall continue to be a critic of nationalisation, but I always try to be constructive, rather than destructive".

My public comments, and a letter which appeared in the Evening Press over my signature, caused an inquest to be held at the next meeting of the Chamber of Commerce Council. Rex Bragg felt that I should have consulted my two Vice Presidents before making any public statement on the matter. However at the end of the discussion the majority of the Council members supported my action.

At the end of my year as President of Chamber, I was nominated for a further term. Again I was unopposed and was re-elected by acclamation. In view of the response, I felt that the members must have been satisfied with the way I had led the Chamber during my year of office, and that gave me the confidence to continue.

It was at that Annual General Meeting that I raised the concept of a Conference Hall for Guernsey. This idea was enthusiastically taken up by members, who envisaged it as a multi-purpose building which could be a financial success and of great benefit to both islanders and tourists. A conference hall, I suggested, could incorporate a sports centre, a dance hall and other amenities. With the support of the membership, I arranged a meeting with the States Tourist committee. That was the start of the Beau Sejour project.

At the Annual General Meeting in 1965, I handed over as President to Frank Stroobant. So ended a very enjoyable two year period in the service of the Guernsey Chamber of Commerce.

My speech at the Annual General Meeting was fully reported, and the 'leader' in the Guernsey Evening Press commented :-

> 'In an outstanding speech, the retiring President of the Guernsey Chamber of Commerce Mr Bill Green, drew attention to the near static position of our Horticultural industry, and the fact that we are approaching saturation point in the field of Tourism. He therefore suggested another way, in which to bring prosperity to the island, that Guernsey should absorb large investment in property in the island. Whether or not this is a good idea, is a matter of opinion, but the fact remains that the Chamber of Commerce is a live body, and it is fully aware of its duties. Its virility is especially marked in the Young Businessmen's Group.

> The ideas of this section of the Chamber, auger a most successful future for that ancient yet 'with- it' body.
>
> Mr Green is a good speaker, and in his speech he was able to put over what the Chamber had done, and in his opinion what it ought to do in the future. Membership is good, but it should be a great deal better, for union is strength, and given greater support this local organisation could do a great deal more for the islands benefit, than it is capable of doing at the present time. As to what the Chamber does, one has only to read Mr Green's report to find out, the Guernsey Chamber of Commerce is a great power for good in the island, and its future seems to be in good hands. If this is so, we may safely believe that the island itself is heading in the right direction, which is consolation indeed.'

Since the war the Chamber's involvement in policy formation within the community, had not been as effective or as great as I would have liked. The French Chambers of Commerce have powers and legal status, which our Chamber has not, so in comparison what we can achieve is limited. Any success we may have, can only be achieved by example and by leadership. To that extent the selection of the President and other officers of the Chamber is of paramount importance. A President who is a good leader ensures a successful Chamber of Commerce. I have known Presidents who have had the necessary leadership qualities and under their leadership the Chamber flourished. Regretfully we have also had Presidents without those qualities. Frank Stroobant had outstanding leadership qualities and proved to be an exceptionally able President.

Chamber's role in the Guernsey business and commercial world is difficult to define or quantify. Over the years I think it has been as much as anything, a sounding board. Of course, one of its main duties is to represent its membership and allow their voice to be heard in the corridors of government.

During my period as President I sought to encourage better relationships with other Chambers, than had previously existed. I felt that in Guernsey we were a little too isolated, particularly from a business point of view. I believed that by working together with other Chambers we would achieve a unity through which we would be better able to talk and negotiate with the various 'Authorities', including the British Government. Unity, I believed, was strength and organisations such as our's could exert more influence than individuals !

I was very keen to bring about a better working relationship between the Jersey Chamber of Commerce and ourselves. I got in touch with Mrs S.Le Brocq, their Secretary and together we set in motion plans for holding the first ever joint meeting between the two Chambers. Regretfully we were not able to hold that historic first meeting during my Presidency. However, after a number of false starts, the meeting was held in St Helier on the 8th December 1965. Our President, Frank Stroobant, led the Guernsey delegation, of which I was proud to be a member. We discussed matters of common interest, including the British entry into the Common Market and the possibility of a Channel Tunnel.

The joint meetings have now become an annual event and I was glad when the Alderney Chamber was invited to participate. In recent years the Isle of Man Chamber also attends the inter island meetings. I like to think that I was partially responsible for initiating this liaison between island Chambers of Commerce.

Chapter 32

DEEP FINANCIAL TROUBLE

On the 27th February 1965, Mabs and I celebrated our silver wedding at La Fregate, probably at that time the best restaurant in the island. A few weeks later I came home from business late one Saturday evening in April and found a chair in the middle of the hall with a note from Mabs. She had left me and said that it was her intention to sue for divorce. I was shattered, I knew that our marriage had been going through a difficult time, largely due to my continuing relationship with a long time girlfriend, but certainly I had not realised that Mabs was about to take such drastic action after twenty five years of marriage.

Mabs had left home and I did not know where or how to find her. I telephoned every friend of hers that I could think of, but no one knew or was prepared to tell me where she was staying. She drove a little Vespa car, so I kept an eye open for that in the hope of finding Mabs.

It dawned on me one day that she might have gone to stay with Mrs De Putron, who lived in a large house, Pierre Percy, in Prince Albert's Road. I drove down to have a look and, sure enough, parked behind a large granite wall was Mabs little Vespa. As I drove down the drive and past the house I recognised Mabs through the window, but as soon as she saw me, she ducked down out of sight. At least I knew where she was living.

A friend of mine with whom I regularly swam, Jim Foster, told me that Mabs was suing for divorce, he had seen the official notice displayed at the Greffe. That was the first time I was aware that Mabs was actually carrying out her threat and taking the matter to Court. I went down to look at the notice in the Greffe, Jim was correct, I was being sued for divorce and Advocate Peter Collas was acting for Mabs. I knew Peter and went to see him and forceably made my views known.

"I learnt about the proceedings from a friend of mine." I said. "When you want to do anything to your property", his premises were adjacent to mine, "you come and ask me if you can put a ladder on my property, yet you haven't the decency to tell me I am being sued for divorce, and I am very upset about it !"

He was apologetic, but pointed out equally forcefully that he was representing Mabs in a purely professional capacity.

Advocate Peter Collas represented Mabs in the Royal Court on the 22nd October 1965 when her petition for divorce was granted.

A report in the Guernsey Evening Press of Saturday, 23 October 1965 read :

> 'Mr Collas appearing for Mrs Mabel Vera Green who's address at the time the petition was filed, was Lyndel, Jerbourg, St Martin's. Mrs Green was granted a provisional degree with costs. Her petition was on the grounds of cruelty by her husband Mr William Green of Lyndel, Jerbourg, St Martin's.
>
> Giving judgement the Bailiff, Sir William Arnold, said it was abundantly clear that here was a marriage that began in February

1940, and only a few years afterwards had began to go off the rails. If it had broken, plainly, it was through no fault of the petitioner who had done all she could through a great many unhappy, and anxious, years to save the marriage.

But it had been said in the authorities that cruelty was a most difficult ground. A marriage that had broken down was no reason in itself to find cruelty. The Bailiff said he had come to the conclusion that over a period of some twenty years the husband had known that his conduct was causing his wife great distress. It was because of an accumulation of incidents he found it proper to make a provisional order that the marriage be dissolved'.

I felt absolutely torn apart and totally shattered. There was no doubt in my mind, I was the guilty party and it preyed on me to such an extent that I virtually hid myself away. I kept myself out of circulation. I withdrew from all my normal activities. My business life was affected as I tried to avoid contact with customers. Whenever I went to the shop, I kept in my office out of the way. It took me a long time to settle down afterwards.

After the provisional order, a settlement had to be agreed between Mabs and me, or rather between our Advocates. Mabs was now represented by Advocate Graham Dorey, and Advocate Le Pelley acted for me. Mabs, understandably, was very bitter at that time, so much so we were writing letters to each other, through our Advocates, which were costing a small fortune. The legal profession was having a very profitable time at my expense.

Eventually I said to Advocate Le Pelley,:

"I am sick and tired of all this costly time wasting, I will make an offer and if that is not acceptable, then the matter of the settlement can go to court. This" and I detailed my offer, "is what I am prepared to do, I will not go any further."

My offer was accepted and the settlement then had only to be formally agreed by the Royal Court.

Part of the divorce settlement was that I would pass Lyndel over to Mabs and that I would move out. In the meantime, once the provisional decree had been granted, Mabs moved out of the room she had rented in Mrs De Putron's house and into one of the flats above the Smith Street shop.

By this time Margaret had left my business. After spells working in Italy and Switzerland, and being a water ski instructor, she was running her own flower arrangement company in the Guernsey. She had been living above her business in the Bouet, but moved into the flat with her mother. Between them, they had only a very limited amount of furniture and household equipment. I believe that they started off with just two beds, a couple of chairs, a table and a cooker. Margaret continued running her business, Floral Art Limited and Mabs gave her a hand. Amid all the sadness of our divorce, Mabs and I were thrilled at the news that Margaret had accepted a proposal of marriage from Tony Talbot-Cull.

As I was due to leave Lyndel I set about finding a new home for myself. Ben Lovell of Lovell and Partners, the Estate Agents, found a new bungalow in Gele Close, Castel, which suited me. In early 1966 I purchased it with a ten year mortgage, the maximum period the bank would allow because of my age. Prior to moving out of Lyndel I worked hard trying to leave the bungalow that had been our home for twenty years, in almost perfect condition. I decorated it throughout and even the garden was in a reasonably tidy condition. It kept me occupied whilst I was trying to to withdraw from all my normal pastimes.

Mabs, some years before our divorce, lost her wedding ring when she was hanging out the washing. I bought her a replacement, but it was never the same. One day while I was digging in the garden, I found the lost wedding ring. I thought it was an omen that might put things right between us but, of course, it didn't.

I had withdrawn from everything, I even gave up going swimming. My friends reacted in different ways, some sought me out and encouraged me to get on with my life, while others totally ignored me. Eric Martin, who will always be one of my special friends, wrote to me, and I still have the letter, saying; "Bill, whatever the circumstances or whatever is wrong, we would still like to see you."

Eric and a group of us regularly went swimming at the Valette pool early in the morning. The fact that they wanted me to rejoin them did a great deal for my morale. I shall always be grateful to Eric for writing such an understanding letter, just when I was at what was probably the my lowest point in my life. I will treasure that letter for as long as I live

I didn't feel like returning to any of my former activities until I was invited back. I was a non-States member of the Water Board. I wrote to the President, Alan Mackay and asked him to excuse me from attending meetings. He wrote back and enquired, in a most tactful way, what type of cruelty had been involved. Mabs had, in the divorce petition sued on grounds of cruelty, which I found very damaging to my reputation. Mabs claimed that she suffered mental cruelty, whereas many of my friends and acquaintances assumed it to be physical cruelty. People thought that I had been knocking Mabs about.

I wrote back explaining that it was mental cruelty and Alan replied saying; "I and the Board would very much like you to come back to Water Board meetings," which I eventually did, but it took me a long time.

For a number of years, I kept as low a profile as possible, withdrawing from nearly all my former activities. I still ran the business, though it was running itself really, Edna Butt was looking after the Smith Street cycle shop while Bert Coutanche was managing the George Street motorcycle garage.

I travelled to various parts of the world, in many ways just to get away from the Guernsey environment. I went to the Canaries twice with an old friend of Dad's, Stan Machin. Richard Moore, who at that time was establishing his highly successful King's Club, also came along. I became very friendly with Richard and Joyce Moore. I went and lived in their house when they were away and looked after their two children. Actually I only supervised the children, because they had a maid who did all the work. On other occasions I visited Los Angeles, and Newfoundland.

An old pal who stood by me during my period of self-imposed purdah was 'Stroo', Frank Stroobant. We had been great buddies back in our school and motorcycling days. He and I had also been closely involved in the Chamber of Commerce. Because we found ourselves very much in the same circumstances, both without wives, we became close friends again.

His wife, Gladys had died in 1959. Prior to my divorce, when Mabs and I had been at odds, he and I spent quite a lot of time together. 'Stroo' is good fun and, although a natural clown, he can also be a thoroughly good friend and adviser. And that is just what 'Stroo' was to me when I needed a good friend and sound advice.

Around this time 'Stroo' met a very glamourous lady, called 'Siggy' who was a divorcee. 'Siggy' originated from Germany, and came to Guernsey with her first husband. After a while 'Stroo' announced that they were going to get married and would I be his best man. I was delighted to accept and was very happy for them both when they were married by the Greffier, in the ballroom of their home in St Martin.

'Siggy' has made 'Stroo' a wonderful wife, he is a very lucky man. I can imagine that he is not the easiest person to live with, but she has coped with him well, although I think the first year or so was a little turbulent at times. I recall getting a number of telephone calls from 'Stroo' to the effect:

"Come and sort us out, we're having a row, it's all your fault, you were my best man!"

As a result of my divorce, which had been very costly, and the cost of the repairs and renovations to the Smith Street premises, I was running an overdraft of around £30,000. That was a great deal of money in those days, and naturally the Midland Bank was concerned. Alec Hooley, the bank manager, became very nervous as to my financial position, so much so that I was having to go and see him about three times a week. He constantly wanted facts and figures so that he could furnish his head office with a constant stream of reports on my situation. I was in deep financial trouble and having tremendous difficulty in keeping Alec and the bank from foreclosing on me.

Before the war, when Dad and Mum were running their boarding house at Seaplane Bungalow, one of their regular visitors was a family called Machin. They returned year after year and Stan Machin became very friendly with Dad. After the war Stan retired and came to Guernsey to live. He and I became good friends and one day we were talking about my problems with the bank. Suddenly he said:

"Ah! to hell with them, here's a cheque for £5,000, put it in the bank."

It was an outright gift, not a loan, but I repaid him eventually. I went into the bank and personally gave the cheque to Alec Hooley. It saved the day as far as I was concerned. Stan Machin, after hearing of the bank's reaction, said to me :

"You tell him that if he wants some more, he can have some more."

I have always been grateful to Stan for his timely help. But for him, I dread to think what might have happened to me and my business.

As a result of my divorce, I for the first time in my life had to look after myself. I had to cook my own meals, wash and iron my own shirts, darn my own socks, do all my own housework - no longer could I look to Mabs, or Mum, to look after my every need.

Edgar and Jane Stacey were very good to me and regularly invited me to Sunday lunch. Jane was a marvellous cook and I really looked forward to Sundays.

I once boasted to Edgar that I was as capable as Mabs at doing all my own cooking and housework. Of course he didn't agree.

"You say you can do without Mabs - just look at your larder, its full of tins - nothing else. I grant you, you're handy with a tin opener !"

"I can do what Mabs can do." I insisted.

"At one time your socks were darned by your mother, then Mabs took over. What happens now you throw them away and buy some new ones"

Defending myself, I responded, "I have bought myself a sewing machine"

"Yes, and look what a mess you make with that, backwards and forwards, up and down, trying to repair the holes. I have seen your socks, with cycle patches, one each side over the hole. You haven't got the touch Bill, you have got it on a motorcycle and you have got it in the water, but not in the house."

The trouble was, Edgar was right.

Margaret, so that she could be near her future husband Tony, sold her company Floral Art Ltd to Mabs and went to live in Oxford. She obtained a position with Jaeger, the fashion company. Mabs enjoyed running her own commercial company, which she carried on doing for about two years before selling it to a friend.

Margaret and Tony Talbot-Cull were married in a Registry Office in Oxford, and held their wedding reception at the Randolph Hotel. I think that Mabs was disappointed that they were not married in St Martin's Church, but as Margaret put it:

"We would have needed a four sided church, as both Tony's and my parents were divorced."

For their honeymoon, they drove all the way to Yugoslavia and back in a little Vespa car that I lent them. The car was loaded down with so much luggage and gear, I'd be surprised if they ever managed to go faster than thirty miles per hour.

Tony was employed at the Churchill Hospital in Oxford, as a medical scientist specialising in Haematology. Later he obtained a position at St John's Hospital in Newfoundland. Margaret and Tony were in Newfoundland for six years and while they were there my two grandchildren, William and Fiona, were born. When each came along, I flew out to see them, trips which I thoroughly enjoyed. When Margaret and her family left Newfoundland, Tony took up a post at Southampton General Hospital.

Chapter 33

A SAD END TO A WONDERFUL FRIEND

In 1966 Mr David died. He was the owner and proprietor of the music shop at 21 Smith Street. It wasn't long before Mrs David, his widow, put the premises on the market. I recalled Alec Hooley's interest in my property and saw the possibility of transferring my business to the other side of the street. There was a back entrance into Forest Lane, a facility which I had never possessed, but always felt my business needed. I approached Mrs David and she expressed her willingness to sell the property to me for £27,500. I then went and talked to Alec, and he on behalf of Midland Bank readily agreed to purchase my premises for £45,000.

I felt that was a good deal as far as I was concerned, it would allow me to obtain more suitable premises and pay off the overdraft that I still had as a result of the improvements I had carried out to my present premises. After mulling the idea over for a few days, I decided to go ahead on that basis.

But before I committed myself to the deal, I needed to ensure that my tenants would be suitably re-located or adequately protected. In the event only one was affected, Mr Percy Rabey who ran the bookshop next door to my cycle shop. Although I was aware that he was suffering from ill health and had talked of retiring, I was deeply concerned for the future of his business. Whilst he had no lease, he had been in business and my tenant for over thirty years. He had the benefit of a low rent and I did not want to do anything which would adversely affect the continuation of his business.

Part of my proposed deal with Mrs David included the shop next door to the music shop. It was run by Mr G.L.Cohen, trading as 'De Paris'. I was able to negotiate with him, that he would vacate the premises on completion of my deal with Mrs David. It was arranged, therefore, that Rabey's bookshop could transfer their business to the other side of Smith Street. Having made all the necessary arrangements, I approached Mr Rabey, and explained my reasons for selling and offered him the tenancy of the shop opposite. Percy Rabey thanked me for being so considerate, but said that he had decided to retire. So all my planning and scheming on his behalf was of no avail.

My Advocates were Martel & Le Pelley and they also acted for Midland Bank. Advocate Le Pelley also happened to be Mrs David's brother-in-law. We all met in the Advocate's Office, before signing the necessary documents and paying our respective deposits, Alec Hooley said:

"Midland Bank's deposit is dependant on us getting change of use of Mr Green's premises as a bank."

"Is that necessary Mr Hooley ?" Advocate Le Pelley asked.

"Yes, last month the Island Development Committee took on powers that allow them to control the change of use of buildings. They haven't used them yet, but just as a precaution, I wish that condition inserted into the contract."

Advocate Le Pelley telephoned Vernon Luff, the secretary to the Island Development Committee, and asked if that was the situation.

"Yes" Vernon Luff said, "that is now the law, but of course the object is to stop a wet fish shop opening up next to a jewellers, or a butchers next to the Town Church or something incompatible like that, but there should not be too much problem with a bank."

But, never-the-less Alec Hooley insisted on the inclusion of the condition. So Advocate Le Pelley said: "Well Bill, you had better put the same proviso on opening a cycle shop in Mrs David's premises," to which I agreed.

What none of us anticipated, was the possibility that I would get permission for the change of use of the Music shop, while the Midland Bank would be refused consent for the change of use of my premises - and that is what happened !

Tom Ogier, the President of the Island Development Committee, had been the Chief Officer of Police in Trinidad before returning to his home island to retire. He was a very formidable character, who had a mind of his own and a determination to get his own way. Over the years, as President of the Island Development Committee, he ruffled many feathers. He was dedicated to the retention of Guernsey's character and looking after Guernseymen in preference to outsiders. A philosophy that I fully supported.

Tom and his Committee wanted to see Smith Street retained as a shopping area and not turned into another Throgmorton Street, where no one but businessmen went.

After we all signed the contracts, we were supposed to complete within two to three months. I received my planning permission for the change of use of the music shop, but Alec was furious at being refused. He went back to the Island Development Committee with various amended applications, but with no success. Unbeknown to me, Midland Bank had further discussions and negotiations with the Committee, during which they were offered five alternatives sites for their bank. Also many details of my business and personal affairs were apparently discussed. I was furious when I learned of these secret discussions and, as I put in writing at the time, 'What dammed right had you to do this... I was never consulted'.

As long as the bank was refused permission, the deposit it had paid me was safe, but my deposit with Mrs David was at risk. I could not complete the purchase of the music shop until I was assured that my sale to Midland Bank was certain to be completed.

One day Mrs David asked:

"Mr Green, are you going to complete the transaction ?"

"Mrs David I can't do that unless I sell my premises and there is this problem with the Island Development Committee."

Mrs David was very good and said:

"I need to sell, so if I dispose of the shop to someone else, below the price you have offered, I will take it out of your deposit and refund you the balance. If I sell it for the same price, then I will refund your deposit in full."

That was very fair because, in law, she was entitled to keep the whole of my deposit, whatever price she obtained for the property.

In the meantime, Alec Hooley, as a result of his negotiations with the Island Development Committee, submitted a further application, in which he proposed to retain two shops on the Smith Street frontage and use the rest of the premises for banking purposes.

One Saturday in October 1967, I was walking down Smith Street, when Mrs David stopped me and said:

"Mr Green, I have sold my premises, and I have received £750 less than your offer, so I will take that out of your deposit and refund you the balance of £2,000".

"Mrs David," I said, "I'm very sad, but thank you very much - you have been very kind and very fair."

On the following Monday, Midland Bank received permission to convert my premises for banking use.

So I had lost part of my deposit, incurred considerable expense in architect's fees, had failed to buy the music shop and was legally committed to selling my premises. After almost sixty years, Greens were being forced out of Smith Street. I felt I had let Dad down. Regrettably, there was no way I could renege on the sale of my premises, other than to repay the Midland Bank their deposit and a further sum to match it, I could not afford a further £4,500. So I was out of Smith Street. I held the Island Development Committee totally responsible for the mess in which I found myself.

Tom Ogier advocated Guernsey for the Guernseyman and what had he achieved ? He'd driven a Guernseyman out of Smith Street and allowed in two English investors ! I had warned him that if, as a result of his Committee's actions, I was forced out of Smith Street, I would 'scream to high heaven', and that is what I did.

I published an advertisement in the Guernsey Press detailing the whole saga. When I submitted the copy, the Press passed it to a Advocate to ensure that it was not libellous in any way. In the circumstances, I was surprised how much of it they passed for publication !

So, on the 29th February 1968, I closed the door and locked up the shop in Smith Street for the last time. Another locally-run and owned business in St Peter Port had closed. It was a very sad day for me and I believe a sad day for Guernsey.

With the sale of the property to the Midland Bank, I was able to pay off my overdraft for the first time in many years. At peak, when I was renovating Smith Street, it had risen to an all time high of £33,000.

I transferred my cycle business to George Street, but it was never the same. The days when almost every islander owned a cycle were over and never to return. Even the motorcycle business had shrunk. At the peak I had employed twenty-one staff between Smith Street and George Street, but by the early seventies that number was well down and profits had also become a lot slimmer.

It was obvious to me that I would have to take up a major car agency if I wanted to stay in business. It was not just my business that was affected, the same decline was happening to every motorcycle business in the island. The national pattern was just the same and, to survive, we all needed a car agency. In Guernsey there were very few, if any, available, most motor manufacturers had been represented in the island for many years. The only agency that was obtainable was Skoda, which was manufactured in Czechoslovakia. A very good car from an engineering point of view, but certainly not the best prospect in respect of potential car sales. So, somewhat reluctantly, I took on the Skoda agency for Guernsey and imported quite a number of their vehicles.

I traded profitably for a number of years before, Paul Le Page approached me in 1973 and said he wished to buy the George Street property and the business. I was also approached by a property developer by the name of Brauch, who at the time, was buying up a lot of property in Guernsey. In my view he was a mysterious character, who was prepared to pay big money for what he bought. He only wanted my property, not the business. He was not a Guernseyman and I didn't like him, so I had no truck with him. I wanted the business to continue, and although he tempted me with a very good price, almost 50% more than Paul had offered, I refused. I was too much of a Guernseyman to sell it to a property speculator. I only wish that over the years other islanders would have had the courage to follow my example.

My daughter Margaret, who at that time was still living in Newfoundland, was the only person who might possibly have wished me to continue to run the business. I flew out to see her and ask if I should sell. She said:

"Yes Dad, sell and retire you have been in business for almost 50 years and I am not interested in taking over".

So that was settled, I would accept Paul's offer of £45,000, and retire. I was sixty three, but still had some unfulfilled ambitions.

After having been seen off by Margaret and her family, I was sitting in St John's Airport in Newfoundland, waiting to catch the plane on my way back home to Guernsey. It was mid winter, it had been snowing very heavily and was extremely cold. After a long wait we were flown up to Gander Airport, with the intention of connecting with the transatlantic flight from Halifax, Nova Scotia, that would take us to Heathrow by way of Shannon.

After being at Gander for some time, we learnt that the Halifax plane was not going to materialize due to the rapidly worsening weather conditions. It was announced that we were going to be flown back to St Johns. I could see the plane we had previously travelled on, it was now covered in snow and ice. How, I thought, are they ever going to get that aircraft into the air and what chance was there of it flying to St Johns. However, the airport authorities wheeled out two de-icing spray units and proceeded to spray the aircraft. While we stood in the warmth of the passenger lounge we watched the ice and snow melt and fall from the aircraft. After that demonstration of de-icing, I felt much happier about travelling back to St Johns.

Back at St Johns the airline announced that they would take us to The New Inn, a local hotel, where we would be put up for the night at their expense.

When it was time to get on the coach to go to The New Inn there was one passenger, a small man, sitting on a cardboard box, who refused all attempts to get him to join the rest of the party. All he would say was:

"London, London," and he refused to budge.

The Airline staff, the Airport officials, all tried to get him to join us on the coach, but still he refused to move. I went over and tried to communicate with him, but he couldn't speak a word of English, so I resorted to sign language. After a while, he responded by pulling the linings of his pocket out, to show me that he had no money and saying:

"Nein geld".

After a while I persuaded him to join us on the coach. He was very reluctant and very hesitant, but he came. He was totally overwhelmed by the whole situation and it seemed that I was the only person who could 'communicate' with him. Next morning we were flown to Montreal and, as our new connecting flight was not due until the evening, I took the opportunity to go into Montreal and look around the City. My new-found friend couldn't be persuaded to join me, he just wanted to stay in the passenger lounge. I sat him down near the entry to the Gentleman's toilet and went into Montreal by coach. After I had spent a very pleasant few hours exploring the City, I returned to the airport and 'my friend' was still sitting where I had left him.

When we arrived at Shannon, in Ireland, he wouldn't get out of the plane. All he would say was:

"London,London".

On the flight over, he showed me a letter, it was written by a Doctor from the hospital at St John's, which explained that he was a Polish fisherman from one of the fishing boat's of the White fleet that fished the waters off Newfoundland. The letter explained that he had recently undergone a serious abdominal operation and would anyone reading the letter please take care of him and help him to get back to Warsaw. He had no papers and no passport. He didn't even know what message the letter contained. I read it and understood it and indicated to him that everything would be all right. He had become my 'baby'.

When we eventually arrived at Heathrow, I managed to take him as far as

Immigration and Customs. There I explained the situation to a Customs Officer, who sent for one of their liaison officers. She was a very charming girl, I told her that I felt responsible for him and wanted to make sure he caught the plane to Warsaw.

"You can trust me to see that he gets on the Warsaw plane," she said, "I will take him through all the passport formalities, it will be OK."

I left him with her and that was the last I saw of him. He wouldn't give me his address, but I gave him mine.

Sometime after, I received a card through the post from him which simply said in English, 'Thank you for good conduct.' As simple as that, and on the card was his address. I was in 'correspondence' with him and his family for almost fifteen years, then I received a photograph from his widow, of him lying in state in his coffin. I found that a touch macabre, but apparently that is what they do in Poland.

After arriving back home in Guernsey, I had a chat with Mabs and she also advised:

"Sell the business".

So I told Paul that his offer was accepted. I was keen to see the business, which first Dad and then I had built up, carried on. I wanted to ensure that my staff, who had always been very loyal to me, would continue to be employed in the business. I took Paul to see many of our suppliers and generally tried to ensure that the change over took place as smoothly as possible. Unfortunately Paul did not have the same interest in motorcycles as I did, motorcycles were not for him, he was happier selling cars. He obtained the agency for Colt Cars and ran a very successful business for many years.

On the day I retired from business, I held a party at a restaurant in Fountain Street, in the same building where I was born. All the staff who were with me when I retired attended. I made a short speech telling them;

"I was born in this building some 63 years ago."

We had an excellent dinner and during the party that followed I made little presentations to each of my staff. I am glad to say I still regularly bump into many of my former employees, who I now proudly number amongst my many friends.

Frank Stroobant and I sold our businesses and retired very much at the same time. One day, 'Stroo' enquired:-

"How have you done Bill, have you sold out all right ?"

"Yes, I think I have done all right."

By todays standards, I didn't have a lot of money, but in those days it seemed more than adequate.

"Each year," 'Stroo' said, "I have re-invested 10% of my income to cope with future inflation."

"Do you think it is necessary to put that much aside,'Stroo' ?"

"Well it won't hurt, I would advise you to do it."

I took his advice, and have tucked away 10% of my income every year, without fail. In consequence my capital is now very much larger than it would have been otherwise. The income from the annual interest I receive is also, in consequence, larger, so I am as comfortably off as I was when I retired. Not by any means a rich man, but comfortable and without any financial worries. That was very sound advice I received from Frank Stroobant.

After I had given up racing I stored 'Old Faithful' my 350 cc A J S, in our garage at Lyndel and forgot about it. The garage was always full of my bits and pieces and Mabs was always on to me to clear it out. Shortly after returning to Lyndel, Mabs telephoned me to say that she wanted the garage cleaned out and demanded that I get the motor bike out of her way.

I sent one of my staff out to Lyndel with instructions to pick it up and dump it into a quarry. It was a sad end to a wonderful friend. I wish now that I had found a way of keeping it. When it went, so went a chapter of motorcycling history. I have few regrets in my life, but dumping that 'old friend' must be one of them !

When I finally retired from motorcycle racing, the 500 cc. A.J.S was cleaned up, serviced in the usual way and stored in my George Street workshops. Charles Pratt, who for years had looked after it between meetings, always made a point of seeing that it was stored away in a clean and serviced condition. Charles had heard me talk of retirement many times, and was always wary that I might change my mind and embark on yet another come back. My racing motorcycle, fully serviced, remained in store until the business was sold to Paul Le Page. I took it home and put it in my garage at Gele Close.

When John Foley created his Motor Museum at the Charroterie, he came and asked me if I would allow him to put my 500 cc. A.J.S on display. I readily agreed and it became part of his Museum. He displayed a photograph of me alongside my racing machine. That photograph was to bring me back in contact with one of my early girlfriends.

Chapter 34

THE BAILIFF REQUESTED THAT WE TOSS A COIN

Even as a comparatively young man, I was interested in 'Island politics', and enjoyed political debate. Dad's interest in current affairs, inevitably rubbed off on me and my involvement with various sports Club's and their administration also kindled my interest in the government of the island.

Before the occupation I was involved with the administration of the Guernsey Swimming Club and in 1938, was elected as one of their two representatives to the States Bathing Pools Committee, which was then under the Presidency of Cecil Stonelake. Whilst the Bathing Pools Committee did not function during the occupation, I was still recognised as a member when it was resurrected after the liberation. In one way or another I have been a member of a States Committee ever since. That may well be some sort of record !

During the occupation I further developed my interest in the States through my discussions with Jurat John Leale. When I was elected to the Constitutional Reform Committee, in 1945, he said:

"I hope that one day you will join us in the States as a Deputy."

Coming from my hero, that was encouragement indeed. From that moment on it was not a matter of if, but only of when. The seed was sown and had taken root.

Louis Guillemette, the States Supervisor, wrote to me on one occasion, and concluded his letter with the comment that;

'I hope that I am writing to a future President of the Board of Administration.'

Flattery indeed and inevitably I was getting keener, although I was never destined to become President of the Board of Administration.

Soon after I joined the Chamber of Commerce Council, I was elected as one of their delegates to the States Advertising Committee. Originally the Chamber had undertaken all the holiday advertising for the island. Later it became a shared responsibility between the States and the Chamber. Before long the Tourist Committee was created to take over and extend the work of the Advertising Committee. I became a member of the new Publicity sub-committee. In 1947 I was invited to join the main Tourist Committee, which eventually became the Tourist Board. I was to continue as a member for, in all, about 35 years. There was a two years break when I lost my place as a non-States member to Squadron Leader Chambers, who was President of the Guernsey Hotel and Tourist Association. When, later, I became a Deputy, I was re-elected as a member of the Tourist Board.

In 1949 I was invited to join the Water Board as a non elected member. Clearly in many peoples mind I was being blooded for future membership of the States. People were always asking when I was going to stand. With my business, my sporting activities and many other interests, I felt that the time had not yet arrived when I could give the necessary time, or do justice to the responsibilities of being a Deputy.

I was very friendly with Frank le Page, who ran the Old Forge shop at Carmel and who was one of the Deputies for St Martin. Together, we became involved in a dispute regarding a right-of-way at Jerbourg. A path which I had always understood to be a public footpath was closed by the adjacent land owner. One day, when I met Frank in the street, I asked him :

"I thought that was a public footpath. Is it right that the neighbouring landowner can close it off, just like that ?"

Frank came down to Jerbourg to see for himself. As a result, he took the matter up and fought quite a lengthy battle in the States and won. The right-of-way was reinstated and the footpath has been open to the public ever since. After he won the battle, he told me that I should be in the States fighting that type of battle on behalf of St Martin's. He was very keen that I should stand at the next election. I think that I would have done so, had it not been for my divorce.

After the divorce, I had moved out of Lyndel and bought my bungalow in the Castel, so I could no longer contemplate standing for the parish of St Martin. Lloyd Robilliard, an old friend, approached me in 1970 and suggested that I should stand for the States in the Castel parish. I was extremely reluctant as I still felt that the public would not forgive me for having been involved in divorce. Lloyd's view was that it was almost five years since the divorce and that it had all been long forgotten.

Lloyd finally persuaded me to stand and he and Lewis Dorey, who I always called Louis, sponsored me by signing my nomination paper. I signed that I consented to be nominated and handed the completed papers in at the Bailiff's Office. Almost as soon as I had left the Royal Court building, I started having doubts that I had done the right thing. The more I thought about it, the more certain I became that I should not be standing at that election. I went back to Lloyd and Louis and told them I had lost heart. Despite much pleading, they both finally agreed that I should withdraw my nomination, but that was easier said than done. By this time nominations had closed.

I went to see the Bailiff, Sir William Arnold, and explained my position to him. Sir William was very reluctant to return my nomination paper. He tried to persuade me let my name stand, as he pointed out that I may have taken the place of someone else who might otherwise have put their name forward. I pointed out that there were two other newcomers, besides myself and that I was not actually displacing anyone. But he was not at all pleased about it and I had to be firm and quite definite in my desire to withdraw. The notice detailing the nominations had been printed, so my name had to be cancelled out.

When election time came around in 1973, I was again pressed to stand in the Castel Parish. Lloyd and Louis signed my nomination form and I burned the midnight oil writing and re-writing my manifesto. There being no political parties in the island, each candidate is obliged to publish his own manifesto, so the electors have some idea what each candidate stands for and proposes to do if elected. I included in my manifesto the fact that I had been divorced. I thought I would let the people of Castel decide, whether or not they wanted a divorced man to represent them in the States.

Looking back now, I realise that I unintentionally misled the electors of Castel, by saying that I was born in 1910, instead of 1909. Why I did not give my correct date of birth I do not know. What I wrote was :

"I was born in 1910 in Fountain Street, which tends to make me rather old to start a States career - your judgement will have to consider this carefully."

I have found several references to my birthday being 1910. My passport states my year of birth as 1910. When I checked my old school records at the Intermediate school, they also recorded my date of birth as 1910. I was beginning to think that I was not as old as I thought I was, certainly I have never felt as old as

I was supposed to be. I decided that there was only one way of confirming my age and that was to check the official record of my birth at the Greffe.

I was taken down into the strongroom and a very old register was located, detailing all the births registered in 1910. There was no record of a Green on August 19th. Then the register for 1909 was produced and there, on the 19th August, was the entry 'William Green', son of William Green. Confirmation that I was both legitimate and born in 1909. The young man who located the register for me commented:

"You're older than you look".

I thanked him for the information, and the remark, and left contented.

Whilst I realised that it was desirable, in order to get elected, to knock on doors, I was very apprehensive as to the response I might receive in view of my divorce. So I never actually canvassed door to door. I fought the election on the basis of my printed manifesto. The bulk of them I posted but with the help of Eric Walters two sons, I delivered some, but only left them at houses with letter boxes. It is surprising how few houses in the island have letter boxes.

Like all the other candidates, I recorded a television interview which helped to spread my message. With the other candidates, I attended the parish public meeting at Beaucamps School and answered questions on a variety of subjects. The speaking experience I gained with the Chamber of Commerce gave me a degree of confidence, that I think a number of my fellow candidates lacked. I was able to take the meeting in my stride. The States House Tenants' Association came out in my support and their endorsement, I was sure, would be to my advantage on polling day.

Eventually, election day came around and once the poll was closed, it was only a matter of waiting for the Returning Officer and his team of counters to do their job. It seemed an interminable time before finally the Returning Officer appeared and read the result in alphabetically order.

William Green	877
Roland Guille	670
Cecil Le Noury	646
William Rowe	832
Wilfred Wheadon	926

When the Returning Officer announced my 877 votes, and then the 670 for Roland Guille, I knew that I had won a seat in the States, as there were only five candidates for four seats. With Roland having fewer votes than me, I knew I was one of Castel's new deputies. I had achieved my long standing ambition to become a member of the States, Guernsey's Parliament. I was gratified to come second in the poll at my first attempt. It gave me renewed confidence, I was a new man and felt that I had again been accepted. I was back as part of the community and my divorce was now well and truly behind me.

So it was with a feeling of achievement and confidence that I attended my first meeting of the States. The Bailiff, Sir William Arnold welcomed members and particularly the new members. In the course of his welcoming remarks, he said :-

> "I would remind old and new members of their duty to the island through the States and of the dignity and politeness which characterises politics in Guernsey. I think it is characteristic of us that we fight no pitched battles here, or anywhere else and that the conduct of the affairs of this island, both in the States and in parish assemblies, is inspired with a deep sense of tradition and dignity and an abiding sense of duty to put first, the wellbeing of the

> people who we represent and the prosperity of the community over whom we are set in authority.
>
> The observance of our rules and procedure, and the courteous exchange of views have always been a matter of good manners rather than the exposition of a lesson learnt from the written word. We do not govern only to ensure freedom, but without it we could not govern.
>
> This is a parliament, one of the most ancient in the Commonwealth, for many centuries it has formed a direct and unbroken link with the Crown. It must surely be a shining example to all civilised people that this link, of which we are so proud, has proved down the years to be a hallmark of our freedom, rather than a symbol of bondage to the Monarchy. Every law that we pass should have, not merely a desirable end, but an absolute justification for its existence, for every law is to some extent an encroachment upon the freedom of the individual. Freedom is not the right to do as we please, but the liberty to do as we ought. And that of course goes for freedom of expression. There are those, I regret, who think that to hurl abuse is the expression of freedom, I disagree profoundly".

That was, in my view, a very profound and deeply considered judgement, which caused me, as a new Deputy, to think very carefully about the role I was about to play in the government of my island.

Very soon after being elected, I went with the President, of the Water Board, Ernie De Garis and Tom Hurst, the Chief Engineer to have a look at a new water treatment plant that had recently been commissioned, near Paignton in Devon. We stayed overnight at an Hotel that had a swimming pool and, of course, I couldn't resist its attraction. I dived into the pool, but it turned out to be shallower than I had realised. I scraped my chest on the bottom and injured my back. After returning home, my back progressively grew worse, so much so that I was out of commission for three months. I simply could not walk. At first I was sure that it was just a matter of determination on my part. I tried to force myself to walk, but I found it impossible, so much so, that I became extremely annoyed with myself.

I began to think that I might have permanently disabled myself. I could only just crawl to the toilet on my hands and knees and when there, it took considerable effort to pull myself up. Margaret came back from Newfoundland to look after me and brought my granddaughter, Fiona with her. The most comfortable position I could find was lying on a mattress on the floor in my lounge. Young Fiona enjoyed having Gramps, as she calls me, near at hand and took great delight in jumping on me. I can still vividly recall the excruciating pain, she thought it great fun, but for a few moments Fiona was not my favourite granddaughter. Finally Doctor Heyworth gave me epidural injections and I never looked back.

My back injury caused me to miss two or three States meetings and a whole string of Committee meetings.

Soon after my election as a Deputy, Fred Short came to see me and asked for my assistance in clearing his name in connection with the Police trials during the occupation. Fred, since his return to the island in 1946 had been working at the Airport.

He explained; "We pleaded guilty to theft because, had we admitted sabotage, we should have been shot, the penalty for sabotage was death." He added "Even the pleas of guilty to theft were forced out of us by torture."

Fred told me that he had been on motorcycle patrol at L'Islet, and was passing the house of a fellow policeman, Sergeant Le Lievre, when he was stopped by an armed German. He was told that he had been arrested and had to go to the Feldgendarmerie headquarters at Grange Lodge. As he was on the police motorcycle he was instructed to drive in front of the German police car. They came along the front and turned up St Julians Avenue. Fred accelerated up the Avenue and turned into Hospital Lane without the Germans following him.

Fred knew that the Germans were bound to search his house, so he drove straight to his home, St Davids', in Steam Mill Lanes, St Martin and collected a revolver and fifty rounds of ammunition that were hidden on the top of his wardrobe, under his white A.R.P. tin helmet. He quickly passed them on to a farmer friend and neighbour, who still had them when the occupation ended. Fred then drove to Grange Lodge and reported to the Germans. Sure enough, his house was searched and, of course, nothing was found. He was released, but a few days later Fred was re-arrested by the Germans and so started, what he described 'a nightmare of pain and torture'.

Taken to the top floor of Ash House, which is adjacent to Grange Lodge, Fred was subjected to hour upon hour of questioning, often from eight in the morning until eight at night. He was interrogated by three of their police, one who sat directly in front of him and two who sat either side of him. The Nazi who sat opposite Fred started the interrogation by taking his revolver out of its holster and placing it on the table. He said pointedly, in broken English;

"These have been known to go off accidentally."

After about eight days the questioning turned to brutality, when one his inquisitors lost his temper and punched him in the face. He recalled;

"I was repeatedly punched in the face, knocked to the ground and beaten with a rifle butt. They smashed my false teeth and split my lip in two. My head was continually banged against the wall and when I lost consciousness, they threw ice cold water over me. Then they made me stand, until I collapsed again."

They made vile threats about what would happen to Fred's wife if he failed to admit his involvement in the 'thieving'. Fortunately his wife had evacuated to the mainland.

"In the end" he said "I lost all count of time. On one occasion I was kept without food for forty eight hours, on another they threatened to pull out my finger nails if I didn't say yes to something he wanted me to admit. At 2 o'clock one morning three Jerry Feldgendarmerie arrived and gave me another beating, I was too weak to try and resist and in any case I would only have been bashed about more if I had tried to do so."

"In the end, like everyone else, I confessed to theft, but the details of the so called confessions were written, not by me, but by the Germans, in German. I was forced to sign and that was the confession which convicted me both in the Military Trial and in the Royal Court."

One of the charges that Fred Short was accused, concerned the breaking and entering of the Essential Commodities Committee Store at Littlefield and Snell premises in Trinity Square. It was alleged that with P.C's Bert Smith and Frank Tuck, he had stolen four cases of tins of tomatoes and a quantity of cooking oil.

Fred was emphatic that the charge was dreamed up by the Germans and that none of them had ever taken anything from the Littlefield and Snell store. I promised Fred that I would do what I could to help, although we both realised that virtually all the possible legal avenues had already been explored.

I went up to see Mr Snell and he told me that none of the goods that Fred and the others were accused of stealing from his store, ever went missing as far as he knew. It was a trumped-up charge by the Germans in order to discredit our Police Force. Fred and others were beaten into admitting to the charges and our Courts accepted that as evidence.

Regrettably, I was never able to get the case reconsidered. The more I investigated the charges and the convictions, the more I became certain that there had been a major miscarriage of justice.

My first three years as a Deputy quickly passed and it was back to the hustings in March 1976. At that election, the number of Deputies elected to represent the Castel Parish had been increased by one, to five. My basic election platform was 'Guernsey First and Last' It was a simple, but effective message which readily went home to the average Guernseyman. I frankly admit that I did not knock on doors as I should have done, my canvassing was confined to saying 'Good Morning' to the bus queues ! Despite that omission, I increased my vote from 877, to 1134 - a very satisfying result as far as I was concerned. It gave me the vote of confidence that I wanted to continue to represent the people of Castel in the States.

The election was significant from two other points of view, first that my previous 'sponsor' Lloyd Robilliard was elected at his first attempt and, secondly, Charles de Carteret, who was one of the Guernsey Labour Group candidates, trailed badly at the bottom of the poll. The Labour Group, who had previously put up candidates in the first election after the war, were again testing the political water. Again none of the candidates they endorsed were successful. The electorate emphatically told them to stop dabbling in the clear blue waters of non political Guernsey.

Three years later, in 1979, I again stood and Lloyd Robilliard and I tied for top place in the election. We both received 1303 votes and, despite a recount, that remained the result. My other original 'sponsor', Louis Dorey also stood and was elected. The election was also of interest, because Eric Walters stood for the first time and surprisingly came bottom of the poll. At the next election he won a place in the States and has since become Castel's favourite Deputy and regularly tops the poll by a substantial margin.

Because there is a protocol about seating, a Deputy's seat in the house depends on his position in the poll, it was necessary for Lloyd and I to decide which of us would occupy Castel's senior seat. The Bailiff, Sir John Loveridge, requested that we toss a coin. I won, but as Lloyd had previously occupied the premier seat, I was reluctant to turn him out of his place, so we agreed between us that he had won the toss and that I would sit in second place.

As the time came around for the election in 1985 I came to the conclusion that it was time for me to step down. Twelve years was a good innings and, if I stood again I would be seventy nine by the end of another term of office, and that, in my view, was too old to properly represent the people of my parish. I had long been a critic of other people who held on too long before they retired. I didn't want to be subjected to the same criticism,- I had stayed long enough.

Inevitably people sought to change my mind - they were keen that I should stand again. It was very flattering to be asked, but I knew that the right time to go is when people still want you to stay. I was approached by two States members who had suggested that I stand as a Conseiller. It was very tempting, it would indeed have been a great honour and in many ways a fitting conclusion to my work in the States and on the Constitutional Reform Committee. However I stuck to my decision and retired from the States, although I missed it dearly.

Listening to the debates which are now broadcast on Radio Guernsey, I would still like to put my oar in on occasions. Looking back now, I don't regret retiring, it was the right time to go. Despite not continuing as a Deputy, I was elected as a non-States Member to the Board of Administration, the Civil Defence, the Constitutional Review and the Gambling Control Committees. That at least was a consolation and allowed me to retain an interest, albeit at committee level.

Being very much a committee man, I believe I made a bigger contribution to the running of the island in committee, behind closed doors, than I did in the open forum of the States. There were two issues, however, which I fought for publicly, the maintenance of the Conseiller system, in which I passionately believe, and the saving of the Valette bathing pools.

Over the years there has been a small vociferous minority in the States, who sought to change the system by which Conseillers are elected. Generally they were some of the newest members, with as yet little experience of the ways of the House and belonging to the anti-establishment platoon. Many of them, with experience, modified and changed their views.

Whilst I was not necessarily against change, I was opposed to change for changes sake. If a system is working well, and over the years the Conseiller system has provided the island with stability and good government, why change. The Conseiller Bench in many ways provides the stabilising influence which in other democratic countries is supplied by a second chamber.

If a better system was proposed which would produce better government for the island, then I would support change, provided that it received the backing of the people of our island. The only occasions when I have ever been tempted to consider change has been at times when one or two of the members of the Conseiller bench have behaved in an arrogant or irresponsible manner. That is no reason to change the system - what is needed, however, is more careful selection of the members of the Conseillers bench.

Over the years, our little island of Guernsey has established for itself, an international reputation for the stability of its government. This in turn has helped to establish and maintain a very prosperous finance industry. Nothing must be done to weaken or destroy that image. Changing our system of government to satisfy a vociferous minority could, in my view, do immense damage to our international standing.

I was concerned that the House could, in an unguarded moment, make a change to our Constitution that would have unforeseen consequences. On one occasion there was a tied vote on the matter of changing the method of electing Conseillers and the Bailiff voted for the status quo, which is, of course, traditional. I came to the view that changes should only be made if they had the support of at least two thirds of the House.

Accordingly, with the assistance of Her Majesty's Procureur who drafted a suitable Requete, I was able to persuade the States to build into the Constitution the need for a two thirds majority before any changes can be made. There was, as I expected, strong opposition from certain Deputies, who saw the move as thwarting their aspirations, which was exactly what I intended. The time it took for my amendment to the Constitution to go through the necessary legal formalities, meant that I had left the States before the process was completed. However I am proud that the safeguard that I proposed is now law and that it is no longer possible for our constitution to be changed by chance, perhaps because one or two members just happen to be on holiday.

In the spring of 1977, the Recreation Committee, who had by that time taken over the responsibilities of the Bathing Pools Committee, published a Policy letter in the Billet D'etat, the States agenda, suggesting that the swimming pools at La Valette should be abandoned in view of the cost of the maintenance required. That was a proposal to which I was totally opposed.

There are occasions when all that is needed is a good speech in the House, to defeat a proposal with which a Deputy disagrees. On some issues the marshalling of public opinion is essential. This was one of those occasions. My assessment of the situation was, that to defeat the proposals, a letter writing campaign was needed, and a well-attended public meeting with a positive vote to retain the Valette pools.

I contacted as many of my fellow swimmers, past and present, as I could, and encouraged them to write to the Press, their Deputies and the President of the Recreation Committee. The response was tremendous.

Jim Foster, one of our regular swimmers, hit just the right note when he wrote, in a letter to the Press, 'That the swimming pools are part of our island heritage'. The Comment column in the Guernsey Evening Press took up our cause and commented:

> 'Letters appearing in the Dear Sir pages of the Evening Press, usually represent the tip of the iceberg of public feeling on particular subjects. This could well be the case in regard to the plan to allow a part of the bathing places to fall into further disrepair to the point of abandonment.
>
> Public objections to the proposal, which comes before the States next Wednesday vary from the placing of the pools within the heritage of the island, to the more practical aspect of their popularity.
>
> While it is true that, with the proliferation of swimming pools all over the island, the need for seaside facilities is not as great as say ten years ago, there are still many people who prefer the salt water to chlorinated'.

When the public meeting that I organised was held at Beau Sejour, over two hundred members of the public turned up as well as a number of States members. I took the chair and the meeting went totally according to plan, everyone present voting in favour of the retention and repair of the bathing pools.

Conseiller Tom Ogier, the President of Island Development Committee, attended and publicly congratulated me for calling the meeting and wished more were held on major issues. Tom commented that he could not understand how anyone could even contemplate abandoning the pools with their tradition and record of giving pleasure, particularly at a time when conservation was the vogue.

By the time the States met to discuss the Recreation Committee's proposals, the letters, the press comment and the public meeting had all but won the day. Every member of the Recreation Committee supported the retention of the pools. The lone dissenting voice was that of Conseiller Peter Dorey, who felt it entirely unnecessary to retain all four pools.

Despite the States decision to retain the Valette Pools, no maintenance work was carried out that summer. By the autumn, the situation was getting so bad that I wrote to the President of the Recreation Committee, Tony Bran, again drawing his attention to the problem. He agreed that temporary repairs would be made to the pools during the winter and that his Committee would ask for a capital allocation to cover major works the following year.

I heard that the Recreation Committee, which was bringing a further Policy Letter on the matter to the States, had asked the Island Development Committee for their views. I learnt also that Tom Ogier and his members were going down to look at the Pools the next morning. I realised that the tide would be up and that they would be able to see little of the maintenance problems. I made it my business to be there when they arrived, so that I could explain what work needed to be carried out. I came away with the impression that many members of the Committee were not very concerned about the pools and would not be speaking in favour of spending money on maintenance.

I was shocked when the Policy letter was issued since one of the options the Recreation Committee suggested was to rescind the previous decision by the States to keep the Valette Pools. It was now proposed to demolish the Horseshoe Pool. One of the weapons in a Deputy's armoury is the use of humour. I decided this was a situation which called for its use.

When the matter was debated in the States, I told the story of having learned that the Island Development Committee was to visit the Valette Pools when the tide was up, which meant that they would be able to see very little of the work that needed doing. I went on;

"But then, Mr President, I have to tell you, that we have a man amongst us with far more power and authority than Canute ever had, because Conseiller Tom Ogier glared at the waters, ordered them to recede and low and behold, six hours later they did."

The States broke down in laughter and I won the day. I like to think I saved the bathing pools.

During my time in the States I served under three Bailiffs, Sir William Arnold, Sir John Loveridge, and Sir Charles Frossard. I think that, from the point of view of presiding over the States, Sir John was in a class of his own. I greatly respected him for his handling of the States, it was absolutely masterly. He was so democratic that no one was ever put into the position that they felt they couldn't speak. It didn't matter how long the States went on debating and I have been in the chamber until seven o'clock in the evening, because Sir John was absolutely meticulous that everyone who had anything to say had to be given the opportunity.

In comparison, Sir Charles, looked upon 5 pm as an absolute deadline which was rarely if ever crossed. I think in fairness, the composition of the House had changed by the time Sir Charles became Bailiff, so too had the desire of members to speak on virtually every issue, whether they knew anything about the subject or not. Sir John had a better States with more responsible people who only spoke on issues in which they were involved, or about which they were knowledgeable.

Sir William Arnold was, in comparison, very much more laid-back and casual, in his handling of the House, he was in many ways an unpredictable man. Sir John and Sir Charles were both men of total predictability. Sir John a stickler for tradition and etiquette, while Sir Charles often took a more light-hearted, and in some ways a more human approach to his high office.

I was a critic of the Housing Authority's policy of 'self build', so it came as a surprise, when its President, Roydon Falla, asked me to join him on the Authority. 'Self build' was a co-operative scheme where a group of people helped each other build their own and each others houses. I had been critical of the policy, because I did not think it would work. People in my view, quickly became tired of building other people's houses. Some schemes succeeded, but many others ran into time consuming difficulties. I was never sure whether Roydon asked me to join the Authority because he wanted my help, or because he believed it was the best way to deal with a critic !

I thoroughly enjoyed my time on the Housing Authority and remained a member when Binney Lincoln became President. Much as I profoundly disagreed with many of her policies, I respected her greatly as an individual. She was totally sincere in everything she tried to do to help people in need of housing.

In 1976, Ernie de Garis retired as President of the Water Board and since I was his Vice President, I naturally hoped to succeed him. I felt that I had the experience necessary to take on the Presidency. At the States meeting both Roger Berry and I were nominated for the position and Roger won. That defeat hurt, particularly being beaten by a young man who thought that he knew 'everything about everything'. I thought I would let him get on with it, so I resigned from the Board.

I became President of the Civil Defence Committee, but otherwise missed out on Presidencies. In retrospect I don't think that is surprising, as I started in the States at an age when other members of a similar age were thinking of retiring.

When Bert Ozanne stood down as President of the Tourist Board, I was approached to stand for the vacancy. I had served with Bert for many years on the Board. He was a typical stubborn Guernseyman and as cunning as a fox. He got things done his way, by any means possible. Bert was ruthless, able and successful - a man with a lot of guts. When he lost his seat as a Deputy for St Peters, he stood for St Peter Port and won. He was a man who never gave up.

I would have very much liked the job as President of the Tourist Board, I believe I could have made a success of it, but I was aware that Bert wanted his son Richard to succeed him. I thought it over and came to the conclusion, that if it went to the vote, Richard would win, so I said 'No'.

Richard Ozanne has been a good ambassador for Guernsey outside the island, but has too often undersold himself and his Board at home.

One of the great characters in the States during my time was without doubt, Cecil de Sausmarez. He and I had long been good friends and I vividly remember a walk we took together along the Jerbourg cliffs. As we walked, Cecil was 'indoctrinating' me with details of the feud that has raged between the Carey and De Sausmarez families for centuries. He told me with great glee, how, as he conducted parties of visitors around Sausmarez Manor, he brainwashed them into 'hating' the Carey's.

When Cecil was conducting a party through the picture gallery, he would say, 'Yes this is Lord De Sausmarez, he did so and so, and so and so, and this is Lady De Sausmarez, his wife, she did so and so, this is the daughter of the De Sausmarez. He would go right around the picture gallery describing all the pictures and would come to a picture with it's face to the wall. Cecil would pass it and go to the next picture and say:

"This is a picture of..." and hesitate.

In doing so he always caused one member of the party to enquire:

"Well what about that one with it's face to the wall ?"

He would delightedly respond by stating:-

"She wanted to marry a Carey !"

In that way he perpetuated the feud between the Carey and De Sausmarez families.

As we walked around the cliffs, part of which had been donated to the island by the Carey family, Cecil reminded me that the Germans had blown up the Sausmarez Monument in Delancey Park. He said :

"The Careys had the audacity to have one of the blocks of stone from the monument carved with their name." and at that moment we came upon the stone. I stopped and read the inscription, indicating that the Carey family had given that part of the cliffs to the island. After I had read the inscription, Cecil said :-

"I often walk these cliffs and I have trained my dog to perform against the stone." And with perfect de Sausmarez timing, the dog performed.

Chapter 35

NO VICAR IS EVER GOING TO SEE ME OFF AGAIN

Elsie Patterson, who as Elsie Stewart had been one of my girlfriends in the nineteen thirties, came back to the island for a holiday with her husband in 1980. One day they visited John Foley's Motor Museum in the Charroterie. My 500 cc A.J.S. racing motorcycle was on display there, together with a photograph of me in my younger days. Elsie recognised me and enquired if I was still alive !

On being told that I was very much alive and now lived down near Vazon, she telephoned me. It was the first time that I had spoken to her for over forty years and amazingly I recognised her voice before she identified herself. I had known Elsie when she was sixteen and I was in my mid twenties. I broke off our relationship when the Reverend Rose expressed concern at the difference in our ages.

The three of us, Elsie, her husband Pat and I met the next day at the bathing pools. Later we went out to dinner and reminisced about old times. Elsie and Pat became regular visitors to the island and each time they came we usually met up for a meal and a chat. Sadly her husband died in December 1982 and, after a number of extended visits, Elsie decided to return to the island permanently.

We have again become good friends and in many ways have taken up from where we were before the Reverend Rose 'intervened'. No vicar is ever going to see me off again.

Not many years ago the Motorcycle and Car Club were holding a motorcycling sprint meeting on the Vazon Coast Road, which is very near to where I now live. Being interested, I walked up and was leaning on the wall watching the races when I noticed a Jersey competitor with a beautiful overhead camshaft AJS,'A' type motorcycle. The model had been out of production for some years. I said to the rider:

"That's a lovely model."

"Yes, I am very proud of it".

"What age is that ?"

"1955."

I said "I had the first overhead camshaft AJS model that ever came out of the AJS works."

"Go on!" he said "When was that ?"

"1928" I replied.

"Oh no you didn't, they didn't make a camshaft model until 1954."

"They made a cam shaft in 1928," I said, "I had the first one that ever came out of the factory."'

"No,no,no!" he said, "You had a push rod, you know what a push rod engine is?"

I repeated "I had a cam shaft."

"No," he said "they never made a cam shaft until 1954."

There was no convincing him, so I went home, which was no more than a two minute walk away, looked out a photograph of my Camshaft A.J.S and went back to the sprint racing. With the help of a Race Marshall, I caught up with the Jersey competitor and showed him my photograph.

"What about that ?" I said

He looked at the photograph carefully, and said :-

"That's a 'cammie' AJS."

"Yes that is a 1928 'cammie' AJS."

"Ah, but there is no date on it".

"There is you know, I am the chap in the saddle."

He looked at the photograph again and then at me, and said;

"Christ!"

"There is another date on it. The bike has girder front forks."

He said "So it has, I never knew they made a cam shaft before 1954.'

"It was 1954 when the first camshaft models were made after the war. But they made camshafts before the war and I had the first one"

Inevitably, a Guernsey occupation Society came into being, and many people who were here during the war became members. For years, all I had wanted to do was forget about the German occupation and everything associated with it. However I was eventually persuaded to become a member of the Society and have attended many of their 'dinner lecture' meetings.

Willie Haggadorn, a former German Signals officer, was the speaker at one meeting. He was stationed in the island right up to the end of the occupation. Willie made a wonderful speech in beautiful English, giving a graphic account of how he was sending signals to German High Command, on the situation in Guernsey, right up to the German surrender. Then he told how, because of his excellent English and knowledge of the equipment, he was employed by the British forces, after they landed, to transmit messages to Allied Headquarters.

Willie Hesse, the German billeting sergeant, who returned to the island after the war to marry Shelia Radford, had died. I invited Shelia, his widow, to the lecture dinner as I thought that she might be interested in what Willie Haggadorn had to say. Being stone deaf, she could not hear him, but was able lip read. Sitting alongside Shelia, I was carrying on a conversation with her by writing little notes and she would speak her reply. I noticed that Mrs Haggadorn was not speaking to anyone. Obviously she could only speak German and looked a bit lonesome. I wrote a note to Shelia,

'Perhaps you could go and have a word with Mrs Haggadorn, because she looks so lonely.'

Shelia looked at the note and then turned to me and said:

"I cannot speak German, I never heard Willie's voice."

I was dumbfounded, a marriage, two children and she had never heard her husbands voice !

A few years ago, I had a letter from a lady in England asking me if I remembered a German sailor who rode into my shop on a motorbike during the occupation. She explained that the sailor, who at the time was avoiding the German police, was her father. She had married an Englishman and now lived in England. Her parents were coming to visit her and during the visit they hoped to come to Guernsey. She said that her father would very much like to meet me again. I wrote back saying that I had a very clear memory of the incident and would love to renew our acquaintance.

I met this ex-sailor, a charming man, when he came to the island with his wife and daughter. During the war he had gone on to become an officer. Now retired, he lived in Bremenhaven. We talked over the incident, we retraced his steps in Smith

Street and we all went to Herm together. I am sure that he had a very enjoyable second visit to Guernsey!

In the early seventies an advertisement appeared in the the Guernsey Evening Press for a position at the Princess Elizabeth Hospital. Tony my daughter's husband, was aware that the position was to become vacant due to the impending retirement of the current post holder. So when the advertisement appeared I sent him a copy. Tony applied and was successful, so they all came back to the island. Sadly however, Margaret and her husband Tony separated and were later divorced.

In recent years my daughter has successfully developed her own travel business. I am a Director of her company and from time to time get opportunities to make business trips to various parts of the world.

One trip I made with her company was to Mexico for the annual gathering of International Travel Agents. Margaret went a week before me, so for my outward trip I met up with a party of Travel Agents at Gatwick. They all asked:

"Where is Maggie ?" and "How is Maggie ?"

Of course I told them she was well and had gone ahead of me. On our way to Mexico we had a stopover in New York where we stayed the night. The next morning we all caught the transit bus back to Kennedy Airport. On the way our party got into conversation with a Yank, who greeted us with:-

"Hi you folks, where are you folks all from ?"

As I did not think that he would have ever heard of 'little old Guernsey', I said:-

"We're from England."

The Yank turned to me and said:

"Gee how's Maggie ?"

Not immediately realising that he was referring to Maggie Thatcher, I said in all innocence :-

"You know my daughter too, do you !"

This Yank thought he had hit the jackpot. For a few moments I was a celebrity.

One memorable trip that I made with Margaret and my friend Elsie, was to attend the ABTA, Association of British Travel Agents, conference in Israel in early 1989. We were based in Jerusalem, a fascinating City steeped in history. The seven Dead Sea Scrolls that were discovered in 1947 are housed in 'Shrine of the Book' at the Israel Museum. The impact that these Scrolls have had on the biblical world can only, in my view, be described as revolutionary. Seeing the Scrolls made a lasting impression on me.

One of the trips which was laid on for conference delegates involved driving out into the Palestinian desert in a fleet of twenty-seven Jeeps. There was a leader and the rest of the Jeeps were driven by members of our party. This was the desert in which Christ spent forty days and forty nights in conditions of severe discomfort and at the end of it he had decided what it was he was ordained to do. It is a fascinating place. One sometime imagines the desert as just a big plain of sand, but that is not necessarily accurate. The Palestinian desert is very uneven and hilly.

We visited the area of the desert where David slew Goliath. There are flints out there which are knife sharp and steel hard. I understood for the first time in my life how David could have achieved his 'against the odds' success.

Lunch with the Bedouin people was the highlight of the days trip. This was absolutely fascinating, although I did not eat any lunch as I did not fancy the menu. A shelter of skins had been erected to give us some protection from the burning sun. This encampment was, we were told, exactly as it would have been two thousand years before. They cooked a kid goat in a desert oven. They offered us such delicacies as sheep's eyes and other traditional fare. It was all very interesting, but not in any way appetising to me. I arrived back at the hotel that evening, extremely hungry.

Our visit included a trip to the Dead Sea, which must be one of the most fascinating places on earth. A unique location that boasts a combination of natural geographical, historical and archaeological phenomena which, for me added up to an unforgettable experience. At 1300ft below sea level it is the lowest place on earth and, as Elsie commented:

"Even you cannot sink any lower than that !"

My daughter swam in the Dead Sea, but I did not. When I saw her floating on the top of the water it put me off. I even had my costume on but still didn't go in, that was not my kind of swimming. Looking back now I am sorry that I did not at least take a quick dip. Margaret told me that the incredible sensation of floating effortlessly on the surface of this remarkable sea has to be experienced to be believed

The Dead Sea is not only unique for being so far below sea level, it is also the saltiest and most mineral laden body of water in the world. Every litre of water contains 2 lbs of salt! The Dead Sea is also famous for its black mud. It is reputed to be healthy to cover yourself with this mud - they call it pelotherapy, or mud treatment.

We visited Bethlehem, where a church has been built on the site of the stable, the original birth-place of Christ. These places are very much tourist areas, but never-the-less you get the feeling of something very special.

Outside of the church in Bethlehem, the church of the Nativity, it was all very touristy. A street trader kept draping beads around my daughter's neck and she kept removing them. Eventually she tore them off and said to the street trader:

"Go away, - I now know why the Lord chucked you chaps out of the Temple."

"It was not me Madam, it must have been some other chap."

The tourist trade has regrettably taken over from religion ! Despite Margaret's protestations, I bought some of the beads. When we returned to Guernsey, I found the same beads on sale in Creasey's at half the price !

Within the walls of Jerusalem is the Church of the Holy Sepulchre, where it is thought Christ was crucified. There is a garden outside the walls, and it is believed that the hymn 'There is a green hill far away without a city wall', refers to this garden. In the Garden of the Tomb, is where the actual tomb of Christ is reputed to have been.

Our Tour Guide told us that, as far as history can ascertain, that was the actual tomb of Christ. It is hewn out of rock and whilst one can appreciate that this could have been excavated at any time, that particular tomb is noted in the history of Jerusalem, as having been there for over two thousand years.

Included in our itinerary was a visit to the Wailing Wall, known as the Western Wall in the Jewish faith. Every Jew is supposed to visit the Wall, once in his life time. I found the garden of Gethsemane extremely interesting, it is an area about fifty paces square, enclosed by a low wall of loose stones and contains eight very old olive trees, believed to have existed at the time of our Lord. Their age, we were told, has been scientifically checked. Christ himself must have looked upon them and now almost two thousand years later I was gazing upon the same olive trees. It certainly gave me a feeling of something very special.

We walked where Christ was reputed to have walked. We visited many of the recognised holy spots. Although some of the information that we were given, is not totally accurate, you have to accept that it is the area where Christ spent much of his life.

Even if you believe that there was no such person as Christ, that he was a myth and that none of the historical events actually took place, then you have to accept that this myth has had a more profound affect upon the human race than any other event in the history of the world. You then have to be logical and accept that a myth, by itself, could not have made such an impact on human beliefs for such a long period of time. Therefore it must have a basis of truth. It doesn't matter whether you have faith or not, it is in my view undeniable that Christ once lived in the Holy Land and that many of those recorded events did take place.

Religion has never played a dominating part in my life, although I do say my prayers every night. I like to believe that there is 'something' after this life. It must, of course, be a spirit world, although I cannot start to contemplate what it would be like. I pray that it exists, because I would dearly like to see my parents again. My philosophy is that if you leave this life with a 'credit balance' then you will probably be alright in the next. What I understand by a credit balance, is that if you have done more good in this life than harm, then you are in credit. My balance must, on occasions have been very slender indeed.

One day, dear old Gibson Nelson, who was at one time my parson, said to me:

"Bill you sometimes come to Church when there is Communion, but you don't take the Sacrament ?"

"No I don't, that's right, Gibson."

"Why ever not ?"

"Well as I understand it, if you intend to take the Sacrament you really mean to lead a better life and to endeavour not to commit your failings again. I admit that I have a few, some of which I enjoy and I don't think I want to give them up just yet."

I thought Nelson was going to drop dead.

For many years a few of us 'old stagers' enjoyed an early morning dip, summer and winter, down at the Valette Bathing Pool. On one cold February morning, only a few years ago, I parked my car in Mount Durand and, together with Ralph Palmer, went down to La Valette with Bernie Amy in his car. Bernie at that time had a poodle which went every where with him.

This particular morning it had been raining heavily and was still pitch black. We went into the changing room and undressed and because it was still dark, and there was no one around at that time in the morning, wc didn't bother with costumes. We enjoyed our swim, and when we came out, the 'blessed' poodle had pushed closed the door of the changing room. It had automatically locked. There we were, three old men, locked out and starkers, at seven o'clock on a cold, wet, dark February morning.

The key to the changing room door and the car keys were in Bernie's coat, which was now locked in the changing room. These three elderly men in their birthday suits could be seen tossing up with a stone, to decide which of them was going to venture up to Jim Foster's house in Hauteville. We knew that Jim, another regular swimmer, had a spare key to the changing room. It fell to poor old Ralph to go, so we draped as much seaweed as we could find around his shoulders and waist and sent him off to obtain the spare key from Jim. Meanwhile Bernie and I were getting pretty cold, so we attempted to keep ourselves warm with some physical exercise. Not a pretty sight !

Ralph, dressed only in seaweed, went past the bottom of Le Val des Terres and the Guernsey Brewery, along the Strand and, by the back way, reached Hauteville and Jim Foster's house. Ralph recounted to us afterwards that he was lucky, he only met two people on his journey and was able to hide in doorways while each of them passed. What they would have thought of this elderly naked man draped in seaweed, darting in and out of doorways at that time of the morning, one cannot imagine - fortunately they did not see him, of if they did, perhaps they were not wide enough awake to realise what they saw !

Bill Green still enjoying his daily swim on his 70th birthday.

Ralph finally, to his great relief, reached Jim Foster's front door and rang the bell. Jim was still in bed, but heard the bell and said to his wife, Ann :-

"Somebody is ringing the door bell at this unearthly hour."

Jim told us "I put on my dressing gown and slippers, lit my candle and went down and opened the front door, to find this 'apparition' draped in seaweed on my doorstep saying;

"Can I have the spare changing room key and a mackintosh, please."

Chapter 36

TELL ME ANOTHER FUNNY STORY

As my eightieth birthday drew near I realised that, quietly and secretly, plans were being made by my daughter Margaret and Elsie, to celebrate the event. Apparently Margaret had decided to have my old 500 cc. A.J.S racing machine restored, as a surprise birthday present. She had planned to get Elsie to 'remove' it from my garage, at Gele Close, where it had been since John Foley was forced to close his motor museum, have it crated up and sent to a restorer in South London.

Elsie did not feel that she could just have the motorcycle removed from my garage without telling me as she thought that I might report its loss to the police. So reluctantly Margaret and Elsie told me of their plan and asked for my agreement.

Of course I agreed, it was a wonderful idea, in fact for years I had dreamt of having it refurbished. Frankly I had neglected it and it was in a very poor and rapidly deteriorating condition. As I was keen to see who was going to carry out the restoration, I suggested that Elsie and I hire a van and personally deliver it to the restorers.

I went up to Herbie Tostevin's old place in Grande Rue, St Martin and hired a Budget van. There was no doubt which company it came from, as the name 'Budget' was plastered all over the vehicle. My old racing machine was loaded into the van and Elsie and I caught the ferry to the mainland.

Driving up the M27 towards London, we called into a motorway service station for a bite to eat and to fill up with petrol. When I went over to pay for the petrol, it was a self service station, the attendant asked;

"What do you think of the Budget then ?"

"Well it goes all right."

"It suits you does it ?"

"Oh yes, but it's a bit tricky to steer."

He gave me a funny look and said:

"Well this country is tricky to steer, you know."

It was only then I realised that it was Tuesday 14th March, Budget Day in Britain and we were talking at cross purposes.

Then I confused him completely by saying :

"The budget is of no concern to me, I will not be effected at all."

He scratched his head and served the next customer.

As I walked to the van, I shouted back:-

"You see, I'm a Guernsey boy !"

We delivered my motorcycle to the premises of the company that was going to restore it to its former glory. I had been keen to meet whoever was going to carry out the restoration. In the past I had carried out a considerable number of adaptations to the machine and to make their job easier I wanted to warn them of some of the problems they were likely to encounter. In fact I doubted whether the engine was any longer capable of being repaired, far less ever being started again.

Originally it ran on alcohol, with a fourteen-to-one compression. Would they, I wondered, be able convert it to run on petrol. I talked to one or two of their mechanics and satisfied myself that they were capable of restoring my prized racing machine.

A few weeks later I received a telephone call.

"What did you do to the connecting rod on this bike ?"

"Well," I said, "I put this high compression piston in and shortened the barrel to raise the compression a bit further than the piston would do it. The conrod was too long, so I found an old Norton conrod which I ground down."

"Oh crumbs!" he said, "I don't know what I'm going to do about that."

"Nor do I."

A few days before my eightieth birthday one of the restorers came over to Guernsey and brought my reconditioned 500cc. A.J.S. with him. They had done a truly remarkable job, it arrived back gleaming and totally restored. All the thrills of motorcycle racing came flooding back to me as I rode it around the private lane near Seaplane Bungalow, where my daughter Margaret and my two grandchildren live. I had not ridden my A.J.S. for something like thirty years, it was quite an exciting moment.

I spent hours that day just riding back and forth, revving up the engine, just like a schoolboy with his first motorcycle. The sound of the exhaust was music to my ears. I really enjoyed myself, having my motorcycle restored was one of the most appreciated birthday presents I have ever received.

Later that day, one of Margaret's neighbours went to see her and complained:

"We have for years put up with all the antics your son gets up to and all the noise he makes, but this new motorcycle of his is the end !."

Margaret, attempting to keep a straight face replied :-

"That is not my son, its his grandfather !"

A few days later, I went down to my insurance broker's office to insure my 500cc. A.J.S., so that I could ride it on the island roads. A very pleasant young man and at my age any man who works in an office has to be a young man, listened to my request and gave me an application form to complete. I went to a separate desk, duly completed the form inserting all the details about the motorcycle and myself that were required.

I took the form back to the pleasant young man, who started checking through the details I had entered.

"William Green - no middle name ?"

"No - my parents only gave me one name."

"Gele Close, that's in Castel if I'm not mistaken ?"

"Yes".

"Fully comprehensive ?"

"Yes".

"A 500 cc Motorbike and an eighty year old rider - tell me another funny story!"

If I live to be a hundred, I shall probably be able to do just that.

My eightieth birthday party was held in the garden at Seaplane Bungalow. It was a magnificent day, the sun shone and the visibility was so good that I could make out the far-distant French coast. Margaret, who masterminded the party, had a marquee erected on the lawn. She and Elsie and many others had conjured up a mountain of food and an inexhaustible supply of drink. Elsie unbeknown to me, had 'borrowed' my Christmas card list and everyone on it received an invitation. Just so that no one was left out, Margaret also placed an advertisement in the Guernsey Press, announcing that my birthday party was being held and anyone and everyone who knew me was welcome.

My family, my many friends, my memories and the setting, all blended in with the magnificent weather to make it as fine a birthday party as this eighty year old could wish.

My prized birthday present, my reconditioned racing motorcycle, had to have pride of place in the centre of the lawn, where it inevitability attracted great interest. I noticed Les Lane carrying out a very careful inspection, no doubt thinking back to the days when he and I were arch rivals on Vazon Sands. Today he lives quietly in retirement in St Martin. Every now and again we get together and put the world to rights over a meal and a glass or two of wine.

Many of my old employees, who came to my party, took great interest in the A.J.S, each no doubt had different memories. Charles Pratt, who lavished so much care and attention on it between race meetings, took out his handkerchief and gently polished out a small smear on the petrol tank. Even in his retirement he had not lost any of his pride in my racing machine.

A voice called out:

"Hello Skipper, when is the next race ?".

It was Derek Holmes, another of my trusted mechanics. There was Mrs Butt, wonderful Mrs Butt who ran the cycle shop so well, standing there waiting for my answer. For once in my life, I could not think of a suitable, spontaneous reply.

As I stood there, still admiring my A.J.S, my thoughts went back to some of my most successful races and to my old Jersey adversary, Sid Logan. Sadly, many years ago Sid suffered a very bad car crash, which has left him with many gaps in his memory. Recently I went over to Jersey to see him in Overdale Hospital. He did not even know who I was and talking about motorcycles did not help. Sid doesn't remember any more.

I noticed 'Stroo', Frank Stroobant standing on the edge of the lawn, looking out to sea. He stood there a long time, all by himself, occasionally raising his arm and pointing in various directions. I ambled up beside him. After a few moments he said:

"This is a million dollar view!"

As we stood there together, I wondered if 'Stroo' was recalling the time when he and so many other islanders were deported into captivity in Germany. I could see the very jetty from where I had watched 'Stroo' climb aboard the M.V. Minotaur with everything imaginable tied to his person. I vividly remembered that occasion, when as he disappeared into the hold of the ship, I called out:

"Cheerio 'Stroo', God bless"

As we stood there gazing out at the clear blue sea, I turned to him and said:

"You have been a good friend to me throughout my life, thank you." and I shook his hand.

Like me, he has always been involved in sport and still is to this day, only now, 'Stroo' enjoys the less athletic sports of snooker and cards and, I am told, still makes a good living from them !

There were so many old friends, many that I had not seen for a very long time. It was a beautiful day and we were able to sit in the garden overlooking the sea, with St Peter Port, Herm and Sark in the background, and talk of bygone days. It was marvellous to renew old acquaintances and listen again to stories of our past. I also remembered the many, many friends who could not be with me. Some were too ill and others had long since passed away. How I wished that Mickey Travers, Ted Laker, Len Rouget, Cecil Hardwick, Artie Selous and a host of others could have been with me, to celebrate my birthday.

Dreamy Stranger, with whom I had so much fun as a boy and young man, and who in recent years had virtually withdrawn from circulation, appeared as a surprise and honoured guest. They don't make friends like Dreamy any more ! Having retired as a Director of John Upham Ltd, he still lives at Merton House, in

St Andrews. Dreamy and I could have reminisced all day, but it was not to be, there were many other friendships to be renewed.

Mabs arrived at my party in her little Mini, her pride and joy, and gave me a birthday kiss, the first from her for well over twenty years - there were benefits of being eighty after all ! She presented me with a most beautiful embroidered scene of myself on my A.J.S, with my helmet and pullover picked out in black and gold. Only someone with artistic talent like Mabs could have designed and executed such a work of art.

There were so many people, old and young, who came to share my birthday with me, that inevitably there were some faces to which I could not put a name. There were, of course, faces that I had hoped to see, that did not appear. Where was my best man and great playmate Ralph Palmer. From time to time during the party, I stood back and scanned the crowd of friends, looking for his familiar face. Regretfully, due to his poor health, he was unable to join me in my celebration.

"And what do you call this then" said Edgar Stacey, my occupation next door neighbour and confidant, pointing to my gaily coloured shorts and wide open sports shirt.

"More comfortable than the suit your wearing !" I responded.

The same old Edgar, with the same brand of repartee. I always enjoyed the verbal banter that inevitably takes place when we meet.

Edgar like us all, has retired, he still enjoys a round of golf, a cigarette and a tankard of ale. He and I reminded each other of some of the antics we got up to during the occupation. We had a good laugh over his radio set. I recalled how he was in constant fear of me being arrested and how in my view there was nothing to worry about.

"You were exceedingly fortunate not to have been arrested, you deserved it and if you don't start behaving yourself, there is still time yet."

Good old Edgar, a great friend and a wonderful neighbour.

After all my guests had taken their leave, many promising to see me on my ninetieth birthday, I went out into the garden and sat down on the seat that I had first sat in as a very young boy. The seat was part of the threewheeler car that Dad built before the first war and in which I was photographed sitting on my Mother's knee. When Dad scrapped the car, he kept the passenger seat and placed it in the garden at Seaplane Bungalow. Dad must of spent many happy hours sitting there, surveying the view that he loved so much. Surprisingly, that seat was one of the few items which the Germans did not destroy during their four year 'conquest' of Seaplane Bungalow.

That seat is now part of my family's history, as in fact is so much of Seaplane Bungalow and it's surroundings. As I sat there I recalled the time when Dad had the original inspiration to buy the land because of the magnificent view it commanded. Dad knew then he would build here, sometime, somehow, something. Of course in those days there were no regulations whatsoever, you could do just what you liked and that was what he did and he liked it.

I recalled how Dad bought the plot for sixty pounds from Mr Le Maitre, a local farmer and how he reassembled the hut from the French seaplane base, to create the home he loved. I could see where Dad had set his initials 'W.G' and the date 1918, in the concrete of the balustrade he built. As my eye followed the balustrade around I came to the point where the two French plaster of paris practice bombs had been displayed. They did not survive the occupation.

Neither did the miniature cannon and cannon balls which had been found in an excavation in town. Dad had placed them on a pedestal and wrote an inscription in the concrete of the pillar. The Germans removed the cannon balls and gun, but had left the pedestal. I tried to remember the exact inscription, but it would not come to mind, so I went over to read it, just once more. It reads :

'Sponge me out and fill my mouth,
and I'll send a ball direct to south'

Dad had mounted the cannon with the help of a compass, so that the cannon was facing due south.

I walked over to the cliff edge and stood on the rock Dad so often stood upon. There stretched below me, was probably the finest view in the whole of Guernsey, which Dad always declared had not changed in a thousand years. As I stood there admiring the majesty of the scene, I rejoiced that it was still as un-spoilt by civilisation, or indeed the German occupation, as it had been when Dad first admired it, probably a century before. As I stood there thinking of Dad having stood there before me, I also thought of future generations of my family, still unborn, who will in years to come, stand on the same rock and enjoy the same magnificent scene. It is the one place in Guernsey which will, I pray, remain unchanged for another thousand years.

As I retraced my steps, the sun caught the Pea Stacks rocks and reminded me of the time when my sister Daisy and I climbed right to the end of the farthest rock. When we reached the rock, Daisy tied a bit of ribbon from her knickers, or drawers as they were called in those days, right on top to show that a woman had been there.

My thoughts of Daisy caused me to turn and look again at my sister's old home, Sen-Sook, standing next to Seaplane Bungalow. Dad bought the plot for Daisy and Mum went out and spent twelve pounds of her own hard saved money, on a two roomed hut, which was my sister's family home when they returned to the island from Siam. Daisy later lived in various houses around the island before her son Ian bought his mother 'Sekondi' in Jerbourg Road. Daisy died in 1978 aged eighty six.

Then all of a sudden a rabbit darted for cover on the cliffs, scared by something or some sound I hadn't seen or heard. I remembered when, as a child I came out in the early morning and clapped my hands, just to see the scores of rabbits run in all directions. I suspect that if I was to come out in the early morning now and clap my hands, I would still see the rabbits run.

As a child I played in the Bassett-Lowke's field, in and around the twenty one trees, which now are long gone. Gone too is the holiday home of the Northampton family, gone also is the flagpole which served as an aerial for Dad's and Mr Bassett-Lowkes early wireless experiments. Today the field, which I now own, looks just like any other field, but to me its different, as I know its history

As I walked back down the road to the entrance of the short drive to Seaplane Bungalow, I looked out at the vast expanse of sea. I thought of the time, during the first war, when Dad and I saw a French seaplane bombing a German submarine, very near the spot where I first set eyes on the Vega coming through the mist. That was the stretch of water in which I boated and swum, that was the stretch of water that has given me so much pleasure over so many years.

Turning into the drive, I recalled the garage that Dad had constructed from a ten foot section of the original French hut. The driveway was so narrow that the only way I could park Dad's car in the garage was to reverse in. Dad however, when returning from his 'club night', would come up the drive at speed and turn straight in. I always expected to see him come out the other end, but he never did. His 'club night' did on one occasion have an effect on his driving. Dad came home with a slightly crumpled Austin '7'. and 'explained' that he had been driving along the Esplanade, when he saw two similar cars approaching him in the opposite direction. Not knowing quite what to do, he decided to go in between the two cars. Then he discovered that there was only one car after all and he hit it head on. That was his explanation and he stuck to it for years.

As I stood in the driveway looking beyond where the garage used to stand before it burnt down, I marvelled at the annex that Dad built, after retiring from the cycle business. Despite being well over sixty, Dad, not only built the eleven bedroomed annex single handed, but he and Mum ran it as a very successful boarding house almost up to the time of his death.

It was to Seaplane Annex that I brought Mabs as my young bride. It was to the Annex that Mabs and I returned with our newly born daughter and it was from there that we had been turned out by the Germans. I could still see in my minds eye the devastation that had been wrought to the property, by the Germans and the cowering soldier we found ‘in residence’ when Mabs and I first returned after our liberation.

Standing there in the drive, I reflected on my eighty years. They had been good years, enjoyable years, years blessed with good health and good friends. I have few regrets in my life. I regret not having a son, I regret not becoming a professional motorcyclist and above all I bitterly regret not having being able to make a success of my marriage.

After turning to take a last look at the magnificent view, I went indoors, half expecting to see Mum and Dad, Mum working in the kitchen and Dad in his chair with his pipe. Instead it was Fiona and William, my grandchildren, Fiona quizzed :-
“What have you being doing out there Gramps ?”

“Oh, just reliving a lifetime !”

INDEX